THE ROOTS OF JEWISH CONSCIOUSNESS, VOLUME TWO

The Roots of Jewish Consciousness, Volume Two: Hasidism is the second volume, fully annotated, of a major, previously unpublished, two-part work by Erich Neumann (1905–1960). It was written between 1940 and 1945, after Neumann, then a young philosopher and physician and freshly trained as a disciple of Jung, fled Berlin to settle in Tel Aviv. He finished this work at the end of World War II. Although he never published it, he kept it the rest of his life.

Volume Two, *Hasidism*, is devoted to the psychological and spiritual wisdom embodied in Jewish spiritual tradition. Relying on Jung's concepts and Buber's Hasidic interpretations, Neumann seeks alternatives to the legalism and anti-feminine bias that he says have dominated collective Judaism since the Second Temple. He argues that modern Jews can develop psychological wholeness through an appropriation of Hasidic legends, Talmudic texts, and Kabbalistic mysteries, including especially the Zohar. Exclusively, this volume includes a foreword by Moshe Idel. An appendix, Neumann's four-lecture series from the 1940s, gives a glimpse of his intended, unpublished Part Three.

These volumes anticipate Neumann's later works, including *Depth Psychology and a New Ethic, The Origins and History of Consciousness*, and *The Great Mother*. In Volume Two, *Hasidism*, his concept of the ego–Self axis is developed in clearly psychological terms. Four previously unpublished essays, appended to Volume Two, illustrate Neumann's developmental psychology, including his theme of primary and secondary personalization. This unique work will appeal to Jungian analysts and psychotherapists in training and in practice, historians of psychology, Jewish scholars, biblical historians, and teachers of comparative religion, as well as academics and students.

Erich Neumann (1905–1960) was a student of C. G. Jung, a philosopher, psychologist, and writer. Born in Germany, he moved to Israel in 1934, where he became a practicing analytical psychologist. His previously published works, including *Depth Psychology and a New Ethic*, have never been out of print.

Ann Conrad Lammers, Ph.D., received her Master of Divinity from The General Theological Seminary in New York and her doctorate in theology and psychology from Yale University. A Jungian psychotherapist and marriage and family therapist, she retired from practice in 2015 to edit *The Roots of Jewish Consciousness*.

"Erich Neumann is cited more than any single psychoanalytic writer in the ever-growing exploration of Kabbalah and psychology. So it is gratifying that his work on Kabbalah and Hasidism can now enrich this vibrant discussion. Neumann's especial contribution is the development of the theme of dual transformation, of the world and of the soul, for Jewish mystical psychology, and highlighting the Hasidic move away from moralism towards radical embracing of the full range of psychic manifestation. This exquisitely crafted project will be of profound interest to all who are concerned with the religious life as such."

—Professor Jonathan Garb, Gershom Scholem Chair in Kabbalah; Chair, Department of Jewish Thought, Hebrew University of Jerusalem, Israel

THE ROOTS OF JEWISH CONSCIOUSNESS

Volume Two: Hasidism

Erich Neumann
Edited by Ann Conrad Lammers

TRANSLATED BY MARK KYBURZ AND ANN CONRAD LAMMERS

Routledge
Taylor & Francis Group
LONDON AND NEW YORK

recollections
LLC

First published 2019
by Routledge
2 Park Square, Milton Park, Abingdon, Oxon OX14 4RN

and by Routledge
52 Vanderbilt Avenue, New York, NY 10017

Routledge is an imprint of the Taylor & Francis Group, an informa business

British Library Cataloguing-in-Publication Data
A catalogue record for this book is available from the British Library

Library of Congress Cataloging-in-Publication Data
Names: Neumann, Erich, author.
Title: The roots of Jewish consciousness / Erich Neumann.
Description: New York : Routledge, 2019. | Includes bibliographical references and index.
Identifiers: LCCN 2018055761 (print) | LCCN 2019010908 (ebook) | ISBN 9781315149905 (Master eBook) | ISBN 9781351369121 (Adobe Reader) | ISBN 9781351369107 (Mobipocket) | ISBN 9781351369114 (ePub) | ISBN 9781138556195 (v. 1 : hardback) | ISBN 9781138556201 (v. 1 : pbk.) | ISBN 9781138556218 (v. 2 : hardback) | ISBN 9781138556225 (v. 2 : pbk.)
Subjects: LCSH: Psychology—Religious aspects—Judaism. | Judaism and psychology. | Consciousness—Religious aspects—Judaism. | Revelation. | Eschatology. | Hasidism.
Classification: LCC BM538.P68 (ebook) | LCC BM538.P68 N4813 2019 (print) | DDC 296.3—dc23
LC record available at https://lccn.loc.gov/2018055761

ISBN: 978-1-138-55621-8 (hbk)
ISBN: 978-1-138-55622-5 (pbk)
ISBN: 978-1-315-14991-2 (ebk)

Typeset in Bembo
by Swales & Willis Ltd, Exeter, Devon, UK

Visit the eResources: www.routledge.com/9781138556225

In memoriam Erel Shalit

Erich Neumann in Ascona, Switzerland: at Casa Eranos, c. 1955.

Photographer unknown. Courtesy of the Erich Neumann Estate.

Erich Neumann (1905–1960) was born and raised in Berlin, the second son of a successful merchant family. At university in Erlangen, where he began his study of psychology, he wrote a dissertation on the "mystical linguistics" of Johann Arnold Kanne, a "forgotten Romantic." Neumann entered medical school in 1928, intending to be a psychiatrist and psychotherapist. That year, too, he married Julie Blumenfeld. Their son, Micha, was born in June 1931.

Eighteen months later, as Neumann was finishing medical school, Hitler came to power. Jews were immediately barred from many positions, including medical internships. Recognizing the dire significance of the moment, Erich and Julie, Zionists since their teens, left for Palestine/Israel in the fall of 1933 with two-year-old Micha. On the way, however, they stopped in Zurich, where Erich underwent eight months of analytic training with C. G. Jung.

After settling in Tel Aviv in 1934, Neumann began to practice as a Jungian analyst and also to write the present work. A daughter, Rachel (Rali), was born in May 1938. In 1940 Neumann finished the first part of *The Roots of Jewish Consciousness*. In 1945, as the war was ending in Europe, he finished the second part. Then, for reasons that are imperfectly known, he laid the whole work aside.

Erich Neumann's previously published writings are read worldwide, including *The Origins and History of Consciousness*, *Depth Psychology and a New Ethic*, *The Great Mother*, *Amor and Psyche*, *Creative Man*, *The Fear of the Feminine*, *The Child* (published by Julie Neumann in 1963), and his many Eranos lectures, delivered from 1948 until his death in 1960. An important early essay, *Jacob and Esau,* edited by Erel Shalit and published in 2015, brings a missing piece of his thought to light. His correspondence with Jung, *Analytical Psychology in Exile*, also appeared in 2015. The two volumes of the present work represent not only the young author's thorough integration of Jungian theory with Jewish religious symbolism, but also his early development of profound theoretical insights, now recognized as the hallmarks of his psychology.

Ann Conrad Lammers, Ph.D., received her Master of Divinity from The General Theological Seminary in New York and her doctorate in theology and psychology from Yale University. A Jungian psychotherapist and marriage and family therapist, she retired from practice in 2015 to edit *The Roots of Jewish Consciousness*. In addition to journal articles and book chapters, her published works include *The Jung–White Letters* (co-editor, Routledge, 2007) and *The Jung–Kirsch Letters* (editor and co-translator, Routledge, 2011/2016).

CONTENTS

ILLUSTRATIONS

FOREWORD

On Erich Neumann and Hasidism

Hasidism is a popular movement, inspired by earlier Kabbalistic views. Emerging in the second part of the eighteenth century, it was constituted of two major dimensions: the social one, as a movement, and the spiritual one, represented by the ideals it adopted, adapted, and sometimes transformed from earlier Jewish sources and other cultures. Socially speaking, it developed rapidly and was divided between an increasingly larger number of sects, each led by the Hasidic Holy Man, the *tzaddik,* or, to use Neumann's terminology, the Great Individual. These inner divisions within the movement were mainly the result of personal and family factors, including rivalry, because leadership soon became an inherited affair. Even in the same family, the different sons established their own "courts" and sometimes even their own spiritual variants. With the passage of time, these divergences became greater, and so also the polemics between different Hasidic rabbis. Developing over more than two centuries, the spiritual divergences also grew, and it became impossible to simply extract from many thousands of Hasidic documents one coherent doctrine, just as it is impossible to do this in the case of rabbinic Judaism or of Kabbalah.

The complexity of different schools and institutionalized courts invited different scholars to read Hasidism with different eyes: as a part of the history of Jewish mysticism, as part of eighteenth-century eastern Europe, under various sociological readings, or else as part of the more global phenomenon of mysticism. And now, in the present work, we have Neumann's fully fledged, original, psychological approach to Hasidism, using examples from its teaching that he employed only sporadically in his other published work.[1]

The first attempts to present Hasidism to the European public, those of Martin Buber, oscillated between the need to account for the major differences between the various Hasidic schools, as evident in the organization of his various books, such as *Tales of the Hasidim*, and the effort toward a more unified vision, as seen in his two other major treatments of Hasidism: *The Origin and Meaning of Hasidism* and *Hasidism and Modern Man*. The conceptual approach in the latter two books provoked a controversy between Buber and Gershom Scholem, which started in the very year of Erich Neumann's death.

Though he could not have been acquainted with the specific formulations used in the controversy, Neumann was certainly aware of the different stances toward Hasidism that had been adopted by the two giants in the study of Jewish mysticism. He knew them both from his readings, and also from his personal encounters with Scholem in Ascona, at the Eranos conferences, and possibly also in Israel. He was deeply affected by Buber's interpretation of Hasidism and was thus, at least implicitly, in tension with the opposite views of Scholem and his school.

Let me offer a more general characterization of these two great scholars' approaches to Hasidism, which were certainly available to Neumann. The differences between Buber's and Scholem's interpretations are quite significant, touching not only their more general attitudes to Hasidism but also the manner in which they thought it should be presented. First and foremost, they differ as to what they conceive to be the most representative literary documents, those that are most pertinent for the description of Hasidism. Buber preferred the Hasidic collections of legends, basically hagiographies, which he translated into German and also adapted according to his spiritual orientation; while Scholem preferred the more theoretical-exegetical literature, and the stricter philological-historical approaches to these texts. Not less important are their different phenomenological understandings of Hasidism. Buber was more concerned with the this-worldly elements of this literature, especially with the concept of worship-in-corporeality, *'avodah be-gashmiyyut*, a value that he understood in an existential manner. Scholem, in contrast, emphasized the other-worldly aspect of Hasidism. The central Hasidic values, for him, have more to do with the concept of the *devequt*, the union or communion with God, the lifting of the divine sparks from the demonic realm and their purification and elevation on high, and *hitpashetut ha-gashmiyyut*, namely the divestment of corporeality, as well as the central place of pantheism. Likewise, he was inclined to see Hasidism more as a contemplative than as a transformative path.

I would describe these two vectors, respectively, as Hermetic and Neoplatonic. The former deals with the attraction of supernal power, divinity, light, or spirituality within this world, by means of the religious acts of the *tzaddik*, who then distributes it to his disciples. The latter is concerned with the return of the soul and the divine sparks to their supernal source, as part of an ascent on high, or the elevation of sparks.

Needless to say, both approaches are found in Hasidism. The two scholars emphasized different elements that are indeed found in this literature, and each presented his selection as more representative. Thus, both scholars were right, although, at the same time, given the controversy that caused them to harden their positions, both were also wrong in not allowing a significant role to elements and literatures that the other camp chose to emphasize. In other words, if we look at East European Hasidism as a conceptually composite form of mystical thought, constituted by a variety of spiritual trends—Kabbalistic, ethical, Neoplatonic, Hermetic, Shamanic, and others—the differences between the interpretations offered by these two scholars are much less a matter of diametrically different understandings, but rather of scholars who each referred, more or less emphatically, to existing elements in the rich and diversified composite.

Various attempts have been made to find a comprehensive, fully articulated, distinct message, to identify a "single" tendency, as proposed by an eminent scholar of Hasidism, Joseph Weiss, or to locate the one "spiritual message," according to Rivka Schatz Uffenheimer, or the "ideal" type of "contemplative prayer," according to both Schatz Uffenheimer and Louis Jacobs. All of these formulations, basically following Scholem, are monotonic pictures, even though they disagree with each other.

The quandary that should haunt the critical understanding of the founder of Hasidism, R. Israel ben Eliezer, the Master of the Divine Name (whose title provides the acronym "Besht"), as well as that of Hasidism as a religious movement, is how to explain, methodologically speaking, the diverse important interpretations that emerged at the beginning of the movement and reverberated in later stages of Hasidism, without harmonizing between them. The question is, in other words, how to avoid reducing this complexity to what I call a monotonic picture, such as now prevails in dominant scholarship in the field, even though each scholar writing on this figure has his or her peculiar image of the Besht.

An awareness of the tensions between different emphases would contribute better to the understanding of the development of Hasidism. So, for example, the "this-worldly," transformative tendencies evident in Hasidism, more than in Kabbalah, may be combined with what Neumann calls the introverted type of Judaism, which means that, in Hasidism, one can discern a propensity to interpret biblical and Kabbalistic topics, figures, and values as referring to inner human powers and processes. This tendency has drawn special attention in scholarship, and it is close to the manner in which Neumann reads Hasidism, as evincing an introversive aspect.[2]

In other words, the complex Hasidic literature has been interrogated by different thinkers in accord with their main concerns. Scholem was interested in Hasidism as the neutralization of the messianic impulses present in the earlier forms of Kabbalistic literature. Buber wrote basically as a phenomenologist of religion. In the present book, Neumann asks different questions, seeing Hasidic texts as a type of document reflecting the psychological development of the individual.

Neumann's picture of Hasidism is filtered, in two senses. It heavily depends on inevitable choices made by Buber from the immense Hasidic literature. During the above-mentioned controversy, the aging Buber confessed that he was a "filter"—to use his term. That is to say, he offered his own, rather subjective, interpretation. His selection from the corpora of Hasidic writings is evident, because Buber drew incomparably more from the hagiographic writings than from the doctrinal literature. This is a major point in the critique addressed to him by Scholem and his school, which privileged the latter.

Neumann's second filter is the linguistic one, for Buber and Neumann both wrote in German, and this means a translation from one culture to another. To these two filters, Neumann added a third, his Jungian interpretation, which means that he selected passages from Buber's selection. Interestingly enough, Jung's fascination with Kabbalah, which he read in Latin translations or was informed about by Jewish scholars in his entourage, is paralleled by Neumann's much greater interest in Hasidism, which he read mainly in German. Below, I shall try to draw some few examples from the more doctrinal Hasidic treatises, in order to illustrate Neumann's insights.

1. To turn to Neumann's own view: His vision of Hasidism, as expressed in several instances, is definitely this-worldly, emphasizing the world-transforming dimension of Hasidism, and thus close to Buber's approach. This approach is also evident in the ongoing organization of the Hasidic sects in eastern Europe and in the expansion of Hasidism in a variety of centers in Central Europe, in the Land of Israel, and in the United States of America, not to speak of the more recent, well-known activities of the Lubavitch Hasidic emissaries, male and female, all over the world. In short, the imperative of the Messiah to the Besht, in the latter's famous *Epistle of the Ascent of the Soul*, "Let your wellsprings flow forth," actually inspired Hasidic missionary enterprises, forms of activity unparalleled in earlier forms of Judaism.
2. Another feature that Neumann attributes to Hasidism, also related to the this-worldly tendency, is its being "on the way," or changing all the time. Indeed, continuous change is a principle of the Besht. The need to renew in matters of religion is evident in discussions related of him: routine was conceived of as the great enemy of a true religious approach. This emphasis on the urgency of spiritual renewal reflects also the more general character of Hasidism as a movement. But we should focus here on the view of the founder of the movement. Let me introduce a discussion reported in the name of the Besht by his grandson, R. Moshe Hayyim Ephrayyim of Sudylkov, who preserved many of his grandfather's teachings:

> This is a great principle concerning the worship of God, that the quintessence is faith, and this is what my grandfather was warning, and this is the root of the entire Torah and worship. . . . Just as agedness causes weakness in all the limbs of man because the faculties, the humors and the circulation of blood that vivifies him are in decline, so, too, in the realm of spirituality, an old and aged one does not draw great delight, or vitality, or something new. This is the meaning of the saying "Every day they should be as new in your eyes," because [in Lamentations 3:23] "They are every morning new, [and] great is your faithfulness," which means that, because they are new every morning, namely that you innovate every day the work of creation, by the dint of it, "Your faithfulness is great." We find, therefore, that the quintessence of every prayer and commandment is faith. [*Degel Maḫaneh 'Efrayyim* (Jerusalem 1994), p. 214.]

3. What can hardly be found in either Buber or Scholem on Hasidism was Neumann's special interest in the archetype of the Feminine, which he shared with Jung, as both somehow believed in this as a form of supreme divine agency. Indeed, Neumann has been described as the theorist of the Great Mother. Following some earlier Kabbalistic views, the role of the Feminine, especially in its divine dimension, is found in a Hasidic master about whom late in his life Carl G. Jung wrote an often-quoted confession to the effect that: "the Hasidic Rabbi Baer from Meseritz, whom they called the Great Maggid" was the person who "anticipated my entire psychology in the eighteenth century."[3] Indeed, Rabbi Dov Baer Friedmann, known as the Great Maggid of Meseritz, a key figure in the development of early Hasidism, was also a major source in Neumann's account of Hasidism, as shown below. The Hasidic master was reported by his disciples to have said:

> In the case of Esther it has been written [Esther 5:3] "What is your request up to half of the kingdom": because the kingdom [*Malkhut*] is constituted by two aspects, since there is nothing which is not constituted by male and female. Despite the fact that on its manifest aspect it is male, it has also on its hidden aspect: female. And in the case of the manifest level of the king it is love, on the hidden aspect it is awe . . . which means that when man comes to God in awe then [His] love is aroused" ['*Or ha-'Emmet*, (*Bnei Beraq*, 1967), fol. 37c].

The Hasidic master conceives of the *sefirah* of *Malkhut*, the feminine divine power that corresponds to the *Shekhinah*, as containing two aspects, a masculine and a feminine, but he immediately applies this principle to everything else, not just to the divine Female. This is a case of what I call "dual ontology," which assumes the male–female divide as constituting a basic structure of reality as such. If I am allowed a strictly literal reading of the text, "half" can be understood as referring to a relationship of equality between the two aspects of *Malkhut*, the Male and the Female. The polarity that was earlier either cosmic or theosophical in several schools of Kabbalah, and also even in some earlier forms of Judaism, has been applied now to two modes of worship, referred to as "out of love" and "out of awe"—a leitmotif in Hasidic literature, construed here in gender terms. It should be mentioned that, in the present book, Neumann refers many times to Buber's volume that deals with this Hasidic master. A similar approach is found in a well-known Hasidic master who was a disciple of the Great Maggid's disciple, Rabbi Abraham Yehoshu'a Heschel of Apta:

> [E]verything in the world necessarily possesses aspects of male and female. This is especially true in the case of the worshiper of God, who has to possess the aspect of male and that of female. . . . namely that of the emanator and of the recipient. The aspect of maleness means, for example, that which is always emanating. By dint of his holiness, and great adhering, and purity of

> thought, he emanates a spiritual delight into the supernal lights, worlds, and attributes. And he has also a female aspect, namely that which is the recipient and draws down to the lower worlds the influx from the supernal worlds and to all [the members of] the community of Israel whatever they need and all kinds of good graces, "like sons, life, and sustenance, healing etc." The aspect of maleness causes influx on high and this influx becomes semen and becomes an aspect of maleness in the female . . . and the female aspect of the *tzaddik* is his faculty of receiving the supernal influx and to draw from above downward all kinds of good things and material issues.
>
> ['Ohev Israel *(Zhitomir, 1863), fol. 81cd]*

When taken together, these two passages, stemming from the same Hasidic school, show that there are feminine aspects in the masculine and masculine dimensions in the feminine, in a manner reminiscent the famous Jungian theory of *animus/anima*. The end of the last quotation deals with the more concrete aspects of the results of worship, which are intended to supply the needs of the Hasidic community, not just to inspire the spiritual attainments of individuals. The active aspect of worship, as drawing down divine influxes, has magical sources, an activity that has been combined with mystical worship out of love. The induction of divine delight—another leitmotiv of Hasidism—assumes an extension of responsibility not just to the human collective and to the individual's soul, but also for the well-being of the divinity. Worship is not a matter of obedience, but a much broader type of effect is related to it, achieved by the spiritual efforts initiated by the Hasidim; it is a path to higher attainments.

These few examples validate the psychological analyses of Hasidic texts, and thus they also support the claims made by Neumann. The fact that Neumann's claims are actually reflected in Hasidic texts illuminates Jung's recognition, late in life, that his approach had been anticipated by the insights of the Great Maggid.

Moshe Idel

Notes

1 More recently, there are additional efforts to apply a Jungian approach, including sometimes Neumann's, to Hasidism, as we can see in the writings of Micha Ankori, Erel Shalit, Sanford L. Drob, Haviva Pedaya, Jonathan Garb, or Ruth Netzer—most of whom had no access to the present monograph—or, in some few cases, also in my studies.

2 See Siegmund Hurwitz, "Psychological Aspects in Early Hasidic Literature," in *Timeless Documents of the Soul*, H. Jakobsohn et al., eds, H. Nagel, trans. (Northwestern University Press, Evanston, IL, 1968), pp. 149–240; Gershom Scholem, "The Unconscious and the Concept *Qadmut ha-Sekhel* in Hasidic Literature," in *The Latest Phase: Essays on Hasidism*, D. Assaf and E. Liebes, eds (Jerusalem 2008), pp. 271, 273–6 (Hebrew).

3 "An Eightieth Birthday Interview," in *C. G. Jung Speaking*, W. McGuire and R. F. C. Hull, eds (Princeton University Press, Princeton, NJ, 1977), pp. 271–2.

ACKNOWLEDGMENTS

Permission to publish text and illustrations was kindly given by the Neumann Estate: Micha Neumann and Rali Neumann-Loewenthal. Primary documents for both volumes of this work are found in the Neumann family archive at the home of Rali Neumann-Loewenthal, Jerusalem. Additional documents, including Erich Neumann's April 1940 lecture and his four-lecture series from 1942 to 1943, are also found in this collection. Access to Erich Neumann's documents, consultation about his life and work, his relationships with Buber and Scholem, and the history of his papers and library were all kindly given by Rali Neumann-Loewenthal.

Warmest thanks are also due to the following individuals. First, to Erel Shalit, for planning and overseeing this project, to which he gave caring attention until his untimely death in January 2018. He gave me his learned advice concerning Hebrew and German and guidance in English translation. During the editorial process, he organized two conferences and a webinar on Neumann's work. His rich introduction to *Jacob and Esau* is an ongoing source of inspiration. As his final act in support of the present work, he shared his electronic files of Neumann's "Torah" paintings, from which the two volume covers were chosen.

Erel Shalit also wisely invited Dr. Moshe Idel to write the foreword to *Hasidism*. Professor Idel generously accepted the invitation and, after Erel's death, prepared the brilliant writing that opens this volume.

Nancy Furlotti, in her commitment to Erich Neumann's work, has supported the entire project from first to last. I am grateful for her advice about archetypal symbolism and her illuminating consultation about Neumann's art and writings. In addition to working closely with Erel Shalit until his death, she kept in touch with Micha Neumann and Rali Neumann-Loewenthal, especially with regard to copyright permissions. After Erel's death, Nancy gave careful oversight to the final stages of editorial preparation. As a contributing editor, she provided the graceful preface to Volume One, wrote the caption for "The transformative serpent" in Volume Two, and, finally, crafted fully half of our online chapter abstracts.

Tamar Kron has given invaluable help on many issues of translation and annotation, especially involving the Hebrew language and many of the sources that underlie Neumann's writing. She advised me on Neumann's relationship with Buber and elucidated important points in Jewish mystical tradition. She and David Wieler, who are preparing the Hebrew edition of *Roots*, have patiently read and critiqued our English translations of Neumann's work, as these evolved in parallel with their own translations. She also helped me to direct the artist's renderings of Neumann's drawings of the Sefirotic Tree.

Mark Kyburz, whose specialty is translation from German to English, had worked previously with Erel Shalit in translating Neumann's *Jacob and Esau*. From the beginning of this project, he has been a member of the editorial team, whom I thank for his professional translation work, faithful collaboration, independent research, linguistic advice, and attention to countless details in the text. Mark and I gradually evolved a collaborative translation process, in which each of us corrected the other's blind spots. The book ventures into such a broad range of fields that it might have been impossible for anyone to translate it alone. I am very grateful to Mark for his systematic approach to Neumann's terminology, and I've continually relied on his skills and resources as a seasoned translator.

Before Mark and I could begin translating, however, we needed faithful transcriptions. For these, I trusted Ursula Egli's patient and exacting reading. We puzzled together over the author's textual obscurities and proofread each other's work. Apart from the third chapter of *Hasidism*, which I reconstructed and transcribed, Ursula wrestled first and hardest with Neumann's faded typescripts and difficult handwriting. Her work is the textual foundation for this edition.

In his wide-ranging thought, Neumann draws on areas of study well beyond those that this editor can claim. I have therefore been fortunate to turn to a circle of scholars who helped me to understand the implications of the text, refine parts of the translations, and write many of the annotations. In what follows, I try to remember every one of these generous people. If I have nevertheless omitted someone, I ask to be reminded, so that I can amend this list at the first opportunity.

When the project began, I had just a few official consultants. In addition to those already named, I am especially thankful to Richard Corney for his consultation on innumerable subjects relating to Hebrew language, biblical translations, ancient Jewish source material, and the history of interpretation.

Everett Fox, whose biblical translations are very frequently quoted in the first volume of this work, advised me at an early stage about Buber's work and thought and the history of Jewish biblical scholarship. In Neumann's *Hasidism*, readers will again note occasional passages from Fox's translations, *The Schocken Bible*, Volume I: *The Five Books of Moses*, and *The Schocken Bible*, Volume II: *The Early Prophets*. These limited excerpts are permitted by the publisher, Penguin Random House LLC, as falling under "fair use" and are gratefully acknowledged.

At an early point, due to the arduous treatment he was undergoing, Erel Shalit realized that I would need auxiliary consultants in some of the areas where he had hoped to guide my work. With his support, in 2016 I turned to Steven Joseph for advice about a challenging theme in Neumann's *Hasidism*. I was also grateful, later on, for Dr. Joseph's reading of my two introductions. Murray Stein helped with fine points in Jungian diction. Thomas Kirsch, while he lived, advised me about Neumann's relationship with James Kirsch. Andreas Jung helped me to locate an obscure reference in Jung's *Über die Energetik der Seele*. Sanford Drob advised me on Kabbalah and Jewish tradition, shedding light on several passages in *Hasidism*. Nomi Kluger-Nash wrote to me about the symbolism of Jonah and the meanings of *t'shuvah*. Lance Owens opened my thinking about Neumann's Eranos lectures and his concept of the "great individual." Robert Segal gave learned advice about the writings of Lucien Lévy-Bruhl; he also wisely directed me to his student, Nico Fehlbaum, whose doctoral work at the University of Aberdeen is on Cassirer and myth, and who gave expert consultation on the writings of Ernst Cassirer. Peter Kingsley kindly advised me about Neoplatonism. Steve Zemmelman referred me to Rabbi Jonathan Omer-Man and Rabbi Dr. Zvi Leshem, and later devoted deep and critical reading to my two introductions. Jonathan Omer-Man gently advised me on the unwisdom of publishing Neumann's unfinished short story, "David and Saul." Zvi Leshem read an early draft of my introduction to Volume One and led me to pertinent readings on the history of the Buber–Scholem debate.

For this project, I have had the pleasure of doing research at several libraries, including: St. Mark's Library, The General Theological Seminary, New York; the library of the Graduate Theological Union, Berkeley, CA; the ETH-Bibliothek, Zurich, with assistance from Yvonne Voegeli at the C. G. Jung-Arbeitsarchiv; the Zentralbibliothek, Zurich; the New York Public Library, with assistance from Eleanor Yadin at the Dorot Reading Room; the library of the Jewish Theological Seminary, New York; the Lillian Goldman Reading Room at the Leo Baeck Institute, New York,, overseen by Renate Evers. Finally, I've spent many hours at the Brandeis Library, Waltham, MA, and I owe special thanks to the Judaica Librarian at Brandeis, Jim Rosenbloom, for his support and guidance.

Christine Taylor, of Wilsted & Taylor, Oakland, CA, provided the line art, representing Neumann's drawings of the Sefirotic Tree, for the second chapter of *Hasidism*.

Funding for this edition came from Recollections, LLC: Nancy Furlotti, President, and Erel Shalit, CEO.

I would also like to thank the excellent team at Routledge, especially Susannah Frearson, who shepherded this work through its editorial process and Heather Evans, who, with Susannah, oversaw its production stage. It was also a pleasure to work with Ellie Jarvis at Swales & Willis, under whose supervision Jane Sugarman did the expert copy-editing, and Vanessa Tamplin created both the general and the scriptural index.

As further explained in my Editorial note (*Roots II,* pp. 277f.), in translating this volume we made frequent use of Olga Marx's previously published translation of one of Martin Buber's collections of Hasidic stories, *Die chassidischen Bücher*. The publisher's copyright permission reads:

party use of this material, outside of this publication, is prohibited. Interested parties must apply directly to Penguin Random House LLC for permission.

Frequently in *Hasidism*, and to a lesser extent in *Revelation and Apocalypse,* Neumann quotes from the Zohar, using sources inconsistent with recent research. In Appendix A, we provide parallel passages (when they could be found) from an excellent English version of the Zohar. Deep respect is owed to Daniel C. Matt, editor and translator, to Marion Pritzker and the Pritzker Foundation for supporting his work, and to Stanford University Press for publishing the Pritzker Edition. I am especially thankful for the following permissions:

Excerpted from *The Zohar: Pritzker Edition*, Volume 1, by Matt, Daniel C. © 2004 by the Zohar Education Project Inc. Published by Stanford University Press. Used by permission.

Excerpted from *The Zohar: Pritzker Edition*, Volume 3, by Matt, Daniel C. © 2005 by the Zohar Education Project Inc. Published by Stanford University Press. Used by permission.

Excerpted from *The Zohar: Pritzker Edition*, Volume 4, by Matt, Daniel C. © 2007 by the Zohar Education Project Inc. Published by Stanford University Press. Used by permission.

Excerpted from *The Zohar: Pritzker Edition*, Volume 5, by Matt, Daniel C. © 2009 by the Zohar Education Project Inc. Published by Stanford University Press. Used by permission.

Excerpted from *The Zohar: Pritzker Edition*, Volume 7, by Matt, Daniel C. © 2012 by the Zohar Education Project Inc. Published by Stanford University Press. Used by permission.

Excerpted from *The Zohar: Pritzker Edition*, Volume 8, by Matt, Daniel C. © 2014 by the Zohar Education Project Inc. Published by Stanford University Press. Used by permission.

Excerpted from *The Zohar: Pritzker Edition*, Volume 9, by Matt, Daniel C. © 2016 by the Zohar Education Project Inc. Published by Stanford University Press. Used by permission.

Excerpted from *The Zohar: Pritzker Edition*, Volume 10, by Matt, Daniel C. © 2016 by the Zohar Education Project Inc. Published by Stanford University Press. Used by permission.

ABBREVIATIONS

Bab Tlm	*Babylonian Talmud*. In English: *The Hebrew–English Edition of the Babylonian Talmud*, Soncino Press (1967–88).
"Besht"	Samuel A. Horodezky, "Baal-Schem-Tob (בעש"ט), Israel ben Elieser," *Encyclopedia Judaica*, v. 3 (1929), cols 835–42.
Beziehungen	C. G. Jung, *Die Beziehungen zwischen dem Bewusstsein und dem Unbewussten* (1921). (CW 7,2)
Bischoff	Erich Bischoff, *Die Elemente der Kabbalah*. Teil I: *Theoretische Kabbalah* (1913).
B&R	Martin Buber & Franz Rosenzweig. German translations of the Five Books of Moses (Pentateuch), six books of history, and the major and minor prophets (1929/1934).
Chassid Büch	Martin Buber, *Die chassidischen Bücher* (1928).
CW	*The Collected Works of C. G. Jung*. Bollingen Series XX, Princeton, NJ: Princeton University Press (1956–79). Twenty volumes.
EJ	*Eranos-Jahrbuch, -bücher* (annual collections of Eranos lectures), Olga Fröbe-Kapteyn, ed. (1933–).
Enc Jud	*Encyclopaedia Judaica (Jüdische Enzyklopädie)* (1928–34). Ten volumes, A–Lyra.
Energetik	C. G. Jung, *Über die Energetik der Seele* (1928).
Franck	Adolf Franck, *Die Kabbala, oder die Religions-Philosophie der Hebräer*. Aus dem Französischen übersetzt, verbessert und vermehrt von Adolf Gelinek (1844/1913).
Geheimnis	C. G. Jung and Richard Wilhelm, *Geheimnis der goldenen Blüte* (1929).
Gnosis	Hans Jonas, *Gnosis und spätantiker Geist*. Teil I: *Die mythologische Gnosis* (1934).

Great Maggid	Samuel A. Horodezky, תורת ה "מגיד" ממזריטש ושיחיתיו. *Torat ha-magid mi-Mezerits ve-sihotav*. (*The Teachings of the Maggid of Meseritz and his conversations*) (1923).
Integration	C. G. Jung, *The Integration of the Personality* (1939).
Jacob & Esau	Erich Neumann, "Jakob und Esau" (unpublished typescript, 1934); *Jacob and Esau: On the Collective Symbolism of the Brother Motif*, Erel Shalit, ed., Mark Kyburz, trans. (2015).
Jer Tlm	*Jerusalem Talmud*. In English: *The Talmud of the Land of Israel: A Preliminary Translation and Explanation*, Jacob Neusner, ed. and trans. Chicago, IL: Chicago University Press (1984–90).
J-N Corresp	*Analytical Psychology in Exile: The Correspondence of C. G. Jung and Erich Neumann*, M. Liebscher, ed. (2015).
Jonas	Hans Jonas, *Gnosis und spätantiker Geist*. Teil I: *Die mythologische Gnosis* (1934).
Major Trends	Gershom Scholem, *Major Trends in Jewish Mysticism* (first published in English), New York: Schocken, 1941.
Müller	Ernst Müller, *Der Sohar: Das heilige Buch der Kabbala, nach dem Urtext herausgegeben* (*The Zohar: The sacred book of the Kabbalah*, published according to the original text), 1932.
New Ethic	Erich Neumann, *Depth Psychology and a New Ethic* (German edn 1949; English edn 1969/1990).
Origins and History	Erich Neumann, *The Origins and History of Consciousness* (German edn 1949; English edn 1954).
Pritzker	*The Zohar: Pritzker Edition*, Daniel C. Matt, ed. and trans. (2004–2016). Twelve volumes.
Probleme der Mystik	Herbert Silberer, *Probleme der Mystik und ihrer Symbolik*, 1914.
Psych & Rel	C. G. Jung, *Psychology and Religion*. The Terry Lectures, Yale (1938). (CW 11,1).
R. Nachman	Samuel Horodezky, תירת רבי נחמן מברצלב ושיחיתיו. *Torat Rabi Nahman mi-Bratslav ve-sihotav* (*The teaching of Rabbi Nachman of Brezlav and his conversations*) (1923).
Roots I, II	Erich Neumann, *The Roots of Jewish Consciousness*, Ann Conrad Lammers, ed., Mark Kyburz and Ann Conrad Lammers, trans. (2019). Two volumes.
Seelenprobleme	C. G. Jung, *Seelenprobleme der Gegenwart* (1931).
Soncino	*The Zohar, Soncino Edition*, J. Abelson, ed., H. Sperling and M. Simon, trans., London: Soncino Press (1933). Five volumes.
Tales I, II	M. Buber, *Tales of the Hasidim*, Olga Marx, trans. Vol. I: *The Early Masters* (1947); Vol. II: *The Later Masters* (1948).
Typen, Types	C. G. Jung, *Psychologische Typen* (1921); *Psychological Types* (CW 6)
Unterweisung	M. Buber, *Des Baal-Schem-Tow Unterweisung im Umgang mit Gott* (1927).

Wandlungen	C. G. Jung, *Wandlungen und Symbole der Libido: Beiträge zur Entwicklungsgeschichte des Denkens* (1912/1925). Revised and expanded: *Symbols of Transformation.* (CW 5)
Wirklichkeit	C. G. Jung et al., *Wirklichkeit der Seele* (1934).

INTRODUCTION TO VOLUME TWO

This introduction supplements my Introduction to Volume One of Neumann's *The Roots of Jewish Consciousness*.[1] The first introduction gives a more complete overview of both volumes, including their genesis and historical setting, and their place among Erich Neumann's publications. It also explores the author's many-sided dialogue with C. G. Jung, his intellectual relationships with Martin Buber and Gershom Scholem, and the reasons he later gave for withholding this work of his youth from publication. Rather than repeat that material here, I refer to it only as occasion arises, while encouraging readers to engage with both volumes.

Erich Neumann finished his first part, *Revelation and Apocalypse*, in 1940, and continued working on Part Two, *Hasidism*.[2] Statements in his "Introduction to the work" (*Roots I*, pp. 7f.) show that he originally thought of the two parts, as well as his planned but never completed third part, as belonging to a single book.[3] By the time he completed Part Two, however, he had come to think of them as separable and had abandoned his plan to publish Part One.

Neumann worked on Part Two, *Hasidism*, through World War II, completing it early in 1945.[4] On the first of October 1945 he wrote to Jung:

> After I had completed a rather large work on Jewish antiquity—On the Psychological History of the Jewish Person—(it is now out of date and only useable as source material), I wrote a book on the psychological meaning of Hasidism for the modern Jew, by which I still stand.[5]

At this point, it seems, Neumann still intended to publish his work on Hasidism. Why, then, did he lay it aside? The reasons are not clear from his letters to Jung, but we can piece them together.

In 1959, he told his friend, Dr. Gustav Dreifuss, that his "scholarly conscience" had stopped him from publishing his two-volume Jewish work.[6] As he had been raised in the German cultural context, he said, he did not truly understand his ancestors' form of life. Also, he now believed that, in writing *Hasidism*, he had relied too heavily on Martin Buber's interpretation of the material, which was so strongly shaped by the general European heritage. He could not rewrite the book, Neumann explained, because he felt that an understanding of the archetypal images in Judaism must grow from a full knowledge of the authentic writings and history of the Jewish people—a knowledge that he just did not possess.[7]

The truth is, it would have been difficult for Neumann to think about Hasidism independent of Buber's influence. He had shaped both volumes of *Roots* around his conviction that, in their highest form, the Hasidic teachings represented the most promising way forward for modern Jews. Moshe Idel's summary observation about Buber could have been said equally of the young Neumann: "Guided by his phenomenological approach, Buber ultimately reached the view that hasidism expressed the quintessence of Judaism."[8] For Neumann, as he contemplated the extremity of Jewish existence in the Hitler years, Hasidic mysticism seemed to offer the truest path toward spiritual and psychological wholeness.

Neumann's explanation to Dreifuss was given in 1959, almost 15 years after the present work was completed. If we bring our attention to the years closer to the book's writing, however, an additional hypothesis arises. For the text of *Hasidism* contains a mystery. While transcribing from Neumann's original typescript, I discovered that someone (presumably the author) had removed a 36-page section from *two* carbon copies of Part Two. Neumann was systematic in preserving all the copies of his work, so it was a shock to discover a large lacuna in two otherwise intact, identical texts.

The removal could not have been accidental.[9] The section in question, "Das Leben in dieser Welt" ("Life in this world"), is integral to the work. The second chapter in *Hasidism* was originally titled, "The transformation of souls, and Life in this world."[10] Now, for some reason, "Life in this world" was missing. This major gap not only posed practical problems but also raised the question, why? If the author had borrowed a piece of his text for use in another piece of writing, why borrow it twice? In Neumann's table of contents for *Hasidism*, "Life in this world" still stands, with all its subheadings. The author's footnotes, in various chapters, still contain cross-references to this section.

The absence of so large a section, and one that was necessary to the volume, posed a serious problem for the publication of *Hasidism*. Even if "Life in this world" could be reconstructed—which, fortunately, it could, because Neumann had saved an "inferior" carbon copy, intact, as well as an earlier version of Part Two—still, what did the author intend to do with this part of his book? Would he publish it today? Should we?

We need to recall that Neumann probably completed his volume on Hasidism just as the war in Europe was coming to an end. That is the implication, it seems to me, of his statement in the letter of 1 October 1945:

> But then . . . the Jewish problem and my work on it ended for me precisely at a time when it became conspicuous in the world in an indescribably ghastly way.[11]

This wording may be interpreted differently, but I cannot read it without thinking of the ghastly visual evidence that became "conspicuous in the world" with the liberation of the death camps in the spring of 1945. I believe that, against this existential background, Neumann may have reread his book, or at least one section of it, with new eyes, for the "missing" section is devoted to Neumann's discussion of the Hasidic response to the problem of evil.

In any doctrinal tradition, theology is almost impossible to write in the face of the Holocaust. Painful internal contradictions immediately arise in any discussion that begins by declaring the goodness of creation and the ongoing involvement of God in human life, and then tries to account for the crushing reality of evil in the world. Hasidic mysticism, in its nonlinear, unitive vision, is perhaps the truest response to the dualistic problem of evil. But there are times when the paradoxical unity of good and evil cannot be spoken of, or, if spoken, cannot be heard.[12] Neumann's "life in this world" contains many passages boldly declaring a teaching that, I believe, he could not bring himself to publish after the war.[13]

Under the subheading, "Evil as a level of good," we find such powerful and difficult sayings as this, from Horodezky's work on the Great Maggid:

> So it is said not only that repentance resides in sin like oil in the olive; that "there is good in all evil"; that "the holiest sparks exist on the lowest level"; and that "goodness is hidden in darkness"; but finally it comes to the saying of the Baal Shem: "Evil is also good, it is only the lower level of perfect goodness."[14]

Then Neumann quotes this meditation by Buber:

> The indwelling glory (*Shekhinah*) encompasses all worlds, all creatures, good and evil, and she is the true unity. How can she carry the opposites of good and evil within herself? But in truth there is no opposition, for evil is the throne of goodness.[15]

Another passage occurs under the subheading, "Accepting the world":

> The task of connecting above and below is based on the principle of *accepting the world*, because "In this day and age, . . . the greatest devotion, greater than learning and praying, consists in accepting the world exactly as it happens to be."[16]

The pages that were removed from Part Two have never been found. My intuition is that Neumann sent them to colleagues, who—he hoped—might help him reframe them for publication. If he did, perhaps he was advised to let them go. It was simply the wrong time to publish a paradoxical, unitive vision of God and the world. In the immediate tremendum of the Holocaust, to speak of a God whose glory unites good and evil, to call evil the lowest level of good, and to say that it is the soul's duty to find the sacred meaning in every event may appear meaningless, or insulting, or pathetically unaware. At some point, I believe, Neumann may have taken Job for his model, and laid his hand over his mouth.

But now, having put his two-volume work aside, he turned to publishing the more directly psychological writings that had been occupying him since the early 1940s: *Depth Psychology and a New Ethic*[17] and *The Origins and History of Consciousness*.[18] Readers familiar with his *New Ethic*, which he completed in 1943, will recognize one of the central themes in *Hasidism*, the paradoxical union of good and evil, folded into it.[19] Several passages in *Hasidism* show Neumann's emerging theory of the ego–Self axis, which he stated publicly in 1952.[20] In his lectures of the early 1940s, four of which are published here for the first time, he deepened his discussion of "secondary personalization," a concept that he had first articulated in *Jacob and Esau* and would develop further in *Origins and History*.[21]

It will be exciting to see what connections scholars and analysts find between the whole of Neumann's "Jewish work" and his famous writings that superseded it.

Ann Conrad Lammers
June 2018

Notes

1 The title, *The Roots of Jewish Consciousness* (hereafter: *Roots I, II*), emerged for me early in the editorial process and gained approval from Erel Shalit, Nancy Furlotti, Mark Kyburz, and Tamar Kron in January 2016. Neumann's own working titles for the book included, at various times, the following: "Ursprungsgeschichte des jüdischen Bewusstseins" ("The origins and history of Jewish consciousness"); "Zur Wiederentdeckung des Judentums" ("The rediscovery of Judaism"); "Zur Tiefenpsychologie des modernen Juden" ("On the depth psychology of the modern Jew"); and "Zur Seelengeschichte des jüdischen Menschen" ("The psychological history of the Jewish person"). *The Roots of Jewish Consciousness* echoes, without repeating verbatim, Neumann's word *Ursprungsgeschichte* (origins and history). That word—or phrase, in English—is firmly associated with his title, *Ursprungsgeschichte des Bewusstseins* (*Origins and History of Consciousness*) (1949) (hereafter: *Origins and History*), which properly stands as an independent volume.

2 Neumann to Jung, 11 May 1940, *Analytical Psychology in Exile: The Correspondence of C. G. Jung and Erich Neumann* (hereafter *J-N Corresp*), p. 156.

3 For a glimpse of Neumann's intended Part Three, we have his series of lectures written in 1942–43, which appear here for the first time (Appendix B, *Roots II*, pp. 190ff.). The starting point for that series was Neumann's lecture of April 1940, which he described to Jung at the time as belonging to the third part of his Jewish work (11 May 1940, *J-N Corresp*, p. 156). Revised and expanded in 1942, the transformed April 1940 lecture became, in 1943, the conclusion to his four-lecture series. (Cf. introductory comment, Appendix B.IV, *Roots II*, p. 256.)

4 These dates rest on evidence in the Jung-Neumann correspondence, as discussed in the Introduction to Volume One (cf. *Roots I*, pp. xxviif.).

5 Neumann to Jung, 1 October 1945, *J-N Corresp*, p. 160. Translation slightly altered, based on the original text of Neumann's letter in *C. G. Jung/Erich Neumann: Die Briefe, 1933–1959* (hereafter: *Briefe J-N*), p. 206.

6 Gustav Dreifuss, "Erich Neumanns jüdisches Bewusstsein" ("Erich Neumann's Jewish consciousness"), *Kreativität des Unbewussten* (*Creativity of the unconscious*), *Analytische Psychologie*, Vol. 11, 1980, pp. 239–47. (Cf. also Introduction to Volume One, *Roots I*, p. xxxvi.)
7 Dreifuss, 1980, op. cit., p. 240.
8 Moshe Idel, "Martin Buber and Gershom Scholem on Hasidism: A Critical Appraisal," in *Hasidism Reappraised* (1997), p. 390.
9 Neumann's surviving papers show that, when he typed his work, he created several identical copies, using (as a rule) three sheets of carbon paper. This gave him two clear carbon copies for handwritten revisions, although the lowest carbon copy remained uncorrected, for reference. The fair copy (the top sheet when typing) seems to have held his final, most careful corrections, suitable to send to a publisher. Thanks to the author's care in preserving all his copies, and his family's faithful preservation of his unpublished papers, we can now compare earlier and later revisions, and even see which version of a text the author intended to be final.
10 Although we cannot be certain of Neumann's intentions, it has seemed important to respect his action in removing "Life in this world" from two of his typescripts. That section is now visually set apart and has been made a separate chapter.
11 *J-N Corresp*, p. 160, alternate translation from Neumann's original text: "Dann aber, . . . war für mich das jüdische Problem und die Arbeit an ihm gerade in einer Zeit beendet, in der es in der Welt in unbeschreiblich grauenhafter Art augenfällig wurde" (*Briefe J-N*, p. 206). (Cf. Introduction to Volume One, *Roots I*, pp. xxviif.)
12 The accuracy of this statement depends, of course, on the spiritual disposition of any given hearer. Israel was predominantly a secular society in the post-war years.
13 This suggestion received early support from Steven Joseph, who supports my hypothesis that Neumann could not find a way to publish his work about Oneness at a time when the dualistic vision of evil was so strongly in the ascendant (Steven Joseph, personal correspondence, 2016).
14 Samuel Horodezky, תורת ה "מגיד" ממזריטש ושיחותיו. *Torat ha-magid mi-Mezerits ve-sihotav* (*The teachings of [Dov Baer] the Maggid of Meseritz and his conversations*) (hereafter: *Great Maggid*), 1923, pp. 15 and 39. (Cf. *Roots II*, p. 105.)
15 Martin Buber, *Des Baal-Schem-Tow Unterweisung im Umgang mit Gott (The teaching of the Baal Shem-Tov in conversation with God*) (hereafter: *Unterweisung*), 1927, p. 86. (Cf. *Roots II*, p. 106.)
16 Martin Buber, *Die chassidischen Bücher* (*Hasidic tales*) (hereafter: *Chassid Büch*), 1928, p. 638. (Trans. by Olga Marx, *Hasidic Tales II*, p. 166. Cf. *Roots II*, p. 111 and note.)
17 Erich Neumann, *Tiefenpsychologie und neue Ethik*, 1949. *Depth Psychology and a New Ethic*, with a Foreword by C. G. Jung. Trans. by Eugene Rolfe, 1969. (Hereafter: *New Ethic*.)
18 Erich Neumann, *Ursprungsgeschichte des Bewusstseins*, 1949. *The Origins and History of Consciousness*, with a Foreword by C. G. Jung, trans. by R. F. C. Hull, 1954. (Hereafter: *Origins and History*.)
19 A key passage in *New Ethic* is the paragraph beginning, "The acknowledgment of one's own evil is 'good'" (p. 114). Jung objected to this whole paragraph, insisting that it made the words "good" and "evil" meaningless (*J-N Corresp*, p. 366). Neumann, who accepted many of Jung's other criticisms, declined to change this passage. (Cf. also Introduction to Volume One, *Roots I*, pp. xxxiif.)
20 Neumann's concept of "the ego–Self axis" was fully articulated in his 1952 Eranos lecture, published in spring 1956 (trans. by H. Nagel), as "The Psyche and the Transformation of the Reality Planes: A Metapsychological Essay." Cf. *The Place of Creation*, edited by W. McGuire, 1989, pp. 3–62 (especially p. 20).
21 In the present work, Neumann discusses secondary personalization in his three lectures of 1943: Appendix B.I (*Roots II*, pp. 205f.); Appendix B.II (*Roots II*, pp. 210–15 *et passim*); and Appendix B.III (*Roots II*, pp. 239f.). In *Jacob and Esau*, the concept is explored in a central passage, pp. 84–98, and by Erel Shalit in his Introduction, pp. xlvii *et passim*. In *Origins and History*, cf. pp. 335ff.

Hasidism

Its psychological meaning for Judaism

> "I have come to show people a new way to come to themselves."
>
> *Baal Shem Tov*[1]

1

THE STRUCTURE OF THE WORLD AS INWARDNESS

1. Form and the individual

The essential task of this work is not only to describe Hasidism[2] or to make it understandable, but also to show the intellectual and historical meaning of this movement with relation to the history of the Jewish person. From the outset, this interpretation makes no effort to agree with previous interpretations of Hasidism, even though it owes a great deal to many of them. Its distinguishing feature is not in adding new material, which might extend the field of study, but rather in seeing the field from a different perspective.

Any inquiry into the contents of a text depends on the inquirer's standpoint, but the richness of the answer lets us judge whether the quality of the question is adequate to the text. Even religious texts may be queried as to the economic conditions or repressed instinctual forces that helped to shape them. Questions of this kind are justified and important, but they are not adequate, that is, they are not aimed at the true nature of the subject. The problem now arises whether the depth-psychological inquiry into a religious text is adequate in this sense. This problem cannot be discussed here to its full extent, but some remarks may be offered, at least with regard to Hasidic texts.

We are investigating these texts for their psychological, not their metaphysical, reality. Using a depth-psychological point of departure, we can focus our interpretation on the phenomena to which the texts testify. Meanwhile the real aim of our interpretation is to reveal the psychic structure of the Jewish person, as expressed in Hasidism. This psychological turn of mind, which says nothing about a deity's existence independent of the human structure, is guided by all the forms and modes of expression that this deity assumes in the psychic structure of the Jew. As the present work will show, the psychological turn is unrelated to any arbitrary, contemporary approach; rather, it results from the Jewish person's own development, stretching from antiquity to modernity, a development that entered a crucial stage in Hasidism.

Our interpretation of Hasidic narratives and teachings refers to a prototypical selection and emphasizes matters that are not the result of statistics, that is, they cannot be said to be most frequent amid the wealth of material. These emphases are valid for the parts of Hasidism that are meaningful in the history of development, that is, for those parts to which a future Judaism will, and must, refer. The problem of the modern Jew has given us some questions to ask, and it is astonishing how many answers to these questions are expressed, at least inherently, in Hasidism.

Some formulations by Hasidic authorities coincide with ours in such detail that one might assume that theirs were also based at least implicitly on a corresponding interpretation. But it is obvious in a general sense that the texts and their psychological interpretation exist on different levels, being two hundred years apart. Whether or not this interpretation is adequate to the texts will become clear in the course of our investigation.

Beside the teachings, textual interpretations, and philosophical formulations that make up our material, a considerable part of it consists of legends, anecdotes, and stories in which the Hasidic perspective becomes visible. Our work refers in particular to these pieces. Even though our interpretation aims mainly to draw out the rationally known contents of the cited passages, it will also be possible to feel their lifelike power, which provides the background[3] and color that a theoretical–psychological reading necessarily fails to convey.

Whereas the world of Hasidism unfolds in the fullness and diversity of these tales, we are pulling it together around key terms and central concepts, the system of which holds the fabric of this world together like an invisible web. The philosophy of Hasidism, as all of this might mistakenly be called, is not, however, the religious or philosophical conception of any single individual, but the product of a spiritual movement. This spiritual movement forms a subterranean current that invisibly nurtures living Judaism—invisibly, because the inner face of Judaism has become disguised by a rigid and lifeless orthodoxy. This current comes to light again as a secret rivulet in the individual, but perhaps also as the gushing source of a beginning, in the dreams, visions, and psychic experiences of the anonymous modern Jew. In Hasidism, it was a current; there this spiritual movement became collective life and form. But even there, it still did not fully understand itself.

For reasons that will be explained, the spiritual revolution of Hasidism—for such it was—did not shatter the long-ingrained form of Jewish existence. Then, when the Jewish collective disintegrated, the individual, who already stood essentially at the center of the Hasidic world, also became the historical destiny of Judaism in emancipation and assimilation. With this historical turn, Judaism entered the field of its crisis, in which it is still found today. With the emancipation of the Jew, a phase begins, the decisive question of which can now be formulated: What is the task of Judaism in the new era of the world, and does it have a task at all? Or does the end of the Christian era also spell the end of Judaism, which can often enough be shown to be the secret background of Christianity, the development of which it unconsciously accompanied?

But before we can raise and answer this question, we must lay open the historical foundation of Jewish inwardness. This foundation is Hasidism.

In one passage about the meaning of "Divine Incarnation," Sri Ramakrishna says the following:

> Just take the case of the ocean. It is a wide and almost infinite expanse of water. But owing to special causes, in special parts of this wide sea, the water becomes congealed into ice. When reduced to ice it can be easily manipulated and applied to special uses. An Incarnation is something like that. Like that infinite expanse of water, there is an Infinite Power, immanent in matter and mind, but for some special purposes, in special regions a portion of that Infinite Power, as it were, assumes a tangible shape in history. That is what you call a great man; but he is, properly speaking, a local manifestation of the all-pervading Divine Power; in other words: an incarnation of God. The greatness of men is essentially the manifestation of Divine Energy.[4]

This thesis could just as well be Hasidic, at least if one considers only the energetic aspect of Ramakrishna's assertion, which derives the concentration of the being known as the "great man" from the all-embracing energetics of divine existence. Even the mystical aspect of this text, which emphasizes the ecstatic, dissolving nature of the relationship between ice and water, would be affirmed, not only by all western and eastern mysticism, but also by Hasidism, insofar as it is mysticism. And in some places, the mystical realm reaches deep into the core of Hasidism.

But the specific position of Judaism, like that of Hasidism, becomes evident only if one emphasizes the crucial differences between it and this eastern–mystical idea. Ramakrishna's statement is uttered from a standpoint where the speaker is almost identical with the ocean. This position can also be attained from a starting point in Hasidism. But—and this contrasts emphatically with Hasidism—in Ramakrishna, existence in the world is mentioned only fleetingly. Compared with the ocean, the scope of worldly existence is far too insignificant, representing only a transient, coincidental change in the ocean's aggregate state. Even if this aspect counts as a divine incarnation, the drop-like nature and unimportance of the individual become glaringly obvious.

In Judaism, in contrast, the world and the individual have quite a different significance, because "God in Godself," his quasi-oceanic existence, transcends all that can be experienced. As creator of the world, God stands at the center of the Jewish worldview, and the creation is said to be the prototypical divine act.

Basically, the religious existence of the Jewish person revolves around this work of the beginning, around its affirmation and continuation by humanity, as the core content of life. Meanwhile, at just the point where Ramakrishna's metaphor involves the truism of the water-and-ice relationship, what is going on is not only the tension and problematic of the intimacy of God and humankind, but also the whole world-embracing, religious-redemptive power of the Jewish mission.

The substantial identity of God and humankind leads Ramakrishna, and India as a whole, to frankly overlook the difference between God and humankind, treating it like a deceptive appearance. When it emerges as an aspect of Hasidism, however, this identity has a different weight entirely. Whereas in India, the world and the human dimension are wrested back from the overwhelming greatness of the divine, a reverse process begins in Hasidism. Here, based on the tension produced by the ineradicable difference between God and humankind, these opposites begin to be synthesized, and thereby confer on humanity an ever-greater depth and an increasingly stronger capacity for illumination.

Contraction as a principle of creation

A basic Kabbalistic teaching, on which Hasidism rests, is that of the *tzimtzum*,[5] contraction, as the fundamental principle of creation.

This *tzimtzum*, which leads to the emergence of the world from the inherently infinite, means a gradual constriction of divine light. Passing through several levels of the world,[6] it results in the most strongly "contracted" world of things, the material world of our existence. At the same time, however, the *tzimtzum* is the principle of individuation or, as we should say now, individualization, because:

> every thing in the world has another *tzimtzum* in terms of quantity and quality.[7]

The creation of the world through *tzimtzum* is one of the basic problems. Associated with it is the problem of boundaries, and that of relativity and contingency, as the essential constituents of the world of existence. Creation through the *tzimtzum* means that the content of the world is all in individualized form, from the differentiation of humans to that of stones and things.

This varying state of contraction corresponds to a self-contraction by the creative divinity, which concentrates its overwhelming totality into the vessel-like individualization of the world's particularity.

The ability of the individual and the world to live is guaranteed only by the divine *tzimtzum*. As a basic principle of creation, contraction is therefore an expression of divine love, for:

> because of this love he contracted himself, as it were, so that his brilliance could be received.[8]

The inadequacy of everything actually world-like as a "something," a finite entity, over against the infinite totality, requires an act of divine self-contraction, so that the contact between the finite individual and infinite fullness does not lead to the catastrophic explosion of individual form, and thus to destruction. Therefore, creation, as the creation of individualized vessels, entails a divine self-concealment. Divine concealment and the individualization of creation are coordinated facts; they are simply different aspects of one and the same event, namely, the *tzimtzum* as the basis of the world. Thus, any view that relates these facts causally, making one depend on the other, fails to recognize the true state of affairs.

The necessary relativity of the individual toward the infinite is nothing negative. On the contrary, it is fundamentally willed and affirmed by God. As a matter of principle, creation involves lifting the individual, finite form out of the unformed boundlessness before creation. The absolute inferiority of the finite to the infinite is as much constituted by this relationship as the orientation of the infinite toward the finite.

Here, the world is regarded as the diversity of vessel-like forms of different sizes, different stages, and varied vitality. Every single thing is affirmed as separate and limited, whereby the continuous movement of everything finite toward the infinite is an endless dynamic process, even though the finite remains confined by an indissoluble contingency, within which this dynamics takes place.

The weight of creation gathers upon the human being, because the principle of contraction culminates in the individuality of the single person.

> Everyone should know and bear in mind that his nature is unique in the world, and no one on earth was ever like him; for if anyone had ever been like him, he would not have needed to be. In reality, however, everyone is a new thing in the world, and he should bring his character to perfection. For because it is not perfect, the coming of the Messiah is delayed.[9]

The purpose and importance of the individual

In every person there is something exquisite, which exists in no one else. Therefore one should honor everyone according to his hidden quality, which he alone has and none of his fellows.[10]

This importance of the individual is a basic principle of Hasidism, at least of early Hasidism. It is revolutionary for a Judaism in which, since the destruction of the Temple,[11] the collective had once again held center stage.

Except for the esoteric doctrine of the Kabbalah, which was more individual in its adaptation, the rabbinical system of teaching had a collective, rational orientation. Its aim was the acquisition of a vast amount of knowledge by the learner, who was graded up or down depending on his ability to learn this subject matter largely by heart and to work through it rationally. This work focused on tracking down questions, that is, contradictions and their refutation, or on finding answers to set problems. The quality of the answer depended on the pupil's authoritative command and ability to interrelate what had been learned and the material to be combined with it. Cultivating the *talmid hakam*[12] was equivalent to cultivating a formal combinatorial thinking type.[13]

In contrast, Hasidism does not seek to cultivate a particular, qualifiable type, because the human totality toward which it looks can be attained by each individual. Therefore, Hasidism makes efforts in a direction that was previously unknown—in this form—in Judaism. Its concern is the care of souls, understanding this term in its widest range of meanings.

The history of Hasidism is the history of the *tzaddikim*, the righteous men, and of their disciples. Leadership—in the proto-Hasidism of the beginning—means the circle-forming, disciple-making power of the "perfect man," whose central radiance surrounds him with force fields of followers.[14]

The unique significance of Hasidism, not only in Jewish history but also in human history generally, is that a large number of mana-personalities[15] emerged and were influential. These were able to teach and live *at the same time* and *near each other*, without involving a church and the apostolic dissemination of a basic doctrine, or different students teaching *one* path or *one* dogma.

The diverse individuality of the *tzaddikim* and their character proves the authenticity of the teaching about the importance of the individual.

> All *tzaddikim* serve, each in a different way, each according to his station, and the one who says, "Only my rabbi is righteous," loses both worlds.[16]

The care of souls

The phenomenon of the diversity of *tzaddikim*, and of the disciples gathered around them, is not accidental. Corresponding to this phenomenon, the individual care of souls is understood as a religious problem, the guiding theme of which is found in the saying that the *tzaddikim* are the "doctors of the soul."[17]

For Hasidism the world is an infinite sequence of the most varied highs and lows, in which every thing and every person occupies a different, individual place, depending on the kind and size of soul or part-soul embodied in that thing or person. The task and challenge for the *tzaddik* are to give each individual what he and he alone needs.

There is a law that the revelation depends on the level of the person to whom the revelation comes.[18] Corresponding to the theory of the *tzimtzum*, that law is generalized here. The circumference, that is, the holding capacity of the vessels, is of crucial importance for the self-revealing one, which must—out of love—confine itself and adjust to the capacity of the recipient. This relationship is emphasized time and again in countless parables of father and son, showing the father's willingness to adjust to the child's nature, age, and power of understanding. And the same relativity of self-adapting consideration, which determines the relationship between God and the world, also determines—as a basic law of the care of souls—the relationship between the *tzaddik* and the people.

> The *tzaddik* always gives light, the hindrance lies with the one who receives.[19]

or

> When the *tzaddik* reveals something, he brings down new souls for everyone who hears the teaching, depending on their level and their capacity to understand. But the teaching has two powers, to kill and to bring to life . . . .
>
> So the teachings of the *tzaddik* come to everyone according to their understanding. There are people who receive a new soul through the revelation of the teaching, and there are those in whom, God forbid, it is the opposite.[20]

Due to this diversity, the difficulty, which is already great in individual instruction, is twice as great when many people are taught at the same time, for the *tzaddik* must speak with great care:

> so that the individual only hears what he needs to, and no more.[21]

Or, as was said about one rabbi:

> On a sabbath, when my room is full of people, it is difficult for me "to say Torah." For each person requires his own Torah, and each wishes to find his own perfection. And so what I give to all I withhold from each.[22]

We are dealing here with an *inner* dissolution of the community as a collective, which is highly characteristic of Hasidism. Even though it emphasizes the community, which forms a feeling-toned unity in prayer and festival, music and dance, communal meals, and communal instruction, it preserves the single person as an individuality. The community does not exist to orgiastically obliterate the human being. Rather, each one should be seized and enhanced by it as an individual. Here, the community is recognized as a threat. Hasidism attempts to overcome the two negative possibilities of forming a religious community. One is that, within a community, the individual can no longer be distinguished—which is the deepest reason for the modern person's declining attachment to the religious collective, which "gives him nothing anymore," regardless of denomination. The other danger is that he is annihilated, regressively, in a collective, overwhelming mass event—which is the intention of all mass movements substituting for religion.

The revolutionariness of this most individual form of the care of souls can be gauged only if it is seen against the background of a collective Judaism, in which the religious potency of the individual is small, whereas that of the collective community is extraordinarily great. One of the sharpest formulations in this respect is the answer given by a *tzaddik* to an inquiring student: "Show me one general way to the service of God." The *tzaddik* replied:

> It is impossible to tell men what way they should take. For one way to serve God is through the teachings, another through prayer, another through fasting, and still another through eating. Everyone should carefully observe what way his heart draws him to, and then choose this way with all his strength.[23]

But one would seriously misunderstand this answer and its attitude toward the care of souls if it were understood merely as a technical–psychological adaptation to the needs of the community. Underlying it is the idea that, just as the human being stands at the center of creation, so every individual is called to fulfill his sacred, unassailable, and irreplaceable place within it. Only when we have clearly established the full extent of the "anthropocentric place of the human being in the world," as Hasidism puts it, can we see the importance that this position in the universe gives to the individual.

Early Hasidism assumes that it is necessary to develop the individual's ability to carry on his indissoluble dialogue with the divine, so that his life, being determined by this individual connection, may be shaped and fulfilled. The indissoluble and irreplaceable nature of this task is most important. The Jew's sovereignty in relation to God—which corresponds to the ancient Jewish notion of the individual's prophetic disposition[24]—is formulated in highly interesting historical–philosophical terms. It is even emphasized with such surprising audacity that it presents the loss of the Temple and the priesthood, and life in exile, as positive things.

> Today, in the time of the galut, it is easier to reach the holy spirit than in the time of the Temple. A parable: When the king is in his royal palace, it is less possible to draw close to him than when he is on his way, for then anyone who wishes may come closer. Even a peasant, who does not know what is proper and cannot come before the king in his royal palace, may come to him in his lodging house and speak to him. So it is today in the galut: if a person is thinking in his attachment to God, he dwells and abides with him.[25]

This is a revolutionary reversal of all the ideas that were otherwise customary, ideas that denigrated any kind of present at the expense of a historical past. It enhances the religious significance of the individual and burdens him with an unparalleled task, because every individual now occupies within the universe an irrevocable place, to which he is bound.

The autonomy of the individual

The *tzaddik* expresses his relationship to the individual—at least in early Hasidism—in that he sees his task *not* as being an advocate, but as awakening the central activity of the individual and leading him to that layer[26] from which the individual's religious autonomy creatively breaks through. The *tzaddik* must help the individual to conduct his never-ending conversation with the divine in his own voice — not the borrowed voice of the *tzaddik*. Thus, it is said about the Rabbi of Ropshitz:

> He rises early in the morning and prays that all those in need of help may find [what they need] at home and do not need to go to Ropschitz and may not be tempted to believe that the rabbi helped them.[27]

Or someone else says:

> Because often, when someone comes to me to seek counsel, I hear how he himself speaks the answer.[28]

The most significant formulation of the problem of inner revelation and of the individual's religious creativity can be found in the following tale:

> A young rabbi complained to the Rabbi of Rizhyn: "During the hours when I devote myself to my studies I feel life and light, but the moment I stop studying it is all gone. What shall I do?" The Rabbi of Rizhyn replied: "That is just as when a man walks through the woods of a dark night, and for a time another joins him, lantern in hand, but at the crossroads they part and the first must grope his way on alone. But if a man carries his own light with him he need not be afraid of any darkness."[29]

This notion of "one's own light," in contrast to the borrowed light, breaks with the whole tradition of being collectively embedded in the certainty of action arising from knowledge, and knowledge from learning. But it also reverses the devolution of Hasidism under the *tzaddikim*, when the enlightening power of the *tzaddikim* is heightened by the uncannily increasing darkness of the masses. Just here, in the period of deterioration, the early Hasidic effort on behalf of the individual as the irreplaceable center of existence is shouldered by the *tzaddikim*, who gather together as the prototype of the individual, taking the burden of this task upon themselves for the sake of a recollectivized, anonymous mass.

In one Hasidic tale,[30] a rabbi who was searching for a treasure in dreams and by wandering far afield meets a stranger, who mocks his trust in dreams and jeeringly reports a dream of his own, in which he had also been promised that he would find a treasure. According to the stranger's dream, the treasure is lying beneath the stove in the parlor of this same rabbi, whose journey across the world had led him to the stranger. The rabbi returns home, after the dream-cycle between him and the stranger has ended, and digs up the treasure in his own parlor. Here is what is said about this tale:

> Rabbi Bunam used to tell young men who came to him for the first time the story of Rabbi Eisik, son of Rabbi Yekel in Cracow [. . .] "Take this story to heart," Rabbi Bunam used to add, "and make what it says your own: There is something you cannot find anywhere in the world, not even at the *tzaddik*'s, and there is, nevertheless, a place where you can find it."[31]

This humility of the *tzaddik* belongs to early Hasidism and corresponds to an attitude that says:

> When I begin talking to someone, I want to hear him speak the highest words.[32]

The most profound justification for this unlimited respect for the individual and his individuality is that every person, not only the *tzaddik*, is a divine vessel. Therefore, any overbearingness is an overbearingness toward the divinity, which has its seat in the one with whom one is talking. If anyone wishes to instruct another,[33] then:

> he should consider that the soul of his fellow man is also bound to the Creator and devoted to him, and that he stands and preaches before *God*.[34]

The divinity of the person with whom one speaks thus grounds the relationship with the Thou and with the community. The Thou relationship toward human beings is deepened by the meaning contained here. Meanwhile, too, seen from this perspective—transcending the world and the human Thou—divinity itself becomes the sole conversation partner, the only one with whom one is face to face.

One of our tasks is to show how this perspective not only is consistent with affirming the world, but also gives that affirmation its prior foundation and background. The crucial emphasis, however, always lies on the central position of the individual as the speaker or the one spoken to.

This religious emphasis on the individual reaches its ultimate point in Rabbi Bunam's saying:

> When I look at the world, it sometimes seems to me as if every person is a tree in a wilderness, and that God has no tree in his world than himself, and no one to whom he could turn than himself.[35]

One might consider this to be a late form of mystical atomization. However, we shall show how in Hasidism the creative interpretation of the world also shines through this conversation, which takes place in solitude at the edge of the world and demands the transformation of the individual.

The *tzaddik*'s evaluation, which he makes in accordance with the concept of the creation of the world in the *tzimtzum*, is not aimed at more characteristics, abilities, or even "things to have," but at the uniqueness of the individual and its fulfillment. The purpose of this demand is that no one shall take another's place. For the fulfillment of the world rests precisely on this, that everyone should find and occupy the place that belongs to them.

> "He who grasps the level of his fellow and lets go of his own will realize neither this level nor that. Many did what Rabbi Simeon bar Yochai did and their hands remained empty; for they were not in this state but only did as he did, because they saw him in this state."[36]

Korah's rebellion against Aaron[37] is explained along the same lines:

> Korah had noticed that whenever he stood on the mount among the singing Levites, great gifts of the spirit descended upon him. This made him believe that if he stood in the inner sanctuary as a high priest burning incense, he would gain even greater gifts. He did not know that the power that he had felt arose because Aaron stood there, and he here.[38]

The Elijah soul

This view is the end of every collective norm, which aims for the fulfillment of general demands of any kind, be it the fulfillment of the law or of a code of duty or conduct, or the acquisition of characteristics and functions, not to mention the general redemptive power of any sacraments whatever. The postulate of self-fulfillment, of finding one's own light, is indispensable. Its realization, however, is not visible, but lies in *that which is concealed.*

> Rabbi Elimelech told about a man to whom the prophet Elijah had appeared. Someone expressed surprise that this could be, since even Master Ibn Ezra, who had a spirit belonging to a far loftier sphere, had—according to his own words—been denied such a vision. "What you say, is true," said the *tzaddik*. "And yet it is as I have said. You know that after Elijah was transfigured, he became the Angel of the Covenant, and is present at the circumcision of every Jewish boy. But how can this be, since circumcision always takes place in the hour after prayer, and many circumcisions occur in the same hour in all parts of the world? I shall tell you how! Elijah moved all the people of Israel with the spirit of turning, so that they fell on their faces and cried out the name of the true God, and because of this he was given the whole soul of Israel. And so, whenever a boy is brought to the covenant, a part of Elijah's soul is present and enters the boy—a big part or a little part, according to the kind of child and the root of its being. And if the growing boy develops his Elijah-soul to the full, then he has a vision of the Elijah-soul contained within him. Thus the man of whom I was speaking made manifest through his good works the small part of the prophet which was within him. But Ibn Ezra did not have the strength to perfect the great part he had been given.[39]

Self-realization, or what modern depth psychology calls individuation, that is, the development of an individual personal disposition, appears here as the Elijah soul. At first, it seems as if this aspect could relate only to the sacred, "good" aspect of the personality, and thus that the intention here, too, is the development of only a partial aspect. But what emerges unmistakably from the overall conception of Hasidism is that it rejects fragmentation into sacred and profane as ultimately invalid. Moreover, as we shall see, rather than excluding the acceptance and transformation of evil, Hasidism includes even this in the development of the Elijah soul.

At all events, what we meant is now more understandable: the dynamics of inner development, the continuous movement of the finite toward the infinite, is preserved despite the indissoluble contingency defined by the limits within which this dynamic unfolds. The development of the Elijah soul, individuation, corresponds to this movement of the finite toward the infinite. At the same time, the contraction of the individual, given by the world and creation, and the specifically different circumference of the Elijah soul, must be accepted as the basis of life to be fulfilled and completed.

> Before his death, Rabbi Zusya said, "In the coming world, they will not ask me: 'Why were you not Moses?' They will ask me: 'Why were you not Zusya?'"[40]

Or:

> Rabbi Bunam once said:
>
> "I should not like to change places with our father Abraham! What good would it do God if Abraham became like blind Bunam, and blind Bunam became like Abraham? Rather than have this happen, I think I shall try to grow a little over and beyond myself."[41]

Wholeness and compensation

We shall encounter the problem of wholeness and completeness on many levels and from many perspectives, part of which is about doing what is difficult for the sake of wholeness. But this, too, this is meant in an entirely anti-ascetic way, as gaining the foreign side of the world and adding it to one's own.

The rabbi who is searching for treasure must go to foreign places and receive the key word from the stranger, with whose help he then raises his own treasure. One must always take the path that leads to the far side of the world, in order to find one's own side and bring the *whole* world to life.

One of Rabbi Nachman's interpretations of the sentence, "I have charged ravens to sustain you there,"[42] is this:

> In the beginning, when one begins to give alms, one must shatter one's cruelty and turn it into its opposite, compassion. This is the main thing about charity. For if someone is compassionate by nature and gives alms because of his compassionate nature, this is not service. There are also animals that are naturally compassionate. The essence of service is to shatter cruelty and to turn it into its opposite, compassion. To this corresponds: "I commanded the raven to nourish you," for the raven is cruel by nature and was made compassionate to nourish Elijah.[43]

Action as such is not the essential thing. What matters is its relationship to human individuality, the inherent nature of the person. Something that is "accomplished," in terms of service and the expenditure of energy, becomes meaningful only when one's own structure is transformed and becomes whole and complete.

> "There are two kinds of men," said one *tzaddik*, "those with black gall and those with light. The dark-tempered sit over the books of the teachings

> and are of a miserly disposition. The light-tempered love company and are generous. Rabbi H. was dark-tempered, devoted to his studies, and withdrawn. His merit did not lie in living for the teachings, but in governing his nature, and giving freely of what he possessed. But once he had done this, and he had learned to live with his fellow-men, his studying was no longer a necessity, but a virtue."[44]

This is not a fundamental rejection of the scholar, the intellectual aristocrat, in favor of the outward-oriented feeling type.[45] The more far-reaching revolution of Hasidism is often reduced, however, to exactly this formula.

The wholeness to be achieved presents itself as a task for every person, irrespective of type. This emergence of wholeness, of the complete human being, can be achieved only gradually in the life of the individual. Only in the course of time does one manage to circumambulate the whole life cycle of one's own nature. This process, which slowly leads to self-fulfillment through the pain of overcoming oneself, is marked by one's own compensation.

Beside the principle of self-affirmation, which says to follow the path of one's heart's desire, there is the other, which counsels taking the difficult path. But the purpose of this difficulty is individual, and not ascetic, in the sense of being outright hostile to the world. On the contrary, even world affirmation can be the "difficulty" to be accepted for the wholeness of the complete person. Inner and outer, joy and suffering, doing and letting happen: only all of this, taken together, amounts to wholeness.

Beside the admonition to the *tzaddik* who grieved that, despite his age, he had not yet done penance—"You are thinking only of yourself. How about forgetting yourself and thinking of the world!"—stands the seemingly opposite insight of one who set out to convert the whole world and ended up only wanting to right himself, in order to serve God in truth.[46] The outer world and the human community are as much a part of this as the soul and as the inner world. One without the other is too little, for what matters, always, is wholeness. And just as no one is called a "perfect" human being until he is male *and* female,[47] so also no one is perfect unless he unites heaven *and* earth, above *and* below.

To the more penetrating gaze, however, it becomes clear that the world to be affirmed is not merely the actual world of objects and facts, but a world that has to be seen and experienced from within.

When the Great Maggid[48] faced the controversial question whether one should first contemplate the greatness of the creator and then become suitably humble, or whether one should instead begin by being truly humble, because knowledge of the creator would then arise of its own accord—in reply to this question, which largely parallels that of whether one should come to oneself via the world or via oneself to the world, he decided:

> These and these are the words of the living God, but inner grace belongs to the one who begins with himself, and not with the Creator.[49]

Thus, to be sure, the value of beginning with oneself prevails on certain grounds, yet even here, the wholeness of the individual—corresponding to the divine wholeness—appears as the goal and end-point of every singular path.

The emphasis on the individual not only applies to every single person, it also extends to the details of the world, to things, to the places in the world, and to temporal details. In every person and every thing lives the contracted divine spark, in varying degrees of strength.

Being pregnant with revelation is not limited to particular things, creatures, and places; Hasidism does away with the separation between sacred and profane. Everything is pregnant with revelation: "The *whole* earth is full of his glory."[50] Every thing, every creature, everything has its hour; revelation is latent in all. Within everything are sparks that are associated with someone's soul.

> Every thing has its hour, and in this hour it must come to the human being, who comes from the same root as the sparks that are in this thing.[51]

Here again, we see the purpose and nature of individuality. To each soul belong different sparks, through the redemption of which the soul is expanded and lifted up. The fact that people vary, in types, ranks, and individualities, means only that for each one, depending on their kind and capacity, a different-sized sector of the world is within reach, pregnant with revelation. The whole world is filled with this pregnancy of revelation. These sparks exist in every thing and every person, awaiting their redemption. To do justice to the world's total pregnancy with revelation, however, the only subject would be all of differentiated humankind.

This great picture lies at the heart of Hasidism like an unspoken secret. An infinite radiant world of revelation lies hidden in created reality. No perceiving subject, however, corresponds to the brilliance of this world diamond, with its inexpressible myriad of facets. It is still concealed, and only a larger or smaller number of the luminous facets of this diamond will become visible to the fulfilled individuality of the individual. Only if a single eye of humanity could be formed from the immense number of human individualities, in their endlessly varied capacity for experience, might that unified eye alone recognize the hidden light of the world diamond. Only such a unified humanity would be the partner for a self-revealing world.

The relationship between the sparks inherent in things and the individual human soul is close and unmistakable. Even the fortuitousness of life proves to be merely apparent.

> One person loves one thing, another hates it and loves something else. And if he makes use of this vessel, or eats a meal even just for his physical needs, then he improves the sparks that are in it, because afterward he serves with this energy, which comes to his body from this garment or food or from some other thing; and with this energy he serves God, and one finds that the sparks in these things are improved. Sometimes it happens that the thing is

> lost, because all the sparks that were in this thing, that belonged to the root of his soul, were improved by him long ago. God then takes the vessel from him and gives it to someone else, for the sparks still in this vessel belong to another root.[52]

The only sparks that belong to the root of the owner's soul are those he has managed to improve and raise. If the human soul cannot redeem the sparks of things any further, the things will be taken away from him, because he no longer has anything to do with them. They are no longer of interest to him; they are not cathected any more by the libido, and he "loses" them.[53] But what has become unimportant and lifeless for one person is still full of content and pregnant with revelation for another, making his soul catch fire. The lost thing is not worthless or useless; rather, the soul is old when it no longer relates to the thing, being unable to see it in a new way.

Thus, *habit* is the enemy that prevents a new relationship with the world and disguises its fullness.

> God says to man, as he said to Moses: "Put off thy shoes from your feet"—put off the habitual which encloses your foot, and you will know that the place on which you are standing is holy ground. For there is no rung of human life on which we cannot find the holiness of God everywhere and at all times."[54]

Everywhere—thus, over the whole earth, in every thing and creature, but also "at all times."

For Hasidism, the world consists of more or less powerful lights of different sizes. Strictly speaking, even the "thing" does not exist as something substantial, but merely as a coordinate quantity, relative to human souls and their stages.

Contraction in time

Even time is dissolved into an infinity of points in the now, which replace an amorphous time continuum. These points are also coordinate quantities, uniquely and inexchangeably relative to the human being.

> Before the Day of Atonement the Rabbi of Ger said to the hasidim gathered around his table: "Hillel, our teacher, says: 'If I am not for myself, who will be for me?' If I do not perform my service, who will perform it for me? Everyone must perform his own service. And further along, he says: 'And if not now, when?' When will this Now be? The Now that is now, this instant in which we are speaking, did not exist at any time since the world was created, and it will never exist again. Formerly there was another Now, and later there will be another Now, and every Now has its own service; as we read in the Book of Splendor: 'The garments of morning are not the garments of

> evening.' . . . No other Now can make up for this Now, for every moment is concentrated in its particular light."[55]

Here, in the application of the *tzimtzum* to time, the absoluteness of the present moment always offers itself to the human being as a new opportunity and task. The human being, newly confronting the now in freedom of choice, is neither reassured by credit nor burdened by guilt for the now that is past. The entirety of the world and of judgment[56] is condensed into the present moment and assigned, always new, to the one who chooses.

In the apocalypse, the historical situation of the end of time and the expectation of the end hung over everything like a weight, and the judgment and the messianic kingdom in the background oppressed whatever this era chose to do. Later, in contrast, the present time began to be relativized, which led to a provisional existence. Upon the past, upon the Fathers, Zion, and the Kingdom, lay the splendor of perfection, fulfillment, and closeness to God. Upon the future, the time of the Messiah, the future Zion, and the coming rule of God, lay the splendor of hope and justification. The present, however, every present, lay in the shadow of intrusive provisionality and the inauthenticity of exile. In the best and highest case, it amounted to expectation and preparation.

Stepping out of history[57] and stepping out of direct revelation are two correlated dimensions. The world of Judaism had become a world of the interregnum. Every turning toward the world, every attempt to gain a foothold, to establish a kingdom in any sense, was rejected *a priori* by the devout as heresy. It was destroyed from the outset, and thus condemned, by the reality of history, but also, for the Jew, by the manifestation of YHWH.

The messiah soul and actualized messianism

A process begins in Hasidism, however, the "actualizing of messianism," that is, a turning away from the future to the present, from there to here, from outside to inside. Elsewhere, we shall demonstrate[58] to what extent Hasidism, after almost 2,000 years, involves a delayed ripening of essential aspects of early Christianity within Judaism.

Clearly evident here is the collective internalizing of the messianic aspect, an internalizing that suggests that messianism is not something that comes at any time, from anywhere, but is a stage of the individual that needs to be fulfilled.[59]

> A man came to the Rabbi of Kotzk and asked how he could make his sons devote themselves to the Torah. The rabbi answered: "If you really want them to do this, then you yourself must spend time over the Torah, and they will do as you do. Otherwise, they will not devote themselves to the Torah but will tell their sons to do it, and so it will go on. For it is written: 'Only take heed to thyself . . . lest thou forget the things which thine eyes saw . . .! Make them known unto thy children and thy children's children.' If you

> yourself forget the Torah, your sons will also forget it, only urging their sons to know it, and they too will forget the Torah and tell their sons that they should know it, and no one will ever know the Torah."[60]

Or, as a corresponding passage says:

> After a sabbath meal at which many fathers of families were present, the Yehudi said: "You people! If any one of you is asked why he toils so on earth, he replies: 'To bring up my son to study and serve God.' And after the son is grown up, he forgets why his father toiled on earth, and he toils in his turn, and if you ask him why, he will say: 'I must bring up my son to be studious and to do good works.' And so it goes on, you people, from generation to generation. But when shall we get to see the right child?"[61]

This actualizing of messianism corresponds to a radical internalizing of the problem of redemption. Redemption is now less than ever an event that comes from outside. It depends on whether every single person fulfills their messianic stage, the messianic stage of their soul, at every moment and in every place, "everywhere and at all times."[62]

> Know that each individual must safeguard the stage of the Messiah that belongs to him, for everyone, depending on his holiness and purity, has his own Messiah stage. And he must be very careful that his Messiah stage is not spoilt.[63]

For:

> The world was created only for the sake of choice and the one who chooses.[64]

And:

> Every human being in the world can become worthy of the highest level, because everything depends entirely on human choice.[65]

Here, we must recall what was said about the Elijah soul.[66] As is well known, Elijah is said to be the precursor of the Messiah. Fulfilling, that is, realizing the Elijah soul is the task of the individual. The arrival of the Messiah depends on this individual realization of the stage of the Messiah. Only thus does the emphasis placed on the individual and his service become understandable. His redemptive function is the crucial fact in the world, from which comes the emphasis on the individual, on the here and now, and the contraction of the world's fate to human service.

This also helps us to understand a passage in a letter of the Baal Shem, in which he reports the ascent of a soul:

> I asked the Messiah: "When will you come, Lord?" He replied: "You will know it by this: when your teachings are spread and become manifest in the world, and when what I have taught you and what you have understood pours forth, and when people will be able to bring about revelations and ascents like you: then the power of the shell will diminish, and there will be a time of grace and healing." And I was amazed and very aggrieved by the great length of time until this would become possible.[67]

Here, the coming of the Messiah is unmistakably seen to depend on the inner level of humanity's soul, for true to Judaic thinking, the collective remains a decisive contributing factor. It is true that the coming of the Messiah depends on the individual's inner development, but everyone must reach this level, not just one or a few.

Place, time, and the individual belong together, inexchangeably and irreplaceably. Everything "is concentrated in its particular light." Just as no present moment can "be made up for by any other,"[68] so no place and no situation can be replaced by another. So, also, in the presence of the divine there is no substitution. When we read:

> I shall not be asked: "Why were you not Moses?" I shall be asked: "Why were you not Zusya?"[69]

this also means that no one else can absolve this sin of not having been oneself. Here, the central position of the human being suddenly turns into the indissoluble responsibility of self-fulfillment. For this self-fulfillment is also the prerequisite and basic condition for the messianic situation, meaning a collective constellation of humanity and the world.

The anonymous character of eternity culminates in the formed moment, the anonymity of the world in "this place," and that of collective humanity in the individual. In just this way, in consciousness the anonymity of the unconscious, and in YHWH the anonymity of the universe, receives form, shape, and the ability to be named.

2. The inner dimension and the way into the hidden

The path of meditation and the path of creation

For any genuine understanding of Hasidism, it is essential to emphasize the inner dimension. Without a psychological concept that takes the reality of this inner aspect seriously and grasps its reality as a constituent part of human existence, one cannot go beyond aesthetic or vaguely religious attempts to appreciate this movement.

The terminology of Hasidism comes from the Kabbalah, from which it takes its constructive basic conception. In another context, we go into detail about this influence and its meaning. For now, let us begin by setting out a fundamental principle that has remained the common possession of the Kabbalah, independent of its varied formulations. This basic law says that the actual, earthly world is a later and lower form of creation, the beginning of which rests in God as the "hidden of all that are hidden," the inside of every outside; also that the spiritual represents the prior form of everything material.

Creation out of nothingness contrasts with creation out of any matter that is given or any that is gained in a mythological struggle. In constituting creation, the divine *tzimtzum* establishes the contrast between nothing and something, where this "nothing" expresses the fact that divinity infinitely surpasses the human power to comprehend. By the principle of negative theology, an individual, created as "something," cannot assert anything positive about the divine. Nothingness is the positive term for a divinity transcending human consciousness. Yet only from the human point of view is it nothingness, that is, beyond all experience, and this does not say anything about the divine in itself.

> According to the kabbalists, that "nothingness" of creation is not (at least since 1200) at all independent of God, but defined by him, his first utterance, which already the oldest texts (Bahir) refer to as nothingness = אין or מחשבה קדמין (thought, original idea) or as the highest *sefirah*,[70] as "*Keter Elyon*" (*the highest crown*), that is, this nothingness is itself emanated, as the first power. It is a nothingness אין only subjectively, from the creatures' viewpoint. Creatures can glimpse it as the highest destination in their return to God even if it cannot be reached in itself. But from God's perspective, it is still rather the fullness of everything that was thought in the original idea, and highly substantial.[71]

Nevertheless, we shall see that a lot may be said about this nothingness, with regard to its relation to the human being and the world. For the moment, we shall stress only the fact that nothingness is identical with the thought, the primordial idea. The sequence of the ten *sefirot* is based on the same principle as that of the four levels in the creation of the world. Regardless of how the sequence is described in detail, or specifically coordinated with the four levels of creation, it is based on the same principle, a descent from the spiritual to the physical.[72]

The relationship of God and world, absolute and material, YHWH and human being, is always harnessed into a symbolism of opposites. One side is called: spirit–inside–above, the other: matter–outside–below. It is only from this symbolism that the "descending" path of creation and the "ascending" path of meditation can be understood. A view that derives the creation of the world from a divine source, which becomes noticeable on the inside, and which one can at least attempt to approach or grasp through meditation, that is, through introversion, must necessarily proclaim the dominance of this inner dimension and of introversion. (Here, we leave aside the early stages of religious experience, the stages of genuine theophanies, in which this inner dimension appeared projected, even though in a structural sense it clearly belongs to the inner aspect of human nature.)

Alongside the path of speculative meditation, which stresses thinking, another path is found everywhere, namely that of emotional meditation, which stresses feeling and the love of God. This is primarily a path of introversion, even when it extends secondarily into love for the world, a love to which the speculative path may also lead. The primary conception of God is gained from the inner experience whereby, in the progressive stages of the meditative and ecstatic path[73] (which will occupy us later), emotional and rational elements are fused together.

The world of appearance and corporeality is the lowest level of creation, furthest removed from God. In it, God is most disguised and hidden, withdrawn the furthest from his actual nature. Even if, by the fundamental teaching of Hasidism, "the *whole* world is full of his glory," and divine sparks are present in the most inferior things, in evil, and even in idols, yet the hiddenness of the divine is not only a constituent element of our world but also its central problem. The other side of the *tzimtzum* is that in creation the deity became contracted, confined, and hidden all at once.

Thus the world is a series of shells, in which every inside is the outside of a lower level of the world.[74] In the innermost of these, however, God still remains hidden, because:

> God is manifest and hidden, that is, what is manifest to us is clothing and appearance, and what is hidden to us is inwardness.[75]

But the degree and extent of God's hiddenness also depend on the human structure, and not least on the structure of human knowledge. So, as Rabbi Nachman says, God is hidden in two ways.[76] If one knows nothing about the hiddenness of God, then he cannot be found, but remains most deeply hidden. If, however, one knows about his hiddenness, he can be found.

The human task in the world is fundamentally bound up with God's hiddenness in it. The world's redemption demands that it be guided to its true nature, in order to make the hidden divinity visible and thus also to manifest the real reality of God, humanity, and world.[77]

Just as Indian mythology symbolizes the world as a tree, the roots of which are above and the top of which is below,[78] the *Ein Sof* is the divine under the aspect of infinity, and the *Ein*, nothingness, is the root and source of the world, of which are our world of things is the final ramification and differentiation. Time and again, Hasidism maintains that things have their roots at the top and that the task is to lead them *up* to their roots. For a connection with the roots of the upper world brings abundance down, nurturing the lower world, perfecting, enlivening, and bringing it to its true reality.

One prototype of this connection with the root is meditation, the inner path that proceeds through levels and by the ecstatic contemplation of the divine. Descending level by level to the individual, the world forms a genetic chain. In meditation, which restores this connection in reascending order, the life principle of the thing and the creature, being isolated in the world, can be guided back to the shared, divine source of life from whom the creation of the world poured forth. One may return to this source through meditation, when contingency and individuation are suspended.

The *tzimtzum* principle, however, as the affirmation of creation in terms of individuation, as the affirmation of God's entering into hiddenness, and as the affirmation of the finite, created world of things, demands something more and other than a regressive suspension of creation in introversion and meditation.

It is true that even this meditative path must be taught and followed, if one is to become conscious of the world's real background and relativize the violent factuality of the material–corporeal outer world, without destroying or suspending it.

In reality, this actual world is full of secrets just as it is full of the divine, except that its outwardness should not disguise its radiant, hidden inwardness.

> The eyes are the highest, very high things, and they always see what is great and terrible. If a person were worthy of capable eyes, he would already know great things from what they see. For they always see, but he does not know what he sees.[79]

Or, formulated objectively:

> Just as the hand held before the eyes hides the greatest mountain, so the small earthly life obscures the view of the immense lights and secrets filling the world, and whoever can pull it [the hand] away from his eyes sees the great glow of the inner world.[80]

Small, earthly life is the daily obsession with the merely real and the banality of the everyday, in which all background is lacking. This same world, the same everyday, and the same reality are revealed as a world of tremendous lights and secrets, if one is capable of seeing into their true nature, that is, if one's gaze is focused on the inner world. But the inward-turning path is typically a path that spiritualizes, for in Hasidism the world rests on the principle of the wind, the spirit.

For an analogical foundation to the complicated, idealistic–speculative world of the Kabbalah, take for example the invisible, spiritual realm, in contrast with the solidity of things. Consider the hiddenness and hidden power of the spiritual, and the striking way that visible actions depend on the invisible thoughts that precede them. We need not discuss here the complicated system of the Kabbalistic world, its philosophy of language and numbers, but a few remarks may suffice to illustrate the spiritual structure of the world as viewed by Hasidism, based on the Kabbalah.

The inner sequence, or the sequence of internalizing, ascends from action to word, and from word to letter, where every letter represents a spiritual power. From the letter, or from the word, the ascending path leads further to the thought, and from the thought to the original idea or wisdom.

Every level in this sequence represents a higher spiritual world. Every level also serves as the outward reality for the level above, while being the principle of life for the one below. This means, for example, that the word serves as clothing and vessel for the letters and the thought, conceiving from them. Meanwhile, the letters and the thought are the word's principle of life. They are its power, its activity in what is done, for the word only lives from the thought. Likewise, the action is clothing and vessel for the word, and the word is the principle of life by which an action occurs, from which it lives. All of this corresponds to God's creative speaking when the world was made.

In this chain, every link begets downward while it conceives from above. The descending act of creation took place in reverse order to the path of meditation, from nothingness through wisdom to action. Meanwhile, meditation not only goes downward, retracing the path of creation, it also rises, uniting the links of the chain, so that the circle of life's current is closed in them. Through this organic connection between the source and the vessels, abundance flows down into the world, while, at the same time, in the upper world, joy is born.

Corresponding to the nature of this sequence, the ascending path is simultaneously a path from the outside to the inside, from the particular to the general, from the contoured to the boundless, from the solitary one, contracted in the *tzimtzum*, to the one who is absolute and infinitely alive.

The inner complexity of this path, which always leads through all worlds and the ten *sefirot*, seems at first to be rationally speculative and unnatural.

The connection with what lies above is sometimes established by means of a conceptual abstraction, or by a shift from the particular to the general. This method does in fact seem quite artificial. If, for example, the idea of beauty, the world of beauty, and God as the creator of beauty are all derived from woman's beauty, then this path is ancient and can be found everywhere. If the upward ascent from the real thing is accomplished through the concept of purpose, this can also appear primitive at first. For instance, a house may be inserted into the original ontological sequence, so that the path to be traveled becomes: place–sleep–peace–strength for God's service–prayer–God. But a spirit lives behind and beside these artificial, somewhat forced and speculative paths of upward connection. And although the method is still often unwieldy, it is a fundamental way of recognizing the essence of existence and penetrating to the realms behind it.

The ancient contrast between the perfection of the mental image and its finite realization in time and space is paradigmatic for the difference between the absolute world of the creative idea, or wisdom, and the factuality that is realized in the *tzimtzum* under the principle of contraction and judgment. This is often exemplified in the difference between the intellectual plan of building a house, and its realization. On the one hand is the thought, the creative beginning. On the other hand, its realization necessarily involves dissection into temporal sequences, individual actions, materials, etc., all of which belong to the ultimate purpose of bringing it to reality.

The historical parallels, and perhaps even the origins of this conception, are obvious. It is, however, important that this conception of the world is not meant in aesthetic or epistemological terms, but in volitional ones. The ideas and the generality, the letter and the thought, are conceived of here as creative powers. The spiritual is the principle of life in all of reality. The inner vitality of every thing in the world consists in the spiritual that is in it, from which it was created, and through which it is connected to the reservoir of creative and spiritual life.

The vitalist concept

Only this vitalist concept enables a real understanding of the meaning of the act of meditation, in which the spiritual connection is not only revealed but also actualized. Nor should the claim that a world corresponds to each of these levels be understood in formal terms. Instead, the central position of the human being within this spiritual, animated world, which is also becoming animated, becomes clear only if one considers that among all of them a latent love relationship, so to speak, is urging toward unification. Under this image is formulated what we describe today as energetic tension. This means:

> The word desires to be attached to the thought.[81]

Conversely:

> The thought longs to have a voice so that it may have its say.[82]

And so it is everywhere. At work between all spheres and all levels of the world are these latent relationships, which need to be actualized, and the center of which is represented by the human being and his spiritual side, his intellect or reason or consciousness, for:

> Human thought is the vehicle to God.[83]

This theory of language is merely one version of a doctrine of the soul and its inherent activity. For, as we shall show,[84] the various worlds and levels of the world are assigned to various parts of the soul. The principle of the hidden inner activity, dwelling within the outer appearance, is a projection of the theory of the soul, which animates the body.

If ancient Judaism depicted the principle of life as the spirit breathing into the material body, which has no life in itself, now it is said:

> The essence of the body's activities is only the principle of life, which is in the body-soul (*nefesh*). For the *nefesh* shows its activity through the body's limbs, and the body has no movement of its own. Everything occurs through the forces of the *nefesh*.[85]

For this reason, crucial emphasis lies on the *sekel*,[86] a term that simultaneously means common sense, reason, and consciousness. It is, so to speak, the organ of mental activity that is specifically human, because it is the vehicle of the act of meditation, of service, and of prayer.

The *sekel* appears in one passage[87] as the "essence of the principle of life," in contrast to the "sleeping stage," which is associated with evil and desire. This marks the recurrence of the familiar Gnostic opposition between the conscious light of reason and the sleepy stupor of worldly existence. But beyond that, the *sekel* is revealed here not only as a rational principle but also as the spiritual principle *par excellence.*

The *sekel* is an organ of the transpersonal, in that it is associated with the *neshama*, the rational soul.

> The renewal of the *sekel* is the renewal of the *neshama*, for the *sekel* is the *neshama*.[88]

That is, the renewal of the principle of consciousness is the renewal of the soul's highest part, the transpersonally rational soul. The spiritual principle, the organ of which is the *sekel*, is also the path to the transpersonal, and the *neshama*, the rational soul, being the transpersonally spiritual part of the human soul, is closely related to the *sekel* as the organ of consciousness.

This rational soul is typically seen as being identical with selfhood or the human "I."[89] Here, however, "I" should not be understood in terms of egoism, in the sense of an encapsulated egocentricity or merely rational consciousness. Rather, it is the quintessence of the individual soul, created in the *tzimtzum* and existing as a subject.[90]

The concept of the *sekel* need not be defined in detail. It is mentioned here only as a symptom, to show how the spiritual nature of inwardness is understood in association with the principle of consciousness, on the one hand, and with the individual soul, the essence of the self, on the other. The ego receives special emphasis in Judaism, both as the center of consciousness and simultaneously as the epitome of isolation in the creation of the world. We shall see that Hasidism, in particular, shifts the spiritual center of gravity from the ego to a deeper level. But even here, as in ancient Judaism, maintenance of the higher principle of reason and consciousness is not only consistent with realizing the soul's deep level but necessarily entailed by it.

The night world

The path to God, as the most hidden of the hidden, is bound to lead into hiddenness and mystery. The path inward is the path into concealment and stillness; it leads into the darkness of that which wants to reveal itself. The nature of this hiddenness contrasts with the visibility and clarity of the human world, the world of things. So the world of introspection, of the inner life or introversion, is always assigned specifically to night rather than day.[91]

This cosmic and natural association of night with introversion also plays a role in Hasidism, if only peripherally. At night, human beings experience elementary solitude, either by plunging into the irreplaceable, unique world, where what is inside unfolds itself in dreams and envelops the isolated ego, or else with fear, as everyday, worldly things are pulled away from the ego, which tries to hide, shivering, from the ever-present world of numinosity that looms up with its summons.

At night, in sleep, the hidden part of the world reveals itself, that is, its spiritual aspect.

> For by day a person sees only the material and thinks that the spiritual is encased therein. But in his dream he sees the spiritual naked, without a shell. It is so: By day the human principle of life is weak, for a person is bound to matter by his body. This is why he does not see the principle of life in material things. But at night the human principle of life divests itself of the body. Then the life principle is strong, and that is why a person can see its essence and from there can reach the level of prophecy.[92]

From this, Rabbi Nachman logically concludes:

> The essence of solitude (seclusion) lies in the night, when the world is free from the bustle of this world. For the day disturbs people and, because they run after this world during the day, it prevents them from attaching themselves to God. And this happens even if a person is not busy himself, and even if he walks along a lonely path outside the town, where no one else walks. Because the place where people walk by day and pursue this world confuses the solitude of attachment to God, even if no one else is walking there at the time. But when one walks alone at night, on lonely paths where no one else walks, and if he turns his heart and consciousness away from all the things of this world and dissolves all of these and comes to the "dissolving," then his soul is united (completed) with the root and thus the whole world is united with him in the root.[93]

This emphasis on introversion might seem to be so ordinary, so required for every form of religious life, that one would not need to claim it for Hasidism in particular. The crucial point for our investigation, however, is not the emphasis on introversion, but the relationship between "that" world, the inner world, and "this" world, the world of pure factuality.

The world of the hidden is always and everywhere divided into various levels, for spirits and demons, heavens and hells, gods and cosmic figures. These forces of the inner world, with their partly revealed, partly shrouded symbolism, surely play a major role in Kabbalistic and Hasidic legends. But whenever this kind of hiddenness emerges, it is visible as fear and anxiety, danger and hostility, even if ritual and exorcism, cult, and magical prayer dare to confront these forces. Almost always, what gives the world of the hidden its color and feeling tone is the uncertainty of consciousness.

Certainty is given by clarity and the light of consciousness, whereas veiled complexities are always full of danger. Opacity, vagueness, unreliability, and secrecy are experienced here as uncertainty and, even more, as dread and seduction, disaster and malice, and the thing that assaults and drags us into darkness. This hidden quality of spirits and ghosts, which tempts us into jungle and swamp, into ocean depths and desert, is the eternal danger that the ego fears. As the evasive, cold, intangible thing, it creeps up fawningly, and as the "other side," the enticingly unattainable, it becomes the evil will-o'-the-wisp that mockingly eludes our grasp with superior and vicious irony.

This Satanic aspect of the unconscious is not foreign to the Jew.

> The *shedim* (spirits) surround human beings like the pile of earth the vine.[94]

The rope, net, and snare of demons are supposedly warded off by the magical certainty of knowledge and law. Just as the positive character of gods and angels is associated with clarity, so the negative character of the inner realm always brings up secrecy, the dark and hidden, the indeterminate and uncanny. Contrary to the veneration of *moira*[95]—the immutable necessity of destiny and the world—this negative character culminates in Gnostic conceptions of the evil demiurge, arbitrary archons, blind fate, and the terrible demon as lord of this world. And it puts faith in the playing child, the inhumanly anonymous "It," chance as the ruler of existence, or better: the secret, senseless, cosmic power of the world, spinning and whirling.

Like a misty veil of danger, this dismal aspect flutters around the inner path of Hasidism that leads into mystery. The *tzaddikim* are also in control of this side. Amulet and exorcism, the healing of the possessed, and magical action twine around their legendary power. Here, as whenever any real experience of inwardness occurs, the reality of demons and of Satan becomes the problem of the holy struggle. The path inward always leads through the dangerous world of unconscious constellations, which threaten every consciousness that engages with them, working to weaken and entice, to overwhelm and tear in pieces.

For, in its spiritual concealment, the nothingness that overarches all levels of the created world is not only the fullness of light that dissolves the boundaries of consciousness in ecstatic experience. It is not only the essence of the principle of life, arising from ineffable mystery. Although it is all of this, it is also that which precedes humankind, history, and form itself.

The prehistoric blessedness of the *Gan Eden*[96] and boundlessness, *apeiron*,[97] belong to the *sefirah*[98] of nothingness, which sends forth the *sefirot* of wisdom, the source of creativity and spirituality, and reason, as the spiritual place of souls and individuals. All this, however, lies shrouded in mystery, not only beyond what can be spoken, but also beyond experience. For an experiencing ego-consciousness that approaches this level is dissolved, as an individual, into infinite divine fullness like salt in the sea. We recognize this process of dissolving from all the paths that ego-consciousness may take, going level by level into the unconscious. On such a path, ego-consciousness is pulled away from the separateness of differentiation into the undifferentiated entanglement of a *participation mystique*[99] with the unconscious, the universal relatedness of which confuses every form.

Before we consider the creative meaning of this nothingness for the world, we must first form a clear idea of how what is created functions for this uncreated, pre-created, not-yet-formed dimension of divinity.

The midrash[100] about the birth of the child[101] speaks of the foreknowledge of the unborn child, which sees all the ends of the world by the light above its head. With this knowledge, it participates in the spiritual world of the source that precedes all form. It still swims in God's radiant ocean of wisdom, from which it is destined to be separated at birth.

Here is what is said about this original knowledge:

> The *tzaddik* finds what has been lost since birth and brings it back to people.[102]

That is, his task is to restore to the living person, one who has grown up as a conscious individual, that existential state of relationship with original knowledge that he possessed before he was alive, when he lacked both consciousness and form. This circular path of restoration is a self-recollection. When one contemplates the primal world of the spirit, this ancient theme emerges time and again as the actual background of the *déja-vu* phenomenon.

But when it is said:

> God makes something out of nothingness, the *tzaddikim* make nothingness out of something,[103]

this reverse process of transformation is not about disintegration. It signifies the newly creative reconnection of one who is created in the *tzimtzum* with creative formlessness, whereby form is preserved and creation maintained.

This is also the context for Rabbi Zalman's answer, when he was asked why he did not want to return to a previous situation under better circumstances:

> Look! Who can be better off than the child in his mother's womb? He need not worry about his food and drink. A light burns upon his head, and all days he learns the entire Torah. But when the child is born, an angel comes and strikes him on the mouth, and he forgets all he has learned. And yet—even if he were able to return, he would not want to. Why do you suppose? Because he has reached his full measure.[104]

This "reaching full measure" is the fulfillment of being created in the *tzimtzum*, in the limitation and contraction that provides form in the first place and that enables the spiritual existence of a differentiated life. Consciousness is the measuring and determining greatness of human existence. It creates a formed world out of undifferentiated and shapeless anonymity, an act, the original meaning of which is expressed symbolically by the myth of Adam in Paradise, naming the animals.

Here emerges the deeper meaning of the fact that the *tzimtzum* is also associated with the characteristic of *Din* (judgment). Being negatively limiting, it thus stands in opposition to the limitless, spreading inflow and outflow of *Hesed*,[105] grace. For this saying also holds true for the *tzimtzum*: *determinatio est negatio*.[106]

The problem of evil in the Kabbalah is many sided. Whether evil is seen as overflowing from the judging and punishing power, whether it exists as a counterhierarchy of impurity, fed by human sin, whether it is said to be the vestige of primordial worlds that existed before our world, and thus represents the husks of the world tree, whether evil is seen as a waste product of the world organism or as the distancing of the creature from the divine[107], each of these views can be understood by depth psychology, because within the psyche each of these aspects is experienced as evil, and as real.

It does not matter that we explain "evil as a counterhierarchy" somewhat differently today, by referring to the principle of polarity in the dynamics of the unconscious, or that we call the "vestige of the destroyed primordial world" an atavism, or define the overflow of the "judging power" as domination by the destructive instinct. Evil still remains the same.

But beyond all theoretical explanations of evil stands its affirmation in Hasidism. This affirmation is linked to the doctrine of creation and to the affirmed importance of consciousness and of the individual.

> The maggid of Zlotchov was asked by one of his disciples: "The Talmud says that the child in the womb of his mother looks from one end of the world to the other, and knows all the teachings, but that the instant it comes in contact with the air of earth, an angel strikes it on the mouth, and it forgets everything. I do not understand why this should be: first know everything and then forget it?"
>
> "A trace is left behind in man," the rabbi answered, "by dint of which he can re-acquire knowledge of the world and the teachings, and do his service."
>
> "But why must the angel strike him?" asked the disciple. "If this were not so, there would be no evil."
>
> "Quite true," the rabbi answered. "But if there were no evil, there would be no good, for good is the counterpart of evil. Everlasting delight is no delight. That is how we must interpret what we are taught: that the creation of the world took place for the good of its creatures. And that is why it is written: "It is not good that the man"—that is to say the primal man God created—"should be alone," that is, without the counter-effect and the hindrance of the Evil Urge, as before the creation of the world. For there is no good, unless its counterpart exists. And further on we read: "I will make him a help meet for him"[108]—the fact that evil confronts good gives man the possibility of victory: of rejecting evil and choosing good, and only then does the good exist truly and perfectly.[109]

The attribute *Din* (judgment), as a characteristic of God and of the structure of the world, means intensity and the feminine, in contrast with *Hesed*, an extensional, "masculine" characteristic. Through this character of *Din*, negativity becomes visible as a world-constituting quality. The existence of the "vessel," the "measure," that is, creation in the light of the *tzimtzum*, must also be understood in its negativity, and for that reason limitation, as the setting of boundaries and the confining of overflow, is associated in principle with *Din*, judgment.

In the psychology of male–female symbolism, which plays a major role in the sexual symbolism of the Kabbalah,[110] the nature of the *Din* attribute will become even clearer.

Only evil, the other side, brings about the energetic tension called life. This contrasts with the paradise before the world, swimming in the will of God, beyond good and evil, the unconflicted submission of which corresponds to a prehuman state.

The rejection of evil, with which the passage cited above ends, is by no means the complete formulation. Already the ironic and strange identification of the woman with evil—for the "help meet for him" that is mentioned in the text is *Havva*,[111] who is about to be created—catches our attention and plainly shows that this problem is not solved through sheer rejection. It is not difficult to see how the problem of evil here is related to the Lilith problem and to the opposition in Jewish antiquity between YHWH and earth.[112]

Here, evil becomes a consciousness-enhancing principle that leads to the affirmation of the world. Only the differentiating power of consciousness makes the human being a human being, and only the world "equipped" with evil is the real world. When fore-knowledge is remembered, it is a new and different knowledge than the old fore-knowledge of the child and of the soul in paradise before the world began.

Along with this affirmation of evil and the world comes the affirmation of time, for the latter is valid only within the world. The course of the world and the passage of time are one and the same, making yet another emphatic contrast to the timelessness of the paradise before the world. This paradise stands still in being, untouched by life's time-determining energetics of becoming.

In Jewish antiquity,[113] the revelation of YHWH was also associated essentially with the passage of time, understood as the passage of history. Here, we find a corresponding association, though on another, more subjective level. The process of history, as a process of destiny, affords the experience of evil and the struggle against it. Only thereby can a consciousness be created that structures and associates itself with the principle of morality, even a principle that accepts evil. Only this consciousness stands in the world with authority, in the genuine, tested stability that comes from experience.[114] This is the practical background of Rabbi Zalman's saying: no one who has "gained his full measure" wishes to retreat.

In this symbol of measure, "one's own measure," the principle of the *tzimtzum* is bound together with that of individuality into a creative whole. The conscious principle of moderation—in contrast to the self-dissolving enthusiasm of ecstasy—is connected here with the divine, creative nothingness, that is, with an openness toward God within. Only in this connection can a vibrant renewal of the Jewish person and of Judaism be guaranteed, by letting go of the traditional givens and their accompanying paralysis, and at the same time by overcoming the threat of a mysticism that is hostile to consciousness.

Hasidism emphasizes consciousness, under the sign of creative individuality. In doing so, it stands in the starkest possible contrast to the rabbinical emphasis on consciousness, which remained formally and rationalistically uncreative, and—due to the rejection of inner religious experience—wanted to remain so on principle.

> The maggid of Zlovchov was asked by one of his disciples: "In the book of Elijah we read: 'Everyone in Israel is in duty bound to say: When will my work approach the works of my fathers, Abraham, Isaac and Jacob.' How are we to understand this? How could we ever venture to think that we could do what our fathers could?"
>
> The rabbi expounded: "Just as our fathers invented new ways of serving, each a new service according to his character: one the service of love, the other that of stern justice, the third that of beauty, so each one of us in his own way shall devise something new in the light of the teachings and of service, and *do what has not yet been done.*"[115]

Therein lies the extraordinary achievement of Hasidism. In line with the prophetic orientation of ancient Judaism, it demanded that the individual preserve the critical dignity of consciousness, while realizing, in ever-new ways, the creative connection with nothingness.

Tzimtzum–measure–form–individuality–consciousness: these are the creative dimensions that stand opposed to the precosmic chaos of formless anonymity. For humanity, by naming the unnamed, and forming and shaping the formless, continues God's act of creating the world.

The danger of ecstasy

Here, we must also consider the struggle of early Hasidism against the danger of ecstasy, and its sharp distinction from mysticism.[116]

Time and again, the ecstatic state is reported as the normal level of meditation of all *tzaddikim*. By no means, then, may we reject this path in itself—quite the reverse. The ecstatic situation is where all existence is reborn. Its continuous realization corresponds to the highest level of being. But—and here again we encounter the Jewish person's radical emphasis on consciousness—just as ego-stability was one of the genuine preconditions for prophecy in antiquity, now one of the preconditions for genuine ecstasy is a focus on the world. It is as if the dissolution of consciousness into nothingness had to be seen essentially as the apex of a parabola, where the soul hurls itself into nothingness, in order to pass through this point and return to the world in the other direction. In one step, the soul is dissolved into nothingness, in a process of retrograde introversion, picking up the creation and lifting it high, and then, in the next step, in a process of progressive extraversion, it comes back through the stages of creation, returning newborn to the world.

The task is to "not allow the flame to burst from the vessel."

> If the righteous man is to serve God in the right way, he must be a man who, no matter what fires he may feel within him, does not allow the flame to burst from the vessel, but performs every tangible action in the manner proper to it. We are told of a holy servant of God who, when he was to fill the lamps in the House of Prayer, was so flooded with fervor that he spilled the oil. That is why it must be regarded as praise when it is said of Aaron that—although he served his Maker with the whole strength of his soul—he saw to the candlestick in the way prescribed, and lit the lamps.[117]

In the same vein, there is the story of a student, aflame with passion, who left his teacher to go to another rabbi:

> His first teacher was aggrieved by this. "I held down the fire with all my strength," he said; "with the *tzaddik* of Apt he will rise in the burnt offering of his heart." The disciple died soon afterwards in the House of Prayer in the middle of saying the prayer "the soul of the living praise your name."[118]

In Hasidism, even early Hasidism, this danger of ecstasy, of mystical self-sacrifice, abandoning the world, is great and very much alive. For just this reason, it seems that a special effort must be made to tie the soul to the earth, pulling it back against its centrifugal force. And this is where Hasidism sees its purpose. Through inner developments in Judaism, the tension between YHWH and earth had come apart. In the process, the spiritual side had become hypertrophied, rabbinism taking the rational and speculative, Kabbalism the ascetic and mystical direction. Given this development, it is natural that the same centrifugal tendency and flight from the world would also be felt in Hasidism.

This conflict erupted early between the Great Maggid,[119] the most important student of the Baal Shem,[120] the spiritual leader of Hasidism, and his son, who was characteristically nicknamed "the angel."

> After his death, the *maggid* appeared to his son and—invoking the commandment to honor one's parents—ordered him to give up his life of perfect seclusion, for whoever walks a way such as this, is in danger. Abraham replied: "I do not recognize a father in the flesh. I recognize only one merciful Father of all that lives."
>
> "You accepted your inheritance," said the *maggid*. "With that you recognized me as your father even after my death."
>
> "I renounce my father's inheritance," cried Rabbi Abraham, the Angel. At that very moment, fire broke out in the house and consumed the few small things the *maggid* had left his son—but nothing besides.[121]

The ecstatic ascent leads to connection with the divine in its aspect as nothingness, to connection with the actual primal ground of the world, which is "absolute unity,"[122] beyond the division into vessels, organs, and individualities, and to the extent to which he rises higher, he expands and is not in the *tzimtzum*.[123]

This ecstatic gazing—there is no question of merging with divinity; the God–human separation is preserved even here—is not seen by early Hasidism as the ultimate goal. To embrace the ecstatic situation as the ultimate meaning of life would mean negating the world, rejecting the *tzimtzum*, and rectifying creation, so to speak, as a divine error.

This loyal attitude toward reality, by which Hasidism counters all mystical and ecstatic excesses, is evident in the humor of the following short tale about a sick *tzaddik*, who refuses the medicine prescribed by his doctor to cure a bad cough, because he fears it might contain a forbidden substance.

> His son pointed out that *treif*[124] may be enjoyed if one's life is in danger. Whereupon Rabbi Chaim exclaimed with delight: "In the world of divine emanation, in the *Olam-ha-Azilut*[125] one does not need a cure!" "This is true," replied his son, "in the *Olam-ha-Azilut* one needs no cure, but there is no coughing there either." Whereupon the rabbi took the medicine.[126]

If ecstasy and the seclusion of ascetic meditation are called heaven, whereas life in the superficiality of this world is called earth, then, according to the Hasidic conception, the task is to connect heaven *and* earth, up *and* down, outside *and* inside, and to live the connection as wholeness. The actual purpose is to unite and understand these opposites, but not to tear apart the polarities and thus to disrupt the unity of God.

> Rabbi Hanokh said: "The other nations too believe that there are two worlds. They too say: 'In the *other* world.' The difference is this: They think that the two are separated and severed, but Israel professes that the two worlds are essentially one and shall, indeed, become one."[127]
>
> [The Rabbi of Rizhny] spoke about the verse: "The heavens are the heavens of the Lord; but the earth hath He given to the children of men," saying: "There are two kinds of *tzaddikim*. Those of the one sort learn and pray the livelong day and hold themselves far from lowly matters in order to attain to holiness. While the others do not think of themselves, but only of delivering the holy sparks which are buried in all things back to God, and they make all lowly things their concern. The former, who are always preparing for Heaven, the verse calls "the heavens" and they have set themselves apart for the Lord. But the others are the earth given to the children of men."[128]

Hasidism is objective enough that it also calls those who stand apart *tzaddikim*, but it sides with the children of men, the people, the earth, against the aristocracy of those who are set apart.

> The Rabbi of Kotzk once said of a famous rabbi: "That's a *tzaddik* in a fur coat." His disciples asked him what he meant by this. "Well," he explained, "one man buys himself a fur coat in winter, another buys kindling. What is the difference between them! The first wants to keep only himself warm, the second wants to give warmth to others too."[129]

But this higher valuation of the non-aristocrat, who helps the children of men, corresponds less to a social stance than to a religious one. It is *imitatio dei*.[130]

For, as we shall see repeatedly, the human being's task lies in the direction prescribed by the essence of the divine: "Holy are you to be, for holy am I, YHWH your God!"[131] Here, too, the generous and merciful quality of *Hesed* is closer to the divine than is the Holy One's self-sufficiency, for even God stepped out of his self-sufficiency to create the world and the human being.

3. The world and nothingness

The inconstancy of what is given

For Hasidism, and earlier for the Kabbalah, this basic fact that the world's creation occurs through God's self-contracting mercy makes the world appear quite different from how we are used to seeing it. The same basic fact shines through everywhere and always: namely, that the world owes its emergence to a divine self-contraction. At every time and every place in the world, the quality of creative mercy, which enables the world's very existence, and the human being's in it, proves itself to be a concealed inwardness.

For the world, as experienced by Hasidism, contrasts with the cage-like world determined by the laws of natural science. The latter, which we are used to calling the world, is randomly animated by the wild beasts in human nature, which keep breaking loose, having gone mad in this cage.

The world of Hasidism rests on the deity's creative nothingness. Its dynamics not only secretly animates every creature and thing in this world, but also can be attained by the human being at every moment, if he breaks through the world's foreground into this nothingness. It is as if the structure of the world becomes transparent to the seeing eye, which now sees the great lifelines through which divine nothingness, always and everywhere, flows in and pervades the world. The inconstancy of what is given, the non-static, incessantly changing, undetermined nature of the world, is the one major, basic religious concept of Hasidism. Life in this world is only possible, so to speak, if one realizes the reality of this inconstancy and adjusts to it.

Creative nothingness

The world lives by continuous repetition of the divine act of creation, creation out of nothingness. This nothingness is the source and regeneration point of all life. The basic fact that the world is based on nothingness can be observed on different levels of the world.

The first cosmic level of this regeneration is the night, which, as we have already emphasized, is affiliated with YHWH.[132]

> Rabbi Shmelke did not want to interrupt his studies for too long a time, and so he always slept sitting up, his head resting on his arm. In his fingers he held a lit candle which roused him when it guttered and the flame touched his hand. When Rabbi Elimelekh visited him and recognized the power of the holiness which still locked within him, he prepared a couch for him and with great difficulty persuaded him to lie down for a little while. Then he closed and shuttered his windows. Rabbi Shmelke slept until broad daylight. It did not take him long to notice this, but he was not sorry he had slept, for he was filled with a hitherto unknown sunny clearness. He went to the House of Prayer and prayed before the congregation as usual. But to the congregation it seemed that they had never heard him before. They were entranced and uplifted by the manifest power of his holiness. When he recited the verses about the Red Sea, they gathered up the hems of their kaftans for fear the waves towering to the left and right might wet them with salty foam. Later Shmelke said to Elimelekh: "Not until this day did I know that one can also serve God with sleep."[133]

This story illuminates better than any theoretical deliberation the contrast between Hasidism, which returns to creative nature, and rabbinism, which tends toward asceticism, excessive consciousness, and alienation from nature.

The world's places of regeneration

The regenerative significance of the night for the soul is formulated most comprehensively in the following Zoharic passage:[134]

> The earthly human being has a primordial shape and form, and yet his existence is not permanent like those upper beings. For the upper forms and figures consist in their (pure) being, without any other (bodily or material) garment into which they are molded, and therefore (as pure forms) they endure everlastingly. The form of the earthly human being, in contrast, is molded into a garment (his body), and therefore only exists for a certain time. And every night the soul takes off its (bodily) garment and ascends, is consumed by that fire, then created anew, and returns to its garment; and therefore they have no duration like those upper forms. And of this it is said: "New every morning"[135]—these are the people who renew themselves every day.[136] Why? Because, as the verse continues, "great is your faithfulness." Your "faithfulness" (this is the *Shekhinah*, that consuming fire from which they renew themselves at night). She is really "great" and not small, because she takes in all (human souls) and encloses them in herself, the higher and the lower ones. She is the great, vast place that contains

> everything and yet does not overflow, as the verse says: "All rivers go into the sea, and the sea does not become full"[137]—all (souls) go to this "sea" and the "sea" takes them in and consumes them, without becoming full, brings them forth again, and they go away. This is why it is said (of the *Shekhinah*): Great is your faithfulness.

This newly creating, alchemical meaning of nothingness, in the full extent of its many-leveled symbolism, encounters us in the answer given by one *tzaddik*:

> Several disciples of Rabbi Nahum of Tchernobil came to him and wept and complained that they had fallen prey to darkness and depression and could not lift up their heads either in the teachings or in prayer. The *tzaddik* saw the state of their hearts and that they sincerely yearned for the nearness of the living God. He said to them: "My dear sons, do not be distressed at this seeming death which has come upon you. For everything that is in the world, is also in man. And just as on New Year's Day life ceases on all the stars and they sink deep into a deep sleep, in which they are strengthened, and from which they awake with a new power of shining, so those men who truly desire to come close to God, must pass through the state of cessation of spiritual life, and 'and the falling is for the sake of the rising.'[138] As it is written that the Lord God caused a deep sleep to fall upon Adam, and he slept and from his sleep he arose, a whole man."[139]

Here, the pseudo-death of depression, the seclusion of spiritual life, Adam's sleep, and the New Year's sleep of death are seen together as the great passage through nothingness, which is the turning point, from which follow new birth and rebirth, the birth of wholeness and of the whole person.

This passage of renewal takes place every night in the rhythm of the cosmos, also every Sabbath and every New Year, uniting the rhythm of the cosmos with acts of hallowing.[140]

Here is what is said about the Sabbath:

> Sabbath means homecoming,[141] for on this day all the spheres return to their true place.[142]

and about the New Year:

> On New Year's Day, just before the ram's horn was sounded, Rabbi Pinhas said: "All creatures renew themselves in sleep, even stones and streams. If a man wants to renew his life over and over, then before falling asleep, he must put from his shape, and commend his naked soul to God. It will ascend and receive new life. But today is the day of the *great* renewal, and deep sleep falls on all spiritual creatures, on angels, and holy names, and the letters of the Scriptures. This is the meaning of the great judgment in which the

> spirit is renewed. And so today, man shall be destroyed in deep sleep, and the renewing hand of God will touch him." After these words, he raised the ram's horn to his lips.[143]

Thus, the day and the year are nourished by the dark, hidden background and draw their strength from it. By nature, that is, by their reliance on nothingness, these providentially given points of regeneration bring renewal to the human world and, beyond that, to the world as a whole. But creating this contact, at all times and consciously, is a specifically human task.

Nature, which Hasidism treats as landscape and natural existence (though not as the law of nature), also plays an especially regenerative role. It is characteristic that rabbinism's alienation from and hostility toward nature are overridden in Hasidism. Sociological observations, which emphasize the decidedly peasant structure of the Hasidic masses, are doubtless correct. One essential fact, however, is that in Hasidism the *am ha-aretz*,[144] who otherwise were present simply as the masses, assumed a specific spiritual power.

Being alone in nature with the "song" of plants and stones, their natural existence devoted to God, helps and regenerates the human being in God's service.

All the field's talking then enters yours and enhances its strength,[145] for nature "also prays" and lifts up the heart; and even trees, bushes, and worldly things offer the *tzaddik* suggestions for service.[146]

This new affinity with nature is merely a symptom of how Hasidism finds its way back[147] to the wellspring of the soul, to creative nothingness, which regenerates consciousness. The intention is to link consciousness back[148] to the creative aspect of nothingness, which today we typically call, just as negatively, the un-conscious. This renewed emphasis on nature includes a stress on wholeness and joy, as well as a relative affirmation of the body. The old ranking is preserved, of course, which sees the body as the "lowest level of the world," but its definite inclusion in the intellectual–spiritual movement—in contrast to asceticism—makes it clear that the world is accepted. And affirmation of the world is a precondition for realizing the "whole person," regenerated in the slumber of nothingness.

The basic conception of the cosmic state of the world, the daily recreation of the world out of nothingness, now has its consequences, as demonstrated to human consciousness by the night:

> May each one embrace the quality of zeal. May he rise up from sleep with zeal, for he is hallowed and has become another; and he is worthy to bring forth in the manner of God, the blessed, when he brought forth his world.[149]

Immediately after the Zoharic passage cited above, we find this:[150]

> If we do not believe that God is renewing the work of creation every day, our prayers and fulfilling of the commandments will become old and familiar and tedious. As it says in the psalm: "Do not cast me off in the time

> of old age,"[151] that is to say, do not let my world grow old for me. In the Book of Lamentations it says: "New every morning; great is your faithfulness."[152]—That the world becomes new to us every morning, that is your great faithfulness.[153]

Buber comments on this passage as follows:

> The Jew's daily prayer professes this faith with the words: "In his goodness, every day, he constantly renews the work of the beginning."[154]

Hasidism's concept of the world

Nothingness breaks into the world, interrupting continuity, and an awareness of this interruption has revolutionary importance. Contrary to the opinion of isolated ego-consciousness, the world does not consist of a solid, rational, or regular structure. A cage-like world of determinism and mechanism rests on the distorting projection of consciousness, which attributes its own rational structure to the universe. The opposing Hasidic thesis begins precisely with *this*, with nothingness, as the basic phenomenon controlling the structure of the world, and, there, consciousness *stops.*

Contrary to what one might assume, however, this stopping of consciousness is not conceived of as its negation. Rather, its seriousness comes from the basic fact—decisive for human consciousness—that consciousness *depends* on being immersed in nothingness, which is not only the end but also the birth and rebirth of consciousness. From there, consciousness re-emerges new, fortified, and expanded. Thus, nothingness is the source of consciousness and its mental contents.[155]

This conception of nothingness, partly or wholly identifying it with wisdom, because the mind has its source entirely in nothingness, corresponds to a psychology and metaphysics of the creative process per se. For indeed, all creativity stems from the unconscious, the deep layer of nothingness, beyond ego-consciousness. For:

> Every being must come to the level of nothingness, after which it can be another thing.[156]

or:

> If the human being wants a new creation to come out of him, he must reach with all his might toward the quality of nothingness; and then God will create a new creation in him, and he is like a spring that does not dry up, and like a stream that does not cease. . . . And this is called wisdom.[157]

This wisdom, the first *sefirah* of the Kabbalists, is the creative incarnation of nothingness; it is the first emergence, from which all emanation occurs, and which is identified in turn with this nothingness.

> For all change in the world is impossible without wisdom, that is to say nothingness.[158]

The emptying of the human being into nothingness makes the higher spiritual activity become creative and advance. This is how one attains the inner revelation of higher wisdom.

From of old, creative people have characterized emptiness, the state of inner reception, as the situation that precedes productivity. The creative person realizes time and again that he is the tool of the contents passing through him, that manifest themselves to him, that appear, cross his mind, come over him, want to be formed, or compel him. In whatever terms this is formulated, these are merely expressions corresponding to an activity going on within, mainly independent of consciousness. There is no voluntary, active way for consciousness to reach it. One cannot be creative through willpower; one can only prepare oneself. The inner activity can then show favor, or it can resist and close itself off.

A crucial trait of Hasidism is that it knows by experience that the world and humankind are not finally determined. The principle "new every day" leads, especially for Judaism, to a revolution of unforeseen proportions.

Guided by consciousness, human beings always tend to erect a structure in which a definite orientation is possible; they try to establish continuity, with the help of which the eruptive, fiery structure of the world is made rigid, and thus usable. One finds one's way more easily through the labyrinth by following the thread of necessity. And even if this thread becomes the rope of determination, strangling life—as original sin or a constellation of the stars, as constitution or sociological conditioning—one still prefers to wither and calcify rather than to fall into the eternal uncertainty of a perpetual new beginning and thus into the hands of the living God. Because it is actually much easier and more suited to the inertia of human nature—and this should not be misunderstood as irony—to resign oneself to one's own conditionality, depravity, and entrenchedness, than to realize that one is really new, and in a new world, every single day.

The basic attitudes that enable "newness every day" include tensing oneself in readiness, having the energy to consider everything possible, and abandoning presuppositions. Soon, however, we must consider the content of this newness of the world and of the human being, because, of course, not even Hasidism can overlook the fact that in some respects continuity of existence exists and must be accepted.

When one considers what tradition and old age mean for Judaism, one begins to understand the import of Rabbi Nachman's saying,

> Being old is not good. One must renew oneself every day.[159]

The connection between nothingness and the world is guaranteed by points of discontinuity. On some level, these correspond to YHWH's irruptive, invasive nature,[160] as it was characterized in early Judaism. This is the creative possibility of the hidden, which intrudes into the world through the human connection with nothingness, creating change.

This connection, and the fundamental, philosophical willingness to regard the state of the world as being always and everywhere subject to change, become clear in the story of "working faith"[161] and miracle, although Hasidic conceptions of faith and miracle go beyond what one usually associates with these concepts.

Ancient Judaism already saw YHWH in decisive contrast to the fixedness of a world determined by fate.[162] Accordingly, Rabbi Nachman says that Israel is only subjected to fate when it sins; otherwise, the saying is true:

> Israel stands above nature;[163]

because

> In truth, God changes nature.[164]

This is formulated by the Great Maggid to contradict the freethinkers, who are convinced that the world runs by the laws of nature.

The world's constitution includes the cosmic existence of night, Sabbath, and the New Year. These disrupt the order of nature, as nothingness invades the order of consciousness, making changes in the world both possible and necessary. But setting aside the constitution of the world, a special task of creating change also belongs specifically to the human being, and to the Jew.

The hallowing of the world in festivals stands between the cosmic and the human, in that, for instance, the Sabbath and the New Year represent a cosmic constellation, and at the same time a sacred task. However, matters are different with the institution of the ritual bath and with prayer.

The meaning of ritual immersion as a rite of rebirth is ancient. Immersing oneself into water signifies a return to the primal waters that dissolve and regenerate.[165]

> This is what the Rabbi of Kotzk said concerning Rabbi Akiba's saying that "God is the waters of immersion of Israel": "The waters of immersion only purify the soul if one is wholly immersed, so that not a hair is showing. That is how we should be immersed in God."[166]

Whereas ritual immersion has always had a particular symbolic power for the Jew, though especially for the Jewish woman, Hasidism also considers it a symbol, because submersion in God is the essential goal of the ecstatic progressive path of prayer. But this connection with nothingness is not achieved through rare, isolated surges of ecstasy; rather, it belongs to the institution of the sacred arrangement of the world, which intersperses times of prayer throughout the day. Thus, the connection is regularly established, and in this way the survival of the world is guaranteed. For this connection with creative nothingness has not only individual but also collective significance; it "brings abundance to all the worlds."[167] It is the most essential challenge for the human being, and especially for the *tzaddik*, with the help of this linking back,[168] to guarantee the continued existence and development of the world and humankind.

Fulfilling this task in prayer demands that one voluntarily commit one's life, because nothingness is at the same time the level of death. Every prayer that advances as far as this level is a voluntary self-surrender. It is the actualized willingness to dissolve "something" in "nothingness," to devote and entrust oneself to the divine transforming power.

> Before praying he should consider whether he is prepared to die in this prayer.

and

> It is a great grace that man continues to live after prayer. According to the path of nature, he would need to die due to his waning strength, for he commits all his strength to his prayer.[169]

After praying and passing through the level of nothingness, the human being is transformed. But prayer also brings blessing to the Divine, by opening new creative paths into the world. When continuity and constancy are perforated like this, God can keep realizing his will on and in the world in new ways.

The following tale shows how real this danger of dying in prayer was thought to be:

> Someone asked Rabbi Shelomo of Karlin to promise to visit the next day. "How can you ask me to make such promise?" said the *tzaddik*. "This evening I must pray and recite 'Hear, O Israel.' While I say these words, my soul goes out to the utmost rim of life. Then comes the darkness of sleep. And when it is day, the great Morning Prayer is apacing through all worlds, and finally, when I fall on my face, my soul leans over the rim of life. Perhaps I shall not die this time either, but how can I now promise to do something at a time after the prayer?"[170]

The offering of prayer realizes in human terms the ever-recurring creation from nothingness, the cosmic power of which comes alive at night, in sleep, and when festivals break in.

Actions that link with nothingness—both those given by nature and those that are humanly intended—constantly bring about new creative influxes of the Divine. Thus, Hasidism considers the law of creative energy, its freedom and spontaneity, to be a basic fact, which conditions the inconstancy of what is given.

The life of the creative psyche continually experiences itself as originating in creation from nothingness. It keeps experiencing the overflowing of the creative current, which far surpasses conscious intention. Consistent with the nature of grace, a state of renewal is greater than the existence that preceded it, and in death and rebirth something more is generated, manifesting itself not only in consciousness but also in the wholeness of the personality.

(This psychic experience does not rule out the possibility that, psychologically speaking, we are dealing with a transformation of primal forces, so that, if one treated the intangibility of nothingness as a constant, the law of energy conservation would still apply. This implies, however, that the transformative energy flows from the depths of the unconscious within the personality structure, along paths that are only partly known to psychology, and so we cannot speak merely of shifts within a personality structure that is assumed to be constant. And it implies that, from the point of view of ego-consciousness and the personality structure, previously nonexistent forces and contents are appearing for the first time, i.e., that this is a manifestation of creation from nothingness.)

Nature and miracle

The relativizing of the world's constancy also finds expression in the relationship between miracle and nature.

> [Rabbi David Moshe] once asked after one of his hasidim who was in great straits and in need of the help of God. The rabbi wanted to know whether that help had been accorded him. He was told that that was not the case, and that the nature of his trouble was such it was hardly possible to imagine that help could come in a natural way.
>
> "Most likely the man has not perfect faith," said the *tzaddik*. When he saw that the hasidim did not understand him, he continued: "At first glance it seems as though there were no reason to separate the natural way from the supernatural. This event was sent by God and that other too was sent by God—so why make a distinction? But the distinction is real nevertheless. You know, when the world was created, the flood of light was so unbounded that the world could not bear it, and the vessels broke. And so the light was limited in order that it might be received and contained. And that is the meaning of the natural way: the limiting of the abundance into the bounded measure of the vessels. Now such a vessel is the readiness of man, and the readiness of man is faith. But just as all men have not the same faith, and no man has the same faith at all times, so the bounds of the natural way differ. He whose faith is stronger, whose vessel is more spacious, is accorded a greater measure of the natural way, for that way reaches to the bounds of faith. Yesterday when faith was small, you had to seek the help you had need of beyond nature, but today your faith has grown great and so all the help you are accorded is possible by the natural way. This is the meaning of what is told of Nahshon, the son of Amminadab: When Israel stood by the Red Sea he leaped into the waters before they were divided, and when they reached his throat, he said: 'Save me, O God, for the waters are come in

> even unto the soul.' He did not cry aloud, he spoke in a gentle voice, for his faith was great, and so everything that took place was natural."[171]

Miracle and nature are related concepts here, depending only on the realized structure within the human being.[172] There is no fixed world, any more than there is a fixed human being, for the human being is "one who walks," and the world is always transforming. How far a person can realize the potential of the world depends on his inner capacity, and this varies according to his scope of consciousness and the relationship of his ego to the creative unconscious, which is always changing. The greater this inner capacity—meaning faith, in the sense of a readiness to realize potentialities—the greater is God's potential to become real and enter the world, which is to say, the greater nature becomes.

Therefore it is said of the "working faith" that its:

> power contributes to the fulfillment of that which is to be.[173]

This is the faith that "moves mountains,"[174] thus, that changes the structure of the world.

To understand this perspective, that the world may actually change, we must refer to the connection that exists between the psychic structure and the outer world. For not only is the image of nature and the world altered by the psychic structure of the one who controls and perceives it. Changes also occur in nature itself and the world itself, because with a different psychic structure, different phenomena become possible and in fact occur.

This concept of the relativity of nature views nature not as a given, but as dependent on the human structure of consciousness and the total human structure. This concept is associated with the idea of a hidden, not fully realized God, whose one attribute and form of appearance is creative nothingness. But this nothingness cannot be identified with God, either; for:

> Even at his most hidden, he is both veiled and visible; his inwardness is hidden from us.[175]

As a liminal concept of nature, a miracle is always that which surpasses faith and exceeds the willingness to consider what is possible. It is also endlessly variable, according to the level of the individual. For the Jew of antiquity, a miracle was the experience of YHWH's way of working, whose indefinable character breaks through the world's rational lawfulness.[176] Here, we confront the corresponding fact, but with an essential difference.

In antiquity, YHWH's way of working appeared to be more or less absolute, a matter of free projection. It took human determination only partially into account, and then only for those who were greatest. But now, in Hasidism, the decisive step is taken, making YHWH's way of working essentially dependent on the total human structure, or at least setting it in a functional relationship with this structure.

At any rate, this process, for which evidence also exists in the Talmud, assumes its most mature form in Hasidism. In antiquity, it was about the absolute freedom of YHWH's power and its functional relatedness with the collective associated with it in the covenant. In Hasidism, a relativity is assigned to the individual, according to his structure and the level he has attained, and, at the same time, the individual relates both actively and passively to his collective and his environment.

The basis of the world's dynamics is just the individuality of the single person, his position on various levels, closer to the center or farther from it, and his movement from level to level. Serious attention to individuality says nothing about stabilizing the possibilities, but instead demands the elastic vitality of ever-renewed readiness. For:

> the receiving [of revelation] takes place at all times. It was given to all equally, but they did not all receive in equal measure.[177]

The basic Hasidic concept does not correspond to a world cosmos or even to a world mechanism, a network of coordinates that fixes every creature at a geographical point within this system of reference. Rather, for Hasidism the world consists of a great, diffusely distributed creative nothingness, within which the points of concentration, in varying degrees of power, reshape and form this unformed energy and cause it to shine. These points of concentration are the world's individuals, created in the *tzimtzum*, having a smaller and greater circumference and varying energy charge. They can also diminish or increase the extent and intensity of their radiance, depending on the level they attain, that is, their ability to enter into contact with divine nothingness. This astronomical worldview is constantly evolving; it flares up and darkens, depending on cosmic and individual constellations. In one sense, it extends from the stones to the angelic and spherical creatures, because all of these represent points of concentration in the world, differing only in their extension. But in addition, this dynamic and transformation also reach beyond time, insofar as the theory of the transmigration of souls carries dynamic development and movement beyond individual life. Rabbi Nachman's words are informed by this basic notion:

> The world is like a spinning die, and everything turns, and man transforms into an angel, and the angel into man, and the head into a foot, and the foot into a head; and thus all things turn and revolve and transform, this into that, that into this, the highest into the lowest, the lowest into the highest. For in the root all things are one, and in the transformation of things and their turning back, salvation is decided.[178]

This formulation no longer corresponds exactly to early Hasidism. But it shows the background against which this movement unfolded and contains many elements belonging to the original conception of Hasidism, though it frames them more rationally.

When the world's essence is conceived of as divine points of concentration, the individual is also emphasized. For on this basis, every individual is a nodal point in the world, a place where nothingness becomes incarnate, changing from anonymous infinity into named finitude.

The primitive person[179] and the animal float in the anonymous sea of nothingness, lacking differentiation, in a fluctuating *participation mystique* with the universe. In this state, neither is a center that could make choices. The sequence of development only later reaches the luminous, concentrated point of ego-consciousness, in which the undefined gains a unique, distinct shape. Only with this discerning ego-consciousness is the individual established, and only in this individual does the deity gain a mirror to see himself in and a partner to talk with. This, however, constitutes the sacred significance of the individual, and, insofar as he is aware of this, he is undetermined and free. For, according to the Baal Shem:

> the human being [has] the duty to remember at all times that he is the son of the king of all kings, and therefore he must not fall [in isolation] [with himself].[180]

To achieve this level of undetermined freedom, unchained and unbound by all the world's conditions and determinations, counts as the fulfillment of the individual at the messianic level.

The theory of sparks

A considerable part of the astronomical image of the world is formed by the theory of sparks, which stands at the center of Hasidic teaching.

> The principle of life is a holy spark, and that is the son of the king. And the spark yearns to be connected to its father.[181]

According to this doctrine, sparks are inherent in every thing, every creature, and every place. The verse:

> The *whole* earth is full of his glory,[182]

is cited with emphasis on the *whole* earth, meaning that there is nothing that does not contain the sparks representing the principle of life that originates in God. This verse is always completed by another, emphasizing the fact that God does not live only in purity and goodness, but that:

> he dwells in the midst of their uncleanness.[183]

The point is not simply that God *also* exists in uncleanness, but that he is *especially* there. For:

> The holiest sparks exist on the lowest levels,[184]

and

> Even in idolatry and all idols there are holy sparks.[185]

Like all symbolism, the symbolism of the spark has many aspects, which can only gradually reveal themselves to us. The first and most fundamental is that of the *principle of life*. It is often said to be the "power of the doer in what is done," the part that comes from God, encapsulated in the husks of physical reality, which constitutes their vitality and capacity for life, without which they could not exist. Crucially, however, this spark is more or less veiled, encased, deprived of its luminous capacity. It has entered hiddenness and invisibility, secrecy and confinement through the compactness of the bodily husks of materiality. Smallness is an image of greatness. Just as God entered contraction and hiddenness in creation, so, too, has the spark, which for this very reason is also called the Son of the King.[186]

However, the principle of vitality, which is represented by the spark, is only the aspect that is most easily seen. Here, it is crucial to recall what was said elsewhere about the direction of the act of creation.[187] That is, creation occurred from above, from the spirit downward, and the principle of life is something spiritual, always and everywhere. This spiritual meaning of the spark must be redeemed, however; its spiritual aspect must be grasped and made conscious.

> The sparks want to join through reason.[188]

For this reason, the human being, the only creature with the gift of reason, is appointed to redeem the sparks. It is written:

> The holy spark, that is to say wisdom, is mixed with all the contents of this world.[189]

and

> Your whole intention should be to lift the sparks to their roots, to the place of supreme holiness.[190]

In everything that this world contains, in all the regions of the world, from stone and thing through plant and animal to the human being, in all situations, from profane, everyday situations to prayer, and to every single letter in the words of a prayer, from good works to sin, everywhere the secret light of the spark is hidden and makes its claim on the human being.

With all its radiant celestial bodies, the astronomical image of the world is dynamic. Here, "dynamic" does not mean the regularity of nature, for this astronomy has no laws independent of the human structure. The flaring up and coalescing, the motion and stasis of these dimensions depend on the psychological intention of the human being and (though not always) on his consciousness.

The psychic freedom of human spontaneity, which resembles the creative freedom of the God who created this world, determines this world and the world of sparks.

Whereas, on the one hand, it is written:

> It is the inclination of *our* soul to lift those broken by the shattering[191] (the sparks) up to their roots,[192]

on the other hand, it says:

> The *sparks* want to join through reason.[193]

The dynamic movement of the world is based on this relationship between the soul and the sparks.[194]

At first, the description of this state of affairs is that sparks exist everywhere in the world, that is, in the external world of things, bodies, and creatures, making their demands on humanity. Irrespective of what these sparks are and how they express themselves, they want something from the human being, and something in the human psyche corresponds to this wanting. It, too, wants to do something with things. The will of the sparks in the world coincides with the will of the human soul; they are fitted to each other. And there is a natural connection between the dynamics of the world's demand and the dynamics of the psyche's direction. It is precisely the world's claim on the human being that makes him what he is, the great mediator and ruler of the world, the ladder that connects the world and God. Between the world, mankind, and God, the great work of redemption to which humanity is called is playing out.

Notes

1 From S. A. Horodezky, "Baal-Schem-Tob (בעש"ט), Israel ben Elieser," (hereafter: "Besht"), *Encyclopedia Judaica* (hereafter *Enc Jud*), v. 3 (1929), cols 835–42. Neumann slightly paraphrases the following passage by Bozina di-Nehora: "In replying to the attacks on him, the Baal Shem summed up the meaning of his mission: 'I have come to show people a new way to come to themselves'." The quotation continues: "Three things are needed in this respect: To love God, Israel, and the Torah, but without castigation and self-torment" ("Besht," col. 838). (Cf. also *Roots II*, p. 100.)

2 A brief definition of Hasidism appears in Buber's 1948 pamphlet, *Der Weg des Menschen: Nach der chassidischen Lehre* (*The Way of Man, According to the Teachings of Hasidism*), (p. 51, n. 1). This note appears as the opening sentence in the English edition: "The name 'hasidism' (in Hebrew *hasidut*, i.e., originally, 'allegiance' and, hence, 'piety') designates a mystical–religious movement which seized eastern European Jewry about the middle of the 18th century and numbers many congregations to this day" (*The Way of Man, According to the Teachings of Hasidism*, translator unidentified, p. 5).

3 *Hintergrund*. A metaphor that Neumann often uses to refer to hidden or veiled realities, or meanings behind or below the surface level.

4 *EN*: Ramakrishna, *Teachings*. [No page is cited. Neumann's bibliography lists only *Teachings*, v. 2, 1920. A one-volume revision includes this passage under the heading, "Avatara (Divine Incarnation): A Fact" (*Teachings of Sri Ramakrishna*. 1971, pp. 45f.).]

5 Hebrew, צמצום: "contraction, constriction, condensation, concentration." In the teaching of the Kabbalist Isaac Luria, the creation began with God's deliberate shrinking of his infinite unity, making room for finite worlds to come into existence (cf. Lancaster, 2005, pp. 98f.; Drob, 2010, pp. 12f.).

6 *Weltstufen*: lit. "world levels." (Depending on context, sometimes translated "worlds.") The concept that there are worlds on different levels, or different levels of the world, is central to Kabbalistic theory.

7 *EN*: Horodezky, *Torat Rabbi Nachman* (*Teachings of Rabbi Nachman*), p. 58. [This work (1923) (hereafter: *R. Nachman*) is published only in Hebrew. Neumann may have made his own German translations of quoted passages. Many thanks to Tamar Kron for checking his references and translations.]

8 *EN*: Horodezky, *Thorat Hamaggid* (*Teachings of the Maggid*), p. 35. [This work (1923) (hereafter: *Great Maggid*) was published only in Hebrew. Neumann made his own German translations of quoted passages. Many thanks to Tamar Kron for checking his references and translations.]

9 *EN*: Buber, *Die chassidischen Bücher*, p. 157. [Neumann's quotations from *Die chassidischen Bücher* (*The Hasidic books*) (1927) (hereafter: *Chassid Büch*) are cited throughout by the German edition. When possible, as noted, English renderings follow the translations of Olga Marx, whose two volumes, *Tales of the Hasidim: The Early Masters* (1947), *The Later Masters* (1948) (hereafter: *Tales I, II*), are organized differently from Buber's book.]

10 *EN*: Ibid., p. 160.

11 "Temple" is ambiguous here. Neumann identifies the destruction of the Solomonic Temple, 586 BCE, as the beginning of the end of ancient Judaism; but he marks the culmination of that process in the destruction of the Second Temple, 70 CE. (Cf. "Introduction to the work," *Roots I*, pp. 8f, nn. 20 and 22.)

12 Hebrew: lit. "wise student." Idiomatic for one who studies day and night. With thanks to Tamar Kron.

13 *eines formal-kombinatorischen Denktyps*: here Neumann modifies the Jungian category, "thinking type" (cf. CW 6).

14 Neumann returns to a theme that was introduced in Part One, with his description of Moses as a charismatic leader (cf. *Roots I*, pp. 17–23). In this and other passages about the *tzaddikim*, he adumbrates the concept of the great individual (*der große Einzelne*). Cf. especially Neumann's 1948 Eranos lecture, "Mystical Man," and his works of 1949, *Depth Psychology and a New Ethic* (hereafter: *New Ethic*), and *The Origins and History of Consciousness* (hereafter: *Origins*).

15 *EN*: Jung: *Die Beziehungen zwischen dem Ich und dem Unbewussten* (*The relationship between the ego and the unconscious*) (hereafter: *Beziehungen*). [Originally published in 1928, this work is printed in CW 7, *Two Essays*. Neumann refers to Part Two, Chapter 4: "Die Mana-Persönlichkeit," pp. 184–208 in the first edition. (Cf. "The Mana-Personality," CW 7, ¶374–406.)]

16 *EN*: *Chassid Büch*, p. 104. [Incorrect citation. Source uncertain.]

17 *EN*: E.g., *R. Nachman*, p. 186. [Cited as p. 109.]

18 *EN*: Talmud. [Reference not found.]

19 *EN*: *R. Nachman*, p. 190. [Cited as p. 180.]

20 *EN*: *R. Nachman*, p. 91.

21 *EN*: *R. Nachman*, p. 180.

22 *EN*: *Chassid Büch*, p. 534. [*Tales II*, p. 248.]

23 *EN*: *Chassid Büch*, p. 481. [*Tales I*, p. 313.]

24 *EN*: Cf. Part One, pp. 43f. [*Roots I*, pp. 27ff.: "The elevation of Moses."]

25 *EN*: *Great Maggid*, p. 160.

26 *Schicht*. A reference to Neumann's concept of the layers of the personal and the collective unconscious.

27 *EN*: *Chassid Büch*, p. 603.

28 *EN's note*: *Chassid Büch*, p. 602.

29 *EN*: *Chassid Büch*, p. 548. [*Tales II*, pp. 62f.]
30 *EN*: *Chassid Büch*, pp. 532f. ["The Treasure," *Tales II*, pp. 245f.]
31 *EN*: Ibid., p. 533. [*Tales II*, pp. 245f.]
32 *EN*: Ibid., p. 29.
33 Birnbaum refers explicitly to "*ethische Lehren*" ("ethical teachings").
34 *EN*: Birnbaum, *Leben und Worte des Balschemm*, p. 98. [Paraphrased, with emphasis added by Neumann.]
35 *EN*: *Chassid Büch*, p. 539.
36 *EN*: Ibid., p. 157.
37 Cf. Numbers 16:1–35.
38 *EN*: *Chassid Büch*, pp. 584f.
39 *EN*: Ibid., pp. 446f. [*Tales I*, pp. 257f.]
40 *EN*: Ibid. [*Tales I*, p. 251.] [This passage is not found in *Chassid Büch*, but in Buber's 1948 pamphlet, *Der Weg des Menschen nach der chassidischen Lehre* (*The Way of Man, According to the Teachings of Hasidism*), p. 17.]
41 *EN*: *Chassid Büch*, p. 539. [*Tales II*, p. 256.]
42 I Kings 17:4, trans. by E. Fox.
43 *EN*: *R. Nachman*, p. 161.
44 *EN*: *Chassid Büch*, p. 642, slightly paraphrased. [*Tales I*, p. 271.]
45 *des weltzugewandten Gefühlstyps*: the phrase refers to the typology that Jung developed in his 1921 volume, *Psychological Types* (CW 6) (hereafter: *Types*). The adjective, *weltzugewandt* (lit. "turned toward the world"), suggests an extraverted feeling type (cf. CW 6, ¶595–600).
46 *EN*: *Chassid Büch*, pp. 593, 595. [*Tales II*, p. 214.]
47 *EN*: *Great Maggid*, p. 115. [Neumann has added emphasis and put quotation marks around his word "*vollkommen*" ("perfect"). That word may be a misinterpretation, however. According to Tamar Kron, Horodezky's word in Hebrew, שלם (*shalem*), is better translated *vollständig* (complete).]
48 Honorific name for Dov Baer of Meseritz (1704–1772), a leading Hasidic rabbi. Cf. also *Roots II*, p. xvii, n. 3; p. 33, n. 119.
49 *EN*: *Chassid Büch*, p. 437.
50 Isaiah 6:3. In the prophet's vision, the seraphim call to each other: "Holy, holy, holy is the Lord of hosts; the whole earth is full of his glory."
51 *EN*: *R. Nachman*, p. 57 [Cited as p. 67.]
52 *EN*: *Great Maggid*, p. 40. [Cited as p. 36.]
53 *EN*: This, incidentally, is an excellent explanation of part of the loss, because not only what is overly cathected by libido is lost (Freud), but also what is emptied of libido.
54 *EN*: *Chassid Büch*, p. 561. [*Tales II*, p. 170.]
55 *EN*: Ibid., p. 637. [*Tales II*, p. 306.]
56 *des Gerichts*: lit., "of the court."
57 *EN*: Cf. Part One, p. 172 [*Roots I*, p. 128: "The loss of earth, inner and outer."]
58 *EN*: See below, p. 170, and Part Three. [*Roots II*, p. 136.]
59 *EN*: All these single aspects already existed in early Hasidism, but they did not merge into a worldview that changed Judaism until Hasidism.
60 *EN*: *Chassid Büch* [page ref. missing]. [*Tales II*, p. 284.]
61 *EN*: Ibid., p. 528. [*Tales II*, p. 231.]
62 Ibid., p. 561. [*Tales II*, p. 170. Cf. *Roots II*, p. 17.]
63 *EN*: *R. Nachman*, p. 108.
64 *EN*: *Chassid Büch*, p. 33.
65 *EN*: *R. Nachman*, p. 17.
66 *EN*: See above, pp. 15f. [*Roots II*, pp. 13ff. "The Elijah Soul."]
67 *EN*: Birnbaum, op. cit., p. 77 [Neumann substitutes *Schalengewalt* (power of the shell) for Birnbaum's *Klipiss*.]
68 This quotation and the preceding, from *Chassid Büch*, p. 637, are first cited above, *Roots II*, pp. 17f.

69 Cf. above, *Roots II*, p. 14 and note.
70 Hebrew: lit. "shoot" (plural: *sefirot*). The *sefirot* are "emanations of God, the central symbols of the Kabbalah. They depict the immanence of God and define the reciprocal relationship between God and man" (Lancaster, 2005, p. 230). They are described in the *Sefer Yetzirah* as "ten archetypal numbers, which define the parameters of space, time, and morality," and whose "transcendent source [is] 'nothingness'" (ibid., pp. 42, 75).
71 *EN*: Scholem, "Kabbala," *Enc Jud*, v. 9 (1932), col. 673.
72 *EN*: Ibid. Cf. also Bischoff, *Theoretische Kabbalah* (hereafter: Bischoff). [In Scholem's *Enc Jud* article, cf. col. 702. In Bischoff, cf. "Die Lehre vom Zimzum" ("The doctrine of the *tzimtzum*"), pp. 19f., especially "Die zehn Sephiroth" ("The ten *sefirot*"), pp. 23–38.]
73 *Stufenweg*: lit. "path through levels." This term, which occurs often in Neumann's discussion of Hasidism, is translated according to context. Here, its meaning is conveyed in the phrase "progressive stages of the path."
74 *EN*: *Great Maggid*, p. 48.
75 *EN*: *R. Nachman*, p. 69.
76 *EN*: Ibid., p. 72.
77 *EN*: The historical connection of this conception with the Lurianic Kabbalah is clear, but it cannot be pursued here.
78 *EN*: Cf. below, p. 101 [*Roots II*, p. 77.]
79 *EN*: *R. Nachman*, p. 63. [Cited as p. 64.]
80 *EN*: *Chassid Büch*, p. 32.
81 *EN*: *Great Maggid*, p. 69.
82 *EN*: Ibid., p. 54.
83 *EN*: Ibid.
84 *EN*: Cf. pp. 64f. and pp. 85f. [*Roots II*, pp. 6, 25, 66ff.]
85 *EN*: *R. Nachman*, p. 51.
86 Hebrew, שכל: "good sense, prudence, insight, understanding, intelligence," and in medieval Hebrew "reason, intellect."
87 Neumann provides no citation for this passage.
88 *EN*: *R. Nachman*, p. 51.
89 *Ichheit*: lit. "I-ness." In the context of depth psychology, the noun *das Ich* is customarily translated "the ego." In the context of Jewish mysticism, however, especially in Kabbalah, the concept of "I" has a particular meaning. Human intellect is linked with the divine Mind. Thus it is possible to speak of "the union of the human 'I' with the divine Essence—the eternal 'I'" (Lancaster, 2005, p. 199).
90 *EN*: See below, p. 107 [*Roots II*, p. 81: "If we begin with the action of choosing . . . ."]
91 *EN*: Cf. Part One, p. 211. [*Roots I*, pp. 153ff.: "Earth and Bull."]
92 *EN*: *Great Maggid*, p. 78.
93 *EN*: *R. Nachman*, p. 143.
94 *EN*: Brecher, *Transzendentales im Talmud* (*The transcendental in the Talmud*), ¶20. [Brecher, 1850, p. 52, under "Dämonologie" (Demonology).]
95 Greek: fate. In ancient Greece, the Fates were worshiped as three sisters, the *Moirai*, with power to spin, weave, and cut off the thread of life.
96 Hebrew: Garden of Eden.
97 Greek: unendingness.
98 Cf. above, *Roots II*, p. 21, n.70.
99 French: "mystic participation." This term, coined by Lucien Lévy-Bruhl, is frequently used by both Neumann and Jung. (Cf. *Roots I*, p. 25, n. 38)
100 exegesis, commentary. The word, from Hebrew (pl. "midrashim"), has crossed over into English usage.
101 *EN*: See above. Part I, p. 133 [*Roots I*, pp. 93f.]
102 *EN*: *R. Nachman*, p. 188. [Neumann's translation changes the meaning of this passage. Tamar Kron advises that, based on Horodezky's Hebrew, it should read: "The *tzaddik* looks for what he has lost, and when he finds it, he looks for the losses of others; and when he finds them, he looks for the losses of the whole world."]

103 *EN*: *Great Maggid*, p. 200. [Cf. also *Roots II*, p. 59.]
104 *EN*: *Chassid Büch*, p. 466. [*Tales I*, p. 265.]
105 Hebrew: also translated mercy, love, lovingkindness. *Din* (judgment) and *Hesed* (grace) are two of the ten *sefirot*, discussed below (cf. pp. 69ff).
106 Latin: determination is negation.
107 *EN*: Cf. Scholem, *Kabbala*, op. cit., col. 688. [*Enc Jud*, v. 9 (1932), col. 689f. In Scholem's encyclopedia essay, cf. "Das Problem des Boesen" ("The problem of evil"), cols 688–93.]
108 The reference is to God's saying, in the second creation story: "It is not good that the human should be alone, I will make him a helper corresponding to him" (Gen 2:18, trans. by E. Fox).
109 *EN*: *Chassid Büch*, pp. 614f. [*Tales I*, pp. 144f.]
110 *EN*: See below, p. 121. [*Roots II*, pp. 95f.: "Love and fear."]
111 Hebrew: Eve.
112 *EN*: Cf. Part One, p. 219 [*Roots I*, p. 160, under "Lilith."]
113 *EN*: Cf. Part One, p. 133. [*Roots I*, p. 93, n. 82, ref to *Babylonian Talmud* (hereafter: *Bab Tlm*): *Hagiga* 12a.]
114 *EN*: See below, p. 121 [*Roots II*, pp. 95f, "Love and Fear."]
115 *EN*: *Chassid Büch*, pp. 581f . [*Tales I*, p. 147. Neumann's quotation from Buber is slightly paraphrased, with emphasis added.]
116 *EN*: Cf. Part One, pp. 148ff. [*Roots I*, pp. 115ff.: "The dangerous ending of the YHWH–earth tension."]
117 *EN*: *Chassid Büch*, p. 581. [*Tales I*, p. 91.]
118 *EN*: Ibid., p. 572.
119 Dov Baer of Meseritz (the Great Maggid): Hasidic rabbi, chief disciple of Israel ben Eliezer (Baal Shem Tov), and propagator of his teachings.
120 Israel ben Eliezer (1700–1760): Rabbi, founder of Hasidism, known as the Baal Shem Tov (Master of the Holy Name), or "Besht"; he lived and died in Podolia, Ukraine.
121 *EN*: *Chassid Büch*, p. 418. [*Tales I*, p. 115.]
122 *EN*: *Great Maggid*, p. 27.
123 *EN*: Ibid., p. 180.
124 Hebrew: "food ritually unfit for eating."
125 Hebrew: "world of divine emanation."
126 *EN*: Bloch, 1930, *Priester der Liebe* (*Priests of love*), pp. 223f. [Also in *Aus Mirjams Brunnen* (From Miriam's well), p. 256. The last sentence is Neumann's interpolation.]
127 *EN*: *Chassid Büch*, p. 575, with added emphasis. [*Tales II*, p. 317.]
128 *EN*: Ibid., p. 542, slightly paraphrased. [*Tales II*, pp. 53–54.]
129 *EN*: Ibid., pp. 600f. [*Tales II*, p. 274.]
130 Latin: "imitation of God."
131 Leviticus 19:2.
132 *EN*: Cf. Part One, p. 211and above, p. 35. [*Roots I*, pp. 153ff, and *Roots II*, pp. 26f., "The night world."]
133 *EN*: *Chassid Büch*, p. 425. [*Tales I*, pp. 187f.]
134 *EN*: Scholem, 1935, *Die Geheimnisse der Schöpfung. Ein Kapitel aus dem Sohar* (*The mysteries of creation: A chapter from the Zohar*), p. 75. [Scholem identifies the source of the passage, slightly paraphrased here, as *Buch Bahir* 19a,b (Zohar I 19a,b). The final sentence, which appears to be Scholem's commentary, is echoed by Daniel Matt's observation that "'faithfulness' is one of the many names of the *Shekhinah*" (*The Zohar, Pritzker Edition*, v. 1, p. 147n). Cf. also Appendix A, *Roots II*, p. 182.]
135 Lamentations 3:23, cited by Scholem.
136 Here Scholem notes the page turn, from 19a to 19b.
137 Ecclesiastes 1:7 (cited as Qohelet).
138 This saying originates in a work by Dov Baer of Meseritz (the Great Maggid), *Magid Devarav le-Yaakov*, originally published 1780. In the critical Hebrew edition of Rivka Schatz Uffenheimer (Jerusalem: Hebrew University, 1976), the saying is

part of a discussion in Section 179, pp. 278f. With thanks to Tamar Kron and to Jim Rosenbloom. Cf. *Roots II*, pp. 91, 113.

139 *EN*: *Chassid Büch*, p. 632. [*Tales I*, p. 173.]

140 *Heiligung*: The main purpose of ritual "hallowing" is to establish the holiness of natural things (such as procreation, home, and death). Buber's term is *Einheiligung* (cf. *Roots I*, p. 42, n.7).

141 *EN*: "Sabbath," from the root *sh-v*, meaning "return."

142 *EN*: *Chassid Büch*, p. 644. [*Tales I*, p. 123.]

143 *EN*: Ibid., pp. 632f.

144 Hebrew: "people of the Land."

145 *EN*: *Chassid Büch*, p. 23.

146 *EN*: *R. Nachman*, p. 186.

147 *Rückfindung*: this word, and its near-rhyme in the next sentence, seem to be examples of Neumann's deliberate use of a "guiding word" ("*Leitwort*"—cf. *Roots I*, p. 138, n. 2).

148 *rückzubinden*: the concept of "linking back" is repeated below, with added emphasis. (Cf. *Roots II*, p. 42 and note 168 below).

149 *EN*: Buber, *Des Baal-Schem-Tow Unterweisung im Umgang mit Gott* (*The teaching of the Baal Shem Tov in conversation with God*) (hereafter: *Unterweisung*), p. 22. [On the title page, this description: "The teaching of Rabbi Israel ben Elieser, called Baal Shem Tov (Master of the Good Name) in conversation with God, from the fragments gathered by Martin Buber."]

150 Tamar Kron advises that this reference to the Zohar cannot be confirmed.

151 Psalms 71:9.

152 Lamentations 3:23. (Cf. above, *Roots II*, p. 36.)

153 *EN*: *Unterweisung*, p. 39 (slightly paraphrased).

154 *EN*: *Unterweisung*, pp. 109f.

155 *seiner geistigen Inhalte*: in this context the word *geistig* may signify "mental," "spiritual," or "intellectual."

156 *EN*: *Great Maggid*, p. 296. [Cited as p. 215.]

157 *EN*: *Chassid Büch*, p. 156 (slightly paraphrased).

158 *EN*: *Great Maggid*, p. 46.

159 *EN*: *R. Nachman*, p. 9. [Cf. also *Roots II*, p. 128.]

160 *EN*: Cf. Part One, p. 64. [*Roots I*, pp. 22f.]

161 *des ziehenden Glauben*: lit. "of pulling faith." Tamar Kron advises that the concept of a faith so strong that it causes things in the world to be pulled, or moved, is specific to Hasidism.

162 *EN*: Cf. Part One, pp. 101ff. [*Roots I*, pp. 62ff.: "YHWH and the Mother Goddess."]

163 *EN*: *R. Nachman*, p. 105.

164 *EN*: *Great Maggid*, p. 12. [Cited as p. 13.]

165 *EN*: See above, "the *Shekhinah* as the sea" [pp. 36f.: passage by Scholem.]

166 *EN*: *Chassid Büch*, p. 565 (slightly paraphrased). [*Tales II*, p. 277.]

167 The theme of abundance flowing downward is introduced above, pp. 24f.

168 *Rück-Bindung*. Neumann's added hyphenation draws attention to the meaning of each part of the word: "back" and (literally) "binding." (Cf. above, p. 38, n. 148) These passages in Neumann's book apparently owe nothing to Jung's published works. In his 1950 revision of *Wandlungen*, Jung writes that one derivation of "religion" is the Latin *religare*, "link back" (cf. CW 5, ¶669), but this discussion was not present in the editions to which Neumann had access when writing. In his 1937 Terry Lectures, Jung explains the word "religion" on the basis of a different Latin verb (CW 11, ¶6).

169 *EN*: *Great Maggid*: *Tefilah* (prayer), p. 144. [Both quotations are found on the same page.]

170 *EN*: *Chassid Büch*, pp. 573f. [*Tales I*, pp. 275f.]

171 *EN*: *Chassid Büch*, pp. 570f. (slightly paraphrased). [*Tales II*, pp. 76f.]

172 Neumann was surely moved by this concept, which he explored in a brief, fictional narrative, "David und Saul," based on imagined events in the first-century lives of Rabbi

Elisha ben Abuyah (ha-Acher) and his disciple, Rabbi Meir. This undated, apparently unfinished piece of writing could not be included, unfortunately, in the present work.

173 *EN*: *Chassid Büch*, p. 606. [*Tales I*, p. 153].

174 Alluding to a passage in an epistle of Saint Paul: "... if I have all faith, so as to remove mountains, but have not love, I am nothing" (1 Cor 13:2).

175 *EN*: *R. Nachman*, p. 69.

176 *EN*: Cf. Part One, p. 140 [*Roots I*, p. 98, where the same statement occurs.]

177 *EN*: *Chassid Büch*, p. 587 (slightly paraphrased). [*Tales II*, p. 278.]

178 *EN*: Ibid., pp. 31f.

179 *der primitive Mensch*: like other writers of his era, Neumann applied the term "primitive" to human beings without pejorative intention.

180 *EN*: Bloch, 1930, *Priester der Liebe*, p. 222. [Also cf. *Aus Mirjams Brunnen*, p. 253.]

181 *EN*: *Great Maggid*, p. 39.

182 Isaiah 6:3, in translation different from B&R. Footnote missing in Neumann's typescript.

183 Leviticus 16:16 (paraphrase). Footnote missing. This verse concerns God's purging of the Israelites' uncleanness and the location of his Tent of Meeting amid their sins. In Fox's translation, the verse ends: "which dwells with them in the midst of their *tum'ot* [pollutings]."

184 *EN*: *Great Maggid*, p. 39. [Cited as p. 35.]

185 *EN*: Ibid.

186 See above, p. 46, n. 180.

187 *EN*: See above, p. 27. [p. 21: "The inner dimension and the way into the hidden."]

188 *EN*: *Great Maggid*, p. 39. [Cited as p. 36.]

189 *EN*: Ibid. [Cited as p. 35.]

190 *EN*: Ibid., p. 40. [Cited as p. 36.]

191 *EN*: According to the Lurianic Kabbalah, the sparks have fallen into the shells of matter, causing the unbounded creative light to break the "vessels."

192 *EN*: *Great Maggid*, p. 36.

193 Ibid., p. 39. [Neumann's note is missing.]

194 *EN*: Later we will consider the difference between the Gnostic, the primitive–animistic, and the Hasidic theories of sparks. See below, pp. 183f. [*Roots II*, pp. 141ff.: "Hasidism and Gnosticism."]

2

THE TRANSFORMATION OF SOULS

1. The levels of the soul and the realms of nature

> The human being should raise the holy sparks that fell when God built and destroyed worlds. He should purify them upward, from stone to plant, from plant to animal, from animal to the talking being. He should purify the holy spark, which is enclosed in a powerful shell. Everyone in Israel shares this basic purpose. It is well known that every spark that inhabits a stone or a plant, or any other creature, is completely formed, has all its limbs and tendons, and that if it lives in the stone or the plant, it is in the dungeon, unable to extend its hands and feet or to speak, but its head lies on its knees. And the one who is able to raise the holy spark from stone to plant, from plant to animal, from animal to the talking being with the good power of his spirit leads it to freedom. No other liberation of the imprisoned is greater than this. It is like one who rescues a king's son from captivity and brings him to his father.[1]

This text, which we must interpret in various stages, leads us to the heart of Hasidism, its worldview, and its image of the human being. But to shed light on the entire background of this text and perceive its inner coherence, we must make several detours through its various interpretive layers.

We are dealing with a gradual process of transformation, which besides the development toward increased *vitality*, from the dead stone to the living person, also emphasizes the development toward increased *consciousness*, from the mute stone to the talking being.

The development from the dead stone—from the greatest impenetrability and encasement, which seems dead to the human being, and in which the spiritual principle of the spark is most hidden—to the talking being, is identical to a development toward human existence. The spiritual principle is most powerful, visible, and creative in the human being, because his speech repeats and renews God's world-creating word and speech. In his word, the world of thought becomes distinct and capable of consciousness.

As elementary things are palpable and massive, their existence is most obvious, even though silent. It is most veiled in its inherent activity; the reality of the spiritually creative principle is hidden in it. This is the world at its lowest level, the silence of which is broken every so often for primitive people when a thing "speaks," that is, addresses them. Such a thing is sacred and revered because the divine dwells within it. In it, the spark has become visible and has been raised upward to its root; it has assumed a redemptive character, and its original state within the divine has become transparent and powerful.

Stages of culture and realms of nature

In the stages of cultural development, with all its transitions and intersections, as human consciousness grows, the revered image of the divine passes through the sequence of natural realms.

The earliest known places of veneration are sacred stones. Veneration of the elements and of the elemental spirits of earth, fire, water, and air preceded that of shrines. Later, the divine was worshiped as an animal, and this development ends with worship of the divine in human form.

Parallel to this sequence, humankind conquers the levels of nature, dominating them through consciousness. In the earliest period, the Stone Age, the elements are joined to the sphere of culture. This age is typified by earthen caves, fire, and stone weapons. Then, the realm of vegetation is incorporated, with hoeing, cultivation of plants, and farming. The domestication of animals comes next, and after that the historical period, the time of human cultures and social relationships.

There is surely an association between the gradual expansion of consciousness through the realms of nature and the worship of the divine under symbols of these realms.

The sacralization of a realm of nature either expresses or leads to a concentration of libido in this realm, and with that a concentration of consciousness. "Sacred stones" show that human beings are so fascinated by the world of stones that they concentrate on it, and that their libido and interest are directed toward this world.[2] As Jung earlier demonstrated, with the help of symbolism the libido is transformed and consciousness is expanded. Any given stage of nature, then, has the potential to become capable of consciousness, so that its contents might be used by consciousness and eventually descend from the sacred to the profane, to be included in human culture.

The psychology of early humans is characterized by a different connection with nature than we are used to today. The notion of *participation mystique* means that what exists between the individual and the object of participation is not a subject–object distance, but an unconscious identity. The boundaries dissolve because no developed conscious system yet exists, i.e., one capable of separation and differentiation. Undefinable identity and contact exist between the natural object and the "individual" human, who is not actually an individual. Whenever modern psychology speaks of projection, i.e., whenever there is "ensoulment" or something akin to it, we are dealing with a *participation mystique*. Thus, participation with a stone, for instance, manifests itself by the vital role played by that stone for the participating individual or group, as talisman, fetish, or idol. It belongs to the living system, and its damage or loss is just as important as the damage or loss of a vital organ. This has a real impact, so it should not be misunderstood allegorically, for losing such a fetish can lead to literal disease and death. The term "auto-suggestion" is merely another way to say that the taboo object is connected to the psychic system. Relics, flags, sacred places, etc., are the remnants of the same facts in our day and age. The psychic outburst of a mass of people when such taboo zones or places are violated proves that this kind of participation is still powerful today.

Participation with an animal also has objective consequences. To give an easily understandable example, human–animal participation leads to the human being taking notice of the animal. Without involving consciousness, this cognizance is both profound and extensive;[3] it is also an essential condition for the domestication of the animal world.

Such participations in the pre-logical stages of consciousness often involve the sacralization of the objects with which participation occurs. As consciousness develops, however, such participations gradually dissolve in one of two ways. One way involves the conquest of nature by consciousness, i.e., its introduction into human culture. The other way is for this realm to become simultaneously represented in the psyche. In the sacred cult object of the stage preceding this differentiation, these two aspects are still connected: the symbolic, i.e., psychic aspect and the worldly, natural one are united in the object.

So, for example, when we seek to understand what the sacred cow means for early humans, we find that what matters is not only the domesticated animal, or even the breeding and mastery of animals, important as this is for an entire stage of humanity. Beyond its meaning as a farm animal, the cow is also a mother symbol. Its domesticated use, as a supplier of milk, also relates in part to this mother symbolism. Thus, the natural object is at the same time a symbolic representation for a psychic constellation, the image of which it offers but does not cause or create. For, as analysis of the mother–cow symbolism shows, the contents that flow into and are gathered up in this symbol are exceptionally numerous and may not be simply deduced from "cow" as a natural object.

An advancing consciousness resolves the original participation with reality in two ways. One way is internally, through psychic representation in the symbol; the other is externally, through mastering the natural stage.

In the organization of the human psyche, in the layers of the unconscious we find, even today, the diverse realms of nature and their symbolism. For all stages of humanity and in every domain of mythology and religion, this symbolism is the same.[4] The layers of the unconscious are oriented anthropocentrically, that is, whatever is closest to human occupies the highest place, whereas in descending order come animals, then plants, and finally the inanimate elementals, whatever is farthest from human. So the stone is said to be inanimate, because it is most foreign to human beings, farthest from their principle of life. In this hierarchy, cold-blooded creatures also appear in opposition to warm-blooded, for a warm-blooded creature is more closely related to the human psyche, and therefore easier to identify with.

Any theory of the transmigration of souls, by claiming that rebirth occurs in everything the world contains, from stones to the gods, thereby declares that it sees all the things and creatures in the world as ensouled in varying degrees, that is, as having souls or parts of souls living in them. When we interpret the statement that the sparks should be purified from stone to plant, from plant to animal, and from animal to the "talking being,"[5] we must start from a concretistic notion and advance all the way to a psychological one. All of these stages coexist and are equally valid.

Many legendary narratives recount the redemption of sparks. These sparks may appear as ghosts, as lost souls, or even as a sacred melody that has been lost, but finds itself again with a shepherd in the galut. The shepherd's melody is heard and recognized by a *tzaddik*, who includes it in his prayer as a *niggun*,[6] and so it is redeemed, taken into the sacred sphere. One essential trait of such redemption stories is that the sparks, having wandered off into meaninglessness, are brought back into meaningful connection and attached to human consciousness. By being lifted out of the randomness of a merely accidental existence and linked to the spiritual, sacral, or psychic wholeness of a higher order, they are guided upward to their roots, their true identity.

This legendary redemption occurs on the objective level, that is, where the relationship between the sparks and the human being is not psychological but concrete. This projected form is serious about the fact that the sparks are personal souls, with their own intentionality. Here, the theory of sparks takes mythological form.

When we view the sparks of the soul as partial souls, in relationship to the redeemer's own soul, we are working on a different level. Whether these partial souls are primarily independent or related individually to the human soul that redeems them, in either case the process of redemption is such that these parts of the soul, previously isolated and shut up in the world, are transformed by their attachment to a human being and receive a different rank in the hierarchy of the living. This path, ascending level by level, may be described, however, as a path through the levels of nature, from the mineral realm to the human, from what is furthest away from consciousness up to consciousness itself.

This theory of redemption means the redemption of the unconscious toward consciousness. Only naming, thus the connection with the spiritual name, with human consciousness, which provides true existence, or, more broadly speaking, the connection with the human soul, releases the silent thing of nature from its anonymity. It releases the un-conscious—the latently captivated embryonic spiritual core of the thing and its essence—into meaning. It leads from possibility to reality and restores the original connection between the part, which has been scattered in outer reality, and the whole, the inwardness of the world, which provides meaning and life.

The soul's teaching about the levels of nature

To understand the transformation through the levels of nature, we must briefly attempt to characterize the symbolic meaning of the various levels and their differences, which must be seen here as different psychic stages. We must see the transformation from stone to human as the reverse of the descending path taken by creation. Just as creation descended from spirit to matter, to the supposedly dead and inanimate, it must now follow the reverse process in ascending order. As cited:

> God makes something out of nothingness, the *tzaddikim* make nothingness out of something.[7]

The *mineral* world is "dead"; it is sheer matter, the meaning of which is its passive usability. It is an unchangeable or barely changeable reality, without its own intention, or any traits of life. In a certain sense, it is specifically feminine, a vessel, material to be formed. It receives its dignity by being classified as part of an overarching context. It is not merely, as the midrash tells us, that the stones desire to support Jacob's head and thus, included in his fate, to form the basis of the ladder to heaven and so to become sacred. The principle of the primary purity of nature,[8] according to which all natural things—regardless of their relationship to the human being—are pure, does not exclude the existence of higher- and lower-ranking natural things. If life is the highest value, and if vitality and the spirit belong together, then water, bound to the plant as sap, ranks higher than elementary spring water. The spark in the water longs to be redeemed, to ascend, to become an integrating part of a higher whole, which is more alive, but thus also closer to God, because in it the deity has stepped even further out of hiddenness into visibility.

The *plant* realm is life of a particular kind. It transforms the elements upon which it depends. It possesses growth, that is, fate, and lives in time. But its imprisonment is unfreedom; it is confined to the narrow sphere of its roots, to which it is entrusted and on which it depends. The plant realm is more magnificent and more mysterious than the realm of stones, because it reveals more of the living secret of the divine, which fulfills and is visible in it.

Each level builds on the one beneath it. Each has its own meaning, but each lower level is also represented in the next higher one. The mineral exists in the plant, the mineral and the vegetative in the animal.

Creation's instinctual and volitional aspects only become apparent in the animal, as movement and self-determination, instinct and character. Here, the active side of the world is attained, and the spiritual side shines through. Although human likeness exists here, consciousness and choice have yet to emerge.

The scale dead–vegetative–animal–human is also alive and understandable to us. The human being is the only talking animal, that is, the living creature in which the world of thoughts, the mental aspect of the world, expresses itself. Like thought, speech is an attribute of consciousness, toward which the whole sequence of nature develops.

This inner symbolism of the levels of nature clearly establishes the path of transformation from the deepest unconscious to consciousness. Beyond the legendarily projected representation, we must now attempt to understand what this redemption of the sparks from nature can mean.

As noted, the sparks have a will of their own, and they place a claim upon the human being, demanding to be redeemed. Depending on the person's capacity, he is called upon by a larger or smaller circle of the world, for which he in turn is responsible.

> Everything that the human being owns, his servants, his animals, his tools, contains sparks, which belong to the roots of his soul and want to be raised up to their origin by him. [9]

Moreover:

> All the things of this world that belong to him yearn to draw close to him with all their might, so that he can raise up the sparks of sacredness that are contained within them. [10]

Here, the spark is said to be in an individual relationship to the single soul. Such a relationship frees the theory of sparks from its worldly projection, so that a broader understanding becomes possible.

The spark is a latent spiritual content that rests enclosed, like an embryo, within every thing and every creature. All that is contained in the world can give birth to revelation, which can break forth from anything and everything. The individual capacity to give birth to revelation, and the nature of that revelation, depend only on the kind, the power, and the intention of the human soul. When a thing, creature, or situation is pregnant with revelation for a soul, the self-revealing spark shows that it belongs to the soul undergoing the revelation. The greater the soul, the greater the portion of the world that demands to be redeemed by it, and the more latent psychic forces exist within it. Hidden in things, as sparks, these latent forces wait to be redeemed and led upward to join the soul.

Revelation is a kindling, inflammatory process, in which the human soul and the spark of that thing that is pregnant with revelation unite, collide, and procreate. The sparks' will to be redeemed, and the soul's to redeem, are two matching and cross-fertilizing directions in the world's dynamic. If it is said that nothing is perfect that is not simultaneously masculine and feminine, then the following makes sense from our present perspective:

> In relation to the brain, every implement and every thing in the house, from small to large, are female.[11]

The "male" activity of the redeeming soul procreates in the vessel's passivity by liberating the spark and making it fertile, guiding it up from its germ-like potential into reality. The embryonic posture of the imprisoned spark, "its head on its knees,"[12] points in the same direction. At the same time, however, in this process of procreative revelation the human soul "conceives" and is female, insofar as it is aroused by the self-revealing content.

When it becomes conscious that the human soul conceives, the self-revealing spark is redeemed on a new level; it demonstrates that it is "male." That is, the human soul realizes that something in the thing desires to ascend, and, at the same time, this thing procreates within the human being, and the human being conceives from it.

Thus, the spark concealed in the thing gradually discloses itself. It is guided upward until it becomes the talking being, a content, a revelation, that can express itself and address human beings. Only then is the spark completely redeemed, connected with its root. Only then does it become the talking being, which can release and express its living, mental and spiritual inwardness.

The path that each spark follows through the levels of nature does not need to be rationally defined here; nor do we need to interpret these levels as being, in some sense, categories of meditation.[13] But still, let us try once again, briefly, to clarify the picture.

A thing, entity, or situation that is simply used by human beings exists on the *mineral level*. It is material, and its authenticity is hidden. But the stony spark inside it is redeemed when it makes contact with the human being and becomes attached to his soul, even if this occurs unconsciously. The hewn stone that is used to build a house is different from the stone that is merely "there" on the mountain. It has entered the story; it has a connection, however slight, with destiny, with human consciousness. It is formed, redeemed from the deepest anonymity of existence.

On the *vegetative level*, the entity is experienced as existence. It unfolds as it is, represents itself, is alive within itself, but lacks conscious direction. It is oriented without knowledge and apathetic; yet it has an inner regularity, which may even be considered beautiful. A stone on the vegetative level—to put it paradoxically—is not simply used, but is recognized as a particular, living existent. A landscape is perceived as a landscape, not as a collection of anonymous natural objects. Here, the spark is already closer to its authenticity. In it something immanently spiritual is evolving; something previously latent and enclosed is becoming apparent. But the direction toward the human soul is still not present, or it operates only unconsciously.

This direction can be felt when a thing or entity comes noticeably to aim toward and speak to the human psyche. Then this thing or entity is on the *animal level*, and the psyche notices its will, its urgency. Animation and movement emanate actively from the thing and communicate its will. Now the will of the spark is perceived. A procreative component moves toward the human soul, and a lively connection begins to operate between the thing and the soul. The spark "reddens" to some degree; it wakens and moves, and its movement is expressed in feelings and affects.

The spark that is enclosed in the stone, that burns invisibly at the vegetative level, here becomes a living feeling. What marks this as a development playing out on the animal level, however, is that the experience may be lived unconsciously, as an affective disruption. This becomes obvious in the following tale, in which the spark of a place has an impact on the animal level, being felt as a disturbance or accusation:

> Once Rabbi Bunam was praying at an inn. People jostled and pushed him, but he did not go into his room. Later he said to his disciples: "Sometimes it seems impossible to pray in a certain place and one seeks out another place. But that is not the right thing to do. For the place we have quitted cries out mournfully: 'Why did you refuse to make your devotions here with me? If you met with obstacles, it was a sign that it was up to you to redeem me.'"[14]

These three levels of nature are stages of existence in the unconscious. Here, things and people are still asleep. The alert wakefulness of consciousness, the ego-centeredness of the subject, still lies dormant. The relationship between the human being and the spark occurs in the unconscious without any active involvement of human consciousness.

But this "existence in the unconscious" does not necessarily represent a lower level. As we shall see, the *tzaddik* who is unaware of being a *tzaddik* is highly esteemed in Hasidism.[15] He ranks higher than the knowing scholar of the Law, though not higher than the knowing *tzaddik*.

Above the animal level lies the *level of the talking being*. At this level, the sparks not only express themselves, but also their specific relatedness to the destiny of the human soul, by which they are redeemed, becomes evident. Whereas up until then the projection of the parts of the soul into the sparks is still taken concretely, as if it were something objective, on this level the process proves to be an event both *in* the human psyche and for it.

Redemption now becomes apparent as self-redemption. The spiritual and inner meaning of the event steps out of concealment. The human being, as a spiritual center and as the representative of spirituality in the world, as the governor in the likeness of God, becomes conscious of himself. Here, the world gains its meaning. Hasidism's anthropocentric interpretation of the world stems from the perspective of this level, which could therefore also be called the *level of meaning*, as opposed to the symbolic level.

Above it lies the *symbolic level,* as the last level that is in some sense capable of expression. On this level, the perspective of meaning has also been overcome. The subject of experience is no longer the ego, as on the level of the talking being. Here the subject is transpersonal. The redemption of the sparks is no longer the redemption of things and creatures, nor of the human being, but the redemption of the Deity. Here the *divine* destiny is at stake, and the destinies of humankind and the world are only fitted into it.

On the level of meaning, the spark has become the light of illumination, the revelation in which the secret meaning addresses the human soul. Here, beyond any affective involvement in the encounter, the spiritual becomes evident. What is meant opens up, and the prisoner is freed, the son connected with the father. On the animal level, the individuality of the place, the personal structure, and the individuality of the ensouled were in the foreground, and, on the level of meaning, the individuality of the experiencing soul was new and important, although, on the symbolic level, even this emphasis is surpassed. It is still present, as the vegetative and mineral levels are present, but it is no longer crucial. On this highest level, there is only one topic, which is the Divine. On this level, the "mournful place" in the story loses its purely individual character. It could be recognized—it is not mentioned in this tale, but in many others—as a symbol of the waiting deity, the *Shekhinah*, who continually makes her claim on the human being, here, there, everywhere, in constantly changing guises and ever new ways.

> Once I was present at a conversation my teacher carried on with a widow. He spoke to her of her widowhood in good, comforting words, and she allowed her soul to be comforted and found new strength. But I saw that he wept and I too began to weep; for suddenly I knew that he was speaking to the Divine Presence, which is forsaken.[16]

On this highest level, the individual event is symbolically surpassed. But this does not mean it is to be understood *only* symbolically, or that the real situation would not occur in actuality. On the contrary, it is only when this widow's uniqueness is taken seriously that the symbolic aspect appears. Then this encounter becomes the revelatory situation: the event becomes transparent, as an encounter between the soul and God. When the human soul realizes and accepts this uniqueness in all its radicality, then, and only then, the universal speaks through the contraction of the individual situation.

God himself speaks, in some sense, only on the symbolic level. Only here did the creative beginning come into its own, creating the world by lowering itself into uniqueness. Here, the divine itself reached a new level.[17]

The level of the soul and of the world: The world's relative transparency

In discussing the transparency of the world, we encounter a problem of relativity, because the level of the soul where the human being stands is closely connected with the level at which he sees the world. Thus, the problem of relativity is constellated, for the visibility of the world, in its authenticity or inauthenticity, depends on the stage of the human being.

Now let us consider this relativity more closely, as it affects the association between the progressive path of souls, or parts of souls, and the progressive path of nature, or—better—the sparks of nature.

On the path, as the sparks of the world were raised from the mineral to the symbolic level, the world became more visible and clear in its reality. From one level to another, it shed its physicality and revealed its spirituality, that is, its essence emerged out of hiddenness into openness, revealing its secret. From one level to another, the husk-like shell of visibility became more transparent, allowing the previously invisible, spiritual form of the principle of life to be seen more clearly through it. In order to remain in the symbol, the task of this path was to gradually reduce the impenetrable physicality hiding the inner light, and at the same time, by making this physicality more translucent, to make the hidden light more visible in its activity.

It is important to understand that this kind of change and transformation also signifies a shift in and transformation of perspective.

It makes no difference how the change is formulated. From the perspective of the thing, one may say: the spark of the thing was raised to the human level.[18] From the perspective of the world, one may say: the world became transparent in this thing at its human level. From the perspective of the human being, one may even say: the soul has raised itself up to the human level. All three formulations are the same. Through one and the same act, change occurs in the thing, the world, and the human being. It would be a mistake, however, to assume that this shift in perspective occurs only within the human being. With this change in the soul, not only does the whole person change, including his consciousness; but also the world changes, and not only the human world.

The redemptive function that human beings have toward the world happens inwardly. In transforming the sparks of the world, they transform themselves, but, in transforming themselves, they also transform the world. This transformation seems to be merely a spiritual and psychic process. But because, as we have seen, the doctrine of Hasidism considers the world and human life a spiritual and psychic phenomenon, and because the bodily and factual dimension is only one *aspect* of reality, and of the world's background, the true reality of the world changes with every spiritual and psychic transformation.[19]

However, this does not mean that the world must be annihilated, even less that one should or may withdraw ascetically from it. Instead, it means that the world should become "transparent," its essence made visible.

> Just as the hand that is held before the eye covers the largest mountain, so small, earthly life obscures the view of the tremendous lights and secrets filling the world, and whoever can pull it away from his eyes as one pulls away a hand will behold the great radiance of the inside of the world.[20]

"Small, earthly life" does not mean life as such, but life insofar as it is small and earthly. If corporeal authority is portrayed here as negative, this refers to its opacity and density, or its existence at what we were calling the mineral level.

The ascent of sparks and of the soul

To understand the reality of the Hasidic world, we must realize that, when the sparks in things are made to ascend, this always involves the simultaneous ascent of the human soul. The soul moves along with the sparks, because these sparks and parts of the soul belong to it, and what causes the ascent of the sparks is that the human soul rises in their service.

One only sees what one is. A person on the mineral level, that is, someone whose soul is dead, closed, and without any movement, whose soul is said to be "in the dungeon, unable to extend its hands and feet or to speak, but its head lies on its knees,"[21] for such a person the world also exists on the mineral level. His unconscious existence[22] and the world's unconscious existence belong together. The world's redemption and self-redemption are joined together like communicating vessels, for one is the projection of the other.

A person on the mineral level not only has a different image of the world from someone on the level of meaning, but his reaction in and to the world is also different. Certain objective connections are associated with his psychic and also his conscious level, and they operate in the world differently. The world realizes itself on different levels through him and in him.

The mineral world is subject to the law of inanimate bodies. Events that happen to a person on the mineral level are blind, and he reacts to these mechanically, as it were, according to the principle of least resistance. When the same events happen on the level of meaning, they are different. To a person at this level, events are not blind; they are transparent, having a meaning that he sees and to which he must respond.

A crucial relativity exists between the level of the world and the level of the psyche. The same event may encounter two individuals. For one—and through him and in him—the world exists on a low level, and so, for him, the event remains material, inauthentic, dead, and meaningless. But for someone on a different level, through this same event the world is revealed and realized. Everyone constantly rises and falls; each person is "one who walks,"[23] and so is different at every moment. This perpetual change constitutes the world's secret life, its inwardness.

But such an event takes place in a world, the inner processes of which cannot be observed. This means that God, too, is always hidden. This world and the other world are one and the same. The point is to make the spiritual, inner aspect of this world transparent and to live it, but not to make a division between this world and the other—between God's world and the emperor's.[24] It is not a matter of choosing God's world as "the other world," or rejecting the emperor's as "this world."

The opposition between the outer and inner world, which had been projected onto heaven and hell, this world and the other, is taken inward. This internalizing of previously projected contents is one of the factors that defines the importance of Hasidism for Judaism. The spiritual essence of the world must be realized by guiding the sparks upward, a process that both makes the world and the divine transparent and allows them to become transparent.[25]

The renunciation of what is physical, factual, and visible does not occur because the physical is a pretense, a deception, or nonexistent, but rather because it is shown to be only a peripheral aspect of reality. The ascent of the soul, with its shifting perspectives,[26] does not mean annihilating the world or withdrawing oneself from it. Instead, it corresponds to an increasingly dynamic and intense relationship with the world, and an entry into what lies behind it.

Throughout, however, a delicate paradox remains, which is linked to the nature of the spiritual and the psychic: namely, this ascent also involves entering hiddenness. That is, this activity need not always become visible to the outside; often it must not become visible at all.

As on all meditative paths, the ascent of the soul eventually leads to nothingness, to an ecstatic situation, which seems to amount to dissolution. But this nothingness is the place of regeneration. It is the creative nothingness, even when all the traits of genuine nothingness are ascribed to it. It exists beyond space and time,[27] beyond oppositions, beyond individual differences.[28] It is said that:

> Whoever makes himself nothing is connected with the highest nothingness.[29]

This level of the ascent, on which "nothingness" is reached, corresponds to the highest level, the symbolic level, on which the ego disappears. Or as we are told:

> The human being must think of himself as nothing and completely forget himself. His prayer should strive entirely toward the *Shekhinah*. He can then reach beyond time, that is, to the world of thought, for there everything is the same: life and death, the ocean and the mainland.[30]

Here, the highest union is achieved, the connection with the divine is made permanent. And thereby the perspective on the world is accordingly transformed. The human being who is transformed and connected with God in this way now experiences the world at the symbolic level, as something done by the divine.

This is a permanent connection only for the *tzaddikim*, who live in continual attachment to God, but it can also be achieved through individual acts of meditation, or prayer, or however the sparks are redeemed.

The four levels of the world in the Kabbalah, and the stages of introversion

Here, it would be well to shed some psychological light on the act of meditation and a few Kabbalistic ideas. Our concern is less to offer a full interpretation than to help readers understand the reality of these contents, by indicating the corresponding psychic states.

As we have emphasized elsewhere, the ascending path of meditation proceeds from existence, from something, from the created, back to nothingness, to the uncreated. Thus, it takes the path that God took, in reverse order, when descending in the creation. That is, the path of meditation proceeds through the four stages of the world and through the ten *sefirot* of the Kabbalah.

The lowest of these four stages, *Assiah*, contains the material shaping of the world, of material creatures and things. It is the world of action and actuality. The next stage, *Yetzirah*, is the world of formation, form, material ideas, angels, and human souls, and also of the seven planetary spheres. The second highest world, *Beriah*, is the world of the basic plan, of the Torah, of original creation, of individual principles. The highest stage, *Azilut*, is closest to the absolute. It contains the *sefirot* as the constituents of the world.[31]

There is a crucial coordination of the levels of the world with acts of meditation and the various stages of introversion. It is a known psychological fact that the stages of introversion, which culminate in ecstasy, are accompanied by a diminishing awareness of the body. Ecstasy is repeatedly described as the soul's detachment from the body, a stepping out of the body, a closer approach to the psychic world of the collective unconscious, in which the soul is dissolved.

The world of consciousness is centered in and tied to the body.[32] It relates essentially to the outer world, and the unity of ego-consciousness rests upon the experience of the body's integrity. Unless it occurs under particular circumstances, every introversion leads to dissociation. That is, the ego then exists as an ego-complex among the emerging partial complexes of the psyche, which confront it in the shape of personalized figures, as in the diminished consciousness of dreaming. Traveling through these worlds of partial souls is described as a passage through the upper and lower worlds, with their geniuses, hierarchies of angels and devils, heavenly palaces, and so on.

These ecstatic visions are accompanied by the libido's turning away from the outer world, by introversion, manifested as a "forgetting of the physical," that is, of the outer world. This stage corresponds to the second level of the world: the soul has reached *Yetzirah*. In terms of the philosophy of language and the technique of meditation, this corresponds to letters uniting as the constituents of a word. Here, the word is the lowest mental instrument. It reaches down to the *Assiah*, the parts of which, the letters, as the principle of life, the spiritual element, and the vessel of thought,[33] are united in *Yetzirah*, that is, they are recognized as elements of spiritual form and connected to each other.[34]

Deeper introversion leads to catalepsy, a state of paralysis, which is a symptom showing that the outer, physical world is no longer perceived at all by consciousness, nor by the psyche as a whole. What mystical language calls the "transposing of the lights" has been achieved here. The sun has gone down on the outer world and risen on the inner, and the light of consciousness has turned from one side to the other.

On this level, where nothing more is heard from the outside—the eye has closed long ago, that is, turned inward—the soul is at the level of *Beriah*. Letters are united with thoughts, and the single idea is connected with a central idea. Here, the person speaks without hearing any more what he is saying. His ego-consciousness has disintegrated, and *IT* speaks out of him.

The next, the highest level is nothingness or wisdom, which are characteristically identical. This is the level of danger, death, ecstatic disintegration. Here, the soul enters the world of *Azilut* and is destroyed or reborn. Crucially, it relies here entirely on grace, or "the faithfulness of God." For its own capacity to act is suspended, and ego-consciousness with it. Here, only the deep layer of nothingness is active, uniting death and life.[35]

This association of the levels of the world with those of introversion is intended psychologically; it makes no claim to describe the Kabbalistic idea. If, for instance, the Kabbalah conceived of the entire sefirotic world as *Azilut*, and if the path of meditation within it should only be traceable as far as the *sefirah* of *Binah*, then our association would seem utterly impossible. However, our reflections are based on psychic experience and its collective symbolism. Instructed by and related to this empiricism, the doctrine of the four levels corresponds to a projection of psychic states, which can be generally verified and compared. Leaving linguistics aside, our statements are justified from this viewpoint.[36]

We had reasons, earlier,[37] to associate "renewal from nothingness," that is, nothingness as the neutral point[38] on the path of meditation, with the *sefirah* of nothingness. On the other hand, the fire of nothingness, alchemically renewing and consuming, has been characterized as the *Shekhinah*, which is not the first *sefirah* but the tenth.

Psychologically, with respect to the ego, the character of nothingness can be represented by any *sefirah* including the *Shekhinah*. This means not only the second *sefirah*, *Hokhmah* (wisdom), the sea, but also the third, *Binah* (reason), as the higher mother, and also the tenth, *Malkhut* (kingdom) and *Shekhinah*, as the lower mother.[39] Originating in primordial nothingness, each part of the sefirotic world possesses this aspect of nothingness vis-à-vis human ego-consciousness, even if it does not correspond, in a spherological sense, to the *sefirah* of nothingness, which is the other-worldly representation of the Infinitely Other at the creation of the world.

The *sefirot* may be called non-pictorial archetypal constellations. They are therefore conceived of as levels, aspects, characteristics, hypostases, principles, emanations, names, lights, and forces.[40] Like every archetype, each *sefirah* owes its nothingness to its energy, which infinitely surpasses ego-consciousness and thus has a disintegrating effect on the ego.

Even if the next section treats some of the *sefirot* as psychic qualities, this needs to be understood as part of our serious endeavor to show how the higher human being,[41] *Adam Kadmon*, who consists of the *sefirot*, corresponds to the lower human being and the parts of the soul. These correspondences are developed along the lines emphasized here. Psychologically, we start from the assumption, discussed below, that the image of the human being was projected onto the sefirotic world.

In what follows, we are not concerned with the inherent meaning of this sefirotic world, referring to it only in order to understand Hasidic and Kabbalistic anthropology. In doing so, we treat the *sefirah* as a characteristic or constituent of the human image, *Adam Kadmon*, that was projected onto the creation of the world and onto the divine.

We also leave aside the Kabbalistic meaning of the *sefirot*, their world-constituting character. The inner justification for this approach can be established retrospectively, once we have made clear what Hasidism means by "the fashioning of God's human form."[42]

2. The parts of the soul and the soul's transformation

Adam Kadmon *and the parts of the soul*[43]

The ascent to nothingness, which occurs through prayer or meditation, and the simultaneous transformation of the world's sparks and of God's reality, conform to a *process of psychic transformation* within the individual parts of the human soul. We have already encountered the basic meaning of the parts of the soul, the *nefesh* or blood-body-soul, the *ruach* or spirit-soul, and the *neshama* or rational soul.[44] We must now discuss in greater detail what happens to these parts of the soul in the transformation process.

According to the Kabbalah, a perfect correspondence exists between the lower human being and the higher, primordial human being, *Adam Kadmon*. The law that everything above is below, and everything below is above, rests on this correspondence.

> The making of the entire world below is modelled upon the world above. To us down here, everything that exists in the upper world seems like a copy, and yet they are both the same.[45]

(The Babylonian origin of this notion is irrelevant in this context. Just as Platonic and Neoplatonic influences receive a different emphasis through their specific conversion by Judaism, the final sentence, "and yet they are both the same," brings into play the micro–macro cosmic identity, the *unitary* aspect, and thus an utterly different conception of the world.)

The ten *sefirot* are commonly represented by a tree, by a human form, by concentric circles, etc. Their most frequent array is shown in Figures 2.1 and 2.2, where two systems operate side by side.

The tree is arranged as a three-part *horizontal* structure:

first *sefirah*: *Keter*—crown

second *sefirah*: *Hokhmah*—wisdom

third *sefirah*: *Binah*—reason

This is the realm of *reason*.

fourth *sefirah*, *Hesed*—grace, or *Gedulah*—greatness

fifth *sefirah*: *Din*—judgment, or *Gevurah*—strength

sixth *sefirah*: *Rahamim*—compassion, or *Tiferet*—beauty

This is the intermediate region, the moral realm of *spirit* and *soul*.

seventh *sefirah*: *Netzach*—eternity

eighth *sefirah*: *Hod*—splendor

ninth *sefirah*: *Yesod*—foundation, or *Tzaddik*—the righteous one

This is the lower realm of *nature*.

These nine *sefirot* are generally contrasted, as the masculine unity of *Adam Kadmon*, with the tenth, feminine *sefirah*, which is *Malkhut* (kingdom) or *Shekhinah* (divine glory).

Next to this division exists a division into three pillars, a three-part *vertical* structure (see Figures 2.1 and 2.2).

The *right-hand* or *masculine* pillar is formed by *sefirot* 2, 4, and 7 (*Hokhmah–Hesed–Netzach*).

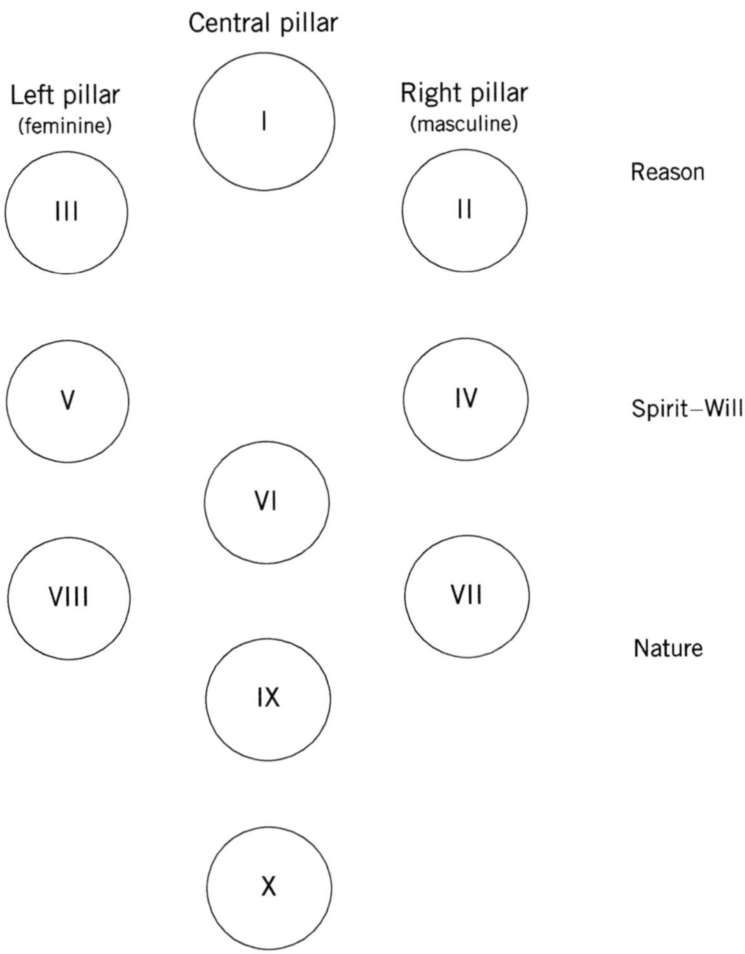

FIGURE 2.1 The Sefirotic Tree (I).

Adapted from drawing © 1940, Erich Neumann. Courtesy of the Erich Neumann Estate.

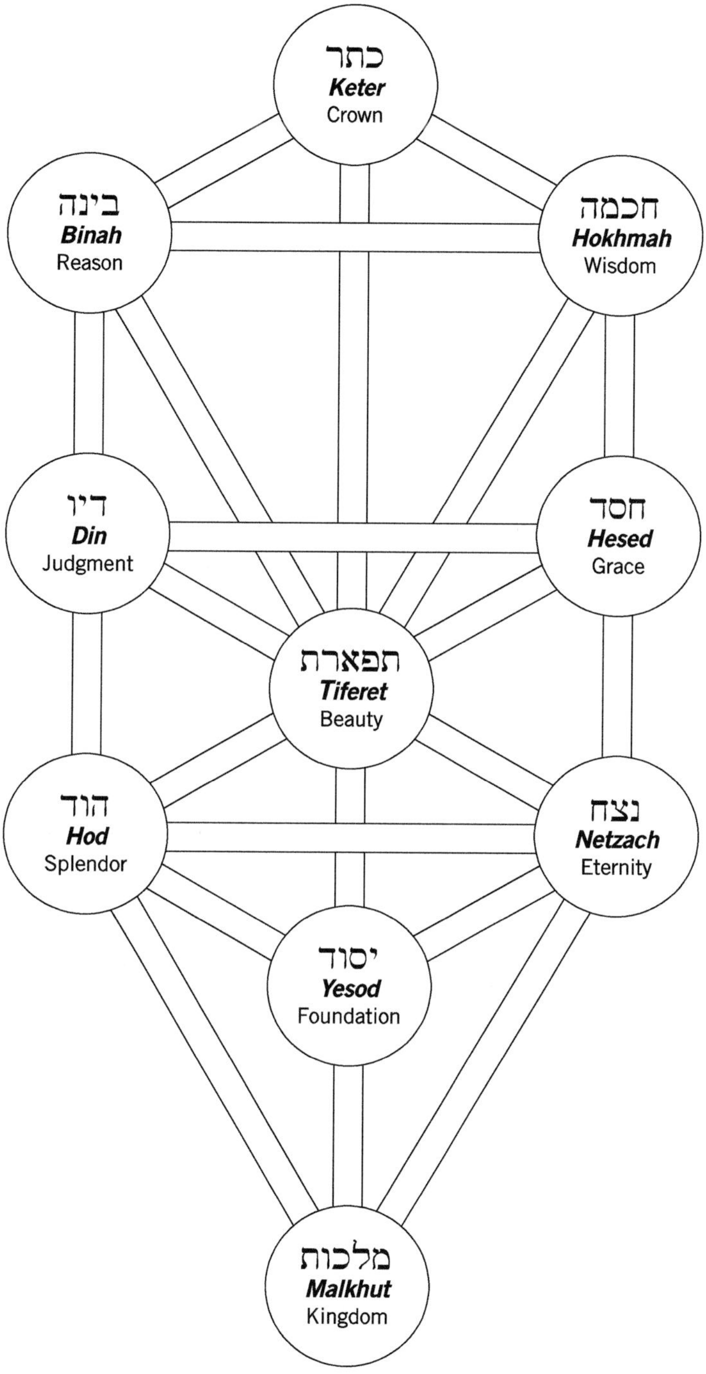

FIGURE 2.2 The Sefirotic Tree (II): based partly on Neumann's hand-drawn sketch of a woodcut (not found) by sixteenth-century German artist Hans Burgkmair. The names of the *sefirot* may vary; shown here are those mentioned most often in Neumann's *Hasidism.*

The *left-hand* or *feminine* pillar is formed by *sefirot* 3, 5, and 8 (*Binah–Din–Hod*).

The *unifying* or *central* pillar is formed by *sefirot* 1, 6, and 9 (*Keter–Tiferet–Yesod*).

Adam Kadmon is the primeval or original human being, the first formed by the *sefirot*. The Gnostic speculations of the Kabbalah are connected with this son of God, the first-born of creation, who made his appearance on the *Merkavah*, God's throne-like chariot in Ezekiel's vision.

> No form, no world existed until the human form emerged; for it contains all things, and everything that exists, exists only through it. Still, the "heavenly human being" must be distinguished from the lower one. The latter could not exist without the former. The entire formation of the universe rests upon the human form. This is the form that is meant when we are told (Ezekiel 1:26) that "a human form" was seen above the divine throne.[46] And likewise, we are told in Daniel (7:13): "I saw one like a human being coming with the clouds of heaven."[47]

Of importance in our context is the attribution of the three parts of the soul—*neshama–ruach–nefesh*—to the three regions of the body—head–chest–stomach—and its three centers—brain–heart–liver, the first letters of which, M (*moach*–brain), L (*lev*–heart), CH (*haved*[48]–liver) may be read as *MeLeCH*, "King," thus designating the royal likeness of *Adam Kadmon*.

We can understand this doctrine of correspondence once we know that *Adam Kadmon* is composed of the *sefirot*, and that the three centers of the body (brain, heart, liver) correspond to the three *sefirot* forming the central pillar of the sefirotic system. These three *sefirot* are the centers of the upper realm of reason, the middle realm of spirit, soul, and will, and the lower realm of nature, that is, the world's spiritual constitution and the human being's physical constitution are in harmony with each other.

The upper center, the brain, belongs to the rational *neshama*-soul, which is coordinated with the three upper *sefirot* of *Adam Kadmon*. It is the highest rational aspect of the world of primeval thought. (The classification of *nefesh* and *neshama* in the Kabbalah varies. Sometimes, *nefesh* is attributed to the tenth *sefirah* of *Malkhut*, *neshama* to the *sefirah* of *Binah*. Crucially, *neshama* belongs to the triad of *Adam Kadmon*'s head and spirit. Even if it is said to stem from *Binah*, it is shaped by the other two *sefirot* in this triad.)

Likewise, the heart center is coordinated with the *ruach*-soul, the psychic and spiritual part, corresponding to the level of the talking being. Possessing a soul, the talking being is set apart from sheer nature, for it possesses a strong spiritual and moral component. This center corresponds to the middle triad of *Adam Kadmon*, but especially to *Tiferet* as the very middle of this triad.

The three lower *sefirot* in the sefirotic scheme correspond to nature and the world and are centered in the abdominal region of *Adam Kadmon*. They correspond to the liver, as the center of the body, which is coordinated with the *nefesh*-soul, which is the blood-soul.

Yesod, the middle of the lower triad and the procreative member of *Adam Kadmon*, is the principle of creative nature.

As noted,[49] the vegetative–animal sphere of life is governed by the *nefesh* part of the soul, in the liver.

We must consider in slightly more detail what is symbolized by the *nefesh*-soul and its related region, the center of which is said to be the liver. This sphere is the world of unconscious life, the aspect of human existence dominated by instincts and drives. That is, it is the dense aspect of the psychic world, where the amoral and pre-moral forces of the unconscious operate, and no division into good and evil has yet occurred. The liver is an archetypal symbol, representing the sphere of drives, where "good and evil" commingle. It is coordinated with the vegetative–autonomous nervous system as the central organ, along with spleen and kidneys.

> The faithful shepherd said: "The liver belongs to Esau's level: This is Edom,[50] who gathers all blood in himself, whether pure or cloudy, and does not distinguish between good and evil.[51]

This biological, value-free zone has a crucial function for life and for psychology, especially with respect to the ancient world. It is the aspect of the unconscious that is closest to life and to nature. Its significant role in the primitive world and in early cultures, in particular for the world of prophecy, stems from the fact, evident from ancient orgiastic and divinatory procedures, that prophecy was aided by these lower centers of the unconscious that the liver symbolizes.

The Zohar takes a characteristically negative view of the *nefesh* aspect. It experiences this instinctual dimension as the shadow, that is, as negative and destructive, and it displays its ascetic–moral tendency and hostility to nature by assigning this region specifically to the Jewish shadow-figure, Edom (from *adom*, "red," related to *dam*, "blood").

This connection emerges in the broadest sense from another text, which follows the passage cited above:

> The heart, however, is Israel, which separates good from evil, impure from pure blood, and only accepts the selected and cleansed, like someone who separates food from waste. When the heart, which corresponds to Jacob, has selected the higher blood, the liver is left with the waste. It rages in the bile, which is hell, which was created on the second day, and is called the death of the strong, the shameful woman, the foreign fire, the hard drudgery, the "foreign service." And because it stirred the wrath of the liver, the rabbis have said that every angry person resembles an idolater. Moreover: no excitement or inflammation of a sick organ exists that does not stem from the bile, which inflames the hollows of the liver and seeks to burn up the entire body.
>
> It [the bile] can be compared with the ocean, whose wrath makes its waves rise up to heaven when they want to burst its boundaries to lay waste to the world—if it were not for the *Shekhinah*, which is to the sick person like the sand that encloses the ocean, so that it does not transgress its bounds. Similarly, the *Shekhinah* encloses and protects the body.[52]

This text extends the opposition between Jacob and Esau to that between the heart and the liver. It also brackets the shadow aspect of Edom with hell, the "shameful woman" (Lilith), idolatry, and the wrathful ocean.

The meaning of this association is discussed elsewhere in detail,[53] but it can be mentioned here. The "shameful woman," Lilith, in whom the Terrible Mother archetype is connected with the negative anima, is most strongly opposed by the *Shekhinah*. This opposition becomes particularly obvious in the contrast between the wrathful and devouring ocean, representing Lilith, and the renewing ocean, representing the *Shekhinah*.[54]

The association of "the ocean that transgresses its bounds" with the system of liver and bile can be compared with our discussion of the "Foundation stone and the waters of the deep"[55] and of Lilith's relationship with these waters. In every case, what is involved is the negative invasion of the flooding unconscious. It makes no difference whether the aspect of shadow or the aspect of anima is dominant, nor whether the danger being emphasized is that of amoral instinctuality or of overwhelming affects.

Both Lilith and Edom emphasize the danger of the unconscious. We have already discussed the link between Lilith and blood, the earth, the black moon, and impurity. This connection and its consequences are further substantiated in various ways in the text that follows.

If the shameful woman is associated with idolatry, this connection is supported by the relationship between Lilith and the sphere of magic and divination.[56] Similarly, the wrathful ocean, which "transgresses its bounds," is identical to the invasion of the waters of the deep, with the appearance and meaning of which we became familiar in connection with the idolatrous dancing around the Golden Calf.[57]

Beyond the medical, Galenic[58] idea of this text, there is the psychological one. The sphere of the liver and the *nefesh*-soul is opposed to that of the heart and the *ruach*-soul, as strongly as Edom is opposed to Jacob. The region of liver and *nefesh* region characterize the part of the unconscious that makes people unconscious. The affect of rage is as dangerous as the overwhelming sexual drive, and the divinatory, orgiastic component of idol worship is as negative as bloody aggression. Just as characteristic of this satanic sphere, however, is melancholy, black-biled depression, which is attributed to the "evil enemy," because, like all flooding components of the unconscious, melancholy paralyzes consciousness and thus threatens and damages the part of the human psyche associated with Jacob and *ruach*. But this aspect, the choosing and free *ruach*-soul, which distinguishes good and evil, is the essential part of the human being, the decision-making part of his psyche.

The ascent of the soul, the ascent of the sparks through the levels of nature, the transformation of the world's aspects, and the stages of the shedding of physicality,[59] all these states are now complemented by the union of the parts of the soul.

> In the three things, *neshama*, *ruach*, and *nefesh*,[60] we find a faithful reflection of the higher unity. . . . For all three form merely a single existence, in which everything is linked as a unity. The *nefesh* as such possesses no light. She is closely related to the body, whose nourishment and functions she governs. . . .

> Over the *nefesh* rises the *ruach*, which governs the former, gives her laws, and illuminates her as far as necessary. . . . Over the *ruach* soul rises the *neshama*, which governs the former and pours upon him the light of life. The *ruach* is illuminated by this light and so depends entirely on the *neshama*.[61]

Sefirot, *elements, regions of the body, and parts of the soul*

Each person is potentially a point at the center of the world. We realize this level every time we succeed in uniting what is lower in us (*nefesh*) with what is higher (*neshama*). Then the light of the indwelling glory, which once shone over the embryo, shines over us once again. But now the original unity is restored on a new basis, for its foundation is the conscious life of the individual.

The human being's exquisite task, his actual service, is to connect above and below, heaven and earth. This is an essentially Jewish idea, which predates the Kabbalah.[62] Here, we encounter another familiar symbolism, that of the elements.[63] Head and brain correspond to heaven, the *neshama* and *fire*.[64] Chest and heart correspond to the wind, the *ruach* and *air*. Stomach and liver correspond to the *nefesh* and earth.

The Zohar tells us that:

> The human figure encompasses everything in heaven and on earth, the higher and the lower entities.[65]

Meanwhile, the *Sefer Yetzirah*[66] had already said:

> Three mothers in the body: head, stomach, upper body. The head was formed from fire, the stomach from water, the upper body from air, which mediates between them (fire and water).

and:

> Three mothers in the world: heaven, earth, wind. Heaven was formed in the beginning from fire, earth from water, wind from air, which mediates between fire and water.[67]

The unity produced the human being unites heaven and earth, that is, *Adam Kadmon* unites with the lower human being, the divine with the human. And at the same time, the higher, heavenly, fiery soul unites with the lower, earthly soul, through the mediation of the spiritual soul whose element is air.

If this three-part division, "God–human–nature," exists throughout the world, in *Adam Kadmon*, and in the human being, then the soul characteristically stands for its middle part, the human being. This soul, then, is the *ruach* or spirit-soul, the *pneuma*, which is seated in the heart, and which seems to be the key characteristic of the human being in his central position.[68]

Ruach ***and*** **Tiferet** ***as the middle***

This part of the soul must be studied together with *Tiferet*, its corresponding *sefirah* in the figure of *Adam Kadmon*. The contents of *ruach* and *Tiferet* must be given their whole range of meanings, in order to understand that they constellate the "human being in the middle," where the middle is also the center of wholeness.

This middle or center contains the place of the heart, whether *ruach* is understood as the human heart, *Tiferet* as the heart of heaven, or the human being as the heart of the world triad, encompassing both nature and the divine.

In its elemental meaning of wind or air,[69] the *ruach* also acts as a mediator between the region above—light, fire, and heaven—and the one below—darkness, water, and earth. This middle place is the power that continually brings together, both in itself and with each other, the transpersonal dimension of a higher collective world and the not-yet-personal dimension of a lower one. The *sefirah* of *Tiferet* (beauty) or *Rahamim* (compassion) in *Adam Kadmon* corresponds to the heart, the seat of the *ruach*-soul in the human being. Thus, by characterizing this *sefirah* as the synthetic and active mid-point of the sefirotic system, we also shed light, by virtue of their correspondence, on the meaning of the *ruach*-soul in the human heart.

Tiferet, located in the center of *Adam Kadmon*, is also called "the heart of heaven." Besides corresponding to the *ruach*-soul of the lower human being, it is also the origin of the human *ruach*. The *sefirah Tiferet* is the heart of *Adam Kadmon*, the middle-most of the middle triad, and also the middle-most *sefirah* in the central pillar. It is thus the actual center of the whole. If, as often happens, one considers the upper triad as detached, *Tiferet* becomes the center and the epitome of the lower seven, which are the forces constituting the world. On the other hand, it is also said to epitomize the lower six, whereas *Malkhut* stands on its own as the seventh. *Tiferet* is not only the middle of the central pillar, but also the middle between the right and left sides of the middle triad. That is, it stands between the *sefirah* of *Din* (judgment), which is on the left and female, and that of *Hesed* (grace), which is on the right and male. Thus, it forms the male–female synthesis, *Rahamim* (compassion). At the same time, as *Tiferet* (glory, beauty), it is the union of these two *sefirot*, *Din* and *Hesed*, which are also characterized in their male–female opposition as *Gevurah* (strength, concentration) and *Gedulah* (greatness, expansion).

The Sefirotic Tree, as depicted in Burgkmair's woodcut (see Figure 2.2),[70] for example, shows the characteristic position of the *sefirah* of *Tiferet*, which emphasizes its character, as heart and mid-point, in yet another way. The upper triad,[71] as a world of its own, is contrasted with the sevenfoldness of the other *sefirot* and forms the top of the tree. *Malkhut*, the tenth *sefirah*, the woman or queen, stands as an object over against all others. But *Yesod*, too, the ninth *sefirah*, unites the powers of the tree in itself and simultaneously forms the site of transition and procreation between *Adam Kadmon* and *Malkhut*. The five middle *sefirot*, at the center of which stands *Tiferet*, form the trunk of the tree, whereas *Yesod* and *Malkhut* form the roots and the earth. Archetypally, the sacred five, the middle of which is *Tiferet*, symbolize centered wholeness, which is also what *Tiferet* proves to be. (A similar symbol

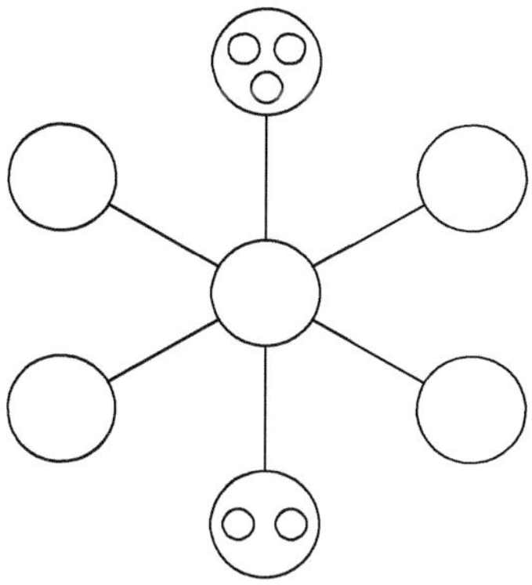

FIGURE 2.3 The *sefirot* as a circle.

Adapted from drawing © 1940, Erich Neumann. Courtesy of the Erich Neumann Estate.

arises from the slightly variant summary of the Sefirotic Tree, in which the three upper *sefirot* are grouped as a triad, just as the lower two are depicted as a polarity, so that *Tiferet* represents the middle of the circle, which encloses it (Figure 2.3).

We can also read the Sefirotic Tree the other way round. Then, we view the upper *sefirot* as descending from nothingness and from creation, so that they represent the upper roots and heaven. *Malkhut* is then the unfolding and spreading, the tree-top pointing downward. But, even considered this way, the middle group of five still forms the trunk of the tree, with *Tiferet* as its center. One important function of this centrally placed *ruach*-soul is choice, or differentiation. This is the place where the opposites meet and are resolved.

> If one wants to gain a sense of the holy unity . . . one must contemplate the flame of a brazier or lamp that has been lit. At first one sees two kinds of light (in the flame), one shining brightly, the other dark blue. The bright light is above and rises straight up, while the darker one is below and provides as it were the seat for the upper one. Nevertheless, both are so closely united that they form a single flame. The "seat," on the other hand, joins with the ignited substance beneath it. The bright light stays the same color throughout. In the darker one, however, one can make out different colorations. Also, unlike the white light, which points only upward, it has two directions: Upward it joins with the bright (white) light, downward with the ignited substance. This, however, is consumed relentlessly and rises (in the burning) constantly (upward) to the higher light. So everything joins together into a complete unity.[72,73]

The middle part, corresponding to the *ruach*-soul, has two directions, one pointing upward, the other downward. Only from this perspective do we begin to understand that this part represents the power of moral discrimination. Upon it rests *choice*, as that for which humanity was created, and also the principle of freedom. This *ruach* part of the soul is really the heart and the center;[74] it is at once spiritual and emotional, judging and determining, neither instinctual nor abstract. It is associated with the principle of gravity, the middle, equilibrium, harmony, balance, and beauty.[75]

Ruach *and* Tiferet *as central activity*

This aspect of choice refers to morality, the decision between good and evil, and to aesthetics, the evaluation of beauty and ugliness, and it emphasizes the principle of the mid-point. It outweighs by far the concept of the *ruach*-soul as *anima*,[76] between mind and body, as found in the schema of Neoplatonism.[77] Here, what is meant by choice is not logical or abstract, but emotional. In this sense, the link between the *ruach* spirit and the feeling heart corresponds exactly to what has led analytical psychology to claim that feeling is a rational function. The character of this part of the soul is important in all its aspects—spiritual as well as emotional, moral as well as active.

It is striking how variously *ruach* and *Tiferet* can be interpreted. For some, the *ruach*-soul is psyche and temperament; for others, it is a moral faculty. Some associate *Tiferet* with volition; others represent it as the highest aspect of moral life or moral perfection. It is also depicted as beauty, through the perfection of the good. The second triad of the Sefirotic Tree, the middle of which is *Tiferet*, is interpreted in another context as the world of feeling. Only a psychological analysis can bring order to these interpretations and make them understandable.

The function of the *ruach*–soul in the heart is related to what analytical psychology calls the feeling function, which expresses itself as evaluation, choice, and ethical and aesthetic activity. It looks in two directions and hence has two faces, for, in evaluating, it decides between good and evil, also between beautiful and ugly. The *ruach*-soul is therefore said to look both up and down, conceiving from the *neshama*, and giving shape to the *nefesh*. Its bidirectionality, which unites acceptance and rejection, shaping and being shaped, makes it the prototype of what is perfect, uniting the masculine and the feminine. And thus its name: "Adam" is said to be the union of A (the symbol of God as wisdom) and *dam* (blood). Although neither without the other can create a perfect form,[78] the unity of Adam connects the higher A, the *neshama*, with the lower *dam*, the *nefesh*.

As the spirit soul, mediating above and below, the *ruach* contrasts as strongly with the transpersonal principle of the spiritual and rational, making up the divine part in the *neshama*, as it does with the unconscious principle of bodily instinct, the impersonal and less than personal, making up the natural part, the *nefesh*.

The region of the *ruach* forms the sphere of humanity and individuality, between the transpersonal collective world above and the pre-personal collective world below. The aspect of individuality is also contained in it, as revealed by the names of the gods that are associated with the *sefirot*:

> When finally everything has been formed and has emerged from that womb (of the third *sefirah*, *Binah*, called the mother),[79] when everything has received its place and now it is time to name the individual, then God names himself YHWH.[80]

And thus the name of God, YHWH, is assigned to the *sefirah* of *Tiferet*.

As the place and function of choice, the *ruach*, "the organ of self-encircling inner human life, the breath of individual psychic substance,"[81] forms the basis of human freedom. The "I-am" therefore belongs essentially to this part of the soul, which explains the coordination of the volitional aspect with this *sefirah* and this part of the soul. The freedom of choice rests upon the will, as the ability of consciousness to manage the energy at its disposal, that is, to deal with it intentionally and selectively.

Only the human being can choose and decide, however, and he can do so only by virtue of his ego, which forms the center of consciousness. Having no ego and no consciousness means having no choice. Once more, we see how strongly Judaism emphasizes consciousness and the ego as the fact constituting the individual.

The "I,"[82] as the mid-point, is the divine self-revelation associated with the king, *Tiferet*. As the basic precondition of the individual and individuality, this "absolute I" is a principle so unique to God that one Hasidic tale considers it presumptuous to respond with "I" without giving one's proper name. Thus, the person referring to themselves as "I" receives the following answer:

> Who is it that dares call himself "I" as befits only God himself.[83]

But the "I" that is meant here is actually not the ego as the center of consciousness, but rather what modern psychology calls the Self. This "I-Self"[84] is the center of the whole. It is the totality, which is established when above and below are connected, when "light fully envelops the human being," when the *yehidah*[85] is realized.

The principle operating in Hasidism is that the parts of the soul must be united with the help of the ego and consciousness, and that only this will establish the human being's original wholeness and centrality. Then, the *yehidah*, the unified or total soul, will also emerge. It is unrepeatable and closely entwined with *tzelem*, the Self, "one resembling a man,"[86] without which no generation can occur. Considering this, the Zohar tells us:

> God created the human being in his image. This image receives us when we enter the world. It develops when we grow, it accompanies us when we depart from the world. This image is a heavenly being.[87]

And thus we are also told:

> The essence of human selfhood, that which is called "I" by the human being, is the *neshama*, which is everlasting.[88]

This psychology of the Self also includes the *tzelem*,[89] which is identified partly with the *neshama*, but appears partly on its own as the *principium individuationis*.[90]

The mid-point is the place of decisive activity, the place of separation and connection, the place where the world's destiny is governed.

As noted, the initial letters of the respective centers and of the parts of the human soul produce the name *MeLeCH* (king). Thus, the *sefirah* of *Tiferet*, as the center, essence, and unification of *Adam Kadmon*, is also referred to as king.

The tenth *sefirah*, the queen (*Malkhut* or kingdom), stands opposed to the other *sefirot* like the object to the subject. It is passive, female, and forms the counterpole to *Tiferet* as the center of *Adam Kadmon*'s active potencies, which become procreative in *Yesod*. Thus, *Malkhut* is a woman, a matron, and a queen; she has no power of her own, but is at once the harmony of the whole and a symbol of God's power over the world. In her is concentrated the entirety of the *sefirot*, and she alone mediates their downward influence.

The procreative union of *Tiferet*, the king, and *Malkhut*, the queen, produces the next level of the world and moreover the world as such. It is only because *Adam Kadmon*'s sefirotic forces are able to procreate in *Malkhut* (the kingdom) that they come to power, and not only they but also the divine. Thus, *Malkhut* is identical with nature, the world, and life. But as the *Shekhinah*, she is also God's immanence, the self-revealing deity, and the world's soul, if we understand this as all the sparks swallowed up in the world and needing to be redeemed, while they simultaneously bring redemption. She is the feminine aspect of God, God's glory, yearning to be united with the other part of God, which is revealed as *Tiferet*, yet hidden as crown or as nothingness.

> The *Shekhinah* is called "this," for she is the world that reveals itself.[91]

The *Shekhinah* is also God's glory in exile. She wants to be redeemed by the human being, and this is his actual task.

> May he do everything he does entirely for the spark of the *Shekhinah* therein, and may he do everything because of the *Shekhinah*, not for himself.[92]

The *Shekhinah* is also the moon, which receives its light from the hidden sun, *Tiferet*, whose light has power in darkness only through the *Shekhinah*. Whereas the *Shekhinah*, the moon, has a luminous character, she is also the hiddenness of the divine in the world, the secretly nurturing, inner principle of the world's life. Thus, it is said:

> She is the mother of all things, and everything that exists on earth suckles at her breast and is blessed by her.[93]

So the *Shekhinah*, as the mother of worlds, is also named Eve. *Tiferet*, as the king and heart of *Adam Kadmon*, directs his relationship toward *Malkhut*, and this creative relationship is the paradigm not only for God's creative relationship to the world, but also—because the human being is in God's likeness—for the creative relationship of the human being to the world. Because of this likeness to God, the human being himself stands as *Tiferet* and king with respect to the world of *Malkhut*. On the symbolic level, the world is the *Shekhinah*, the immanence of God. So the redemption of the sparks redeems not only the world and the human being, but also the divine. For whenever the human being manages to raise the spark from the bowl to nothingness, this is also God's union with the world, and the *Shekhinah*'s with *Tiferet*, which brings blessing to God, the human being, and the world, all together.

Tiferet, the *sefirah* at the heart of *Adam Kadmon*, has a central, active character, as the sun and as YHWH. Centrally located within the lower human being, it corresponds to the mid-point, the *ruach*-soul. Human activity actually flows from the *ruach* part of the soul, which connects what is above with what is below and procreatively produces the union of God and the world.

If we begin with the action of choosing, then the *ruach* part of the soul is essential. If, however, we begin with the ontological aspect, then *neshama*, as the highest part of the soul, is the essential actor. We must recognize that redemptive action can proceed from below as well as from above, and that these movements are causally related: the lower movement causes the upper, and vice versa. But a more profound approach also shows that, despite its significance, this causal relationship is merely superficial. Even here, when seen from the highest level, the divine activity encompasses everything.

The essence of this middle location of the region of *ruach–Tiferet* is its aspect of totality and connection. Its oneness unites the various aspects and simultaneously forms a reality beyond them. One essential symbol of this union is the hermaphroditic character of *Tiferet*. The principle of the balance,[94] governing worldly life and the system of the *sefirot*, is the law of polar opposition and its union through synthesis.

Placed as a fundamental law over every union and alliance, even that of *Tiferet* and *Malkhut*, the king and queen, is the balance, the creative union of masculine and feminine, on which the life of the world depends.

> When the balance did not yet exist, they (king and queen, the procreators of the lower worlds) did not yet see each other face to face, and the original kings died from lack of food. This balance hangs in a place that "is not" (nothingness, equivalent to *Keter*, crown, the highest *sefirah*).[95] It has no support but itself. . . . It bears and will bear everything that is not . . ., everything that is, and everything that will be.[96,97]

In the perfect individual, the polarity of *Din* and *Hesed*, male and female, good and evil, is united and overcome. This defines the essence of *Tiferet*, the heart *sefirah*, and of *ruach*, the heart part of the soul.

Ruach *and* Tiferet *as ego–Self*

In *Tiferet*, as in the *ruach*, the basic male–female polarity is synthesized, which governs the world. Therefore, *Tiferet*, the king, also represents the principle of the hermaphroditic *Adam Kadmon*.

> Every form in which one does not find the male *and* the female principle is imperfect. The Holy One, the Blessed, only makes his abode where both principles are completely united. The blessings only come down where this union exists, as it is written (1 Moses 5:2): "And he gave blessing to them (both) and called *their* name: Humankind!"[98] (not: humans). This teaches that the name "human" applies only to both together, man and woman in their union.[99]

Thus, *Tiferet*, as the mid-point and synthesis, is also the place where "the colors blend."[100] Its symbol is the rainbow, the symbol of the covenant. For red, associated with the left pillar of the Sefirotic Tree—being the color of *Din* (judgment) and of Edom (see above)—and white, the color of the right pillar, which has the character of light, combine with the green of the central pillar to form a unity in *Tiferet*.

This aspect of connection, unity, and totality is characteristic of the multicolored center of *Tiferet* and *ruach*. The Self, with its richly symbolic forms of appearance, perhaps becomes most obvious in the *tzelem*, the inner *Adam Kadmon*, God's image in humankind. Appearing at the moment of procreation, it accompanies the human being through life, develops with his development, and does not leave him when he departs from life. The Self characteristically has the aspect of the effective middle of the King, the totality, the union of opposites, and the hermaphrodite. But the symbols of the Tree of Life (see the Sefirotic Tree), the food of life, and salvation, are also associated with this central region.

> This region where all the colors unite is called *Tiferet*.[101] Here the whole body attains salvation, and a tree, tall and mighty, splendid and beautiful, grows. "The animals of the field found shade under it, the birds of the air nested in its branches, and from it all living beings were fed."[102] He has a right and a left arm. The right one is life and love, the left one death and strength.[103]

The abundant and manifold symbols appearing here in unison are characteristic of the Self. *Tiferet* is the king and, as the creative principle, also the sun, over against the queen *Malkhut*, as *Shekhinah*, who is also the moon. At the same time, however, *Tiferet*, the center, is also the sacred five, the six, and the seven. As the six, it is the unity of the six *sefirot*, the primordial force within the six directions constellating space,[104] and thus the center of the higher forces. As the five,[105] it is the centered totality, the middle of the middle. As the seven,[106] it is the union of the lower powers of the world, which are connected with [. . .][107] and appear archetypally as the sacred seven.

The Self still appears under the same symbolism today, in the psychology of the modern person. But here let us review what this aspect of unity and totality means for the three parts of the soul.

Within *each* part of the soul is contained, in latent form, the aspect of unity, of totality, that is, of the Self. But it is modified differently in each. In the *nefesh*, it is the unity of the body, which always reacts as a whole, although on an unconscious level. In the *neshama*, the part of divine reason, the Self is at its purest, most detached, and most inhuman. This part of the soul is therefore said to be realized only in old age.[108] The aspect of connection and productivity is most obvious in the *ruach*. It represents the human task in the world, which is to produce the Self through human activity, in relation to God, the world, and oneself.

This ego-Self emerges or appears when the choosing and decision-making activity of consciousness, which belongs to the *ruach*-soul in the heart, has combined with *neshama* above and *nefesh* below. On the other hand, even if the divine part of the human soul, the *neshama*, is considered as a son who emerges from the union of *Tiferet*, the divine king, and *Malkhut–Shekhinah*, the divine queen, this generation of the Self does not conflict with our previous remarks. The complexity of these aspects simply confirms that their psychological content has a single meaning.

In terms of the process of creation, the human Self is brought forth by divine self-union; it is the product of the connection between God's active, masculine aspect and his feminine, worldly aspect, the *Shekhinah*.

In terms of production and ascent, the Self is the son born of the human connection, on the level of *Tiferet*, with the world, on the level of *Malkhut*. That is, it is a product of the individuation process, the engagement between the human being and the world.

In terms of the union of the soul, the Self is a result of the connection of *ruach* with *nefesh* and *neshama*. That is, it results from individuation within the human being, as a process leading to wholeness.

Part of this path of union occurs meditatively on the higher level, with the help of consciousness. On the other hand, it stands directly opposed to the ego as the egocentric mid-point of a solely rational and self-reflected consciousness.

The Self is surely related and joined with the ego in the manner of likeness (the image of God); yet, at the same time, it stands paradoxically opposed to it. This becomes obvious if we consider the dangerous character of the Self. If a human being has not completed the process of union, YHWH manifests himself in *Tiferet* as a consuming fire. The only human being who is spared from facing the Self as an overpowering and annihilating spirit archetype is one in whom above and below are united. If the Self can make its appearance as the middle of a person's established wholeness, it inflicts no harm, but, to an isolated ego-consciousness, it shows the aspect of death and annihilation.

The danger of Gnosticism in Jewish antiquity[109] and the danger of ecstasy in Hasidism[110] are characteristic in this context.

This is formulated in the Zohar as the "consuming nature of blue." In the above text, about the flame, this forms the midpoint of *ruach* and *Tiferet*, between the white light above and the *nefesh* below, the part that is matter and body.

> Therein lies the secret meaning of blue. This blue light, containing the whole, needs to be unified with another thing, which is dead in itself, in order to join with the white light. These two kinds of light are also distinct, in that the lower light changes over time. Sometimes, it is blue, sometimes black, but it also turns red again; whereas the white light never changes, but remains constant. The blue light combines itself in two directions: upward with the white light, downward with the thing beneath it, through which it is enabled to shine in the first place. And in combining with what is below, it eats and devours its foundation. The blue light devours what it is connected with and what it rests upon, because its nature is devouring:[111]
>
> Upon it depend, therefore, the consuming of everything and the death of everything. It consumes what is attached to it from below. But the white light above never consumes nor destroys; in itself it remains unchangeable. Thus Moses says: "For YHWH your God—he is a consuming fire" (Deut. 4:24). This is quite literally the case. It eats and consumes whatever dwells beneath it. Therefore Moses says "your God" and not "our God," because Moses belonged to that white light that neither consumes nor destroys.[112]

The danger of the blue light is then most especially highlighted:

> All colors are favorable in dreams, except for blue, which also has a consuming nature. It signifies the Tree of Death, whose rule over the lower world causes destruction and consumption for everything beneath it. But one may point out that this color also rules in heaven. After all, how many throngs of beings live there above and continue to exist! But notice, all these higher beings are enclosed in the blue light. Not so the lower beings, whose condition is coarse.[113]

The threat posed by the color blue, in which *Tiferet*'s Tree of Life becomes a Tree of Death, can only be banished if the blue light combines with the unchanging white light, and if the flame then burns upwards in perfect union:

> And because it is the nature of this blue light to consume everything attached to it from below, so it is written, for the occasion when the offering is accepted and the flame burns as one: "And fire of YHWH fell and consumed the offering-up."[114] Thus it is recognized that the light burns in a unified combination. Joined with the white light, the blue light consumes all the fat pieces of the offering, which it is able to do only when it has risen, and everything is combined with the white light. Then peace is established in the worlds, and everything is bound together into *one* unity.[115]

This Zoharic text still highlights the *neshama*, the higher part of the soul. With its ascetic, spiritual emphasis, it only brings in the lower dimension, *nefesh* and nature, as "dead matter." In another Hasidic text, discussed below,[116] we will observe a further development, in that the emphasis has shifted downward. That text, too, concerns the symbol of the flame, with the thornbush as its base but, here, the base is affirmed and integrated quite differently. In contrast to the material that is consumed in the Zoharic text, the fact that the thornbush remains unconsumed is the central point of the event.

As we have pointed out more than once, the stance of the Kabbalah is often in stark contrast to rabbinism; nevertheless, the two are still deeply associated through their spiritual–ascetic emphasis. But Hasidism, despite its Kabbalistic heritage—or better, due to its directness and substance, which permitted it to become a religious folk-movement—still exists as a religious folk-movement, beyond the aristocratic isolation of spirit common to Kabbalah and rabbinism.

An essential inner grounding for Hasidic reality is based on the union of the parts of the soul, their specific nature, and their connection with the sefirotic system. Most especially, as we shall see,[117] the great image of *Adam Kadmon* and his central role as the Self are realized on a new level in Hasidism. The form and meaning of the *tzaddik*, and the central human task of "working on God's human form," can only be understood against the background of this Kabbalistic psychology, which we have outlined as a union of the parts of the soul.

Notes

1 *EN*: *Unterweisung*, p. 28. [Neumann also cites key portions of Buber's passage in other contexts. Cf. *Roots II*, pp. 61, 65.]

2 *EN*: In addition, the fact that the sequence of venerated objects is identical for all of humanity proves that the selection of sacred objects is not externally determined, by accidental, "momentary" gods. Rather, the hierarchy of cultic objects is determined by developmental stages in the structure of human consciousness.

3 *EN*: See Lévy-Bruhl's various accounts of the connection between primitives and animals and, in contrast, Maria Hornstein's discussion of humans and animals in *Reich der Seele*. [Cf. Lévy-Bruhl, 1927, *Die Seele der Primitiven* (*The primitive soul*), pp. 24–45. In Hornstein: "(The dog) is the bearer of his master's unconscious . . . because these animals have a distinct ability to take up transferences from the unconscious" (*Reich der Seele*, v. 2, 1937, pp. 119f.).]

4 *EN*: See C. G. Jung's *Seminar* and, among others, Heyer's *Organismus der Seele*. [Perhaps referring to Jung's discussion of archetypes in his *Dream Seminars* and *Vision Seminars*, to which Neumann had access in typescript. For example, in the *Dream Seminars*, v. 4, Winter 1930, pp. 81–6, Jung comments: "In our day, dragons are great machines, cars, big guns. These are archetypes now, simply new terms for old things. These new things are words for images, just as the old things were words for images. The mythological idea of the dragon is probably derived from the idea of huge saurians . . ." (p. 83). Cf. also Jung's discussion of ancestors as archetypes, and the archetype of the Mithraic cave, *Visions Seminars*, v. 6, Spring 1932, typescript, pp. 110f. Also cf. his discussion of "lived" and "symbolic" archetypes, ibid., pp. 158–64. In *Der Organismus der Seele*, Chapter 12, "Jungs analytische Psychologie II," Heyer discusses Jung's typology, anima and animus, archetypal and mythological figures in the collective unconscious, and the spark of the self, as related to individual psychological development (pp. 135ff.).]

5 Cf. above, *Roots II*, p. 55.

6 Hebrew: "tune." In Hasidic tradition, a tune based on a sacred text.

7 Cf. above, *Roots II*, p. 29.

8 *EN*: See Part One, p. 60. [*Roots I*, pp. 37f.]

9 *EN*: *Unterweisung*, p. 30.

10 *EN*: Ibid., p. 31.
11 *EN*: *Great Maggid*, p. 116.
12 Cf. above, *Roots II*, p. 55 (from *Unterweisung*, p. 28).
13 *EN*:This path through the levels of nature could be shown to parallel the path through the sefirot toward firmly assigned categories and contents.
14 *EN*: *Chassid Büch*, pp. 539f. [*Tales II*, p. 256.]
15 *EN*: See below, p. 114. [*Roots II*, p. 90: "Life in this world."]
16 *EN*: *Chassid Büch*, p. 505. [*Tales II*, p. 118.]
17 *EN*: *Chassid Büch*. [Source not found. Citation omits page number.]
18 *Menschstufe*. Neumann refers to this concept again, *Roots II*, p. 112.
19 Reciprocal transformations in the soul and the outer world are discussed above under the category of miracle. Cf. *Roots II*, pp. 41, 43ff.
20 *EN*: *Chassid Büch*, p. 32. [Also quoted above, *Roots II*, p. 23.]
21 Cf. above, *Roots II*, p. 55 (from *Unterweisung*, p. 28).
22 *unbewusst-Sein*: a play on words, used twice in this sentence. By breaking *Unbewusstsein* (the unconscious) into its component parts and capitalizing its final syllable, Neumann calls attention to the word *Sein* (existence).
23 "*ein Gehender*": cf. above, p. 44.
24 Perhaps alluding to a Gospel passage in which Jesus is challenged, "Is it lawful to pay taxes to Caeser?" He replies, "Render to Caesar the things that are Caesar's, and to God the things that are God's" (Mark 12:13–17).
25 *EN*:Through this act, in the self-same process, another, lower level of the world and of God's immanence is realized as a historical event, while existentially, another level of the world and of God's immanence becomes visible as a revelation of existence. It could be said that the activity of the human soul, contingent upon time and space, establishes a new reality of the spatial–temporal world; and it could just as well be said that this activity lays bare various stages of the world's and of God's immanence, which have been eternally present, though more or less veiled.
26 *Verschiebung der Aspekte*: lit. "shifting of aspects." In earlier passages, Neumann discusses the natural and symbolic aspects (cf. above, pp. 59f.) and the shift from one aspect—or perspective—to another, when the sparks ascend (p. 64).
27 *EN*: *R. Nachman*, p. 69. [Cited as p. 60.]
28 *EN*: *Chassid Büch*, p. 148.
29 *EN*: *Great Maggid*, p. 185.
30 Ibid.
31 *EN*:This classification changes in the Kabbalah; see Scholem. This scheme is uncompleted. [Scholem discusses the *sefirot* and cosmology in "Kabbala," *Enc Jud*, v. 9, cols 673–88. Cf. especially col. 686.]
32 *EN*: See Part One. [Page reference omitted.]
33 *EN*: *Great Maggid*, p. 66.
34 *EN*: *Great Maggid*, p. 145.
35 *EN*: See above, pp. 49/50 [*Roots II*, pp. 36f., "The world's places of regeneration."]
36 In Neumann's original, a typewritten note follows this paragraph: "Another similar correction may be inserted here." The planned correction is unwritten.
37 Cf. *Roots II*, p. 37, concerning the sleep of the New Year, and pp. 42f., concerning (re)creation from nothingness.
38 *Indifferenzpunkt*: lit. "point of indifference." The psychological point of balance between death and life.
39 *Malkhut* (kingdom) and *Shekhinah* (divine glory) are both feminine. They are alternative names for the tenth *sefirah*, and together they represent the lower mother. (Cf. below, *Roots II*, pp. 80f.)
40 *EN*: Scholem "Kabbala," *Enc Jud*, col. 674.
41 In Lurianic Kabbalah, the whole of creation is contained in the archetypal human figure, *Adam Kadmon* (Lancaster, 2005, pp. 118f).

42 *EN*: Cf. p. 199. [*Roots II*, p. 171.] [The phrase echoes Genesis 1:26, interpreted by Buber as meaning that, as God created humanity in his image, the goal of human life is to strive to become the image of God (Buber, 1932, *Reden über das Judentum: Gesamtausgabe*, p. 109).]
43 In Neumann's typescript, this subheading reads: *Adam Kadmon und Seelenteile.* As the archetype of *Adam Kadmon* is hermaphroditic (cf. p. 97, n. 38), Neumann may have avoided the possessive pronoun.
44 *EN*: See Part One, pp. 206f. [pp. 150f.: "Body-soul and blood."]
45 *EN*: Zohar II 20a, Bischoff, p. 99. [Cf. *Roots II*, Appendix A, p. 184.]
46 "... and seated above a likeness of a throne was something that seemed like a human form" (Ezek 1:26).
47 *EN*: Zohar III 144a, Bischoff, p. 103. [Cf. *Roots II*, Appendix A, p. 187.]
48 Under the convention that we have adopted for this book, the Hebrew letter Het is transliterated "h" at the beginning of a word or syllable (*haved*), and "ch" at the end (*melech*). Another conventional transliteration, used by Neumann and others, renders Het as "ch" in either position.
49 *EN*: Cf. Part One, p. 209. [*Roots I*, p. 152.]
50 *EN*: See author's accounts of the symbolism of the Jacob–Esau opposition, *Jacob & Esau*, parts I–III. [Related to the red lentil pottage for which Esau sold his birthright, Edom is another biblical name for the elder son of Isaac. It may also refer to Esau's descendants and the country where they lived.]
51 *EN*: Zohar III 234a, Müller, *Der Sohar*, p. 163. [Ernst Müller, 1932. *Der Sohar: Das heilige Buch der Kabbala, nach dem Urtext herausgegeben* (*The Zohar: The sacred book of the Kabbalah, according to the original text*) (hereafter: Müller). Cf. *Roots II*, Appendix A, Zohar III 232a,b and 234a, pp. 187f.]
52 *EN*: Ibid. [Müller folded commentary into Zohar III 232a,b and 234a, including his reading of a verse from Proverbs. Cf. *Roots II*, Appendix A, p. 189, n. 8, where the verse from Proverbs is covered in a footnote.)]
53 *EN*: See Part One, Appendix IV: Lilith. [*Roots I*, pp. 157ff.]
54 *EN*: See above, Part Two, p. 50. [*Roots II*, pp. 36f.]
55 *EN*: See Part One, p. 187. [*Roots I*, p. 140: "The foundation stone and the waters of the deep."]
56 *EN*: As established in Part One, Appendix IV: "Lilith." [*Roots I*, pp. 157ff.]
57 *EN*: See Part One, p. 33 *et passim*. [*Roots I*, pp. 23ff., "The Golden Calf."]
58 Alluding to the theory of the four humors, first developed by the Roman physician and philosopher Galen in the second century CE.
59 Cf. above, pp. 63f.: "On the path, as the sparks of the world were raised."
60 Paraphrase. The original passage reads, "three things: spirit (*neshama*), spirit-soul (*ruach*), and the life of the senses (vegetative soul, *nefesh*)."
61 *EN's note*: Zohar II 142a, Bischoff, vol. I, pp. 110f. [Paraphrased. Cf. Appendix A, *Roots II*, p. 186.]
62 *EN*: Homburger, "Urmensch I" ("Primal humanity"), *Realencyklopädie*, p. 1006, references. [Source not found. *Paulys Realencyklopädie* (1926), contemporary with Neumann's writing, contains no article by Homburger and none titled "Urmensch."]
63 *EN*: See Part One, p. 205. [*Roots I*, pp. 148ff.: "Wind symbolism."]
64 *EN*: See below, pp. 129f. [*Roots II*, pp. 101ff.]
65 *EN*: Zohar III 144b, Bischoff, pp. 102f. [The cited passage is not found in either the Pritzker or the Soncino edition of the Zohar. With thanks to Tamar Kron for her additional searches.]
66 The *Sefer Yetzirah* (*Book of Creation*), written in the third to sixth century CE, is described as "the earliest extant Hebrew text of systematic speculative thought on cosmology and cosmogony" (Wigoder et al., eds, *Encyclopedic Dictionary of Judaica*, 1974, p. 636).
67 *EN*: *Sefer Yetzirah* III 4 and 6, Bischoff, pp. 68f.
68 *EN*: When Buber translates this *ruach* soul as *Gemüt* (temper) (above), this hints at its difference from *neshama*, the rational soul; but it blurs the main characteristics of *ruach*

rather than clarifying them. [Maybe referring to an earlier passage from *Chassid Büch, Roots II*, pp. 14f. Below, *ruach* is associated with *Gemüt* (temperament), but without mention of Buber: cf. *Roots II*, p. 78.]

69 *EN*: See Part One, p. 205. [*Roots I*, pp. 148ff.]

70 Hans Burgkmair (1473–1531), a German painter and woodcut printmaker, produced elaborate, symbolic images. The woodcut to which Neumann refers has not been found. Figure 2.2 shows the *sefirot* approximately as drawn in Neumann's typescript.

71 Based on a sketch in Neumann's typescript, Burgkmair's woodcut showed the upper three *sefirot* smaller than the rest and grouped closer together.

72 *EN*: Zohar I 51a, Bischoff, p. 99. [Cf. *Roots II*, Appendix A, p. 183.]

73 *EN*: The same passage is translated by Müller, who (unlike Bischoff) emphasizes the consuming nature of the blue part of the flame. Cf. below, p. 111. [*Roots II*, pp. 83f.]

74 *EN*: Cf. above, p. 91 [*Roots II*, pp. 69ff.]

75 *EN*: Jung, *Types*, Definitions: Feeling. [In the first edition of *Types* (1921), Jung describes extraverted feeling (pp. 509–16) and introverted feeling (pp. 554–60). He also defines feeling as such (pp. 624–28). Neumann deleted an early version of this note: "Note the striking similarity with the feeling function in modern depth psychology on the one hand (Jung, *Types*, Definitions); also the concept of the anima, below."]

76 A Latin term, meaning "wind, air, breath, soul, or life." Here, the dominant meaning is "soul." The anima is a key concept in Jung's psychology, related but not identical to its Latin meaning. Cf. also *Roots I*, p. 38, n. 89; p. 54, n. 147.

77 The leading Neoplatonist philosopher, Plotinus (204–270 CE), taught that the soul mediates between intellect (*Nous*) and body (K. Corrigan 2005, *Reading Plotinus: A Practical Introduction to Neoplatonism*, especially pp. 38ff. With thanks to Peter Kingsley). Neumann's criticism of the ethical aspect of Neoplatonic theory, tangential to his argument, could have been prompted by a recently published Eranos lecture: Andreas Speiser, "Der Erlösungsbegriff bei Plotin" ("The concept of redemption in Plotinus"), *Eranos Jahrbuch 1937*, pp. 137–54.

78 *EN*: *Great Maggid*, p. 153.

79 The parenthetical phrase is Neumann's insertion.

80 *EN*: Zohar III 65a, Bischoff, p. 91. [Paraphrased, with significant addition by Neumann. Cf. *Roots II*, Appendix A, p. 187.]

81 *EN*: Müller, *Der Sohar und seine Lehre* (*The Zohar and its teaching*) (pamphlet), p. 32.

82 "*Ich*": in its noun form, this word in German means both "I" and "ego." In a psychological context, it is translated "ego." In a biblical or spiritual context, as here, recalling the divine "I am" (Ex 3:14), it is translated "I."

83 *EN*: *Chassid Büch*, p. 565. [*Tales I*, p. 200.]

84 *Ich-Selbst*: the translation "I-Self" is required by context. Elsewhere, we translate this key phrase, "ego–Self." Neumann's term, "die Ich-Selbst Achse" ("the ego-Self axis") had not yet emerged as a distinct theoretical concept, but he approaches it in his 1942 lecture, "The religious meaning of the path of depth psychology" (*Roots II*, Appendix B.IV, pp. 256ff.). "The ego-Self axis" was first clearly defined in Neumann's 1952 Eranos lecture, "The psyche and the transformation of the reality planes: A metapsychological essay" (*The Place of Creation*, 1989, pp. 3–62).

85 Hebrew: in Lurianic Kabbalah, the highest (fifth) level of the soul.

86 Referring to the messianic vision in Daniel 8:15 (cf. *Roots I*, p. 100, n. 119.)

87 *EN*: Zohar III 104a, Adolphe Franck, *Die Kabbala* (1913) (hereafter: Franck), p. 170. [Cf. Appendix A, p. 187 and note.]

88 *EN*: *R. Nachman*, p. 51.

89 Cf. above, notes 80, 81.

90 Latin: "principle of individuation."

91 *EN*: *Great Maggid*, p. 17. [Cited as p. 21.]

92 *EN*: *Great Maggid*, p. 15. [Cited as p. 8.]

93 *EN's note*: Zohar III 10b, Franck, p. 146. [Cf. Appendix A, *Roots II*, p. 186.]

94 *der Waage*: lit. "of the (pair of) scales."
95 The parenthetical phrase is Neumann's insertion in Bischoff's text.
96 *EN*: Zohar II 176b, Bischoff, p. 101. [Cf. Appendix A, *Roots II*, p. 186.]
97 *EN*: Müller's translation, which places the emphasis elsewhere, ultimately amounts to the same: "For as long as no balance existed, one could not see face to face. . . . This balance hung in a place that did not (yet) exist. Things that did not (yet) exist were weighed there. The balance exists through corporeality. It was not grasped. It was not seen. Into it went, and into it go things that did not exist and yet existed and will exist." Zohar III, ibid., Müller, p. 188.
98 Genesis 5:2, trans. by Fox, emphasis added by Neumann.
99 *EN*: Zohar I 55b, Bischoff, pp. 100f. [Cf. Appendix A, *Roots II*, p. 184. (Neumann mistakenly cites this passage to Zohar II 176b. Thanks to Tamar Kron for correcting the citation.)]
100 *EN*: Zohar III 296a, Bischoff, p. 124. [Cf. Appendix A, *Roots II*, p. 188.]
101 Müller has "*Herrlichkeit*" ("glory"). Neumann substitutes *Tiferet*.
102 Müller cites Daniel 4:9. In the NRSV, the verse is found at Daniel 4:12.
103 *EN*: Zohar III 296a, Müller, p. 122. [Cf. Appendix A, *Roots II*, pp. 188f.]
104 *EN*: Scholem: *Geheimnisse der Schöpfung: Ein Kapitel aus dem Sohar*, op. cit., p. 34.
105 *EN*: See above, p. 101. [*Roots II*, pp. 76, 77.]
106 *EN*: See above, p. 100. [*Roots II*, p. 76.]
107 A handwritten phrase, inserted here between lines of typescript, is only partly legible. Before Neumann corrected it, the final clause was to have read: ". . . *und als Sieben ist sie die Einheit der unteren Weltkraefte, die archetypisch als heilige Sieben auftreten, also Zentrum der unteren Maechte*." (". . . and as seven it is the union of the lower powers of the world, which appear archetypally as the sacred seven, thus the center of the lower powers.")
108 *EN*: See below, p. 159. [*Roots II*, p. 126: "The soul of old age."]
109 *EN*: See Part One, pp. 148ff. [*Roots I*, pp. 115ff.]
110 *EN*: See above, p. 44. [*Roots II*, p. 67.]
111 Cf. above, note 73, contrasting Bischoff's and Müller's translations of this passage (Zohar I 51a, Müller, p. 322). Cf. Appendix A, *Roots II*, p. 183.
112 *EN*: Zohar I 51a, Müller, p. 322. [Cf. Appendix A, *Roots II*, p. 183.]
113 *EN*: Zohar I 51b, Müller, p. 239. [Cited as p. 322. Cf. Appendix A, *Roots II*, pp. 183f.]
114 I Kings 18:38, trans. by Fox.
115 *EN*: Zohar I 51b, Müller, p. 239. [Cf. Appendix A, *Roots II*, pp. 183f.]
116 *EN*: Cf. below, p. 134. [*Roots II*, pp. 106f.]
117 The Self is discussed at length below. *Adam Kadmon*, mentioned as a Self-symbol, *Roots II*, p. 124, is explored more fully, *Roots II*, pp. 155f.

3

LIFE IN THIS WORLD

This chapter originally formed the conclusion of Chapter Two. At an unknown time and for unknown reasons, someone – presumably Neumann – removed the 36-page section comprising "Life in this world" from two of his hand-corrected typescripts.[1] *Judging from its survival in the author's table of contents and internal cross-referencing, however, this section remained integral to the work. Its uncertain status is marked here by a grey sidebar along the left margin.*

Unknowing and belief

The danger of Jewish intellectualism, with its ideal of knowledge, is known in Hasidism and despised. The world that Hasidism represents is adapted to perpetual movement, and, in this world, the vitality of "one who walks" is opposed to the safe and rigid path of knowledge and its righteousness. Hasidism, with its great tolerance, surely also respects knowledge and aristocratic withdrawal as a path, even if a dangerous one, but it places special emphasis on "good unknowing" and "good uncertainty."[2]

"Good unknowing" is the simple person's life without knowledge, lived in wholeness and unconscious obedience. It is the life of the invisibly devout, the hidden, who lead lives of humility, unaware of their own chosenness.

Those who lead a good life, the visibly devout, the visibly set apart: of them it cannot be said that they are not good, devout, or just. But they are public, *merely* public, and in that sense they do not correspond to the divine inner essence, which is hidden.

Therefore, the naive, the foolish and slow-witted, children and villagers, the wordless and the unconscious, especially those who hide from the outer world, are closer to God than the obviously righteous.

What is emphasized here is not so much the difference between conscious and unconscious, but between self-conscious, that is, conscious of one's ego, and unselfconscious. The simple man is conscious that he is oriented toward God, but unconscious that he is one of the righteous. Later, we shall say more about this opposition to the rabbinical ideal of knowledge, and it will become clear how a stress on consciousness can be consistent with a rejection of knowledge. Preference for the simple results not only from the privileged place that feeling is given over intellect, although this also plays a part; it rests far more on the simple man's wholeness, the unbroken continuity and orientation of his life. Highlighting this aspect leads Rabbi Nachman to such crude and, especially for Judaism, such paradoxical formulations as:

> It involves wisdom and great effort to be like an animal.[3]

And in contrast:

> One can be a scholar and a great scoundrel.[4]

These statements, and many others, emphasize the primacy of belief, secure adherence to God, over knowledge, because:

> Through believing one becomes wise.[5]

Knowledge, and doing the right thing through knowledge, leads to self-assurance, which is one of the most dangerous forms of closing oneself off from God. This is the greatest danger, because the human being's task is to let God into the world, for God dwells, as one *tzaddik* replies:

> wherever one lets him in.[6]

This reply contrasts pointedly with the "correct" rejoinder to the same *tzaddik*'s question about God's dwelling place:[7] "What a thing to ask! Is not the whole world full of his glory!"[8]

This may be a statistical truth, so to speak; it is certainly a static one. It says how things are, to be sure, but only in the strictest sense. In actual fact, at all times and in all places, God's presence must be established, realized, and made manifest in new ways by human activity. Life is therefore a constant beginning and a constant surrendering to God. The human being stands on a higher level than the angel only because the angel stands still, whereas the human being walks. The human being changes according to the inner vitality of God and his world. He rises from one level to another, and, as we shall see, he can rise even when he falls. For the falling is for the sake of the rising.[9]

Therefore, Hasidism also embraces the following Talmudic saying:

> Those who are perfect in righteousness cannot stand in that place where those stand who turn to God.[10]

In the passage that follows this statement, the problem of the lost son is readdressed on another level, when a pupil asks:

> "According to this, one who has been stainless from youth comes after one who has transgressed against God many times, and cannot attain to his rung?"
>
> The *tzaddik* replied: "He who sees a new light every day, light he did not see the day before, if he wishes to truly serve, must condemn his imperfect service of yesterday, atone for it, and start afresh. The stainless one who believes he had done perfect service, and persists in it, does not accept the light, and comes after him who ever turns anew."[11]

This answer shifts the problem to such a high level that, in a sense, the disciple's basic question remains unanswered. For, as before, the answer decides against "the *tzaddik* in a fur coat"[12] and for the righteous, who are devoted to human beings and to the earth. Hasidism is radical and serious enough to answer the question about the stance of the sinner, vis-à-vis the righteous, in favor of the sinner. For in the typically paradoxical view of Hasidism, sinning and adhering to God are not mutually exclusive.

Joy and wholeness

The saying:

> A joyous free spirit is more esteemed in heaven than a sad *Hasid*,[13]

indicates the great revolutionizing of values, whose most beautiful formulation perhaps occurs in the following tale:

> In Lublin lived a great sinner. Whenever he wanted to talk to the rabbi, he readily consented and conversed with him as if with a man of integrity and one who was a close friend. Many of the Hasidim were annoyed at this, and one said to the other: "Is it possible that our rabbi, who has only to look once into a man's face to know his life from first to last, to know the very origin of his soul, does not see that this fellow is a sinner? And if he does see it, that he considers him worthy to speak to and associate with?" Finally they summoned up courage to go to the rabbi himself with their question. He answered them: "I know all about him as well as you. But you know how I love gaiety and hate dejection. And this man is so great a sinner! Others repent the moment they have sinned, are sorry for a moment, and then return to their daily folly. But he knows no regrets and no doldrums, and lives in his happiness as in a tower. And it is the radiance of his happiness that overwhelms my heart."[14]

The importance of joy is a central Hasidic theme. Once we understand this, we can see the new system of values in Hasidism, which takes the place of the old. So we are told:

> Melancholy is the evil enemy,[15]

and even:

> When the Evil Urge wakens desire in man, he is not concerned with plunging him into sin, but with plunging him into despondency by his way of sinning.[16]

Or:

> Even the noblest bitterness verges on melancholy, and even the meanest joy springs from holiness.[17]

This valuing of joy as a central human attribute is related to the entire Hasidic worldview and must be understood from that perspective.

Joy is valued because creation is affirmed. Joy says yes to the world as it is, and this affirmation is not a theoretical, but—crucially—a substantial act, involving the totality of the human personality and uniting the personality into wholeness. The world is arranged so that joy is a strengthening and life-enhancing principle, and experienced as such, whereas grief and melancholy cause a lowering of the energy of life, in fact, a depression.[18] Joy affirms God's declaration about the world, and "God saw that it was good" (Gen 1:10). The human being and God are moving in the same direction. The state of joy, which corresponds biologically to an enhanced state of life, also links the affirmation of the world to a state of well-being and self-affirmation. Moreover:

> The human being must not forget that he is a king's son.[19]

Grief and melancholy, on the other hand, unavoidably involve the negation of life, feelings of illness, and low self-esteem. According to one saying in the Zohar, the snake, Satan, the evil impulse, and the angel of death are all one and the same.[20] Against the unity of the joyful human being stands the dividedness of the grieving and melancholic person, who turns against himself and thus adopts an anti-vital, even life-destroying course. It is no coincidence that this dividedness is also expressed in language, in that "doubt" and "despair" are fundamentally associated with "two,"[21] that is, with splitting, whereas joy lives on the level of faith, beyond all doubt.

> It is a law that one must use all one's strength to make oneself very strong, so as to always be joyful. For human nature tends toward melancholy and grief, due to misfortunes and the bad events of our time, and everyone is full of sorrow. One must therefore force oneself with all one's might to always be joyful and to derive pleasure from everything whenever one can, even from pranks and jokes.[22]

And the heart, once again, the center of beauty, balance, and wholeness, is where joy has its source.

> The essence of joy lies in the heart,[23]

And:

> Joy opens the heart.[24]

But when the heart opens, the human being becomes whole, which alone makes genuine kindness possible and effective. This goodness no longer comes from the loudness of the prayer's fulfillment, but from the quiet certainty of the heart. This inward-leading path becomes apparent in the three stages of transformation that were undergone by one *tzaddik*'s quarrelsome wife:

> From this moment on, she grew quiet. And when she was quiet, she grew happy. And when she was happy, she became good.[25]

This enhancement of the process of life through joy simultaneously enhances the spiritual *ruach* aspect. For:

> When joy is heightened, spiritual power grows.[26]

And even more basically:

> You must know that melancholy cannot guide the brain in the way it wishes to go; for that reason it struggles to still its thinking. Only through joy can the brain be led, as it wishes, to the stilling of thought. For joy is the world of freedom, and through joy people are set free and guided out of the galut. Therefore, when one's joy is connected with one's brain, then both brain and thoughts are free, rather than in the galut. Then one can lead the brain as it wishes, and still its thinking, because the brain is free and not in the galut.[27]

Wholeness in the state of joy is an entirely physical experience. This process of union also involves the *nefesh* part of the soul, the body-soul, for it is the special character of this experience of wholeness that it connects spirit, soul, and body. For this reason, especially at festivals, community plays a role in Hasidism, with music and group dancing, eating and drinking.

The body is united through dance and music, but here again, we are dealing with a heightening of the process of life, which is meant to increase consciousness, not to stupefy it. As we noted above, the deepest ecstasy corresponds to a disappearance of the principle of consciousness in introversion. But at the same time, it signifies that consciousness is heightened, not stupefied, for in returning one can, if one wishes, report one's experiences in the ascent. One does not awaken dismal and weakened, as from the poison of drunkenness.

> One must keep away from drunkenness and take particular care not to drink more than one can take, in order to avoid getting drunk. For it is good to drink a little if necessary, in order to expand one's thinking.[28]

The joy of the unified person gives him an obvious connection with and openness to God, which only the *tzaddik* possesses at a higher level. The high valuation of such a person forms the background to countless Hasidic reports, in which the simple person, the stupid child, the fool, and the ignorant appear as God's favorites. This is not because God has a particular preference for the weak and the wayward, but because the wholeness of their individuality is unbroken and can work itself out unbefuddled by self-consciousness, conceit, ambition, or reflection. Their Elijah soul, small or strange as it may be, realizes itself in joy. Their piety is hidden, and thus it touches the hiddenness of the divine.

> There are two kinds of love. One loves his clever son's actions and speech and boasts about them; the other loves his son whatever he does or says. It is the same with God's love toward humankind. If a proven man fulfills commands and does good deeds with great wisdom, God loves his actions and is present in all his deeds; and thus the outer appearance of the worlds is bound to God. But if the proven man himself is attached to God, then God loves him for himself. Even if he does not accomplish his deeds wisely, but walks the earth with great simplicity, and is attached to God, God loves him for this very reason. And thus the inwardness of the worlds is lifted to God.[29]

The saying,[30] that heaven prefers a cheerful free spirit to a sad Hasid, clearly expresses this substantial and personal valuation, as contrasted with a moral judgment, which places greater weight on partial traits, partial attitudes, or partial behaviors. The fact of the happy sinner's cheerfulness guarantees a more perfect human figure. It guarantees unity in the parts of the soul and the forms of life, because this unity is not darkened by sin. We are told that the joyful sinner "lives in his joy as in a tower." The splendor of his joy, and thus of his hidden value, outshines all the sin that the world sees and takes note of. But the sorrow of the sad Hasid exposes his inner split, and this break in his personality, which has kept God's unity from shining through, is not balanced out by his "being Hasidic."

Love and fear

Joy comes from the heart, and in *Tiferet*, the *sefirah* of the central pillar, where the right and left sides of the tree come together, the positive character of the "right" always prevails. So love for God comes from the right, the masculine side, the side of grace.[31] Grace is a higher attribute than the fear of God, which stems from the left pillar, that of judgment. Joy belongs to love, just as grief belongs to fear. When grief and guilt feelings gain the upper hand, it is the same as when fear does. But we are also told:

> Love and fear are called male and female.[32]

And if the feminine prevails, it is always some form of evil.

Love and the masculine correspond to the divine principle, bounteously giving and streaming forth. The feminine, as the receiving, desiring, and suffering principle, is—like fear—associated more with deficiency.

> Love and fear are also called hands.[33] Love is the right hand, and fear is the left. Imagine a woman and a small child. The left hand wards off, the right one draws close. For the strength to draw close is greater in the right hand. It is the power to embrace and approach. What one wants to give, one gives with the right hand.[34]

Surely, the broken heart and the fear of God's greatness are attributes that must not be lacking in human life. But love and joy are greater. For fear alone can lead to melancholy, thus to unhappiness and sin. On the other hand, fear represents the feminine, humanly fulfilled attitude toward God, whereas love for God is a matter of grace, which does or does not exist but cannot be achieved through effort.

> Love, which is at a higher level than fear, is given to you by heaven. Fear must come from *you*,[35] fear before the sublimity of the infinite divine.[36]

Only both attributes together constitute the perfect masculine–feminine attitude. They complement and complete each other, establishing balance in *Tiferet*, which is the beauty and compassion of the perfect and balanced whole.

The feminine principle

Here, too, the opposition between feminine and masculine is not yet understood in entirely balanced terms. Although the feminine is no longer negative, it is not yet adequately developed either.

In the ancient opposition between YHWH and earth, the earth confronted YHWH as the feminine dimension of nature, which only gradually came to have a negative constellation. For Jews, Christians, and Gnostics, the archetype of the negative Mother and the anima, representing the natural and earthly aspect of the unconscious, became the basis for a negative image of woman, whose instinctual, divinatory, and orgiastic aspect, destructive to consciousness, is seen in the image of Lilith.[37]

The left side of the Kabbalistic tree is feminine. Detached from the positive, masculine side, it is the origin of the "other side," meaning evil. Here, too, the masculine conception of the story of creation remains in effect, according to which the female is secondary, originating from the side of the male, Adam. For even though Adam is seen as a hermaphrodite, his maleness still predominates.

In the Kabbalistic and Hasidic concept of human wholeness and of *Adam Kadmon*, a new countermovement begins to be apparent, leading to an emphasis on the feminine principle that is completely new in Judaism. This shift, which can realize its full development only in the modern Jew, is reflected in the growing importance of the symbols of *Malkhut* and the *Shekhinah*.

This shift is moving in the direction of eliminating the polar opposition between the sexes, in which the individual is identical with one side of the sexual polarity. Previously, even in the Kabbalah, marriage was seen as the union of two sexual polarities to form a hermaphroditic, transindividual being, which still consists of two persons. In contrast, when the parts of the soul are united, this process is introjected within *one* individual. Here, based on the model of *Adam Kadmon*, male and female combine within *one* individual to form a whole. This means, however, that a new image of the human being begins to constellate itself, one no longer centered on polarized sexuality, but instead on *Adam Kadmon*'s hermaphroditic character.[38]

Hasidism no longer considers old age a particular phase of life, but instead symbolically, as an energetic state. This is not just a manner of speaking; it signals a different evaluation of age. Similarly, the form of human existence that is male and female[39] is gradually ceasing to be seen merely as the characteristic of a sexual person. A major concern for us in Part Three[40] will be what it means for Judaism, and especially for the Jewish woman, to stop identifying the individual with a single sex.

This shift does not alter the fact that, symbolically, the feminine is identified largely with evil, and the masculine with goodness. Our previous remarks suggest, however, that the vessel-like, confining, limit-setting character of the feminine is a key constituent of the world, which represents the dimension of nature as distinct form that of the spirit. In this regard, it is especially important to see the role that evil plays in the Hasidic worldview. It is shell, husk, materiality, corporeality; it is also passivity, overly heavy judgment, and contraction; it is grief, melancholy, stupefaction, and sleep. All these aspects contrast with the activity and spiritual vitality of the divine.

As shell, husk, materiality, and corporeality, evil thwarts transparency, makes things dense and heavy, and takes inwardness captive. As overly heavy judgment, contraction, and feminine passivity, it prevents the expansion of light, the active raising of the sparks. It resists upward and inward movement by remaining motionless, holding tight, and creating distraction. Grief, melancholy, and stupefaction are the psychic states close to death, which inhibit mental activity, the vehicle to God, whether through discouragement and awareness of sin, or through despair and paralysis. When such discouragement is constellated, the human being becomes less and less able to cope with the world that Hasidism sees. His melancholy makes him less and less conscious of being a king's son, whereas more and more of the endless series of situations, challenging him in the present moment, glide past him unfulfilled. This danger—which is characteristic for the Jewish person—is considered so great that one *tzaddik* dared speak the following words on Yom Kippur, which epitomizes the "Days of Awe" for Judaism, because it brings fear and trembling, the confession of sin, and the pronouncement of destiny:

> He who has done ill and talks about it and thinks about it all the time does not cast the base thing he did out of his thoughts, and whatever one thinks, therein one is; one's soul is wholly and utterly in what one thinks, and so much a man dwells in baseness. He will certainly not be able to turn, for his spirit will grow coarse and his heart stubborn, and in addition to this he may be overcome by gloom. What would you? Rake the muck this way, rake the muck that way—it will always be muck. Have I sinned, or have I not sinned—what does Heaven get out of it? In the time I am brooding over it I could be stringing pearls for the delight of Heaven . . . . And so on this day before the Day of Atonement let us feel a withdrawal from sin and a strengthening of the spirit, feel it in our innermost heart and not through forced ecstasy, receive it in our hearts for all future time, and be merry. *Let us recite the list of our sins as quickly as possible*, and not dwell upon it, but rather dwell upon the words of the prayer: "And thou, O Lord, shalt reign, thou alone . . . ."[41]

In order to understand the enormity of this revolution, we must compare this disposition and attitude toward life with the ascetic excesses of Luria's Kabbalah, to which Hasidism otherwise makes such strong reference: not only should one eat one's bread in tears, put ashes on one's head, and suffer the four types of death every night. The horribly sadistic punishment meted out for violating the commandments casts the deepest Middle Ages in a friendly light. We can imagine what an immovable burden hung over the soul of this Judaism, in its consciousness of sin and fear of hell:

> He who was angry must fast for 151 days, he who has drunk wine that has been touched by a non-Jew, 73 days. . . . He who offers a Jew forbidden food or meat from dead animals will be transformed into the leaf of a tree, which is carried around by the wind, in great pain.

Here is another example:

> [One of Luria's pupils reports:] My blessed teacher Luria once saw how a man who had died long ago was tormented before he could be raised up to a particular place in heaven, because he had violated a Sabbath regulation. *For this man did not notice that some ashes had unintentionally gotten into his shoe, and he had gone out onto the street like this on the Sabbath. And so he was punished.*[42]

A significant number of Hasidic leaders experienced for themselves not only the liberating and renewing breakthrough of the new Hasidic feeling for life, as taught by the Baal Shem, but also the new experience of God, in contrast with the old, ascetic, Kabbalistic experience.

The teaching of the soul

One of many stories in this respect is Baal Shem's reception of the Great Maggid, the second great Hasidic leader:

> Rabbi Baer was a keen scholar, equally versed in the intricacies of the Gemara and the depths of the Kabbalah. Time and again he had heard about the Baal Shem and finally decided to go to him, in order to see for himself if his wisdom really justified his great reputation.
>
> When he reached the master's house and stood before him, he greeted him, and then—without even looking at him properly—waited for teachings to issue from his lips, that he might examine and weigh them. But the Baal Shem only told him that once he had driven through the wilderness for days and lacked bread to feed his coachman. Then a peasant happened along and sold him bread. After this, he dismissed his guest.
>
> The following evening, the maggid again went to the Baal Shem and thought that now surely he would hear something of his teachings. But all Rabbi Israel told him was that once, while he was on the road, he had had no hay for his horses and a farmer had come and fed the animals. The maggid did not know what to make of these stories. He was quite certain that it was useless for him to wait for this man to utter words of wisdom.
>
> When he returned to his inn, he ordered his servant to prepare for the homeward journey; they would start as soon as the moon had scattered the clouds. Around midnight it grew light. Then a man came from the Baal Shem with a message that Rabbi Baer was to come to him that very hour. He went at once. The Baal Shem received him in his room. "Are you versed in the Kabbalah?" he asked. The maggid said he was. "Take this book, the *Tree of Life*. Open it and read." The maggid read. "Now think!" he thought. "Expound!" He expounded the passage which dealt with the nature of the angels. "You have no true knowledge," said the Baal Shem. "Get up!" The maggid rose. The Baal Shem stood in front of him and recited the passage. Then, before the eyes of Rabbi Baer, the room went up in flame, and through the blaze he heard the surging of angels until his senses forsook him. When he awoke, the room was as it had been when he entered it. The Baal Shem stood opposite him and said: "You expounded correctly, but you have no true knowledge, because there is no soul in what you know."
>
> Rabbi Baer went back to the inn, told his servant to go home, and stayed in Mezbizh, the town of the Baal Shem.[43]

When the Baal Shem says:

> I have come to show people a new way to come to themselves,[44]

this is a path of the soul, about which we are told:

> There is no man who is not incessantly being taught by his soul.[45]

This teaching of the soul, "whose intention is to raise the sparks up to their roots," is the new thing that Hasidism brought and still must bring to Judaism.

When we say that knowledge may, indeed must, have a soul, this means that, beyond abstract or intellectual knowledge, the reality of the psychic background must be open to view. Its visible reality must seize the whole personality, not merely be the focus of rational consciousness. If the divine sphere, the inner vitality of the spirit, has been touched, even slightly, the first indication is a state of passionate feeling, of being possessed and struck by the experience. In asceticism, the personality is also engaged, but in that case there is a cost, which is the suppression of vitality. But in Hasidism, the state of possession has to grip the whole person, in a process involving every part. The astronomical worldview, as we have called it,[46] conceived of the world's essence as follows: in the primordial twilight, human action brings forth force fields, concentration points of psychic energies, which blaze up and spread. This worldview demands constant change from each person; it demands constant renewal and a passion for life, which only a living and creative soul can accomplish.

Thus, Hasidism values passion—even when it is sinful and negative—more than tepid goodness. The habitual, the average, the pleasant, even if these are good, are remote from the divine. For the deity on his new level still has YHWH's old "fieriness." Unconditional devotion and wholeness of reaction, even if one is going the wrong way, bring one closer to God than going the right way at a measured pace, for one only needs to change direction.

Not only are we told:

> Just as oil is hidden in the olive, so repentance is hidden in sin,[47]

but, also, one could almost say that the greater the sin, the greater the opportunity. It is written:

> Someone commits a transgression. If he is used to its consequences, he will not be roused to repent. But if he has committed a great transgression, then he will be roused immediately, because the holiest sparks exist on the lowest level, and when he reaches this level, the spark draws him quickly to his root, and when he rises up to the root—then it is said: Where the repentant are standing, the completely righteous cannot stand.[48]

Here we are moving dangerously close to the boundary line, verging on the abyss, of all the sects—ranging from the Gnostics and the Sabbatarians to the followers of Rasputin—which hope to achieve redemption more quickly through sinning. Nevertheless, we shall avoid crossing that line.

The dialectical principle, as frequently formulated in the Kabbalah and in Hasidism, is basically a psychological law, the reality of which is even demonstrated in the principle of evil and repentance.

Thus the phrase:

> A song of David when Nathan, the prophet, came to him, as he had come to Bathsheba,

is interpreted as follows:

> David returned to God and said his psalm to him with the same passion with which he had gone to Bathsheba. That was why God forgave him on the instant.[49]

Similarly, a *tzaddik* spoke about two opponents of Hasidism, one of whom angrily threw a newly published Hasidic book on the floor, whereas the other picked it up because, after all, it contained words of the Torah. And he said: "The angry one will become a Hasid, but the mild one will always remain an opponent."

The same mystery speaks to us from the apocryphal saying of Jesus of Nazareth:

> Whosoever is near unto me is near unto the fire.[50]

It is as if a state of possession in itself signified nearness to God. For a moved and animated soul will at some point perceive and follow its inherent law and be hurled, by the dialectical principle of the soul, from the depths of sin into repentance. A tepid soul, on the other hand, is less soul-like by nature. Despite its correct opinions, evil lurks within its tepidity and its habitual moderation in the form of heaviness and stagnation. It is less permeable, less agile, less accessible to itself. When we come to examine the inherent activity and meaning of the sparks,[51] we shall be able to formulate this aspect more precisely.

The aspects of movement and passion are linked to those of consciousness and alertness. This becomes most obvious in the symbol of sleep, as is frequently used by Rabbi Nachman. We should understand this rejection of sleep symbolically. That is, we should not confuse it with the rejection of sleep by Kabbalistic asceticism, which relies on the same basic principle but concretizes it. The contrary Hasidic movement, which celebrates the renewing power of sleep, does not oppose Rabbi Nachman, for whom sleep is identical with unconsciousness, heaviness, indifference, and habituation. Thus:

> He is more hallowed who is further from sleep.[52]

Alertness and a sharp gaze characterize anyone who fights YHWH's wars, who accepts the fight, the evil impulse and the world. But he can accept them only because he chooses and decides with an alert consciousness, and penetrates the depth of darkness and sin, fall and failure, with the power of his consciousness, until he reaches the kernel of light that is the spark, redeems it, and leads it upward as the liberator, and thus extends the kingdom of God in the world.

> This is the service man must perform all of his days: to shape matter into form, to refine the flesh, and to let the light penetrate the darkness until the darkness itself shines and therefore is no longer any division between the two. As it is written: "And there was evening and there was morning—*one* day."[53]

Only then will darkness become transparent in its hidden brightness, and able to do its work. Only then will evil become visible in its connection with good.

Fire and fieriness underlie the whole theory of sparks, with their characteristics of kindling, blazing, and passion. Passionate feeling, raised to ecstasy, melts the diverse parts of the human soul together into a whole, and then the personality, unified in joy, is governed by a consciousness that is enhanced but undiminished by ecstasy.

Repentance[54]

The basic law of the human being as "one who walks," and for whom every place and every present offers a task, turns the world into a place of probation, which constantly confronts him with choices and decisions:

> The world was only created for the sake of choice and the one who chooses. The human being, the lord of choice, should say: The whole world was created for my sake alone. Every person should therefore always and everywhere ensure that he redeems the world and fills its deficiency.[55]

For this reason, *repentance* means neither penance nor atonement in the usual sense. Instead, it is the inner consequence of the fact that the world is new every morning, and the human being with it.

> He who sees a new light every day, light he did not see the day before, if he wishes to truly serve, must condemn his imperfect service of yesterday, atone for it, and start afresh. The stainless one who believes he had done perfect service, and persists in it, does not accept the light, and comes after him who ever turns anew.[56]

Basically, the world is built to accommodate human repentance, which belongs to its adequate realization. However, this is not because the human being is evil and always does the wrong thing, but because the world is so infinitely varied that only the inexhaustibly diverse ways in which the human being accepts the world can do justice to it. In undergoing contraction, God reveals himself to humanity throughout the world; this is the only way he can be perceived. But at the same time, this means that his appearing comes about only through an endless series of life situations, fulfilled in reality. The hidden light of a specific situation is revealed, and God's lordship in the world made visible and real, only by tirelessly breaking open the shell of the divine that was given to this situation in the *tzimtzum*. Here, repentance means the constantly new realization of today, the here and now, which disavows yesterday, the there and then. If it is executed in reality, repentance means a process that seizes and transforms the entire personality, not one involving only an insight or a feeling. Repentance, as a transformation process, plays out between God and the human being and leads to an essential change, which is called forgiveness.

When a *tzaddik* asked how someone can tell that God has forgiven a sin, he received many answers. The only correct answer, however, is the one given by the *tzaddik* himself, which coordinates the reality of repentance with that of forgiveness: one can tell, because one no longer commits the sin.[57] This answer is highly characteristic of the reality of what we are discussing here, in that we are not discussing moral or theological concepts, but outlining and describing processes that actually constitute human life.

When a human being is put to the test, it always concerns his specific situation. For this reason, each person is always contained in the unconditionality and newness of the present moment. This is a radical reversal of the doctrine of the helpful merits of the fathers.[58] Not even one's own merits from yesterday are helpful, for the new situation demands an absolute, not a historical, commitment. This antihistorical concept represents a revolution against the merits of the fathers, against tradition, and against relying on the past for security. Taken together with what we have called actualized messianism,[59] it constitutes a basic teaching of Hasidism.

Neither the past nor the future has priority over the present, which is fulfilled by the secret, divine light. Actualization places the individual at the center of destiny, for the world and also for God. All that matters is this individual and his existence in the here and now. The Christian doctrine of redemption, according to which the Messiah has already come, and the doctrine of pre-Hasidic Judaism, according to which he has yet to come, are both abolished here. Individual life actualizes messianism, and the messianic stage of the individual actualizes the work to be fulfilled.

That is also how we should understand the end of the distinction between sacred and profane. In the past, we had the holy land, the holy city, the holy temple, and the holy priest, but now, this is the statement that matters: "The *whole* world is full of his glory."

The radicality of this turn remained partly hidden even to Hasidic self-awareness, or, at least, its full implications were not obvious. But when the Great Maggid says:

> Look, today, in the days of the galut, it is easier to reach the Holy Spirit than at the time of the Temple,[60]

And when the Baal Shem says:

> Every place is right for prayer,[61]

in contrast to the Temple Period, these are symptoms of a radical transformation in the inner principle of Judaism.

The introversion of sacrifice

The introversion of sacrifice, which had already begun when the prophets replaced sacrifice by prayer, is now completed by the people's self-sacrifice, by which they lead themselves upward toward nothingness.

> Once on a Sabbath, Rabbi Moshe of Kobryn was standing before the Ark and praying the Additional Prayer, which is a substitute for the offerings of Sabbaths and feast days. When he said the words: "Lead us into our land and there we shall prepare unto thee the offerings that are obligatory for us," he fell to the floor in a faint. They had great difficulty in reviving him, and he finished the prayer.
>
> That evening, Rabbi Moshe spoke again at his own table: "There in our land we shall bring the special offering for this sabbath, for here we have no sanctuary and no service by sacrifices." And he kindled at the words and cried aloud: "Lord of the world, we, we, we ourselves shall bring ourselves to you in place of the offering!"
>
> Then all understood why in the House of Prayer he had fallen to the floor as if all life had left him.[62]

The ecstatic character of sacrifice is dominant in these reports. This represents a danger, as in the story of the disciple who died, while praying, "in the burnt-offering of his heart."[63] As noted, however,[64] this internalizing of sacrifice does not necessarily lead to an ecstatic dissolution of life. On the contrary, it may end in a rebirth out of nothingness, which is life's regeneration.

It is important to note, again, the new level on which a genuine self-sacrifice occurs. It no longer projects part of the sacrificer outward onto a sacrificial animal; rather, the sacrifice is internalized, as an offering that takes authentic hold of the person. With this internalizing, the original relationship between God and humankind, which occurred in the early period by means of sacrifice, is realized anew.

But now it is independent of cult and ritual, based only on the relationship of the individual to the divine.

The weight of destiny, both for God and for the world, is thus placed on the individual and his life. He is anointed, in his irreplaceability, as the mid-point of the world. However, just as the individual's new decision is not lightened, nor is a false decision balanced out, by his own merits, let alone anyone else's, so a new repentance is undiminished by an old transgression.

"New every morning"—that is what is meant by the total rejection of the past, and with it the total rejection of original sin. Every human being, at every moment in his life, stands in new unconditionality before God. He can repent anew, perform his service, and show himself to be the king's son. For the soul and the world, and their relationship with the divine, were constructed for this end alone. Traditions of merit or knowledge, possession of attributes and attitudes, none of these can safeguard the human being who faces his task with good unknowing and good uncertainty. For:

> He who is aware of the danger is helped by God, so that he will not fall. He who feels safe and who feels that his path is smooth is close to falling.[65]

On the other hand, no evil nature exists, no ill situation, no inadequate disposition, in short no negative condition that would excuse a lack of personal commitment. For everything is pregnant with revelation, and the world shows that it is filled with God's glory by being, everywhere and all at once, a place of redemption and a place of fulfillment.

Although God hides behind garments, these are also full of his glory. The garments, as shells, are only the outside of a hidden inwardness, which must become transparent. As we have seen,[66] this transparency corresponds both to an act of knowledge and to an act of realization, in which, all at the same time, human inwardness is transformed and heightened by the union of the parts of the soul, the nature of the world is transformed and heightened by the raising of the sparks, and God's relationship to the human being and the world is transformed and heightened by both.

Evil as a level of good

So it is said not only that repentance resides in sin like oil in the olive, that "there is good in all evil,"[67] that "the holiest sparks exist on the lowest level," and that "goodness is hidden in darkness,"[68] but finally, it comes to the saying of the Baal Shem:

> Evil is also good, it is only the lower level of perfect goodness.[69]

The sentence about loving God with one's *whole* heart is interpreted as loving God with both the good and the evil impulse, as is the sentence: "Recognize him on all your paths."[70] Moreover, it is said:

> Everything that exists in the world, the pure and the impure, he uses for his service.[71]

Evil is outwardness, but on the inside it is spiritual, and thus, like everything else, it is meaningful, if and to whom it becomes transparent in its meaning. Thus, Isaiah's sentence is realized yet again: God is the creator of evil *and* good. And the serpent, evil, is not an opposing force but an angel, a messenger of God. For it is written: "God also dwells in its impurity."[72]

In the verse, "Love your neighbor as yourself. I am YHWH,"[73] the root, "your neighbor," is replaced by "your evil," which sounds the same.[74] The verse is then read and interpreted as follows: "Love your evil as yourself (as you behave, so shall I). I am YHWH."[75] Here, evil means both the evil from which the sparks are redeemed and also suffering, which must be accepted.

To accept evil, to have the strength to experience evil as the lower stage of goodness, the lower as the basis of the upper, earth as the basis of heaven, the *nefesh*-soul as the throne of the *neshama*-soul, and to unite both sides in this experience, this is the actual service for which the human being was created. For this he was made lord of the earth, to make the unity of God real, as the creator of heaven *and* earth.

> The in-dwelling glory (*Shekhinah*) encompasses all worlds, all creatures, good and evil, and she is the true unity. How can she carry the opposites of good and evil within herself? But in truth there is no opposition, for evil is the throne of goodness.[76]

The human being corresponds to this state of affairs between God and the world, but he is the node and nucleus, the mid-point of this polarity, which must be brought into harmony through him.

> As the glory encompasses all worlds, good and evil, so they were contained in Moses. When God called Moses the first time, he did not answer, "Here I am," because he was lost in astonishment. How then can the union take place? For when God revealed himself in the thornbush, that is, in evil, as the lowest level, all the fountains of fire opened, from the uppermost down to the depths—but the thornbush did not burn, nor was evil consumed. How could this happen? But God called a second time: "Moses!" Then in Moses himself the lowest level joined with the highest, and he said: "Here I am."[77]

Only his "Here I am" makes Moses really present. After establishing his totality, he exists as an ego-Self that can respond to God's call.

The progressive path of the sparks and the soul, as well as the establishment of wholeness with the help of the *ruach*, these two interrelated processes form the background of our interpretation. What is essential here, and what persists, is the basic discovery that "the thornbush did not burn." That is, the sheer fact of evil—the underside, the shell, the contraction, the negative aspect of "this world"—is transformed only from time to time. At most, it may be brought to light and made transparent in its inwardness; it cannot be fundamentally eliminated.

Now, the task of higher service is to free the sparks even from evil, from the "alien" thoughts that sneak into prayer, from the disturbances and hindrances caused by the world's suffering and the blows of fate, in order to break through the inhibitions and the opacities of lower human nature, through corporeality and the shadows, to penetrate to inwardness. Time and again, we hear the parable of the guards watching over the king's treasure. The inferior guards drive away the thieves, who keep returning, but the good ones capture the thieves and render them harmless, by attacking evil itself.

Sin and evil belong, equally, to the necessary ingredients of existence; they are given along with it. Rightly perceived, they are not only a necessary, but also a crucial part of this existence. At the level of meaning, they are spiritually important for the human being. At the symbolic level, they are spiritually important in what they say about God. The experience of evil is the element through which not only is goodness revealed, but also the human being is made human, as one who chooses.

The serpent of paradise

Only the knowledge of good and evil leads to consciousness, for consciousness means differentiation, in contrast to swimming in the undifferentiated state before the world exists. For this reason, consciousness and the ego are associated with the decision-making *ruach*-soul. One *tzaddik* says:

> The sins which man commits—those are not his great crime. Temptation is powerful and his strength is slight! The great crime of man is that he can turn at every moment, and does not do so.[78]

According to the Great Maggid, God even enjoys a person's sin, if he then repents and raises the sparks.[79] To God, only directional human *activity* matters, and—provided this activity exists—good and evil are only relative quantities belonging to it, for, just as God can rejoice in sin, a good way of thinking can lead to sin, if it is misunderstood. This becomes clear in the following profound interpretation of the Fall, which reveals the assignment and nature of the serpent:

> Adam's real sin was that he worried about the morrow. The serpent set out to reason with him: "There is no service you can perform, for you cannot distinguish between good and evil and are unable to make a choice. Eat of this fruit and you will be able to distinguish; you will choose the good and receive the reward." That he gave ear to this, that is where Adam was at fault. He worried that he would not be able to serve, yet at that very hour he had his service: to obey God and to resist the serpent.[80]

This basic situation of sin has to reveal the real nature of evil more deeply than any other situation. What seems especially insidious about the trap that is set for Adam is that the serpent tells him something that is correct in an essential way, because service is really about choosing. So how should Adam have resisted the serpent's challenge? Isn't this deceitful temptation truly "devilish," and isn't it evil of God to allow this trap to be offered as a temptation? This question arises because, for good reasons, we reject the dualistic approach, according to which the serpent is God's adversary. A deeper interpretation of this piece teaches what it means to say that evil is God's messenger, an angel.

Once the serpent poses its question, the human being inescapably faces the real choice, to reject or accept the serpent. Even if, especially if, he had refused the choice presented by the serpent, he would have chosen and would have raised the spark, by deciding not to choose. This situation is inescapable. Therefore the serpent is in paradise by right; it is a true messenger of God to the human being, and not a foreign intruder.

No evil God lured Adam into the negative. Actually, human beings can be put to the choice only through temptation. As he had been given a directive—not to eat—he was unconsciously in the very situation of choice that he believed he lacked.

But what is the meaning of the serpent, the character of which, as a *malakh*,[81] becomes clear when it confronts the human being with a decision? For it is a messenger, even if the human being did not understand the message. The serpent, the salvific character of which is unmistakable in Gnosticism, but also in ancient Judaism, represents the drive toward knowledge, which arose in the human being because the human drive toward knowledge and consciousness is just as powerful as the drives toward power and sex. This drive for knowledge approached the human being with its imperative: "Know, distinguish, choose, be conscious." But when he fell victim to this drive, the human being became—unconscious. Being overrun by any drive makes one unconscious, and, in Adam's situation, being conscious meant entrusting himself to YHWH's inner directive, not suppressing it.

The profound ambiguity of consciousness, especially for the Jewish person, clearly shows through this interpretation. One of the most frequent ways through which the Jewish person becomes unconscious is precisely by overemphasizing the conscious principle and rationalism. His rationalism makes him lose contact with the unconscious, and thus, unknowingly, to be governed by it.

The claim that isolated consciousness and radical rationalism make the human being unconscious only seems paradoxical. Both the normal and the sick psychic life of the individual and the collective repeatedly prove that closing oneself off to the unconscious makes the unconscious powers, which are now no longer controlled by consciousness, gain control over consciousness as well. This occurs not only in the neurotic symptom, in complex reactions, in compensatory invasions of the affects and flooding by the unconscious. It can be demonstrated that every isolated conscious attitude destroys itself by constellating the compensatory counterprinciple in the unconscious. Thus, long before the actual victory of the "counterprinciple,"

FIGURE 3.1 The transformative serpent: in the painting the serpent descends from above into the natural earthly realm, out of the blue sky realm held in puffs of white clouds. It traverses through a round, gold disc at the very center of the painting, perhaps representing the symbol of wholeness that bridges the upper and lower realms. On the left—the unconscious side—is a tree with red dots, perhaps referencing apples. This tree has its branches in the sky and roots on earth, forming an *axis mundi*. The serpent is green, the color of nature with its transformative power. Its head contains red, gold, and blue, the colors that represent the lower, middle, and upper realms that are at play in this painting. The serpentine movement of this intruding, challenging energy is overwhelming, consuming the entire page. It is inescapable, descending to the earthly realm, depicted by the animals on the left and the rising or setting sun over the blue waters on the right. It is a cosmic, otherworldly serpent compared with the sliver of red on the far left that slithers upward toward the tree of life from the black lower left corner of the painting. The movement of the messenger from above points to the chalice-like shape, a vessel of transformation, held in the red of deep human emotion, the blood of life that when transformed sends sparks upward, back to the soul and being of God. (*NSF*)

Note: This figure is shown in color on the front cover of the paperback edition and can also be found in the eResources for this book: www.routledge.com/9781138556225.

the conscious attitude is largely governed by those powers, the existence of which is doubted by consciousness. Thus, for instance, the saints are governed more by the sex drive, which their consciousness radically negates—as shown by their temptations and fantasies—than are those who consciously live their sexuality.

As significant as consciousness may be, and despite all the emphasis it receives in Judaism, there are states, especially creative ones, in which an intervention of consciousness, the drive for knowledge, prevents progress and production. Everything has its hour, and here, once again, it comes down to human choice: either to allow an upwelling from the depths or to intervene with a conscious interruption.

The human situation of choice means that every instinct must be governed, but not suppressed, and that being governed by an instinct makes one unconscious, that is, unfree. As Hasidism has realized, everything can be both good and evil, and, for just that reason, everything depends on the human being's choice and alertness:

> [The Rabbi of Kobryn taught:] The soul says to the Evil Urge what Abraham said to Lot: " . . . If thou wilt take the left hand, then I will go to the right; or if thou take the right hand, then I will go to the left." The soul says: "When you try to lead me left, I will not heed you and go to the right. But should you by any chance advise me to go right in your company, I'd prefer to go left."[82]

One such typical piece of advice was the serpent's: "go to the right." As a symbol of the drive toward knowledge, the serpent advised Adam to expand his consciousness through the knowledge of good and evil. But, in following the serpent, Adam put himself in the sharpest possible conflict with his inner directive, YHWH's prohibition, which lived within him. Now his consciousness split off from this directive, and so, when his consciousness expanded, it expanded toward evil. Even if Adam had rejected the serpent, he would *still* have come to know good and evil. But in that case, he would have assigned his drive toward knowledge a place below the inner directive, not above it. Then his ego-consciousness would not have split off negatively from the Self; rather, it would have developed in conformity with the Self's directive.

But this now constellates the new unfathomability of life, in that right and left are no longer fixed points of orientation. Goodness can be at work in evil, and evil in goodness. Everything depends on human choice. This Hasidic concept of the world, this ethical outlook, is fundamentally opposed to the rabbinical principle: "Transgression causes transgression, fulfilled commandments cause the fulfilling of commandments." The static world, carefully dissected into a white, right-hand part and a black, left-hand one, through which people wander, has given way to a world of dynamic, dialectical vitality, moving in concentric circles around the transforming, rising, and falling human being. It rises and falls with him, challenging and being fulfilled by him, expanding and contracting according to his range and his activity.

The old certainty and security provided by an outward orientation, in which things, actions, and attributes were labeled "good" and "evil," is past and has made way for a dialectical twilight, in which only one's "own light" of firm inner connection can show the path. Only one thing matters here: to have the mid-point, to mind one's center of gravity, to keep one's balance. So, in the story, when one condemned man was asked by another how he had run on a rope across the chasm, he replied:

> I don't know anything but this: whenever I felt myself toppling over to one side, I leaned to the other.[83]

Sure enough, the world is a chasm, and the threat of sin is everywhere. But on the other hand, sin is also part of the world as a typical human characteristic, because hiding within it is the precious spark of repentance.

Only now, when the real meaning of evil has emerged, does the aim to unite heaven and earth also become understandable in its deepest sense. There is a refusal to be merely "heaven," separated from this material world and from evil. That is not the demanded perfection or completeness or "wholeness."[84]

> In truth, what is essential about wholeness is to be above *and* below, in heaven *and* on earth. Only both together, above *and* below, make a whole world.[85]

There is a saying about the letter: each sign contains the three: world, soul, and the divine.[86] This saying holds true in general, as we have seen.[87] In *Adam Kadmon*, it is the triad of three realms that governs, with *Keter*, *Tiferet*, and *Malkhut* as the central pillar. But there is also a group of three, with the human being in the middle as the soul, between the world—meaning the outer world of things and sparks—and the divine residing in the inner world, its hidden place of revelation. And the union, the joining of heaven and earth, which occurs through the human being, connects the outer world (earth) and the inner world (heaven), the lower soul (earth) and the upper soul (heaven), and *Malkhut* (earth) and *Tiferet* (heaven), all in one. It thus realizes the true, original unity.

Accepting the world

The task of connecting above and below is based on the principle of *accepting the world*, because:

> "In this day and age," said Rabbi Mosche, "the greatest devotion, greater than learning and praying, consists in accepting the world exactly as it happens to be."[88]

This acceptance of the world is described in countless narratives, where the "negative" is accepted by the most diverse levels of consciousness. Whether suffering is accepted as good suffering, or someone no longer perceives suffering at all[89] and only sees the good,[90] whether someone asks whether there is really any evil,[91] or yet another maintains that poverty is what he needs,[92] or whether a blind man refuses to be healed because he "sees what he needs to see,"[93] it is always a question of working through the world from a certain perspective, because the world reveals its inner face depending on the level of the human being. We are to consider the world a task, as the Great Maggid puts it:

> The law of things is: everything that a person sees and hears, and all events that happen to him, come to stir him up.[94]

That is, everything happens to set the human being in motion, to awaken his psychic activity. Only when we see this do we realize how fully the *whole* world is pregnant with revelation, waiting to become visible and reveal its inner, hidden light. Thus, accepting the world should not be misunderstood as being quietly and fatalistically passive, but as an achievement, in which inner psychic tension enables the human being to extract meaning from everything he encounters, to redeem the sparks.

When sparks are raised to the "human level,"[95] they deliver to the human being not only their meaning but his as well. They begin to speak. When this happens, it has a practical use, which is to raise up a thing that seems meaningless—something on the mineral level, as it were—so that it reveals its hidden meaning. This psychic achievement is in accord with the creative and active principle of human life and the human psyche, which alone makes it possible to accept the world.

But no recipe or established certainty exists for acceptance, either. In one situation, suffering must be accepted, as what Meister Eckhardt calls the "fastest horse to perfection," but, in another, the opposite is true.

> A woman who lived next door to Rabbi Moshe Leib lost one child after another before they were a year old. Once when she was in the *tzaddik*'s house, she cried aloud: "A God who gives you children just to take them away again is not good: he is a cruel God!" Rabbi Leib's wife scolded her: "That's no way to talk! What you should say is: 'We cannot fathom God's mercy, and what he does is well done.'"
>
> "Oh, no!" said the rabbi, who heard them talking from where he sat in his room and came out to join them. "You must not be resigned. Take courage, woman, and take strength. A year from now you will have a son, and in time to come I shall lead him under the bridal canopy." And so it was.[96]

It was not as if the *tzaddik*'s wife had said something wrong. But her advice was trite;[97] she lacked genuine engagement and did not truly enter into the situation. Thus, this *tzaddik* fulfilled in action what he had expressed in another context:

> But to what end can the denial of God have been created? This too can be uplifted through deeds of charity. For if someone comes to you and asks your help, you shall not turn him off with pious words, saying: "Have faith and take your troubles to God!" You shall act as if there were no God, as if there were only one person in all the world who could help this man—only yourself.[98]

This acceptance leads not only to a knowledge of psychic death as a state of transition and birth, for:

> the falling is for the sake of the rising,[99]

but also, on a higher level, it leads to accepting even God-forsakenness:

> "Noah walked with God."[100] He was so attached to God that every step that he took seemed to be guided by God, as if God stood opposite him and put his feet right and led him like a father who teaches his little son to walk. So, when the Father moved away from him, Noah knew: "This is so that I learn to walk."[101]

At first, this seems only to be about the simple, child-like level of faith, which plays such a major role in Hasidism as the religious emotion of the simple person, who stands and walks in his faith, in the uncomplicated wholeness of his actions. He lives his everyday life, and his loyal fulfillment of the law does not correspond to a conscious rabbinical "life," but is embedded in a given form of existence, in a natural life, which moves within the law as the peasant's does within the landscape. He does not think of it as special or outstanding, but is unconsciously surrounded and shaped by it. Hasidism considers the secret implicitness of his piety a deeper form of life than the clever person's public eagerness to keep the law. We are told not that "God walked with Noah," but that "Noah walked with God."[102] The image of the child should not obscure a much more profound matter.

The human being's decision brought about this bond with God. And this decision-making power is so great that to some extent it even compensates for God's absence. Noah's attachment is irrefutable. Not even God can refute it, because both his existence and his nonexistence are encompassed by Noah's comprehensive faith. Even the stage of God forsakenness, of total divine darkness, is accepted, as extending one's own existence and making it independent. For after Noah has walked alone, he is another person, not one who is merely "walked." As he experiences even the situation of God-forsakenness as guidance, he redeems the evil that had confronted him at first in this forlornness. This is the "continuous attachment" of the *tzaddikim*, whose life is so unshakably connected with God's that the boundaries between them begin to blur. A person who lives this way can do anything. He exists on the other side, in nothingness, and "may move to where he likes,"[103] because the world unveils and reveals itself to him at a depth that is always true to itself. He is not only beyond good and evil, because the deity is always and everywhere transparent to him, but also, in a strangely paradoxical way, what allows him to withdraw into hiddenness is precisely that he seems to become wholly one with this world, part of the earth.

In a dialectical self-cancellation, he once again becomes so inconspicuous that one does not notice that he is a Hasid, or even a *tzaddik*. This self-cancellation already manifests itself outwardly, for example in prayer. The Hasidim prayed differently from other Jews. With their ecstatic prayer, they broke the normal, orderly Jewish form of praying, by jumping up and down and shaking themselves, entering a state of arousal, which strengthened their concentration. But this excitement disappears again in the final stage, where the Hasid becomes inconspicuous. About this stage, we are told:

> The human being is able to enjoy everything that is good and to mortify himself with pleasures. He is able to look wherever he wants and not to lose himself beyond his radius of four cubits, because in all things he is aware of God's secret name. He is able to stand motionless in prayer, so that no one notices his service, yet secretly his spirit burns, and he cries aloud amid the silence.[104]

Here, heaven is so connected with earth, their unity so fully achieved, that from the outside one sees only earth, the normal, inconspicuous person. In secret hiddenness, meanwhile, the inwardness of the world, of heaven, is always powerfully at work.[105]

On this highest level, where the human being attains the symbolic level in his unified wholeness, the very world of the human being, his action and his daily life, becomes a symbol. In everything visible, the invisible becomes transparent; the world of thought becomes transparent in every action, and the spiritual, living inwardness in everything material.

We have already mentioned the story of the *tzaddik* whose conversation with the widow was experienced by his disciples as giving comfort to the grieving *Shekhinah*. Here, the world is fulfilled on the symbolic level. The *tzaddik* perceives the One in everything. He sees only:

> the divine nothingness which gives life to the world.[106]

But he does not see it in its abstraction and unity, but instead in the diversity of its expression and utterance. For this level, the words of the Chorus mysticus (*Faust II*) hold true:

> All things corruptible
> Are but a parable;
> Earth's insufficiency
> Here finds fulfilment.[107]

The world as symbol

Here, everyday action becomes a symbol. It remains the content of this world, while at the same time it means something else, with which it is identical. In one case, Enoch the shoemaker, by joining the upper to the lower leather, joins together heaven and earth. In another, the Baal Shem, by cleaning the vessels at his inn, purifies the creature, which is also called a vessel. In another story, the gatekeeper's question, "For whom do you go?" strikes the *tzaddik* like an arrow, because he understands the guard's question as God's question. It is always the same: the world is a symbol, which comes to the individual as God's messenger, to bring him revelation. When its symbolic character is made real in action, in the redemption of the sparks, it proves that the world is not just the place of revelation, but also of fulfillment.

The level of meaning is always anthropocentric. On this level, God's dialogue about the world takes place with human beings, for the human being is that place in the world toward which the world refers and which it addresses. Here, the human becomes God's true partner, but, at that very moment, the world loses its foreignness. It no longer confronts the ego as a world outside.

The whole world becomes a cipher, the readable content of a meaningful reference. The more inward the world, the more its secret becomes transparent, and the more spiritual and meaningful it becomes, until—amid the greatest psychic tension—the dualistic structure of world and humanity, the dualism of outside and inside, above and below, animate and inanimate, meaningless and meaningful, is entirely dissolved in God's oneness. The human being is then on the highest level, where he experiences the world's oneness and lives its symbolic character by realizing its transparency. The integrated human being corresponds in his wholeness to this unified world. On this level, the level of enduring attachment to the divine, the triad of God, soul, and world. is combined into a three-part unity, the central place of which he occupies.

This world is now an inner world. Its true character has finally revealed itself: it is a spiritual and divine, but also a psychic, world. Everything external in it is not a deception, disillusioning and annihilating; rather, the external has become foreground, and transparent. The true background of this world, as the story of its creation teaches, is spiritual and divine, a reality that human beings can fully experience, however, only at this level.

The individual continues to exist in the world, and is not annihilated by ecstatic flooding, but is preserved in his individuality, while also being connected with his upper root. In the same way, the individual is preserved and emphasized as an individual, although he now stands beyond the *tzimtzum* and its contraction into mere individuality. The law that everything outside is inside now holds true for this world, which is not so much taken inward as returned to its correct and original place.

Every event that appears to come to a person from outside, if we look into its reality, reveals that it is related to something inside the person. In fact, its source is a director of destiny, located within the human being, although not in consciousness. Thus, on a higher level, acceptance of the world becomes self-acceptance. Human foreignness in the world is transformed into such nearness that knowledge of the world becomes self-knowledge. For the dimensions of outside and inside are united and no longer opposed.

> The human being fears things that cannot harm him, and he knows this; and he desires things that can bear him no fruit, and he knows this; but in truth it is something in himself that he fears, and something in himself that he desires.[108,109]

The human being to whom the world occurs on this level is called a *tzaddik*. The many great, central figures of the Hasidic movement stand at this level.

The *tzaddik* is the complete human being; he is the living embodiment of what each individual would have to fulfill.

Notes

1 Neumann typically used carbon paper to create up to four identical typescripts. He revised the carbon copies before transferring changes to the fair copy. As a result, although he removed a section, "Das Leben in dieser Welt" ("Life in this world"), from two typescripts, a copy still remained. A hypothesis about Neumann's reasons for removing this section is offered in my Introduction to Volume Two, *Roots II*, pp. xxviiff.
2 Cf. below, *Roots II*, p. 167.
3 *EN*: *R. Nachman*, p. 84.
4 *EN*: Ibid., p. 187.
5 *EN*: Ibid., p. 85.
6 *EN*: *Chassid Büch*, p. 562. [*Tales II*, p. 277.]
7 The story tells of a rabbi who tested his educated dinner guests by asking this question, to which they gave the "correct" answer.
8 *EN*: *Chassid Büch*, p. 562. [*Tales II*, p. 277.]
9 *EN*: Ibid., p. 632. [*Tales I*, p. 173. (Originally a statement of the Great Maggid. Cf. *Roots II*, p. 37, n. 138; p. 91, n. 9.]
10 *EN*: Ibid., pp. 630f. [*Tales I*, p. 218. (Cf. also *Roots II*, p. 100.)]
11 *EN*: Ibid., p. 631. [*Tales I*, p. 218f. (Cf. also *Roots II*, p. 40. The *tzaddik* in the present encounter is the Rabbi of Berditchev.]
12 Cf. *Roots II*, p. 35.
13 *EN*: Bloch [1930], *Priester der Liebe* (*Priests of love*), p. 35. [Also in *Aus Mirjams Brunnen* (*From Miriam's well*), Bloch, 1966, p. 282.]
14 *EN*: *Chassid Büch*, pp. 481f. (*Tales I*, pp. 315–16.)
15 No citation. A related passage is found in Bloch, *Priester der Liebe*: op. cit.: "Melancholy leads to a fall, to the abyss, to sin; for sadness in itself is sin, the finespun net of the cunning tempter, meant to create a wall of separation between human beings and God" (p. 35). (Cf. also *Aus Mirjams Brunnen*, op. cit., p. 282.)]
16 *Chassid Büch*, p. 481. [*Tales I*, p. 315.]
17 Ibid., p. 351.
18 *eine De-Pression*: by breaking the word, Neumann emphasizes "pressure."
19 Cf. *Roots II*, p. 45. Paraphrased from a saying of the Baal Shem. Cf. Bloch, *Priester der Liebe*, op. cit., p. 222, and *Aus Mirjams Brunnen*, op. cit., p. 253.)
20 *EN*: Paraphrase, from Bloch, *Priester der Liebe*, p. 27: "Yet Satan, the evil impulse, the messenger of death—all are one, says the Talmud—uses every means at hand to prevent redemption." [Also cf. *Aus Mirjams Brunnen*, op. cit., p. 275.]
21 Neumann's point is clear in German, involving the words *Zweifel* (doubt), *Verzweiflung* (despair), and *Zwei* (two).
22 *EN*: *R. Nachman*, p. 161. [Cited as p. 162.]
23 *EN*: Ibid.
24 *EN*: Ibid.
25 *EN*: *Chassid Büch*, p. 438. [*Tales I*, p. 245. (A story about Rabbi Zusya and his wife.)]
26 *EN*: *R. Nachman*, p. 162.
27 *EN*: Ibid.
28 *EN*: Ibid., p. 163.
29 *EN*: *Unterweisung*, p. 50.
30 Cf. above, *Roots II*, p. 92, n. 13.

31 *Gnaden-Seite*: the side of the Sefirotic Tree where *Hesed* is located. Neumann translates this *sefirah* as *Gnade* (grace). (See Figure 2.2, *Roots II*, p. 71.) *Hesed* may also be translated as "mercy," "love," or "lovingkindness."
32 *EN*: *Great Maggid*, p. 115.
33 *EN*: *Din* (fear) and *Hesed* (love) form the left and right arms of *Adam Kadmon.*
34 *EN*: *Great Maggid*, p. 173.
35 Tamar Kron advises that Horodezky cites Deuteronomy 10:12.
36 *EN*: *Great Maggid*, p. 171.
37 Jung's 1938 Eranos lecture, "Psychologische Aspekte des Mutterarchetyps" ("Psychological aspects of the mother archetype") includes the following passage, which supports Neumann's argument: "All these symbols can have a positive, favourable meaning or a negative, evil meaning. An ambivalent aspect is seen in the goddesses of fate (Moira, Graeae, Norns). Evil symbols are the witch, the dragon (or any devouring and entwining animal, such as a large fish or a serpent), the grave, the sarcophagus, deep water, death, nightmares and bogies (Empusa, Lilith, etc.)" (*EJ 1938*, p. 411; CW 9i, ¶157).
38 *EN*: See Part One, pp. 145ff. [*Roots I*, pp. 100ff.: "The messiah as a symbol unifying heaven and earth."]
39 Cf. above, *Roots II*, pp. xvii, 15, 96f.: "male and female."
40 Neumann did not write the planned Part Three.
41 *EN*: *Chassid Büch*, p. 638. [*Tales II*, pp. 306f., with Neumann's emphasis.]
42 *EN*: Horodezky, *Mystisch-religiöse Stroemungen*, pp. 29f. [Neumann's emphasis.]
43 *EN*: *Chassid Büch*, pp. 406f. [*Tales I*, pp. 99f.]
44 *EN*: Horodezky, "Baal Shem Tov." [*Enc Jud*, v. 3 (1929), cols 835–42. (Cf. epigraph, *Roots II*, **p. 1** and note.)]
45 *EN*: *Chassid Büch*, p. 591. [*Tales I*, p. 121.]
46 Cf. *Roots II*, p. 45.
47 *EN*: *Great Maggid*, p. 193.
48 *EN*: Ibid., p. 41.
49 *EN*: *Chassid Büch*, p. 630. [*Tales II*, p. 51.] [The first part of the cited passage is attributed to Rabbi Aaron Leib of Primishlan. The interpretation is Rabbi Shalom's and is included in the Marx edition as cited.]
50 *EN*: Hennecke [1924], *Neutestamentliche Apokryphen*, p. 35. [Trans. by R. F. C. Hull, CW 12, ¶297. Neumann knew this saying from Jung's "Traumsymbole des Individuationsprozesses" ("Dream Symbols in the Individuation Process"), *EJ 1935*, pp. 116f.]
51 *EN*: See below, p. 192. [*Roots II*, p. 144, under "The new experience of God."]
52 *EN*: Eliezer Steinmann, "Rabbi Nachman of Brezlav," *Davar* 11.X.40, p. 33. [*Davar* was a Zionist labor journal. Year and page missing in Neumann's typescript. Passage located by Erel Shalit and Tamar Kron.]
53 *EN*: *Chassid Büch*, p. 578. [*Tales II*, p. 59, emphasis added. (Cited as p. 478.)]
54 *Umkehr*: lit. "return," based on Hebrew *tshuva*. (Cf. *Roots I*, p. 62, n. 166.)
55 *EN*: *Chassid Büch*, pp. 33f.
56 *EN*: Ibid., p. 631. [*Tales I*, pp. 218f.]
57 *EN*: Ibid., p. 637. [No page cited. Tamar Kron located this passage.]
58 Cf. below, *Roots II*, p. 167.
59 Cf. *Roots II*, pp. 19f, p. 128. (On Glatzer's concept of "actualized (or activated) history," cf. *Roots I*, p. 97, n. 106.)
60 *EN*: *Great Maggid*, p. 160. [Cf. also *Roots II*, p. 167.]
61 Cf. "Baal Shem Tov," col. 839. (Footnote missing in Neumann's text.)
62 *EN*: *Chassid Büch*, p. 573. [*Tales II*, p. 168. (Neumann mistakenly cites *Great Maggid*.)]
63 *EN*: See above, p. 45. [Roots II, p. 33, n. 118, citing *Chassid Büch*, p. 572.]
64 Cf. *Roots II*, p. 104.
65 *EN*: *Chassid Büch*, p. 594. [Neumann mistakenly cites *Great Maggid*.]

66 Cf. *Roots II*, pp. 65f.
67 *EN*: *Great Maggid*, p. 15. [Cited as p. 40.]
68 *EN*: Ibid., p. 39. [Cited as p. 213.]
69 *EN*: Ibid., Introduction, p. 15. [A related thought occurs in Bloch, *Priester der Liebe*: "'Neither evil nor goodness comes from above.' Commenting on this verse from Lam 3:38, Rabbi Zusya said: 'There is nothing evil, for even that which man considers evil, is good.'" And from *Midrash Tanchuuma* to Genesis: "Many events seem evil to us simply because we fail to recognize the profound connections . . . . These are cases in life that appear misfortunate. Only years later does 'goodness' emerge and man is full of joy" (ibid., p. 22).]
70 Paraphrasing Proverbs 3:6: "In all your ways acknowledge him."
71 *EN*: *Great Maggid*, Introduction, p. 16.
72 *EN*: *Sifre Nashim* P 1. [Tamar Kron advises that Neumann's citation is incorrect. There is no "Sifre Nashim," and the cited passage is not located in *Seder Nashim*. The correct source is Leviticus 16:16.]
73 Leviticus 19:18. In Fox's translation: ". . . but be-loving to your neighbor (as one) like yourself, I am YHWH!"
74 Richard Corney advises that the two words are close in Hebrew: *re'aka*, "your neighbor"; *ra'aka*, "your evil." For both, the root is *Resh-Ayin*: רע.
75 *EN*: *R. Nachman*, p. 75.
76 *EN*: *Unterweisung*, p. 86.
77 *EN*: Ibid., p. 87.
78 *EN*: *Chassid Büch*, p. 629. [*Tales II*, p. 257. The *tzaddik* is Rabbi Bunam.]
79 *EN*: *Great Maggid*, p. 193.
80 *EN*: *Chassid Büch*, p. 584. [*Tales II*, p. 291.]
81 Hebrew: "angel" (lit: "messenger, one who is sent").
82 *EN*: Ibid., p. 615. [*Tales II*, p. 162.]
83 *EN*: Ibid., p. 546. [*Tales II*, p. 60.]
84 *EN*: Same root as the word for "peace." [Annotating the word *Vollendung*, which Neumann has used in the quotation that follows, his translation of a Hebrew passage by Horodezky. The Hebrew word for peace is שלום (*shalom*), the root of which, שלם, also occurs in the word שלמות (*shlemut*), "wholeness." With thanks to Erel Shalit and Tamar Kron.]
85 *EN*: *R. Nachman*, p. 192. [Neumann's emphasis. Tamar Kron advises that the key words are שלמות (*shlemut*), "wholeness," and עולם שלם (*olam shalem*), "a whole world." To translate *shlemut* as "wholeness" in German, the expected word is *Ganzheit*. Erel Shalit points out that Neumann's choice, *Vollendung*, connotes "consummation," which suggests more fully the meaning of the Hebrew root.]
86 *EN*: *Unterweisung*, p. 65.
87 Cf. Neumann's discussion of "the letter," *Roots II*, pp. 23ff., and "*Adam Kadmon* and the parts of the soul," *Roots II*, pp. 69ff.
88 *EN*: *Chassid Büch*, p. 638. [*Tales II*, p. 166. (The statement is that of a Hasidic rabbi whose prayer was hindered by his extreme poverty.)]
89 *EN*: Ibid., p. 435. [*Tales I*, p. 237. (Referring to Rabbi Zusya.)]
90 *EN*: Ibid., pp. 432f. [*Tales I*, p. 237.]
91 *EN*: Ibid., p. 639. [*Tales I*, p. 318.]
92 Ibid.
93 *EN*: Ibid., p. 539. [*Tales I*, p. 256 (slightly modified).]
94 *EN*: *Great Maggid*, p. 175.
95 "*Menschstufe*." Cf. above, *Roots II*, p. 64, n. 18.
96 *EN*: *Chassid Büch*, p. 515. [*Tales II*, p. 89.]
97 *es war geprägte Münze*: lit. "it was a minted coin."
98 *EN*: Ibid., p. 609. [*Tales II*, p. 89. (Cited as p. 515.)]
99 *EN*: Ibid., p. 632. [*Tales I*, p. 173. Also cf. above, *Roots II*, p. 37, n. 138; p. 91, n. 9.]

100 Genesis 6:9.
101 *EN*: *Unterweisung*, p. 45.
102 Genesis 6:9. In Fox's translation: "In accord with God did Noah walk."
103 *EN*: *Chassid Büch*, p. 597. [*Tales II*, p. 73.]
104 *EN*: *Unterweisung*, p. 48.
105 *EN*: See above, p. 119. [*Roots II*, pp. IIBb-7f, under "Joy and wholeness."]
106 *EN*: *Chassid Büch*, p. 471. [*Tales I*, p. 271.]
107 Goethe, *Faust*: Part Two, trans. by Philip Wayne (London: Penguin Books, 1959, p. 288).
108 *EN*: *Chassid Büch*, p. 33.
109 *EN*: How this world looks at the level of meaning, when it is negatively experienced by a consciousness *not* at that level, is depicted in the work of Franz Kafka. Rabbi Nachman provides a key to this work, which emphasizes *Din* over *Hesed*: "If a person does not judge himself, all things judge him, and all things become the messengers of God" (*Chassid Büch*, p. 35). [After completing his medical studies, Neumann wrote commentaries, unpublished to date, on Kafka's stories and novels, giving them a Kabbalistic interpretation (Löwe, pp. 74ff.). Neumann also refers to Kafka in his lecture of 1942 (cf. Appendix B.IV, *Roots II*, p. 265, n. 5).]

4

THE HUMAN BEING AND THE NEW IMAGE OF GOD

1. The *tzaddik*: An image of the human being

Hiddenness

Earlier, the very hiddenness of the *tzaddik* was recognized as the original feature of his being. In his hiddenness, he is more inward and closer to God. His likeness to the divine is deeper at this level, where he represents the hidden principle of the life of the world, and not its visibility.

This is why we are always told that the *tzaddikim* refused the order to reveal themselves. It goes so far that, when one *tzaddik* was ordered to show himself to the world, he even asked God how he had sinned![1] This resistance is not the same as a prophet's reluctance to accept his mission; nor is it a fear of the world and other people, for, in the Hasidic period, someone seen as a *tzaddik* was revered in the community. Rather, this resistance reflects the bitterness of one who must depart from his inner intimacy with the divine, going out into the world, into a lower level of God's reality.

The parable plays an important role in Hasidism, not just as a means of instruction, but also in its symbolic meaning. Time and again, we are told that the parable is the covering assumed by the father's superior reason, to adapt to the son's limited understanding, and that the *tzaddik* speaks in parables, too, to make himself understood by simple people. The *tzaddik* speaks in parables as God does, for the parable is *tzimtzum*, contraction, concealment of light. The whole world is also a parable, in which God's light is hidden. The world reveals its allegorical nature, as a symbol, only to those who stand on the highest, the *symbolic* level.[2] Only here, and only if the son's understanding has expanded from one level to the next, is God's wisdom revealed, on the level of nothingness, as the father's more genuine and more direct spiritual aspect. But to a limited understanding, God's light in the world is concealed more and more densely from one level to the next, so that it may be grasped at least as a parable. This is life in the world, and this is what the human being experiences and learns from it.

Just as the task is "not to allow the flame to burst from the vessel,"[3] that is, not to detach and free the spark, the spiritual inner dimension, from its clothing and physicality, but to make the husk transparent and the spark visible, even so should the allegorical nature of the world be seen through, while at the same time it is lived. Only a life that accepts the manifest and the secret world, both at the same time, not renouncing one for the other, can do justice to the character of the world as parable.

Therefore the sparks, the world, and the human being are redeemed in daily life, in the midst of ordinary things, indeed even in the midst of evil. For just as "God dwells in its impurity,"[4] so, too, does the *tzaddik*. For "the holiest sparks exist on the lowest levels." God is in hiddenness, and so the true *tzaddik*—just like the spark—is in hiddenness.

Ancient Jewish wisdom holds that the world rests upon thirty-six hidden righteous men. Judaism always knew that inwardness and hiddenness are closer to God than what is manifest.

> There are people who have no public power, but nevertheless secretly rule their generation.[5]

The hiddenness of the true *tzaddik* consists in moving among ordinary people and attending to the fallen, the hidden, and the damaged. There he says and does profane things, but, in his permanent attachment to God, he redeems the sparks from within these people. Thus, he follows a double path, one profane and public, the other sacred and concealed.[6]

But this highest level is not for everyone. Only the one who has achieved nothingness "may move to where he likes,"[7] because:

> If the *tzaddikim* contemplate their roots and attain to nothingness, they can serve God on all levels.[8]
>
> Some say that, because the *tzaddik* is great in the upper realm, he cannot oversee and attend to the people of the world, for he is far from the world. In reality, it is not like this. On the contrary. If the *tzaddik* is very great, he can care for and oversee the world all the more. For is God not sublime and far removed from the world, and nevertheless oversees the whole world down to the last detail? For he who is truly "present"[9] cannot be everywhere at the same time. Because what else is "being present" than being here, and not there. For instance, if he is at some divine service, he cannot observe the world. But if he is "nothing," then there is no place where he would not be, for he has no place at all. Therefore, the more wholly the *tzaddik* enters into nothingness, the more he can oversee and observe the world. He should not be said to be in a high and far-off place, for he has no place at all.[10]

At this level, the *tzaddik* goes about in the world completely unnoticed. He is unconditioned, beyond place and time, and simultaneously, being himself beyond the limits of individuality, he grasps and understands all individuality. His very lack of place, that is, his escape from the contraction of the individual principle and the bias of the merely personal, enables him to oversee the conditioning of other people's individuality. This ability is the basis for the care of souls,[11] which seizes an individual as the capacity to convey to others what is coming toward them. This capacity also allows the *tzaddik* to perceive the heavenly typology of each individual soul, recognizing which of the four corners of the heavenly chariot it comes from: lion, ox, eagle, or human being.[12]

When one stands in nothingness, undetermined and without contraction, it means that he can redeem the sparks everywhere. He sets no condition and makes no selection, and so he dedicates himself to the world and to his work. His undetermined state makes his actions unconditional. Thus, when one disciple was asked what was most important to his teacher, he replied:

> What he happened to be doing at the moment.[13]

And if, in general, it is said:

> "And there is not a thing that has not its place." And so man too has his own place,[14]

then on the highest level, one reaches nothingness, where there is no place.

> If the human being has a heart,[15] he possesses no place at all, for on the contrary, he is the place of the world. For in the heart is divinity, as it is said, "The rock in my heart." And it is said of God, "See, the place is with me," for he is the place of the world, and the world is not his place. And that is why, if someone has an Israelite heart, he may not say that this place before him is not good. For him there is no place at all. On the contrary: he is the place of the world, the world is not his place.[16]

This is the background for the principle of accepting the world, of redeeming through acceptance whatever one encounters, every place, every moment, every situation. Thus, the *tzaddik* in a fur coat[17] and the secluded stand on a lower level, along with those who seek out one part of the world and distinguish good from evil. They are unable to guide the rejected parts of the world upward and redeem them. Their soul is not strong, their ascent not high, their willingness not open enough.

The unconditionality of the person on the level of nothingness means that his will and the divine will are reciprocal in determining, complementing, and fulfilling each other, and are ultimately inseparable.

On the one hand, the person in nothingness, the *tzaddik* on the higher level, is so "emptied," so lacking in private intention, that he "stands before God like a messenger, prepared for his master's every command."[18] His sojourn in this world is likened to that of an envoy searching for the king's treasure, which is hidden in a village, and who acts and dresses like a villager to avoid detection.[19]

But this saying also applies to him:

> The *tzaddik* decides, and God carries out,[20]

for not only does he direct the destiny of the world, but the divine itself surrenders so much to his influence that we are told, almost blasphemously:

> God is man's shadow and, like a shadow, he does everything that man does.[21]

This central position of the *tzaddik* expresses itself in revolutionary formulations, exploding the boundaries of ancient Judaism, such as:

> The *tzaddik* may tear down other people's fences to make way for his path,[22]

and:

> sometimes his foundation is the suspension of the Law.[23]

In the *tzaddik*'s hiddenness, we recognize his secret identity with God. God's being-in-himself corresponds to the *tzaddik*'s being-in-himself, and God's hiddenness, in and before the world, corresponds to that of the *tzaddik*. In this same way, on the next level, the self-revealing *tzaddik* stands under the sign of his identity with the divine. Just as God created the world under the sign of mercy, contracting himself in the process and emerging from his inwardness, so, too, in a like process, the *tzaddik* must tread this divine path of creation and reveal himself.

As Hasidism declined, the *tzaddik* became a mana-personality, a proxy for the human image that offered itself for the fulfillment of every individual Jew. The decline from early Hasidism to tzaddikism consisted precisely in the way the representative *tzaddik* took over the task assigned to the individual in his irreplaceability before God.

In the *tzaddik*, however, one can discern the religious image of the human being that emerged in early Hasidism as a central problem. Later, we shall describe how the multitude showed itself unequal to this assignment, how they projected the messiah level, which the individual was called to fulfill, onto the leader-like mana-personality of the *tzaddik*, and how the psychic constellation, repressed in this way, continued to operate in the Jewish history of ideas.

The tzaddik *and* Adam Kadmon

The *tzaddik*, as the complete form of the human being, has realized the universal human core, namely, the "Godlikeness of the human being within himself,"[24] that of *Adam Kadmon*, who must be realized in his completeness and united in his parts. This development and orientation are natural to the human being; they are inherent and correspond to his psychic structure. In the view of Hasidism, the whole world is built like this. The structure of the world and that of the human being depend on each other in a way[25] that not only enables interaction and renders it fruitful, but also allows the world and the human being to fulfill themselves. What modern psychology calls the psychology of the stages of life[26] suggests that this development of the human being by stages is not exceptional; nor is it an extreme case, which only a few ever achieve, while it remains unattainable for the average person. Rather, it represents a natural development.

Although not yet referring to the stages of life, the following passage associates the parts of the soul with father, mother, and the deity:

> Rabbi Zusya taught: God said to Abraham: "Go out of your country, out of your birthplace, out of your father's house, into the land that I will show you."[27] God says to man: "First, get you out of your country, that means the dimness you have inflicted on yourself. Then out of your birthplace, that means, out of the dimness your mother inflicted on you. After that, out of the house of the father, that means, out of the dimness your father inflicted on you. Only then will you able to go to the land that I will show you."[28]

The path indicated here is that of introversion. But an interpretation that would seek to exhaust the meaning of this brief piece of Hasidic teaching would need to probe deep into the world of its psychic background and its primordial images.

Three worlds are involved here: the world of the ego, the world of the mother, and the world of the father. The world of the soul, of the deep unconscious, becomes accessible only when our own world, the darkness of our ego, is abandoned. It is only when we have left this personal layer behind that we enter the realm of the mother. This realm signifies the world, nature, instinct, constitution and substance, elementary connection, the place of origin.

Then we come to the world of the father, the spiritual world, the world of tradition and values, knowledge, and orientation. This is the place of spiritual origin and spiritual conditionality, which is formed by everything that the father determines, from the spirit of the times to the state, from the educational ideal to collective duty.

All of this is darkness. It is the path through our own layers, through our own casing and outwardness, through the conditionality of inauthenticity. What is "inauthentic" here is the foreignness imposed on us by time, race and people, family, constitution, and type. Our core structure, which the narrative refers to as our "own light," and psychology as the "Self," is obscured. This Self is the land that "God will show,"[29] for in it divine revelation approaches the human being with unclouded directness. Characteristically, this path is one of contraction: it leads from "your land" through "birthplace" to "house." The periphery becomes smaller, or so it seems.

We are dealing with curiously interlocking perspectives. On the one hand, the path leads from the ego through the mother and the father to God; thus, it is a path of continuous expansion. On the other hand, we find contraction, the narrowing of the periphery. After this progressive concentration, leading from land to place and finally to the house, into confinement, a sudden and almost violent change occurs. All at once, the confining curtain parts, and there reappears "land," "the land that I will show you." This time, however, it is the other land, the land of God, as opposed to the land of the ego.

This is the path of turning,[30] from outside to inside, from extraversion, which stands in the sign of the ego and the world, to introversion, which stands in the sign of the Self and the soul. The turning point is reached when even the father's house has been abandoned. Only there, where the human being stands alone and lost, where all connection is overcome, are all origin and conditioning suspended. Only there, where the human being reaches the level of nothingness, being free of root and ground in the negative sense, can the call of God reach him, and the way into God's land is revealed. But the person who is thus separated and freed is God's friend,

> just as one stranger is another stranger's friend, because they are both strangers on earth.[31]

Another statement about foreignness sounds quite Gnostic. For someone is said to have behaved like a stranger, following King David's words: I am a sojourner in the land.[32]

> Like a man who came from afar, from the city where he was born. He is not contemplating honor, nor anything for his own good. All he is thinking of is to return to the city where he was born. There is nothing that he can own, because he knows: it is foreign, and I must go home.[33]

But is this not the "heaven," the seclusion of which Hasidism rejects?[34] According to Hasidism, it is part of human nature to develop such an attitude over the course of life and of aging. It is intrinsic to human nature, and not just to the nature of the Jewish person. For "going into solitude" is not only a basic Kabbalistic idea, but also one that is found in China and India. It is a primordial human idea.

In the extreme case, this foreignness in the world probably also corresponds to the seclusion from which Hasidism distances itself, but the essence of which we must now understand differently. Separation from the world here means separation from the demands and standards of the ego. It is total devotion to the transpersonal aspect of the divine.

At the "symbolic level," the human being no longer lives for himself, but for the Other, with which he is dialogically identical in a particular and paradoxical manner. This creates the distance from the world that looks like foreignness.

The Hasidic conception endures, because in being foreign there is a commonality with God, preserving the orientation toward the world and toward making God at home in the world. This orientation is complicated, not negated, by the human aging process, among the symptoms of which is withdrawal from the world, but which, on the highest level, never abandons the contact that determines the world. In the process of aging, the human being withdraws into God's hiddenness. But, as we have seen, this hiddenness must not be confused with the passivity of powerlessness. The effect of withdrawal on the world is often uncertain, but its reality is seen in its effect on the divine.

The inner purpose and necessity of this development in human life, this orientation toward solitude as a characteristic typical of aging, are not the result of a teaching or a religious faith. Rather, they concern the working through of a basic fact. This fact is death, as the goal and end of all human existence.

The soul of old age

Corresponding to death, as the end-point of human development, there is an arc of life. This arc, as we see in the fundamental ideas of many times and peoples, reveals not only a sinking down, in the sense of aging, but also the reverse, a rising up, in the sense that the inner, spiritual aspect comes to the fore. According to this concept, in the beginning the human being's inner, spiritual essence is covered over and boxed in by his relationship with world and ego, whereas his real core, the Self, becomes transparent only gradually in the process of aging.

> A person's life has three ages. The first is youth, during which he pursues his passions; the second is middle age, in which his passions for this world are not so strong; the third is old age, in which he has no passions at all. And this is because the human being has three "partners." In his youth, he has many passions from the part of his mother dwelling in him. In middle age, he does not have so many passions, because the mother's part in him has now been completed. Beyond that, however, he still has passion from the part of his father that remains within him. But in old age, he no longer has any kind of passion, for that is God's part.[35]

Closely related to this principle of the aging process is the fact that arcane teachings—teachings about the essence of things, the world, the human being, and the divine—are made accessible only to older people. The Kabbalah, for instance, is not to be studied before the age of thirty or forty.

The initiation rites of puberty always stand under the sign of the collective and are oriented toward life. It is a ritual of rebirth into life. The initiation of older people stands under the sign of an orientation toward death. It is a ritual of rebirth out of life. In these higher initiations, the crucial elements are immortality, the vanquishing of death, and detachment from the world.[36]

According to the Kabbalah, the higher soul associates itself only very gradually with the human being. Both grow together slowly at first. It is not until the time of manhood, the middle years, that the *neshama* is completely wedded to bodily matter.[37] Its acceptance is achieved only gradually, and thereafter it determines the last third of life.

The attribution of the three thirds of life to the mother, the father, and God corresponds to the three parts of the soul (*nefesh*, *ruach*, *neshama*), the essence, connection, and unification of which were discussed above.[38] The fact that the natural development of the phases of life is oriented "from the bottom up" is as important as it is understandable. It corresponds to a naturally developing attitude, according to which the focus gradually shifts from bodily and worldly outwardness to spiritual and divine inwardness.

Thus, aging basically involves a renewal of the principle of life, a shift in emphasis, but not a process of rigidification or depletion. As maturation advances, it proceeds first from the dominant *nefesh* dimension of the mother, the youthful period of life that is governed by the instincts, the body, and the prevailing "feminine" aspect. Next comes the *ruach* dimension of the father. The spiritual principle prevails here as the individual way the mature person in mid-life takes hold of the world. The moral and spiritual principle of the father connects above and below. It chooses and decides, standing in a mainly spiritual world of professional activity, tradition, and work for the collective.

All of this is centered on the ego, however, in its self-realization as the tool of individuality. Only in the development from *ruach* to *neshama*, from the paternal to the divine part of the soul, does the shift from ego to Self naturally begin. Here, the transpersonal and religious problem starts to become decisive, as the dimension of ego and world recedes, and that of spirit and soul[39] comes clearly into view.

The self-consciousness of the soul comes from the priority of the spiritual and psychic dimension, which existed before the world. When they awaken, the soul and the spirit experience themselves as something underivable. The soul can understand itself historically, in the sense that it has undergone phases of development and phases of being unconscious of itself. Yet it experiences itself as constituting the world rather than being constituted by it. This fact becomes increasingly obvious from one stage to the next, and, as the phenomenon of the Self comes ever more into play, this awareness of the *apriority* of the soul becomes increasingly strong.

Thus, the history of religion and mythology[40] is a history of the soul's coming to consciousness.[41] This idealistic bias regarding the *a priori* existence of the psychic and the spiritual has an advantage over the materialistic bias, in that every experience of matter is ultimately an experience of something foreign, whereas every experience of spirit and soul is an experience of oneself. As the soul progresses and ascends toward self-consciousness, it understands its path through life as leading toward itself. The path is one of self-contemplation, of finding oneself, returning to the starting point, and coming home.

Judaism came to overemphasize the *neshama*, the soul of old age, and the psychology of old age, a fact with consequences still evident today in the psychology of Jewish individuals. This is why we shall need to discuss, for example, a compensating psychology that exclusively emphasizes the instinctual character of the immature psyche. Such a form of compensation is as understandable as it is dangerous.

One of the foundations for the idea of being foreign in the world and coming home to oneself is that the maturing person of every period learns that he can come to himself and attain freedom only if he leaves behind his passion and entanglement in the world and distances himself from it, as from something alien to his true being. But this does not mean the renunciation of passion or an ascetic hostility toward the world. It is a legitimate sign of psychic maturity when the world is "seen through," that is, when it gradually becomes transparent, as symbolized by the parts of the soul gradually shifting in their dominance. Maturity corresponds to a process of purifying and clarifying one's personality, during which the Self is gradually revealed as the product, and simultaneously the secret director, of a destiny that is lived out in all its instinctiveness and passionate conditionality.

The fact that the spiritual aspect emerges naturally as a foundation of the human being means that the three parts of the soul are normally, if only unconsciously, united in the course of time as a person's life unfolds. Viewed teleologically, it seems as if it had been important to nature that the human being should reach the point where the three parts of the soul would unite. Or, in another formulation, it seems that the human being and the world had been arranged to mirror each other in such a way that a qualitatively changing consciousness should emerge, and finally that the spiritual aspect should become dominant. So even the average, unconscious person, in the course of a natural life, would live out all three parts of the soul, one by one. In the sequence of experience, he would come to unite them, establish their natural hierarchy, and unfold them as a reality, inward and upward.

Hasidism, however, demands that the Jew should constantly and consciously achieve this development, which occurs unconsciously in the normal human being over the course of time.

According to one idea of history, human development pursues a necessary process of salvation, leading to the messianic age. This theory is a projection, corresponding to the factual case of an individual life that passes through time to a God-governed old age. In contrast, the "actualization of messianism" demands that the time component be eliminated, or at least relativized. Every moment is now one of messianic fulfillment, every place is one of fulfillment, and the union of the parts of the soul is possible at every age and stage of life.

Maturity, and the accompanying dominance of the higher parts of the soul, seems to make such a life's work easier to achieve. On the other hand, the young, passionate person might be able, more easily than the older one, to satisfy the other demand, that is, to be new every day. So the sentence that is revolutionary for Judaism, "being old is not good,"[42] also holds true for Hasidism. The Hasidic demand for consciousness does not expect that the task of unification should fulfill itself automatically, as a matter of natural process, but that it is achieved by the individual, consciously, at all times and everywhere. The person who actually fulfills this demand is the *tzaddik*.

Earlier, we explored the connections between the human being and the world, and the human being and the spark, on the one hand, and the human being and

God, on the other.[43] Through the example of the *tzaddik*, these connections become concrete. Over the course of Hasidism, the *tzaddik* became a detached figure, a mediator between above and below, where what was below now also came to include human beings. Originally, however, the intermediary position implied that every person redeemed the world, not just a prominent figure. Thus, the very same process that we found in the development of prophecy[44] now also recurs in Hasidism.

As the prophetic potential of every individual had once led to the rise of a delegated institution of prophecy, to relieve the collective from the individual gift of prophecy,[45] so now the latent capacity of every individual to become a *tzaddik* led to the institution of tzaddikism. At the same time, however, this brought about a deterioration, for the people, who had been an assembly of individuals, now changed into an amorphous mass without form, consciousness, or responsibility, which flocked around the *tzaddikim*. For reasons we shall explore below,[46] this development was much more dangerous for Judaism now than the parallel development had been in antiquity.

It is said:

> The *tzaddik* is a plant that pulls sparks out of the earth.[47]

Likewise:

> If one sows seeds in the earth, then all the forces in the earth are drawn into the seed and bring it to fruition. Thus the zaddik draws the sparks in this world, which belong to the roots of his soul, from the things in the world, and guides these sparks up to God.[48]

The naturalness of the process is emphasized here. For just as the plant draws on the energies of the soil for its unfolding, and as these unfold with the plant in its development, so the earth's life is centered on the *tzaddik*; he is its development, and it is his foundation. But the analogy extends even further. For just as the plant lives from above *and* below, and between above and below, and just as its vitality connects the air and the earth, so the *tzaddik* exists in this intermediate and intermediary space of above and below. If the *tzaddik* is also called the "pillar"[49] and the "path,"[50] this refers to his crucial position in relation to the lower worlds and the divine. For to reach the lower worlds, the influence of the divine must pass through him, the support of the upper and the lower worlds.

Here the central position of the *sefirah Tiferet* and the *ruach* part of the soul is recapitulated. The *tzaddik* represents *Tiferet*, the king, in the world. Like *Tiferet* and *ruach*, he stands between above and below, and is therefore also the heart of the world and of the covenant. And just as *Tiferet* and *ruach* symbolize wholeness, so the *tzaddik* is the corresponding human symbol of wholeness and completeness.

The synthesis of opposites

As described above, the polarity of male and female is a dominant principle throughout the Kabbalah. At the same time, it teaches that every perfect and complete form must be both male *and* female. The polar opposition between male and female does not merely exist above and below, but also *between* above and below. The upper, spiritual worlds embody the expansive, procreative principle of grace, whereas the lower, material worlds embody the intensive, conceiving principle of judgment.

Ultimately, this male–female opposition is also an application of the opposition between *Hesed* and *Din*. The closer the upper world is to creative nothingness, the more spiritual and procreative spontaneity is in it. By contrast, the closer the lower world stands to *Malkhut*, the more contracted and conceiving it is. This hierarchy within the worlds represents one of the coordinate axes, apart from which, however, every creature on every level can assume a male or a female attitude, depending on its capacity to choose.

Every entity is normatively female toward the higher, and male toward the lower. Thus, every entity combines male and female, and in that sense we read:

> Each person must beware of being "female" in relation to things. That is, he should not be inflamed by passions, nor derive pleasure from them, for then he is female in relation to the passions. One should only be female toward God.[51]

Because:

> As a male person, you should overflow, just as God overflows (influences). But you should not do this with the intention of receiving a reward, such as honor or the like; for the one who serves in order to be rewarded is like a woman who conceives.[52]

The redemption of the sparks rests on this interaction between male and female, between the world and the human being. For one who is aroused by the world, who "conceives" from it, is female, whereas one who awakens and redeems it is male. The energy of the world is generated by this dual capacity, in all entities and things, to be both male and female at once, and so to be realized in relation to the world and to God.

The double sexuality of the world and the human being is formulated most clearly in the saying:

> It is clear that the inwardness of the male is female, and the inwardness of the female is male,[53]

which derives from the primary, prehistoric double sexuality of *Adam Kadmon*, who was created male *and* female according to the biblical text. The polarities of outer and inner, above and below, human and world, spirit and nature, whose relations we have tried to describe on several occasions, are represented in their world- and life-propelling energy under the symbol of male and female. The deep meaning of sexual symbolism in the Kabbalah stems from this basic aspect, which also always implies the symbol of union.[54]

Rabbi Nachman places the fundamental principle of polarity most prominently at the center of his worldview. In doing so, however, he highlights only a basic feature of the Jewish worldview. His affirmation of "conflict" and many related comments are almost identical with Heraclitus's basic ideas. According to Nachman, two recurring ideas are that "War is the father of all things"[55] and that the world is "an ever-living fire, with measures of kindling, and measures going out."[56] Eternal recurrence, the circling wheel of the world, the world as a constant process of transformation and as something that is moved without a final purpose, and the conflict between polarities as the basic energetic tension of this movement, forms the background of Nachman's concept of existence.

Conflict and duality are ultimately identical to the evil inclination, as the mover of life. Through the dialectical principle, it prevents the world from standstill and growing old. By creating obstacles, difficulties, and separations, it forces the soul to engage its energies in order to overcome them.

The *tzaddik* represents the dimension of wholeness and oneness. This is his inner meaning, on the subjective level, as one who unites the parts of the soul. It is also his objective, outer meaning in healing human beings and the world, connecting God and the world, above and below. This character of making whole is described:

> The *tzaddik*'s characteristic is connection. Like a seal that binds two things into one, that can no longer be separated, so the character of the *tzaddik* connects worlds and brings down abundance from primordial wisdom to the lowest level.[57]

A characteristic of the *tzaddik* is that he restores and permanently establishes the original male–female wholeness, not only within himself, but also in the world.

> Every thing is both male and female, and so it naturally needs a thing that unites it. That is the *tzaddik*.[58]

The *tzaddik* possesses this whole-making healing function as the "doctor of those whose souls are sick."[59] He can provide a new understanding and a new *neshama*.[60] He does this by awakening the sparks in the human soul, by leading the individual to repentance and to himself, and by letting him discover and realize his own psychic level. His task is to lead the individual to his own light. He must ensure that the individual "does not think the Rabbi helped him,"[61] but, as in the tale about the treasure, that he understands there is something he cannot find anywhere in the world, not even with the *tzaddik*, and yet that a place exists where he may find it.[62]

This was the *tzaddik*'s highest task in early Hasidism. It is and always was the highest demand that can be placed on an individual.

Tzaddikism

On this level, the communication between the *tzaddik* and his disciples still involves the master's focusing on every disciple's *tzaddik*-like quality, his messiah level. The only goal is to awaken the fundamental movement of repentance in the disciple's soul, which leads the individual to the fulfillment of wholeness and thus to radiance, to being a *tzaddik*.

The union of the male and female aspects, of grace and judgment, is fulfilled in the original potencies of the *sefirot*, in *Tiferet* or *Rahamim*, that is, in mercy.[63] And this is the *tzaddik*'s specific quality, his function in relation to the world and human beings, because he transforms *Din* into *Rahamim*, judgment into mercy.[64] This is his redemptive function, and serves as a model for the redemptive function that makes the person a person, toward himself, the world, other people, and God.

Later, when the process of deterioration led to the abdication of the masses and ever-increasing emphasis on the *tzaddik*, his function also changed. The mediating figure of the *tzaddik* now stands in for the irreplaceability of the individual before God. The *tzaddik* now represents humanity, which, in turn, is represented before God by Israel. Not only in the consciousness of the awestruck masses, but also in the self-esteem of *tzaddikim*, the *tzaddik* now becomes an oversized, superhuman, and transpersonal figure. Earlier, it was emphasized that the *tzaddik* depended on the people, on their willingness to receive, and on the historical situation. Even now, the *tzaddik* is seen to depend on the fall and rise of Israel, because

> The *tzaddik* receives his strength from Israel.[65]

But the *tzaddik*'s self-identification with *Adam Kadmon* leads to an obvious inflation.[66]

The individual is now regarded as a part and branch of the trunk, which is represented by the *tzaddik*, and only through his participation with the *tzaddik* is he able to live. Now, in particular with Rabbi Nachman, the *tzaddik*, alone among his kind, becomes a cosmic entity and really the foundation of the world. He is now identified completely with the *sefirah Yesod*, *Adam Kadmon*'s point of procreation.[67] This *sefirah* is also called "*tzaddik*," and—as *Yesod*—is the foundation of the world, of which may now be said:

> Even all the *tzaddikim* are merely its branches, each according to his level. Thus, each *tzaddik* can be its branch, and also the branch of a branch.[68]

The same archetypes also re-emerge in association with the conception of the mediator and the redeemer, whose image they typically surround, identifying him as the tree of life, the fruit of salvation, or the redeeming heavenly food. The image of the original *tzaddik* and his branches is the same as that of the grapevine with the grapes, which appeared in the early Christian era,[69] where Christ is the vine and his disciples are the grapes.[70] The *tzaddik* is now no longer merely the root of Israel and "the souls of all are his branches and conceive from him."[71] Rather, he also represents them in suffering,[72] and even in repentance,[73] because he bears the basic responsibility for everyone.

But beyond this, he actually represents the divine. He is the "doer in what is done," which otherwise was only said of God. The good done by the individual comes from him, because, in his relationship to the *tzaddik*, the individual is merely like the pen in the writer's hand.[74] Thus the brain of every individual conceives from the *tzaddik*, who is superior and represents the general brain.[75] The separation of life and death[76] does not apply to him; he can lift the dead to a high level,[77] and so on and so on.

In Rabbi Nachman's case, this extreme tzaddikism led to the creation of a kind of sect, which culminated in his ordering that his grave be worshipped. So, at least in this respect, extreme tzaddikism contradicted the intentions of early Hasidism.

The doctrine of the *tzaddik* leads to the view that:

> in every single *tzaddik* who is truly a *tzaddik*, there is a revelation of the Messiah.[78, 79]

Messianic actualization was meant to apply to every individual, and the arrival of the Messiah—at least according to the Baal Shem, the founder of Hasidism—depended on whether the messianic level was fulfilled in everyone. In tzaddikism, however, the principle of messianic actualization became shrunken, applying only to the representatives, the *tzaddikim*. In this way, however, the basic importance of Hasidism for Judaism, its message to the individual, and its restoration of the inner revelation in the ascent of the individual soul, begin to be lost again.

2. The relationship of God and human

Jewish antiquity and Hasidism

The basic law, which also underlies the *tzaddik*'s power, is the fact that the divine makes itself dependent on human activity. This teaching, that "the Unconditioned submits to conditionality," actively develops the teaching that above and below are mirror-images. It is not simply that the lower is like the upper, or that the structure of the human being corresponds to that of *Adam Kadmon*. Rather, corresponding to the fact that the upper creates the lower, there is also a sense in which the lower creates the upper.

If God's cooperation with the prophet was already crucial in Jewish antiquity, and if intact and alert consciousness is one of the conditions of genuine prophecy,[80] then the same principle takes effect in Hasidism at another level.

Later, we shall consider the differences, and what they reveal about the process of development. At any rate, it is clear that the wholeness of the individual plays a role here, as it did in another way with the ancient prophets, enabling a partnership with the divine. In neither case could this collaboration be limited to a mystical I–Thou relationship, for it represents the central core of God's very relationship to the world.

The anthropocentric emphasis, already very important in ancient Judaism, became even stronger in Hasidism, where its meaning was generalized. At an earlier time, the prophet was the only individual. Now, individualization has progressed so far that, at least for early Hasidism, every Jew is an individual, predestined for partnership with YHWH.

Hasidism is certainly aware of the changed situation in the world, that is, the fundamental difference between the Hasidic Jew and the Jew of antiquity. The subjection of ancient Judaism to ritual and law no longer holds true in modernity—and Hasidism marks the beginning of Jewish modernity. Against the many passages in Jewish scriptures that attribute dominance to the era of the Fathers, a contrasting sense of the world emerges in the revolution of Hasidism, which establishes, for the new era, unprecedented freedom in relation to the divine.

Everyone, not only the priest, can realize the relationship with God. But even the contraction of sacrality to the holy precinct of *Eretz Israel* and the Temple is relativized by the actualizing of messianism. Because, as the Baal Shem says:

> Every place is right for prayer.[81]

The replacement of the messianic era by the "here and now" goes in the same direction.

> The *tzaddik* can "make a change" at any time, whenever he wishes, which not even the High Priest on Yom Kippur can do.[82]

This formulation is most revolutionary, when we remember that the moment when the High Priest leaves the Holy of Holies on Yom Kippur and, speaking for God, tells the people, "I have forgiven," represented the pinnacle of the religious year and the climax of the religious covenant between God and the people.

Rabbi Nachman most clearly conveys his awareness of this historical change, which signifies the end of the provisional life in the galut and of "living in the meantime," when he mentions a secret, which he wants to tell "again," and that has only been told once, namely before the First Temple. He continues:

> Although this was once told before, it is a complete novelty, an entirely new thing. For of course, much has happened between then and now. At the time it was told as was right for the time; but now it must be told as is right for now.[83]

He then adds more generally:

> For I am treading a new path, which no one has gone before. Although it is very old, it is also completely new.[84]

The relative dependence on the human being, into which the divine has voluntarily entered, becomes evident in the Old Testament, even outside of prophecy as such. It is already seen in Abraham's legal dispute over Sodom, Moses' defense of the people, and other passages. But the bond between the *tzaddik* and the deity leads to a condition that we could describe as partial identity.

The connection of heaven and earth, achieved in the *tzaddik*, signifies that this union and partial identity exist universally in the non-ecstatic condition of daily life. It follows that statements about the *tzaddik*'s effect on God appear merely to continue the old saying:

> The *tzaddik* decides, and God carries out.[85]

Thus, we are told:

> The *tzaddik*'s will is God's will.[86]

Or:

> The *tzaddik*'s word is attached and connected to his root. It is really like the word of God, through which the heavens were made.[87]

The activity of the upper world passes through the *tzaddik*. He is the mediator, the point of transition, and the executive organ of divinity. But his function as the path or channel does not exhaust his importance. When he establishes the connection with the upper world, the *tzaddik*, like anyone at all, knows what will happen:

> The human being is part of the divine above, and if he attaches his thoughts to what is above, he is able to know what happens there, for all things that are happening above pass through his thoughts.[88]

But even this prophetic knowledge, consisting of passive awareness, is only a partial aspect. More importantly, the divine can be actively affected by human beings, and divine activity then responds. This principle might be called "human activity as a prior cause."[89]

Later, we shall consider the consequence of this causal aspect and its transformation, in the context of the new relationship in Hasidism between God and humanity. We would need to describe how far the primacy of the spirit in Jewish antiquity could include both the emphasis on consciousness and the recognition of inner revelation,[90] and what this emphasis on consciousness meant compared with all divinatory, ecstatic movements, which animated the unconscious wholly unsupervised. The loss of the YHWH–earth tension[91] led to a shift, in which the primacy of the spirit yielded to the dominance of rational consciousness. This process shaped the psyche of galut Judaism and, through its calamitous rejection of all inner revelation, eventually resulted in a shrinking of the basis of life and in splitting consciousness dangerously from the creative foundation of the unconscious.

Hasidism moves contrary to this process, reconnecting with the inner structure of Judaism that had emerged in antiquity. It does so at a new level in the history of ideas, to be sure, because the Jewish people are now 3,000 years older. But whereas the basic conception is similar in both periods, at the same time the respective emphases of their orientations toward the dominant mental layer are nearly opposite.

In antiquity—and for prophecy, as well—the chief emphasis is to develop, support, and expand the system of consciousness. What endangers this system is powerful flooding from the dimension of earth, with its negative instinctuality, from which ego stability can be rescued only by consciousness. Structures of morality are the triumphant walls, the task of which is to contain the threat of the unconscious. And the ego, as the image of God and the center of life and realization, being conscious of its responsibility, bears a true character of holiness and separateness. Unlike the irresponsible person, tossed back and forth by the unconscious and continually carried away in the ocean of *participation mystique*, the ego stands here in the freedom of individual choice.

Hasidism moves in the opposite direction. Although still emphasizing consciousness, it dethrones the ego and pure rationalism. In discovering the soul, suspending the old values, relativizing morality, and turning toward irrationalism, feeling, and nothingness as the creative origin of revelation, as well as toward evil and the world, nature, and inwardness, Hasidism offers a saving countermovement against the withering, freezing, and constriction that now threaten the Jewish person from the other side. It moves against this danger of sterile encapsulation in pure rationalism, and against the paralysis of an ego reasoning that has lost its foundation. Separation from life, nature, and the body has disconnected this ego reasoning from the renewing power of the creative. and its dialecticism, formalism, intellectualism, traditionalism, and atrophied content would have meant Judaism‘s suffocation.

The rational conscious system was still maintained, not only in rabbinism, but also in the Kabbalah. The emphasis on speculation, morality, and knowledge, but also on Gnostic asceticism, in which conscious tension implacably opposes the natural inclinations, forms part of the emphasis on the ego in galut Judaism after the time of antiquity.[92] It is not until Hasidism that the focus shifts from the ego to the superordinate center, the mid-point of the human being, which modern depth psychology calls the Self.

The Copernican revolution

The Copernican revolution in the development of Judaism, which begins with Hasidism, displaces the ego from its position at the center of the world. The cosmic universe that emerges consists of the unconscious, organized in hierarchical levels, with the sun of the Self at its center, around which circles the earth of the ego-complex.

Strikingly, however, this Copernican revolution does not contradict a new anthropocentric thesis, which highlights the human being as the bearer of consciousness, that is, as the bearer of a specific spiritual function, against the cosmos of the unconscious. Moreover, this anthropocentric emphasis is stronger, because the human being is now seen as the location of this center of the world, as the specific region of the Self's revelation and dominion. The dialogue between the human and the divine proves to be a dialogue between the ego and the Self, in its human–cosmic constellation. As such, it is a matter of destiny, not only for the human being, but also for the divinity that is realized both in him and by him.

> Concerning the verse in Scripture, "I stand between him and you," Rabbi M.[93] said: The I stands between God and us. When the human being says "I" and presumes to utter his Creator's word, he separates himself from him. But when one offers his "I," there is no longer any wall of separation. For of him it is written: "I belong to my friend, and his desire is toward me." If my I has become the possession of my friend, his desire is toward me.[94]

This offering of the "I" differs not only from the ego's identification with the Self in the ancient mysteries,[95] but also from its dissolving in a state of ecstasy. The essence of this offering is that ego and Self, I and God, are joined, thereby removing the wall that separates the system of consciousness from the one outside this working center.[96]

It is the task of prayer[97] to break through this wall of separation; it is the task of meditation and of ascent. By the attachment of union with the root, consciousness is opened. This is the point of the offering, through which God, the conscious system, and the human being become available. For God, as one *tzaddik* replied, lives "wherever one lets him in."[98] Through this sacrificial act, God's rule in the world is extended. Unlike the mysteries, however, this offering of identification is not an ego-inflation, in which the ego identifies with the Self. Rather, in this identification, the ego experiences itself as part, vessel, and instrument of the transpersonal.

No ecstatic dissolving of the ego occurs here, in which the basis of experience, the ego, becomes dust before the overpowering God-Self. Instead, this ego experiences itself and its preserved activity as part of a higher activity. The human being does the will of God as self-evidently as the hand does the human will, as one parable put it, although the human being experiences himself not only as the hand, but also as the will of the agent. Thus, the offering of the "I" is not a sacrifice of ego or consciousness. Rather, it is about becoming transparent to oneself on the symbolic level. The ego experiences itself as an event of the Self.

Once again, the state of affairs fulfilled here is the connection of the feminine, of ego-consciousness opened to the divine, with the masculine, the activity of ego-consciousness that affects the divine. We find the most complete formulation of this Copernican revolution in the following tale:

> The rabbi of Kotzk asked a self-assured youth: "Can you learn?" "Yes," he replied. "Do you know," the rabbi then asked, "the meaning of the word Torah?" The youth fell silent. "The meaning of the word Torah," said Rabbi Mendel, "is: *It teaches*. But you believe you can learn by yourself—so it hasn't taught you anything yet."[99]

This saying is expanded by another:

> "There is no man who is not incessantly being taught by his soul." One disciple then asked: "If this is so, why don't men obey their souls?" "The soul teaches incessantly," Rabbi Pinhas explained, "but it never repeats."[100]

The creative activity of the soul, teaching and giving meaning, advances here toward the ego. The conscious ego, with its "I learn" and its self-assured narrowness, is here confronted by a superior entity, in the face of which it must open itself, accepting instruction.

This creative activity of the higher spiritual world, the world of the soul, stands in the sign of unrepeatability, being "always new, different at every turn." The unforeseeable answers of the soul, with their fiery, blazing, and subsiding revelation, are alive for one occasion only and must always be understood anew. They live in opposition to the repetitive world of consciousness, for this world is governed by fixed and constant dimensions, crystallized in an immutable paralysis. This repeatable world of knowledge and fixed values constitutes the old, pre-Hasidic world of rabbinism, the abstractness of which tended to exclude vitality more and more, while accommodating to a rigid, yet seemingly well-ordered conceptual framework.

Two directions exist side by side in Hasidism, trying to coordinate the soul's creative force into a new and living connection with the ego, and thereby to regenerate the world of consciousness. One direction is prophetic and ecstatic, which emphasizes consciousness, but nevertheless places such a strong accent on the superiority of the Self that the ego almost disappears in it. The other is the direction of formation, inspired by the *tzaddikim*, which aspires to a process of unity and wholeness. Here, the higher center constellates itself as the mid-point, from which, by offering the ego, the sacred connection between divine and human identity arises to become the new center of the world. Here, the goal and meaning of life are the reflection of the image of God in fulfilled wholeness, the union of above and below.

> For the human being is only half of a form. He is only blood, "DaM." And on its own, A (the symbol of the beginning and the divine) is not a complete form either. But truly, when they adhere to each other to form a unity (ADaM), a complete form arises.[101]

This, once again, is the universal mystical doctrine of the emptying of ego-consciousness, combined here with the doctrine of the creative word, which now becomes generalized and speaks from the human being. The doctrine of the prophetic and creative quality of connection with the deity, in which divine utterance comes from the human mouth, is based on the Kabbalah's cosmic theory of language. As discussed above, this theory holds that the world descended from the world of thought through the world of the word to the factual world of things, moving step by step, clothing and restricting itself, from inwardness to outwardness. The words of the Great Maggid should be understood in this sense:

> I am teaching you the best way of saying Torah: If you lack all feeling of yourself, but your ear hears the world of the word speaking to you, and not speaking your own words; and as soon as you hear your own words, you immediately break off.[102]

This is not a form of mystical glossolalia, that is, speaking in tongues. Saying Torah is identical here with a form of teaching, in that the "it teaches" requires clear consciousness, in that the Torah itself speaks, and in that human wholeness, the Self, can express itself when the union is achieved between the creative unconscious and consciousness.

This prophetic–ecstatic orientation, in which the speaker is attached to the upper spiritual world, proceeds from the state of inspiration, the name of which comes from the spirit's "in-breathing." The concept of inspiration corresponds exactly to the in-breathing of the spiritual principle of life, through which the human being became a human being at his creation. Thus, the psychology of the creative process ultimately constitutes the religious and spiritual background of Hasidism and defines the ego's new relationship with the Self within it.

The meaning of creative nothingness as the birthplace of renewal and meaningfulness, and as the ritual bath signifying the rebirth of ego-consciousness, was discussed above.[103] But this nothingness is only "nothingness" to the ego in its limitation; on the other hand, it is also wisdom, meaning not anonymous indeterminacy, but intangible significance and substance.

From this perspective, the world in its sinking becomes less substantial and less wise, or rather, its content and wisdom become more veiled. But as one ascends closer to the source of nothingness, the wisdom content of all the worlds becomes more transparent. In the same way, to one standing on the symbolic level,[104] the inwardness of the world becomes tangible. And if, on this level, the ego experiences itself as an event of the Self and as part of a superordinate whole, then we see the formulations that attribute the real activity of life no longer to the ego, but to the background of the world and the soul.

> Whenever any kind of wisdom enters human reason, it comes from the world of thought. But who brings this thought into reason? He is hidden and completely unknown, he is the crown, which is called nothingness, which is called primordial reason.[105]

Or vice versa:

> He who himself is nothingness attains the higher wisdom.[106]

Nothingness or wisdom is not an abstraction, nor a general formula, like a demonized concept or hypostasis, but it is the valid formulation of the fact of creativity in the non-ego, the unconscious. From that place, where consciousness encounters something unknown, intangible, and indeterminable, a nothingness, from there comes every thought and idea, every notion, and every image. All the contents of consciousness and everything the human being creates have their origin where the Hasidic system of the world locates nothingness, wisdom, or primordial reason.

The aspect, "it teaches," implies that an activity springs from this upper world, that the incessantly teaching soul is not an object of ego-consciousness. On the contrary, even this soul is a subject, which produces consciousness and makes it its object. We encounter the same problem here. That is, how can inner revelation—the productive activity of the unconscious, as the communication channel of the divine—be reconciled with the dignity of consciousness and stand opposed to the ego's ecstatic disintegration?

Revelation is made possible only by ego-stability, in that, as a transcendent function, its synthesis overcomes the heightened tension between consciousness and the unconscious. This prophetic form of revelation is adapted to a time and a stage of humanity for which everything depends on protecting consciousness from flooding by the unconscious.

In the era of Hasidism, when Jewish consciousness had become cramped, the problem of reconciling revelation with the dignity of consciousness was constellated differently. It would be an exaggeration to claim that Hasidism consciously aimed at what modern depth psychology refers to as individuation. Nevertheless, it formulated and accentuated all the principles that belong to the path of individuation. In particular, this means the principle of wholeness, which always comes up, and the principle of the union of opposites. But it also appears as the center, the totality of the psyche, the Self, in the symbolism of the mid-point as *Tiferet*, king, heart, and *Adam Kadmon*. There, it is endowed with all the attributes that reappear in modern people as the symbolism of the Self.

This process toward wholeness, including evil, that is, intending to unite the whole personality with all its parts, also enables inner revelation as an expression of the Self. At the same time, however, it not only preserves the activity of consciousness and the ego, but also crucially depends on it.[107] An integral element in this process toward wholeness is the individual and his conscious activity, which before all else enables the progressive path of union.

Hasidism and Gnosticism

In this context, it is important to be clear about the meaning of the Hasidic theory of sparks. We need to specify its characteristics, as compared with the primitive and Gnostic spark theories. For early humans, the belief that the world and objects are universally endowed with souls, and alive, corresponds to a primitive theory of sparks, even if not formulated as such. The human soul or parts of souls cannot yet construct a counterweight to the world. The world's dominant power, enlivened by projections, is too great. Unconscious fragmentation of the soul disempowers the human being, so that he only gradually begins, helped by spells, magic, and ritual, to withdraw projections from the world. Through introjection, he takes charge of his dispersed soul-sparks and increases his psychic power over the world. This process occurs with the help of the discriminating ego-consciousness, which is being systematically constituted. But ego-consciousness must also resist the increasing strength of the inner dimension. The struggle that had existed between the human being and the world, which was enlivened by his projections, now shifts inward. It becomes the ego's struggle with the unconscious, strengthened by the sparks that once enlivened the world but are now introjected into the psyche.

This process finds its most obvious, albeit one-sided, expression in the Gnostic theories, in which all consciousness-enhancing spiritual elements are regarded, dualistically, as sparks dispersed in the world. These sparks belong to the human being's divine authenticity and are fettered, caught, and buried in an evil world that causes unconsciousness.[108]

The renunciation of the world, as the prescribed path to redemption, proceeds under the symbol of "gathering oneself" from fragmentation. The soul's ascent occurs here with the help of the sparks gathered from the world, and the ecstatic Neoplatonic path continues this Gnostic path of healing.[109] The Hasidic theory of ecstatic ascent also depends on Neoplatonism and its offshoots, but it is crucial to note that the Gnostic emphasis and orientation differ completely from Hasidism.

Gnosticism goes only half as far as Hasidism. Its rejection of the world is supposed to be about extracting bits of light from the evil world, leaving it below and behind as evil, and thereby restoring the original duality of light and darkness, which had been mixed and confused. Here, the human being is a warrior for the light. His task is to restore the separation in everything. In a sense, he must analytically dissect the mixture of the world, so that, out of the multiplicity of elements, he can gather and bring back the positive ones to their place of origin.

This path of redemption, which leads out of the world, also exists in Hasidism. It is the ascent to nothingness and is characterized by the activity of the *tzaddikim*, who from "something" make nothingness. However, it constitutes only one, regenerative part of the path, which must be followed by the other, creative part, radiating back into the world. Thus, in Gnosticism, and especially in Manichaeism, redemption, as the connection with the upper world, anticipates death, whereas, in Hasidism, this connection is a rebirth, a passing through death, a repetition of the creation. It repeats the divine act, which from nothingness makes something.

The restoration of the original duality in Gnosticism stands opposed to the restoration of the original unity in Hasidism. Redemption and leading the sparks upward are here not an analytical but a synthetic act, in that the union of heaven and earth becomes ever broader, clearer, and more real. Evil is not left behind, nor is it defeated by goodness, which would simply be another form of dualism. Rather, for the ascending soul, evil proves to be only a veiled, hidden goodness. Indeed, when the latent energy hidden at the lowest levels is freed by its awakening, it is the greatest of all.

This contrast finds its strongest expression in the human being's position in the world. According to Manichaeism, human existence amounts to a "series of assaults on life," on the substance of the light that is mixed with everything:

> Since the whole outer world is ensouled to a greater or lesser degree, the fruit laments when it is picked, the earth suffers when it is broken by the plough, the air whistles sharply when it is divided, the water is soiled by the bath one takes in it.[110]

The human position in Hasidism is the opposite. Here, he is the mid-point and redeemer. Things are ensouled, and for this very reason they desire to come to the human being. It is only in him, through his psychic and spiritual activity, that they find their correct place and are redeemed. Without the human being, they are trapped, dead, and meaningless in their authenticity. They receive language only from the human being, by addressing him, and their inwardness becomes transparent through that of the human being who accepts them. In this life-affirming, realizing function, the human being and his prototype, the *tzaddik*, become the world's place of fulfillment. He makes the world holy. By speaking the blessing over the broken fruit, for instance, he raises the purity of nature to its "hallowing."[111]

The integration of the living into the human circle of hallowing increases the original affinity that everything living has with God. The purity of nature represents a latent, unconscious holiness, which is only elevated to a revealed, conscious holiness by the human being. Just as nature can only become "impure" through its relationship with the human being,[112] only this relationship can make it holy. For Judaism and Hasidism, the human being's specific salvific task is to make the world holy by redeeming the sparks.

In another context, we shall return to other essential differences between Hasidism and Gnosticism. Now, let us focus on what it means that the sparks are redeemed, not for the development of the world but for that of the single individual.

The Gnostic saying:

> I am you and you are me, and where you are, I am, and I am scattered in all. And from wherever you want to, you may gather me; but by gathering me, you gather yourself,[113]

could be interpreted in Hasidic terms, despite its subjective mysticism, if even the end and goal of individual development were not reversed. In Gnosticism, individual development is a process of differentiation, in that not only is the world broken up into its original elements, but this process also continues within each person. Once again, we are dealing with differentiation, with the separation of the authentic spiritual elements of light out of their state of confusion, their fall, and their seduction. Elements that are thereby purified are led back to their origin, reversing the process of creation and abolishing worldly and human existence, which must be rejected.

In Hasidism, on the other hand, we are dealing with a process of integration. The sparks are gathered and introjected into the soul, which thereby ascends. This introjection of psychic contents, previously projected into the outer world, leads to a process for the soul, in which it expands, unifies, and becomes whole. At the same time, the ascending soul stretches worldwide, encompassing ever-greater layers of existence. The redemptive process leads to a wholeness, the essential symptom of which is joy, as an expression of existence that affirms the world and life. The soul's ascent also leads to a connection with the place of origin, that is, nothingness, as the divine expression closest to the world. But this "bringing back what was lost from birth,"[114] is not the last stage, but only the second to last.

The oneness and wholeness established in this process of integration never existed before. It is something unique and new, which entered the world with the human being, with every human being. The union of above and below, the raising of the world to different levels of transparence, is a unique process happening within the world. It depends on the human being's structure of consciousness and on his unique constellation as an individual. Involving the human being, the world, and God, this process of integration confirms, expands, and elevates the creation, human existence, and the world. For nothing pre-worldly, nothing uncreated, and no angelic being can execute this process. It is possible on account of the lower aspect, being in the world, and the danger that arises from evil and the negative "earth." Its ultimate goal is to resynthesize the tension between YHWH and earth, which came apart in ancient Judaism.

For the human being, this integrative process means a development of personality, which also includes the lower aspects of his personality. "Lower" here means what is evil and foreign to him; it is where the sparks are most concealed from him, and the divine least visible. It is what he rejects and negates. As we have seen,[115] this aspect, which was still sacrificed in Jewish antiquity, was given an opposite meaning in Hasidism:

> Even in idolatry and in all idols, sacred sparks exist.[116]

This view has the widest implications because, as noted earlier, it completely revolutionized moral and traditional values. The radical nature of this revolution places the greatest demands on the vitality of the individual, because it rules out every definable orientation that would provide secure knowledge. This personality development in Hasidism, aiming at wholeness, calls on the intuitive and feeling capacity of the Jewish person to constellate the wholeness that is pregnant with revelation. Only a shift of focus makes the new revelation of divinity possible, that is, the shift from ego to Self. But this also means a shift away from the conscious and mental attitudes of pre-Hasidic Judaism, a fact recognized and acknowledged by Hasidism and expressed in the un-Jewish sounding saying of the Maggid:

> And every incomprehensible thing is a real part of God.[117]

That is why Hasidism insists that the conscious and common attitude must be compensated for by its opposite,[118] and why it so firmly emphasizes the development of this "other side," which necessarily belongs to wholeness. Meanwhile, it refuses to acknowledge any position once acquired as having a fixed value.

With its strong emphasis on the vitality of energetic tension and on the creative process that alters existence, and with its rejection of everything existing and fixed, everything unchangeable and habitual, Hasidism also needs to highlight all those factors in the individual's life that are suited to his revolution and transformation.

This tendency toward passion and ecstasy, which is restrained in the service of the creation and its renewal, even leads to affirming violence rather than adaptation.

> When a *tzaddik* told a man, "I have no key to open you," the man exclaimed, "Then pry me open with a nail!" From this time on, the *tzaddik* is said to have praised the man very highly.[119]

Hasidism's profound insight, which enabled a renewed experience of God within Judaism, was that genuine religious experience does not occur when the human being is in a place where he feels safe and knowing. Rather, it assails him when he is alone and vulnerable, for the soul grows more deeply in its attachment to God, not in the marketplace, not in the bustling and sheltering community, but in silence, in the menace of the everyday.

This does not mean that there is no security and nothing but assaults, nor that this experience is possible only in solitude and not in the community. Hasidism emphasizes and confirms the opposite. But when new irruptions and moments of solitude continually occur, the fact is proven—it must always be relearned—that, inside the human being, the place of the world's fulfillment, if he desires to become a totality, "all the fountains of fire must open, from the highest to the lowest."[120]

3. The new experience of God

Here, a new religious experience certainly broke through in Hasidism. Our task is to differentiate it from what had previously appeared in Judaism as religious experience. Equally clear, however, is that, although it occurs in another form and on another level, this new experience involves the very same YHWH who takes hold of human beings in the Old Testament, invading and transforming.

Central to both experiences is the statement to King Saul after his anointing: "You will be changed into another man."[121] But Hasidism rules out what was still felt in antiquity as a state of partial possession, or possession by the Holy Spirit, which had transformed the whole personality only for the great prophets (and then not always). For Hasidism focuses above all on the process leading to wholeness.

Although, at its high point, Jewish prophecy is marked by the ego-stability of consciousness and the revelatory irruption of the transcendent function, alongside these, almost always, there is also the quality of mission. That is, human personality is overwhelmed by the deity.

In prophecy, the message is crucial, and, even though the individual form of the prophetic messenger must be moved and transformed, yet it must not be entirely melted down and recast. For all that matters is his capacity to bring the message to the people. For the Hasidic *tzaddik*, life as a whole is not the expression of unique or frequent states of possession by God, but of a continual attachment to him. In the absence of Temple, land, and folk customs connected to the world, the basis from which God's power radiates into the world is the life of the individual, his everyday and his feast days, his acting and his thinking.

And yet all those basic experiences that characterize the experience of YHWH in antiquity recur in Hasidism: here the divine is addressed in reality, and this address is considered to synthesize tradition and personal inner experience. It combines the prophetic and the Hasidic consummation of faith: "*Our* God *and* the God of our fathers."[122]

Over the course of human history, and also the history of Judaism, the relationship between God and humanity became more and more clearly centered on the human being. Once only the object of God, but having gradually become his partner and counterpart, the human being is ultimately the actual arena on which and in which divine power unfolds. The world becomes increasingly free of God, increasingly an outer world and free of revelation, and the human being becomes increasingly filled with God and pregnant with revelation. For with the introjection of theophanies, formerly experienced outside, the soul grows heavier and heavier with God, and the inward migration of the divine is more and more evident.

The human being has become the place of fulfillment, not only for the world and for himself, but also for the divine. Because—and here we approach a chapter that is doubtless as difficult as it is significant—the divine itself, as the immanence of God, the *Shekhinah*, in the world, in the sparks, is waiting to be redeemed by humankind.

This seems to be a Gnostic aspect, for the mourning *Shekhinah*, trapped in the world and separated from divine transcendence, almost needs to be called the world's soul, which is in the galut, in exile. In this, she very much resembles the Manichean *Jesus patibilis*,[123] suffering in the world and existing in all bodies, who is fastened as the suffering aspect of the redeeming God onto the cross of matter. He, too, represents the soul of the world.[124]

The feminine aspect of the divine

Unquestionably, the *Shekhinah*'s development, from the original historical dimension to a cosmic and universal one, reaches its height in Hasidism. Nothing more remains of the *Shekhinah* that went into exile with Israel after the historical event of the destruction of Zion:

> The *Shekhinah* is called "this," for she is the world that reveals itself.[125]

Moreover:

> The *Shekhinah* encompasses all worlds—inanimate, plant, animal, and human—everything created, the good and the evil. The *Shekhinah* is the true union.[126]

In its feminine aspect, as the *Shekhinah* or as *Malkhut*,[127] the deity needs human beings and makes demands on them. When the world becomes transparent to the human being on the symbolic level, as a divine event, then, working in and through him, the divine in some sense reaches a new self-awareness.

Even if the sparks' vitality, their inner principle of life, does not spring exclusively from the projected parts of the human soul, yet their vitality is due, to a considerable degree, to this self-dispersal by the soul into things of the outer world. As we have seen, the process of gaining consciousness corresponds in part to introjecting and internalizing these parts of the soul. This also entails an extraordinary emphasis on the human being, as well as a surge of lively energy.

Although we note the crucial importance of humanity in redeeming and raising the world, especially the importance of human consciousness, we must remember that the Hasidic theory of sparks has wider implications. Even if the essential human task consists of raising the sparks from the dead, mineral level, the sparks also have an activity of their own in relation to the world and its people.

The sparks do not signify only a potential redemptive energy, one that can animate the soul and life of a human being; they may even flood them. If we look more closely, we see that the human being's whole psychic existence depends on this inherent activity of the sparks, and their intention to approach him.

We have said that the dynamics of the world's claim, as symbolized by the sparks, and the orientation of the human soul, are aligned with each other and connected by nature. And if it is true, as we read, that the desire for a thing stems from the divine spark within it,[128] then the energy of the human soul derives from the spark's own activity. A person's disposition and destiny thus depend on the inherent activity of the sparks, which represent the living principle of the world.

What drives and moves a person may be a beautiful landscape, lust for power, the constraint of relationships, or the inner movement of the soul itself. In every case, he is exposed to and at the mercy of the sparks' inherent activity. Stimulating him, they demand something of him and his aroused emotion. For the human being, as an ego, is the object of all this excitement, and, to begin with, as long as he is unconscious, it dominates him. The more unconscious he is, and the more his ego-consciousness exists on the mineral level, the more strongly the disunified activity of the sparks will act upon and in him, yet without his being able to redeem them. Redemption requires an active, conscious process, an activity in relation to which objects on the mineral level are once again feminine. Only an intensifying, widening human consciousness can get beyond the inherent activity of things and their sparks.

Calling a human being unconscious is the same as saying that he is governed by the inherent activity of things and entities, and that the inherent activity of his consciousness is smaller than that of things, and subservient to them.

In the sparks' ascent and redemptive process, which leads to wholeness, the inherent activity of consciousness becomes increasingly greater, the activity of the sparks is absorbed by the soul and fused with the inherent activity of the human soul, which is connected with consciousness. As in the ascent from the mineral level to the symbolic, this process progressively expands consciousness and strengthens the soul.

But a paradoxical and characteristic reversal occurs when this ascent reaches its peak. Up until then, the world's anthropocentric dimension was given reality by an increasingly active consciousness. And the world, reaching fulfillment in the human being, proved so dependent on the human being's "masculine"[129] redemption that even the activity of the sparks could appear partly as a projection of the human soul. But now, on the highest level, although the human being keeps his central place in the world, the ego is deprived of its place as the mid-point in the personality.

When the widened consciousness recognizes the world as a divine event, it can also recognize itself and its process of rising as a divine ascent. Then the human being experiences his own existence, in particular and in general, not as produced by the ego, but as shaped by the Self. This is the point of which it is said: "The individuated ego senses itself as the object of an unknown and superordinate subject."[130]

From determination to identity

The divine destiny in the world, which depends on humanity, now changes from an aspect of determination by the human being to a relationship of identity with him. Once again, we are dealing with the developmental stages of the relationship between God and humanity, and at the same time with a shift in perspective. The idea that the Unconditional allows itself to be conditioned had led, from the human perspective, to the principle that we have called "human activity as a prior cause."[131] Repeatedly, from all perspectives, we have observed that Hasidism centered itself around the human being as the mid-point of the world.

This anthropocentric worldview is plainly evident in this passage:

> Perverted humility may lead a person to turn away from the service of God. Self-abasement may keep him from believing that human beings bring fullness to all worlds through prayer and teaching, and that even the angels are nourished by human teachings and prayer. If he believed this, with what fear and joy would he serve God, attending to every movement and every word, so that he would speak and act in the right way.
>
> The human being should focus his intention on being a ladder, its foot resting on the ground, its head touching heaven, and know that all his gestures, business, and speeches leave traces in the upper world.[132]

At its lowest level, this activity may be formulated causally. For example, every act of repentance, leading to the suspension of a negative judgment, belongs to this causal aspect. Its most primitive form, found in all early religions, is the magical and ritual coercion of the divine. Magical action and ceremony, sacrifice, and formulaic prayers used for exorcism all correspond to this view.

Repentance, as turning back to what is willed by the deity while excluding what is negated, is a higher level. For the divine and the human here grow more intimate, in that the purely external execution of divine prescription associates itself with a corresponding disposition, meaning a conscious psychic act, which was not required on the magical level. At the level of magic, there exists an unconscious participation, a total possession, where the sacrificer is identical with the sacrifice and with the divine. Insofar as no modern mechanization of this process is involved, it requires no inner intention or disposition, simply because on this level there is still no detached inner world, no division between inside and outside. Rather, no differentiation has occurred yet between inside and outside. Instead, the original unity of the human being and the world still exists in the outer act of offering.

The causality of repentance, on the other hand, entails renunciation, which is to say, a capacity for self-direction. It depends on choice, a decision for or against the divine, on the basis of a fundamental partnership. This introversion, as a disposition in the act of repentance, experiences itself positively toward the divine. With this realization, the relationship between God and humanity becomes more intimate, and their connection, hence their mutual dependence, clearer.

Over the millennia, the divine "migrates inward," going from a place somewhere in heaven, totally detached from humankind, and moving into the human being and a partial identity with him. Crucially, in this migration, the step of introversion makes divine action dependent on the human disposition, or at least causes it to react to it.

But the Hasidic formulation goes much further. The saying:

> God's eyes are on the *tzaddikim*,[133]

is not only interpreted as meaning that God oversees the world through the *tzaddikim*, because he has handed over its supervision to them. Rather, it is even said:

> Just as the son's childish idea directs the father's reason to these things, so do the ideas of the *tzaddikim* in relation to God. For God thinks what they think, and if they think with love, they bring God into the world of love.[134]

We now understand the Baal Shem's supposedly blasphemous sentence:

> God is the human shadow and, like his shadow, he does whatever the human being does.[135]

The insight, "I am like you, God," the derivation of which from the verse, "Love your neighbor as yourself, I am YHWH" we have already come across,[136] is not theoretical, but is a very powerful insight. It means that whatever happens to us at the hands of the divine is exactly, and only, what we ourselves are.

As a special application of this sentence, divine revelation depends on the nature of those to whom it occurs. This is the basic principle of the *tzimtzum*, according to which it is an act of divine grace that God does not reveal himself in his uncontracted and unbearable absoluteness, but only relative to the individual's capacity, his ability to understand.

The tale about the man who became unfaithful to his *tzaddik* illustrates this view and its application: a man always came to one of the Great Maggid's disciples, gave him a donation, and his *tzaddik*'s prayer made him rich. One day, hearing that his *tzaddik* had gone to visit the Great Maggid, he was surprised that his *tzaddik* also had a *tzaddik*. Thus, he decided to visit the greater one, which he did, and soon afterwards he fell into poverty. How could this be, he asked his *tzaddik*, the Maggid's disciple? Wasn't the Maggid the much greater *tzaddik*? He was told that so long as he gave his donation to the unworthy disciple, without being concerned about it, God did exactly the same. But when the man began making sure that he gave his money only to worthy recipients, God did the same, and so he fell into poverty.[137]

Here, we see that, just as the Unconditioned submits to conditionality, there is a law of correspondence: above and below are taken with equal seriousness, so much so that, from this perspective, one could almost say that God is unfree. This concept, that God enters voluntarily into dependence, is a basic Jewish idea.

In Jewish thought, even the rejection of God's direct revelation receives divine approval, in favor of the principle of responsible consciousness.[138] In like manner, it is said that God loves the *tzaddik*'s boldness more than he loves submissiveness to his will.

The saying that the human being must always be masculine[139] is applied also to the upper world and the divine. In relation to these, the human activity of meditation and prayer must be "prior," that is, determining.

> When the force of procreation stirs first in the woman, a male child will be born, and the male is the image of compassion.[140] When the movement first awakens below, God's attribute of compassion rules.
>
> Of this it is also said: "*I* will awake the dawn."[141]
>
> And of the Day of Atonement, it is rightly written: "On this day, a cover is laid over you." Even if they themselves did not waken to it, atonement was awakened from above, "to purify you from all your sins."[142]
>
> Yet now follows the word befitting salvation: "*Before*[143] God, purify yourselves."—Even *before*[144] God stirs you to action, you should bestir yourselves.
>
> Thus Rabbi Akiva says: "Happy are you, O Israel![145] *Before* whom are you purified, and who purifies you? Your father in heaven." The earliest beginning is yours. For when the force of procreation first stirs in the woman, a male child will be born.[146]

And, as Buber adds, in his appendix to this passage: "*In the beginning*[147] the world was created. This is interpreted as: For the sake of its beginning."[148]

This recalls the association of *Din*–judgment–female, on the one hand, and *Hesed*–grace–male, on the other, and the connection between these two: *Rahamim*–compassion–*Tiferet*.[149] The eternal play between God and humankind appears here in the symbol of marriage, in which the lower, the one standing under judgment, the human being, is the female, in whom "the force of procreation stirs," which here takes possession of the male attribute of beginning. To this movement of conception and procreation, the divine, the higher, responds with its attribute of grace. It responds to the male attribute of the female, and "the child" is born, the synthesis, the bond between male and female, upper and lower, heaven and earth, God and humanity: *Rahamim*, compassion.

Unquestionably, the model for this marriage is, as everywhere else, the heavenly marriage, which takes place between king and queen, *Adam Kadmon* and the world, *Tiferet* and *Malkhut*. It is the mystery, which, as the secret of the world, reveals the great play of love between the deity and his *Shekhinah*. This secret, which interprets the process of the world as the play of Shiva with his Shakti, is revealed in the Zohar as the highest revelation by the dying Rabbi Simon bar Yochai. In his final words, the master, whose work the Zohar claims to be, interprets the very essence of the relationship between humanity and God as a cosmic and theosophical event. The marriage between YHWH–*Tiferet* and *Shekhinah*–*Malkhut*, as a lower image of the connection between *Elohim* and YHWH, corresponds to the marriage between YHWH and Israel in general, and between God and humanity in particular. Once again, however, what is essential is the prior, male activity of the "female" human being.

The beginning lies with humanity. Conscious human activity, the ego, awakens the dawn, above, the overflowing grace of which then fulfills the worlds, causing the flooding grace of fulfillment to stream toward the human beginning.

It is interesting to note that the phenomenon appearing here at the level of introversion is the same one that, on the primitive and the magical level, corresponds to rites in which human beings make the sun rise.[150] In that case (for instance, with the Indians), the day only begins, the sun can only start to rise, once the prior human ritual is performed. In the same way here, the "dawn," the inwardly ascending sun of the transpersonal Self, is awakened by the preceding activity of the human ego.

The causal aspect has changed and has become an inner psychic act, uniting above and below. Above and below are merely domains of inwardness, in which the qualities differ. The closer the path leads to God, the further inward it reaches. Thus, to make sure the inner dimension would be recognized as the reality of the world, the contact between God and the human being was also primarily internalized.

In the tendency toward union, the parts of the soul become one through prayer, a process that unites the human being simultaneously with God and with the world. Inwardly, the various levels show themselves, and the divine, coming toward the human being, no longer has a detached, foreign, or external aspect. In the developmental process that causes the outer world to become as transparent as the inner, the divine, too, proves to be inner.

On the symbolic level, everything becomes transparently a process concerning the existence of the divine. Human existence proves to be identical in part with divine existence, and aspects of causation, union, and identity once again merely correspond to various levels of change in the relationship with God.

God's human form

This transformation eventually leads to identity with the divine—which of course is always only partial. In the process in Hasidism that leads to this identity, we must especially note two distinct aspects.

First, this process depends on dethroning the ego from the human mid-point and the emergence of the Self as the divine center of wholeness. Second, it requires a radical heightening of the principle that "the Unconditioned submits to conditionality",[151] for it culminates in the "fashioning of God's human form"[152] by human beings.

The process of shifting emphasis from the ego to the Self lives in the superiority of "it teaches" over "I learn." It shines in its own light, which also brightens the path for the ego, which has gone astray in darkness. It is the path to the hidden treasure in one's own neighborhood, the transformation by prayer, in which the separating wall between the ego and God is torn down, allowing God to enter. But the principles of leadership and acceptance are also based on this transformation.

Only when the short-sightedness and outward focus of ego-consciousness are replaced by the far-sightedness and insight of an ego that subordinates itself to the Self can the human being see through the palpable negativity burdening the world, be it suffering or sin. He can grasp the inner meaning, that all things are related to the whole, only when the divine symbol of the Self emerges as the epitome and center of this whole. What appears to be an isolated, negative fact becomes acceptable and meaningful, if its negative meaning proves to belong to the whole and to be related to it. The ability to accept ultimately rests on seeing something that seems incomprehensible and incapable of being worked through, whether as a part, as an event, or as a blow of fate, placed into a larger context of wholeness, where it becomes meaningful.

The soul's ascent through the various levels always establishes a larger context of wholeness, a union, in which the sparks hitherto isolated and encased in the things of the world shoot together into a great flame of illumination, and the accidental and seemingly meaningless facts of life prove to be meaningful and related aspects of a destiny.

The more incoherent and lacking in wholeness a person is, and the more the parts of his soul are falling apart, or at least unrelated, the more he will experience the world, too, as incoherent and disintegrated. But one who unifies his soul on its ascent (recalling here the three symbolic parts of the soul), and in whom a new center of wholeness emerges, provided that he subordinates himself as an ego to this center of wholeness, will also experience the world as new, and as a whole.

On the highest level, where the ego, without being dissolved, is paradoxically identical with the Self, on this symbolic level this Self–ego union experiences the world as the destiny of the Self–ego, the destiny of God. This is analogous to the way the ego normally experiences the world as the destiny of the ego. But the ego can only experience partial aspects of the world, whereas the ego–Self wholeness is able to experience more extensive aspects, closer to wholeness.

In its heightened form, the ego's connection with the Self, as if with a deity dwelling in the human being, leads to an experience of divine identity. Now this experience is neither mystical nor ecstatic, but one in which the relationship of God and human becomes an inner psychic process, while still preserving personality.

The saying:

> The prayer a man says, the prayer, in itself, is God,[153]

already leads to this identity, in which the one who prays, the prayer, and the one who is prayed to are indissolubly united in the act of prayer. It could seem overly daring, here, to entertain the idea that, in the prayer of the human being, God himself prays, or that the power of human prayer is the power of the indwelling deity. But this idea of the human being's tremendous elevation is confirmed a few lines further on:

> When a man who is praying thinks his prayer is something apart from God, he is like a suppliant to whom the king gives what he has begged from him. But he who knows that prayer in itself is God, is like the king's son who takes whatever he needs from the stores of his father.[154]

The following account links the concept of identity to the developmental path in a complicated, yet enlightening way:

> Rabbi Shneur Zalman told: "Before I went to Meseritz [that is, to his master, the Great Maggid], my service was based on reflection, and from this arose my love and my fear of God. In Meseritz I mounted to the rung where awareness is, in itself, love and fear.
>
> When I first heard the holy maggid say, "God's attribute of mercy is our love of God; God's attribute of rigor is our fear of God,"[155] I regarded this as an interpretation. But then I saw that it is so: The mercy of God is the love of God, the rigor of God is the fear of God.[156]

The naive reflection on the saying of the Maggid is that the human being sees that God is powerful—and fears him—and that he sees that God is gracious—and loves him. A causal relationship is established between the two dimensions, God and the human being, by making God's strength the cause of human fear. This is the level attained by Rabbi Zalman before he meets the Great Maggid. It is both rational and moral.

The second level is the one where Rabbi Zalman regards as an interpretation the Maggid's saying: "The mercy of God is the love of God, the rigor of God is the fear of God." God's power is related to the human being, in the sense that his grace, entering the world, becomes love for God, whereas his strength becomes fear of God. Here, strength is no longer an object, nor is fear a reaction to this object. Instead, one is interpreted as the other. There exists an identity, if only in the interpretative sense. We can substitute one for the other, for one mirrors the other.

The new, higher level, however, is the recognition of a real identity. The human love of God *is* God's attribute of grace. One is constituted by the other. It may also be said that God's attribute of grace does not exist beyond the human love of God and, conversely, that no human love of God exists beyond God's attribute of grace.

The causal aspect leads to the statement that God has mercy on the human being because he loves him, or that in his love for God the human being experiences God's mercy. But this view posits a duality, which can exist only if the ego, separated from the Self, is observed and acted upon, and then the love and fear of God arise "as a result." This is a temporal process, and subject to causality.

In reality, however, "if consciousness itself is love and fear," then no observing, self-distancing duality exists between ego and Self, or human and God. Rather, the identity of God and human is realized *uno actu*; so one and the same thing is called, as God's attribute, grace, and as the human attribute, love of God. Both are merely two aspects of a basic phenomenon, two designations given from two sides. Just as the same bridge extends north if it is seen from one bridgehead, and south from the other, so the same thing that, viewed from God toward the human being, is called "grace," is called "love of God" when viewed from the human being toward God. But what is real is only the unifying bridge, the transition, connecting the two polarities. What is powerful is only the energetic movement, the psychic emanation, which can equally well be designated grace or love.

Hasidism does not go so far as to say that, without human consciousness, none of God's attributes exist. Indeed, according to the Kabbalah, upon which Hasidism rests, the construction of the world shows the connection between the world's structure and the divine attributes, for the creation is understood as constituted by God's attributes in the *sefirot*. But the fact that the Kabbalah created and saw this construction of the world in the human image, the image of *Adam Kadmon*, suggests that this image of the hermaphroditic human psyche was cast onto the world's creation as a colossal projection, to be experienced there. In the same way, astrology experienced the human structure, symbolized in the zodiac and projected onto heaven, and alchemy experienced it, symbolized in the elements and projected onto matter.

It is important that in Judaism the chronological process is stressed in precisely this way, as the process of creation and of history. We have already emphasized this aspect,[157] and we shall return to it. For the moment, let us only point out the connection between the process of world history and that of becoming human.

The two processes, as time sequences, are mutually related. for the fulfillment of the world is closely tied to human integration. This applies individually, in that individual wholeness represents the redemption of the world. but it also applies more generally. for the fulfillment of the world has this same double meaning as a messianic process.

In the historical process, up until the messianic age, not only the world "fulfills" itself, but so does the human being. For the Messiah, as the fulfilled image of the perfect human being, comes to earth to complete the world's development and that of the human being, both at once. Curiously, the identity between God and the human being, which secretly enters Jewish consciousness in Hasidism, can be illustrated with the symbol of *Adam Kadmon*. We must recall, however, that any such statements can refer only to the deity's immanence in the world, the *Shekhinah*. But this part can only ever be experienced outwardly, because God in his reality is never reached by human statements; he is and remains the most hidden of all that is hidden.

> Our sages said: "Know what is above you." This is how the rabbi of Apt expounded those words: "Know what is above, is from you." And what is it that is above you? This is what Ezekiel says: And upon the likeness of the throne was a likeness as the appearance of a man upon it above." How can this be said with reference to God? For is it not written: "To whom then will ye liken Me, that I should resemble him? But the truth of the matter is that it is we who make a "likeness as the appearance of a man." It is the likeness we shape when we serve with devout hearts. With such a heart we shape a human likeness for our Creator, for him, blessed be he and blessed be his name, who can be likened to none. When a man is merciful and renders loving help he assists in shaping God's right hand. And when a man fights the battle of God and crushes Evil, he assists in shaping God's left hand. He who is above the throne—it is you who have made him.[158]

Gathered here are all the elements we have discussed, and more than these. On the whole, the formless takes form, in a process that is centered on the concept of the *tzimtzum* and the meaning of the individual. Simultaneously, however, this is the process in which God becomes human, emerging from unconscious creative hiddenness and anonymity toward the structured and world-forming visibility of conscious existence and action.

The role of humanity and of the Jew, its representative, is to make God's human form a reality, a process with four aspects that are realized simultaneously. By taking form in this way, the divine becomes human, that is, it realizes its attributes, which, as we have seen, are also the attributes of humanity.

In human compassion, God's grace becomes real. The divine assumes human form through the human being, for only by and through humankind can the true nature of the divine be realized on the symbolic level. Only in consciousness, that is, in human beings, can compassion be experienced as grace. In the animal, or on the animal level, divine power is trapped in the dullness of unconscious existence, where it realizes only its animal, not its human, form.[159]

The second thing to be realized in the human being is his authenticity, his Self, the *Adam Kadmon*, which emerges as the center of his integration. It is written:

> The human being is both the content and the highest level of the Creation; he was therefore not created until the sixth day. No sooner was the human being created than everything was completed, not only the upper world, but also the lower world. For the human being contains everything; he unifies all forms within himself.[160]

This refers to the *Adam Kadmon*, in whom the world and the human being were created. As God's image, and his presence in the world, he is "the heavenly *adam*, who created the earthly *adam*."[161]

But at the same time, it is said of him:

> The true human being (*adam*) is the soul.[162]

And of Ezekiel's heavenly chariot and the one enthroned upon it:

> The bones and veins are an image of the heavenly chariot, of the forces within, of God's servants. But these are merely clothing; for within lies the profound mystery of the *heavenly* human being. Everything is mysterious, below and above. Hence: "And God created the human being in his likeness." The mystery of the earthly human being is like the mystery of the heavenly human being.[163]

When the Talmud says:

> The earthly human being and God are twins,[164]

this refers to the identity between God and the human being, whose symbol is *Adam Kadmon*, and about whose creation we are told:

> Thereupon, we also learned to interpret the secret of the words: "The earth brings forth the living soul." "The earth" is the community of Israel; "the living soul" is the soul of the upper primordial human being.[165]

The Kabbalistic statement that "the only world that endures is the one formed in the human image,"[166] and that everything was only "made for the sake of the human being," refers to this higher *adam*, *Adam Kadmon*. Our deliberations, however, have shown that, in terms of depth psychology, *Adam Kadmon* represents a symbol of the Self, projected onto the process of the world's creation.

Although this symbol begins to be internalized in Hasidism, that process seems only to have become complete in the development of the modern western Jew.

Third, as God takes form this way, the true order of the world is realized, for it is characteristic that the world was created in the image of *Adam Kadmon*, who represents the unity of the *sefirot* and the constellation of their powers. The world fulfills itself as *Adam Kadmon* takes shape, because the truth of things and the essence of the world are realized only by the human being, who fulfills and redeems the sparks within them.

We have frequently come across these three aspects, which are all fulfilled simultaneously. The fourth, however, merits particular attention because it can help us better understand, once again, the emphasis on the passage of time, that is, Judaism's focus on history.

To form God's right hand—recalling that *Adam Kadmon*'s right hand is related to the *sefirah* of grace—is not an allegory, but a statement about the state of the world. God's right hand will not rule the world, nor will this part of God's human form be materialized, until the attribute of grace rules in the material world, really and powerfully, in all people everywhere.

At this point, the difference becomes clear between the Jewish religious conception and all others, including the Christian. Divine as well as human realization is linked with a change in the world, and, if action is outwardness, this only means that true action draws its origin and its life from inwardness. True, this often means that it is hidden and invisible, but not that it is not occurring. Even in Hasidism—in fact, precisely there—the aspect of God's reign in the world, the kingship of God, is maintained, though deeply concealed within.

The development of humanity is identical with the evolution and transformation of God's form.[167] This process must be fulfilled not only in every day and age and by every individual, but also by every community, for the sake of every time to come. Because—and this defines the meaning of Hasidism for a reawakening Judaism, and perhaps even for a reawakening humanity—the individual is not kept unconscious here at the expense of the collective, but nor is the collective denigrated for the benefit of the individual.

The work on "God's human form," his immanence in humanity, is the service performed to make God visible in the world and in the human being. The process by which God becomes human, which belongs to the history of humanity, reaches a new level in Hasidism.

Notes

1 *EN*: *Great Maggid*, p. 109. [Cited as p. 108.]
2 Cf. Neumann's discussion of the levels of nature, *Roots II*, pp. 59ff., especially the "symbolic level," *Roots II*, pp. 62f.
3 *Chassid Büch*, p. 581. [*Tales I*, p. 91. (Cf. *Roots II*, p. 32.)
4 Statement paraphrases a verse cited above. (Cf. *Roots II*, p. 121.)
5 *Chassid Büch*, p. 35.
6 *EN*: See above, p. 146 [*Roots II*, pp. 111ff.: "Accepting the world."]
7 *EN*: *Chassid Büch*, p. 597. [*Tales II*, p. 73.]

8 *EN*: Ibid., p. 148.
9 "*da-seiend*": lit. "here-being," based on the word *Dasein* (existence).
10 *EN*: *R. Nachman*, p. 190. [Cited as p. 157.]
11 *EN*: See above, pp. 9ff. [*Roots II*, pp. 8ff.: "The care of souls."]
12 *EN*: *Chassid Büch*, p. 601. [*Tales I*, p. 279.]
13 *EN*: Ibid., p. 579. [*Tales II*, p. 173.]
14 *EN*: Ibid., p. 607. [*Tales II*, p. 72.]
15 *EN*: See Part Two, pp. 91ff. [*Roots II*, pp. 69ff.: "The parts of the soul and the soul's transformation."]
16 *EN*: *R. Nachman*, p. 157.
17 Cf. *Roots II*, p. 35.
18 *EN*: *Chassid Büch*, p. 148.
19 *EN*: *Great Maggid*, p. 235.
20 *EN*: (text missing). [The quoted saying, "Der Zaddik beschließt, und Gott führt aus," is a paraphrase of Bloch's "Der Zaddik beschließt—Gott erfüllt es", in *Priester der Liebe*, p. 135. Cf. also *Roots II*, p. 135.]
21 *EN*: *Enc Jud*, "Besht." [Horodezky, "Baal-Schem-Tob," col. 838.]
22 *EN*: *R. Nachman*, p. 184.
23 *EN*: Ibid., p. 92.
24 *EN*: *Great Maggid*, p. 108.
25 *EN*: See Part Two, p. 66. [*Roots II*, p. 48.]
26 *EN*: Jung, "Die Lebenswende" ("The stages of life"; lit. "life's turning-point"), *Seelenprobleme der Gegenwart* (*Current psychological problems*) (hereafter: *Seelenprobleme*). [Papers from this 1931 collection were published in *Modern Man in Search of a Soul* (1933). Neumann cites Chapter 9 in *Seelenprobleme*, pp. 248–74. Cf. "The Stages of Life," CW 8.16, ¶749-95.]
27 Genesis 12:1. As quoted from Buber's story, this verse contains anomalies. In the original text, God addresses Abram (not yet called Abraham). A Hebrew word, usually translated "kindred," is rendered by Buber as *Geburtsort* ("birthplace"). In the Fox translation, this verse reads: "YHWH said to Avram: Go-you-forth from your land, from your kindred, from your father's house, to the land that I will let you see."
28 *EN*: *Chassid Büch*, p. 592. [*Tales I*, p. 244. Marx's translation of Genesis 12:1 departs from Buber's text by translating *Geburtsort* as "kindred." We have restored Buber's word, because Neumann refers to it in what follows.]
29 *EN*: Elsewhere, we shall discuss the connection between this path and the modern person's path toward individuation, from the shadow (the ego's obscurity) through the anima (the world of the mother) and the old man (the world of the father) to the Self (the land of God). [Neumann's note originally referred to Part Three. The reference is deleted by hand.]
30 *Umkehr*: the word also means "repentance." Cf. *Roots I*, p. 62, n. 166; and *Roots II*, p. 102, n. 54.
31 *EN*: *Chassid Büch*, p. 139.
32 Possibly a reference to Psalm 39:12b: "For I am thy passing guest, a sojourner, like all my fathers."
33 *EN*: *Chassid Büch*, p. 138.
34 Cf. *Roots II*, p. 34.
35 *EN*: *Great Maggid*, p. 109.
36 *EN*: Author, "Entwicklung und Psychologie der Lebensalter" ("Development of consciousness and the stages of life"). [Cf. Appendix B.II, *Roots II*, pp. 209ff. Cf. also *Origins and History*, Part D, "Centroversion and the Stages of Life."]
37 *EN*: Molitor [1839], *Philosophie der Geschichte*, op. cit., v. 3, p. 520.
38 Cf. *Roots II*, pp. 69ff.: "*Adam Kadmon* and the parts of the soul."
39 *Seele*: the word means both "soul" and "psyche." The preceding passage concerns Kabbalistic concepts of the soul, so we translate *Seele* accordingly. Here, because Neumann brings "ego" and "Self" into the discussion, the meaning of *Seele* arguably shifts to

"psyche." For the sake of coherence, we have stayed with "soul," but readers should bear both meanings in mind.

40 A modifying clause in this sentence, deleted by the author, reads: "as Hegel described in various ways."

41 *EN*: Author: "Die archetypischen Stadien der Bewusstseinsentwicklung" ("Archetypal stages in the development of consciousness"), I. "Die Psychologie des Mythos" ("The psychology of myth"). [Perhaps referring to an early draft of *Origins and History*. In the first edition (Rascher, 1949), the work's first part was titled, "Die archetypischen Stadien der Bewusstseinsentwicklung" ("Archetypal stages in the development of consciousness"), and its first subsection, "Die mythologischen Stadien der Bewusstseinsentwicklung" ("Mythological stages in the development of consciousness"). Cf. *Origins and History*, Part A, pp. 1–130.

42 *EN*: *R. Nachman*, p. 9. [Cf. *Roots II*, p. 40.]

43 Discussed in previous chapter. Cf. *Roots II*, pp. 55–69, "The levels of the soul and the realms of nature."]

44 *EN*: See Part One, pp. 43ff. [*Roots I*, pp. 27ff.: "The elevation of Moses and the introduction of prophecy."]

45 Cf. *Roots I*, p. 29, citing Deuteronomy 18:15–18, "which places the prophet in the midst of the people and thus simply shifts onto him, in some sense, the people's own capacity to receive direct revelation."

46 *EN*: See below, pp. 226ff. [*Roots II*, pp. 173ff.: "The psychology of assimilation."]

47 *EN*: (text missing). [Tamar Kron cites a related statement in *Great Maggid*, p. 203, which she translates: "The *tzaddik* binds everything that is, in mineral, plant, animal, and speaking (beings), and draws the sparks."]

48 *EN*: *Great Maggid*, p. 26.

49 *EN*: Ibid., p. 207 (saying 27).

50 *EN*: Ibid., p. 204 (saying 24).

51 *EN*: Ibid., p. 117.

52 *EN*: Ibid., p. 116.

53 *EN*: Ibid., p. 115.

54 *EN*: We cannot demonstrate this principle here. We can only refer to its consequences, for instance, in Romanticism (Baader), and also to the independent concept of anima and animus, established empirically by modern depth psychology (C. G. Jung, *Beziehung*). [Neumann may be referring to Franz von Baader's essay on Jakob Böhme, for whom *Einung* is a central concept, involving male–female symbolism and the analogy of impregnation (Baader, 1855, p. 389). In Jung's *Beziehungen*, Part Two, "Individuation," includes a chapter, "Anima und Animus." (Cf. CW 7.2, ¶296–340.)]

55 *EN*: *Herakleitos von Ephesos*, trans. by Diels, No. 53, p. 29.

56 *EN*: Ibid., No. 30, p. 25.

57 *EN*: *Great Maggid*, p. 199.

58 *EN*: Ibid., p. 117.

59 *EN*: *R. Nachman*, p. 186. [Cited as p. 181.]

60 *EN*: Ibid., p. 91. [Cited as p. 194.]

61 *EN*: *Chassid Büch*, p. 603 (paraphrased)

62 *EN*: *Great Maggid*, p. 37.

63 *EN*: Ibid., p. 203.

64 *EN*: Ibid.

65 *EN*: *R. Nachman*, p. 180.

66 *EN*: Jung, *Beziehungen*. [Perhaps referring to the 1928 edition, pp. 194f.: "I have never yet seen a fairly advanced development of this kind where at least a temporary identification with the archetype of the mana-personality did not take place. It is the most natural thing in the world that this should happen, for not only does one expect it oneself, but everybody else expects it too" (CW 7,2, ¶389).]

67 In addition to being translated as "foundation," the *sefirah Yesod* represents the phallus of *Adam Kadmon.*
68 *EN*: *R. Nachman*, p. 183.
69 The image of the grapevine appears in graphic arts in the first century CE, as well as in biblical texts, for example, in Jesus' saying: "As the branch cannot bear fruit by itself, unless it abides in the vine, neither can you, unless you abide in me. I am the vine, you are the branches" (John 15:4f).
70 *EN*: Cf. Jung, *Wandlungen*. Cf. also Baumann, "Tier und Pflanze als Symbole," *Zentralblatt für Psychotherapie*, vol. 10, no. 3. [These references apply only in a general sense. The 35 indexed references to Christ in *Wandlungen* do not include any mention of vine and branches. And, although Hans Baumann's paper discusses cultural and psychological meanings of animal and plant symbology in the ancient and medieval periods, including Romanesque images of Christ with animals, and Gothic depictions of the Cross as a tree, the specific image cited here, of Christ as vine and his disciples as branches, is not included.]
71 *EN*: *R. Nachman*, p. 179.
72 *EN*: Ibid., p. 185.
73 *EN*: Ibid., p. 184.
74 *EN*: Ibid., p. 195.
75 Ibid., p. 199.
76 Ibid., p. 182.
77 Ibid., p. 183.
78 Ibid., p. 184.
79 *EN*: Striking correspondences exist between Indian and Hasidic conceptions. This is a clear parallel to the Indian *bodhisattva*. We must, however, forgo this opportunity to discuss these correspondences in detail.
80 *EN*: See Part One, pp. 79f. [*Roots I*, pp. 47ff.: "The depth of the revelatory layer and the conscious attitude."]
81 *EN*: *Enc Jud*, "Besht." [Horodezky, "Baal-Schem-Tob," col. 839.]
82 *EN*: *Great Maggid*, p. 207.
83 *EN*: *R. Nachman*, p. 32.
84 *EN*: Ibid., p. 11.
85 *EN*: *Great Maggid*, p. 200. [Citation should probably read: Bloch, *Priester der Liebe*, op. cit., p. 135. Cf. above, *Roots II*, p. 123, n. 20.]
86 *EN*: Ibid., p. 200. [In Tamar Kron's translation, Horodezky's statement reads, as here: "The *tzaddik*'s will is God's will." This statement may be a precursor to the German saying paraphrased above.]
87 *EN*: Ibid., p. 201.
88 *EN*: Ibid., p. 107.
89 "*die vorläufende Aktivität des Menschen*": lit. "the human activity that precedes (goes before)." Neumann evidently coined this phrase, to refer to the impact of human actions on the divine. (Cf. also p. IIC-69 in working translation.) Sanford Drob advises that the theological concept is "theurgy."
90 *EN*: See Part One, pp. 79f. [*Roots I*, pp. 47ff.: "The depth of the revelatory layer and the conscious attitude."]
91 *EN*: See Part One, pp. 166f. [*Roots I*, pp. 123ff.: "Shrinking the tension between YHWH and earth: The anti-Gnostic threat."]
92 For Neumann, the time of Jewish antiquity ends with the destruction of the Second Temple in 70 CE. (Cf. *Roots I*, p. 8, n. 20 and p. 60, n. 160.]
93 In Buber's text: "Michal of Slotschow."
94 *EN*: *Chassid Büch*, p. 566.
95 *EN*: See Part One, p. 157. [*Roots I*, pp. 116ff.: "The danger of intuition."]
96 Neumann's lecture, "The path of depth psychology and consciousness," discusses the "wall" that separates an emerging consciousness from the powers of the unconscious (cf. Appendix B.III, *Roots II*, p. 241.)

97 *EN*: *Great Maggid*, p. 143.
98 *EN*: *Chassid Büch*, p. 562. [*Tales II*, p. 277. (Cf. also *Roots II*, p. 91.)]
99 *EN*: Ibid., pp. 589f.
100 *EN*: Ibid., p. 591. [*Tales I*, p. 121.]
101 *EN*: *Great Maggid*, p. 153.
102 *EN*: Ibid., p. 1, epigraph.
103 *EN*: See Part Two, p. 48. [*Roots II*, pp. 35f.: "Creative nothingness."]
104 *Symbolstufe*: Cf. *Roots II*, p. 62, under "The soul's teaching about the levels of nature."
105 *EN*: *Great Maggid*, p. 47.
106 *EN*: Ibid., p. 47.
107 *EN*: Author: "The path of depth psychology and consciousness." [Cf. Appendix B.III, *Roots II*, pp. 235ff.]
108 *EN*: See Part One, pp. 153f. [*Roots I*, pp. 115f.: "The Gnostic threat."]
109 *EN*: Jonas, *Gnosis und spätantiker Geist* (*Gnosticism and the spirit of late antiquity*): v. 1, *Die mythologische Gnosis* (*Mythological Gnosticism*) (hereafter: *Gnosis*), pp. 139f. A two-page section titled "Sich-selbst-Sammeln" ("Gathering oneself") begins: "At this turning point in history, the path of renunciation of the world appears in this image, among others: *Gathering oneself out of the multiplicity of the world*" (*Gnosis*, p. 139).]
110 *EN*: Puech, "Der Begriff der Erloesung im Manichaeismus" ("The concept of redemption in Manichaeism"), *EJ 1936*, p. 255. [Cited as p. 139. This passage occurs in Puech's third lecture, titled "Die Verwirklichung und die praktischen Mittel der Erlösung" ("The realization and the practical means of redemption").]
111 *EN*: See Part One, p. 60. [*Roots I*, pp. 37ff.: "The affirmation of nature and nature's purity." First reference to Buber's term *Einheiligung* (hallowing), cf. *Roots I*, p. 42, n. 107.]
112 *EN*: Ibid. [*Roots I*, p. 37.]
113 *EN*: Jonas, *Gnosis*, p. 139.
114 *EN*: *R. Nachman*, p. 188.
115 *EN*: See Part One, p. 89. [*Roots I*, p. 55, "the almost sacral emphasis on consciousness."]
116 *EN*: *Great Maggid*, p. 39.
117 *EN*: Ibid., p. 107.
118 *EN*: See Part Two, p. 17. [*Roots II*, p. 14: "Wholeness and compensation"].
119 *EN*: *Chassid Büch*, p. 601. [*Tales I*, p. 277.]
120 *EN*: *Unterweisung*, p. 87.
121 *EN*: I Sam 10:6. [Trans. by E. Fox.]
122 *EN*: *Great Maggid*, p. 120 (emphases added).
123 Latin: Jesus (who is) capable of suffering.
124 *EN*: Puech, op. cit., p. 235.
125 *EN*: *Great Maggid*, p. 17.
126 *EN*: Birnbaum, op. cit., p. 86. [Birnbaum's text continues: "In actual fact, however, evil is the seat of goodness."]
127 *EN*: See above, pp. 133f. [*Roots II*, pp. 104f.: "The introversion of sacrifice."]
128 *EN*: *Enc Jud*, "Besht." [Horodezky, "Baal-Schem-Tob," col. 838.]
129 Here and elsewhere, "masculine" is a figurative term, defining an entity as active.
130 *EN*: Jung, *Beziehungen*, p. 207. [Referring to end of Jung's final chapter, "The mana personality" (cf. CW 7, ¶405). Cf. also *Roots I*, p. 28, n. 50.]
131 Cf. above, p. 135.
132 *EN*: *Unterweisung*, p. 26.
133 *EN*: *Great Maggid*, p. 201.
134 *EN*: Ibid.
135 *EN*: *Enc Jud*, "Besht." [Horodezky, "Baal-Schem-Tob," col. 838. Cf. also *Roots II*, p. 123.]
136 *EN*: See above, p. 136. [*Roots II*, p. 106: "Evil as a level of good."]
137 *EN*: *Chassid Büch*, pp. 434f. [*Tales I*, pp. 238f.]

138 *EN*: See Part One, pp. 169f. [*Roots I*, p. 125, n. 42, under "Law and rabbinism," on the *bat kol*.]
139 That is, active, from the Hasidic understanding of symbolic maleness (activity, causation, generation) and femaleness (passivity, receptivity, conception).
140 Ascribing a masculine "force of creation" to the woman at the moment of conception may seem contradictory. Sanford Drob advises that paradoxes of this kind are fairly common in Kabbalistic thought, where maleness and femaleness, understood symbolically, have more than one level of meaning.
141 Psalm 108:2. The "I" is the psalmist, who continues: "I will give thanks to thee, O LORD, among the peoples," etc.
142 This part of the Yom Kippur prayer declares that God's activity precedes that of humans. The next statement once again supports the main theme, that human activity precedes and determines the activity of God.
143 *vor*: "before" in the spatial sense.
144 *ehe*: "before" in the temporal sense.
145 "*Heil euch, Israel!*" (lit. "Salvation to you, Israel!") Erel Shalit advises that this translation follows the wording of Rabbi Jonathan Sacks.
146 *EN*: *Unterweisung*, pp. 100f. [paraphrased].
147 "*Im Anfang*": "In the beginning." This phrase (in Hebrew, *Bereishit*), rather than "Genesis," is the name of the first book of the Bible in Hebrew. B&R, following Jewish tradition, name the books of the Pentateuch by the first word or phrase of each.
148 *Unterweisung*, p. 117.
149 Cf. above, *Roots II*, pp. 69ff. and p. 76.
150 *EN*: Jung seminar, "Sonnenaufgangsmagie" ("Magic sunrise ritual"). [Probably referring to Jung's dream seminars of 1928–30, which were then available in typescript. The Elgonyi tribe's sunrise ritual is discussed in "Winter/Spring 1929," p. 113, and "Autumn 1929," pp. 52f. (Cf. McGuire, ed., C. G. Jung, *Dream Analysis: Notes of the seminar given in 1928–1930*, 1984, pp. 220f and 330f.) The same ritual is described in Jung's essay, "Die Erdbedingtheit der Psyche" ("Determination of the earth by the psyche"), published first in *Mensch und Erde* (*Man and earth*) (1927), then in *Seelenprobleme der Gegenwart* (*Current psychic problems*) (hereafter: *Seelenprobleme*) (1931). (Cf. CW 8, ¶329.) Neumann discusses sunrise rituals further in his 1943 lecture, "Symbols and stages of conscious development," Appendix B.I, *Roots II*, pp. 196f.]
151 Cf. above, *Roots II*, p. 133.
152 The phrase echoes Genesis 1:26, as interpreted by Buber, in *Reden über das Judentum*, op. cit., p. 109. Cf. above, *Roots II*, p. 69, n. 42.
153 *EN*: *Chassid Büch*, p. 574. [*Tales I*, p. 125.]
154 Ibid., p. 574. [*Tales I*, p. 125.]
155 There are many ways to interpret the Hebrew names of the *sefirot*. Buber's text refers to the fourth *sefirah*, which is both *Hesed* ("grace") and *Gedulah* ("greatness"), and the fifth, which is both *Din* ("judgment") and *Gevurah* ("strength"). (Cf. above, *Roots II*, pp. 69ff.) In her translation, Marx renders *Gnade* (lit. "grace") as "mercy," and *Macht* (lit. "power") as "rigor."
156 Ibid., p. 467 (paraphrased). [*Tales I*, p. 266.]
157 *EN*: See Part One, pp. 138f., and above [missing citation]. [*Roots I*, pp. 96ff., under "Apocalypse and redemption in time." Neumann's other reference may be to *Roots II*, pp. 18f., under "The messiah soul and actualized messianism."]
158 *EN*: *Chassid Büch*, p. 567f. (slightly paraphrased). [*Tales II*, p. 117.]
159 *EN*: See Part Two, p. 74. [*Roots II*, pp. 61f., under "The soul's teaching about the levels of nature."]
160 *EN*: Zohar III 48a, Franck, p. 166. [Cf. Appendix A, *Roots II*, pp. 186f.]
161 *EN*: Zohar II 70b, ibid. (slightly paraphrased). [Cf. Appendix A, *Roots II*, p. 184.]
162 *EN*: Ibid., p. 167. Also in Bischoff, p. 37: "'What really distinguishes the human being is his soul,' according to the Zohar (I 191a), 'the body is merely its dress.'" [Cf. Appendix A, *Roots II*, p. 184. Cf. also *Roots II*, p. 172.]

163 *EN*: Zohar II 76a, Franck, p. 167. [Here, Neumann omits the final word in Franck's translation: *adam*. Below, he repeats the end of this passage, elaborating it by adding *Adam Kadmon*. Cf. Appendix A, *Roots II*, p. 185. Cf. also *Roots II*, p. 171, n. 21.]

164 *EN*: *Bab Tlm Sanhedrin* 46b. [Tamar Kron advises that the statement occurs in Rashi's comment on the cited tractate.]

165 *EN*: Zohar II 12a, Müller [1932], p. 217 [Cf. Appendix A, *Roots II*, p. 184.]

166 *EN*: Zohar II 205b, Bischoff [1913], pp. 34f. [This Zoharic citation is perhaps an error. No equivalent text has been found in the Pritzker Edition.]

167 *EN*: Ibid., pp. 40f. [Neumann's typescript lacks a textual connection for this footnote. In Bischoff's volume, the cited section ("Der himmlische Mensch": "The heavenly human being") compares the metaphysical foundations of the Zohar with the theosophy of Jakob Böhme and the philosophies of Schilling and Hegel, all exploring the theme of a higher unity.]

5

HASIDISM AND THE BIRTH OF THE MODERN JEW

1. The place of Hasidism in history

Redemption by the God-man constituted the mystery of the entire Near East, with its dying and resurrecting son-deities. This role, together with the redeeming descent of the incarnate god—from the mediating function of the Pharaoh to the Gnostic *Nous*—is united in Christ.

But by uniting Christ with the historically unique figure of Jesus, Christianity, especially in its Pauline modification, actually annihilated the historical process. For early Christianity believed that the last days had arrived with the coming of Jesus Christ. From this point of view, church history is a long-term attempt to reconcile the unique fact of salvation, the death of the redeemer, with the still ongoing historical process.

This fact, which increasingly undermined Christianity, that all life had to be related to a salvation event at a certain time in history, was a disastrous legacy of Jewish messianism, which early Christianity—in a historical error—viewed as having been fulfilled. The later symbolizing view takes the death of Jesus symbolically as the saving act of Christ, the son of God, who became human and died for humankind. By separating Christ from Jesus, his historical projection, or making a detour around the conflict, this symbolization is one of the deepest causes for the insecurity of Christianity.

Mysticism and Protestant quietism sought to keep Christianity in harmony with human evolution through the imitation of Christ, and by identifying the Christ of "Christ in us" with the Self. This solution is a living development within Christianity, but it is the end of the Church.

The disintegration of Protestantism into a myriad of sects is an example of how the community can become atomized, until only individuals remain. This atomization could be a great opportunity for the development of the individual, but it can also lead to complete ruin.

For the religiously atomized individual is at the mercy of the collective power of the people and the state, and in danger of being swallowed by it. In this way, a progressive de-Christianization is taking place today, because the collective movement of modern man entails an obvious regression to earlier pagan levels, against which the individual cannot defend himself, or only with great difficulty. Thus, this process is especially affecting the Christian peoples, who—as peoples—are not actually Christian, and whose Christian culture has fallen into decay.

The Christianization of the Jew

Paradoxically, Judaism seems to be different. At the time of early Christianity, Judaism had arrived at its Christian stage,[1] when religious revelation became individualized and internalized. This led to the formulation of the heavenly kingdom *in* the human being, and to a rejection of cultic law, and consequently to an emphasis on direct revelation. All of this occurred as a direct extension of the prophetic concept.

Furthermore, in the messiah,[2] there appeared a new conception of the human being as the unifying symbol resolving the tension between heaven and earth. In this new conception, the likeness of God and humankind, their "twin-like nature," became the center of the redemptive event. Early Christianity then gave concrete form to this introversion of the messiah, specifically through Jesus.

The anti-Jewish Christian Church, with its strongly Gnostic and pagan elements, had lost the foundation of life in soil, people, and Temple. Its emergence now led to a recollectivizing within Judaism, in the course of which the previously achieved stage of development had to be abandoned.[3]

This recollectivization negated the individual and inner revelation, and resulted in a form of galut Judaism, the religious liveliness of which was in continual conflict with dogmatic, systematizing rabbinism. One may understand that this process was partly necessary, but that insight makes no difference to the negative consequences of the development, or the way it stunted Judaism.

The biblical canon is proof of a long and lively religious development, in which the Torah, the prophets, and the particular problems posed by Job and Kohelet[4] represent the most varied stages of religious development. Whether one gives higher value to one or another level, this fact of canonical development testifies to a living religious current within the Jewish people. Recollectivization, however, entailed a thorough going acceptance of the long-established tendency to view everything only as the interpretation of a revelation that was concluded once and for all. Any new possibility of revelation was consciously excluded.

It was not until Hasidism, and before that to some extent in the Kabbalah, that this recollectivizing was suspended. This enabled, on a new, inner level of history, a reconnection with ancient Judaism in its primal Christian form, which saw religious individualism as the core of religious revelation.

With Hasidism, which had the mana-figures of outer redemption in its *tzaddikim* and the inner figure of the messiah in *Adam Kadmon*, the Christianism of Jewish individuals took a new historical form. Here, at last, the primal Christian teaching of Judaism reaches maturity: that the son of man is the redeemer; the heavenly kingdom is within; the world is to be accepted, and suffering with it. This teaching now appears, not projected onto the figure of a mediator, but as the central and personal task of each individual.[5]

The Christianization of the Jew then becomes, among modern Jews, a Protestantization. This parallel becomes visible in the fact that Protestants and Jews, unlike Catholics, have many of the same crises and developmental processes in common.[6]

But already the evolving dominance of *Adam Kadmon* in the Kabbalah, the emphasis on the dimension of *Hesed*, the importance of the female aspect of the deity, which plays a similar but even more strongly repressed role in medieval Judaism than in Christianity, the role of asceticism and martyrdom, which is characteristic of pre-Hasidic Judaism, all of these traits correspond to an unconscious Christianization in Jews of the Middle Ages. These features are alien to Jewish antiquity but typical of medieval Christianity.[7] This fact, which cannot be demonstrated here, but only hinted at, does not mean that Judaism was outwardly influenced by Christianity, which it fiercely excluded as a matter of principle. Rather, it is the result of a process of inner spiritual development, which continued within Judaism beyond primitive Christianity, just as, after early Christianity, it also determined the course of Christian development.

The significance of this process can be recognized only when the Christianization of non-Jewish peoples is revealed to be highly at risk, while paradoxically, at the same time, the Christianization of Judaism is becoming increasingly clear.

The transvaluation of Hasidism

We have already discussed the transvaluation of values[8] that had prevailed up to now within Judaism. But we must summarize it here once again, for only in this way can we see the historical position of Hasidism. Only by comparing the positive content of ancient revelation as a whole with the almost complete loss of revelation in the galut period of the Jewish Middle Ages can we perceive the broad significance that it has for Judaism when revelation re-emerges, with its new possibilities and new content. This re-emergence takes place in Hasidism. The underground tributary stream of truly powerful revelation, which—having been rejected and only partly received by official rabbinism—was handed down from haggadah and midrash to the Kabbalah, spread among the people in the messianic and pseudo-messianic movements. But only in Hasidism did it become a religious renewal that shaped the people as a whole.

Within Judaism, with its ancient adherence to inner revelation and also to the primacy of consciousness, development moved in the direction of rationalism, which ruled out creative religious revelation. A leading feature of rabbinism is the dominance of reason, but the breakdown of the relationship between consciousness and the creative unconscious led to a dogmatic rigidity of consciousness and life. Psychologically speaking, at that point two sets of symptoms merged into each other.

On the one hand, after the ancient period, Judaism is dominated by the rational, ascetic, and moral directive of consciousness, with its overemphasis on the male component. On the other hand, at the same time, it shows clear traces of the unconscious rule of the mother archetype.[9]

The castrating, infantilizing dominance of the mother archetype in every dogma, in every "mother church," paralyzes consciousness in its active, masculine, enlightening aspect, in its tendency to transform the contents of the unconscious. This dominance then leads in Judaism to the often sterile, formal, *pilpul*[10] rationalism, in which consciousness no longer reconquers the contents of the unconscious but only demonstrates its own sterility.

In this state, consciousness, which has completely cancelled its relationship with the unconscious, appears to be in charge. In reality, however, we are not dealing here with a free system of consciousness, such as we see in the Enlightenment and to some extent also in the modern human being, who constructs a new worldview and a new world for himself, unconditionally and progressively. Rather, this consciousness is enslaved to the Torah, a dogmatically controlling system of contents, in relation to which consciousness does not move freely, nor does it behave in the active, masculine manner that is appropriate to its nature. Speaking in archetypal images, consciousness usually plays the role of the masculine hero in relation to the feminine unconscious, that is, it enters into the womb of the unconscious, where it is always in danger of being swallowed. In repeated forward thrusts, it liberates new contents, causing the unconscious to conceive and give birth to them. Castrated consciousness, on the other hand, despite its rationalism, moves within the womb of the Torah like a child-fish, giving up its own masculine principle and suspending its lively creative relationship with the unconscious.[11]

Dogmatic paralysis also means a complete paralysis of life. When we hold up the old values and contrast them with the assertions of Hasidism, we once again see the whole, fundamental opposition that exists between moribund rabbinism and the new life that Hasidism brings.

When static references to the Law are transformed once more into a dynamic relationship with existence, it is a signal that a relationship between consciousness and the creative unconscious is everywhere being sought, established, and called for as the supreme religious principle.

The creative relationship with the unconscious can be discerned in the way the sparks enliven the world, and in the relationship to the divine everywhere, which must be established at all times and places. As the place of revelation is separated from the Temple and Zion, from the ritual and the cult, and transferred to the world and the everyday, so the time of revelation is separated from times of prayer and festival, and transferred to ordinary time. Parallel with these, the priestly function, separated from the *cohanim*,[12] Levites, and cult officials, has been transferred not only to the *tzaddik*, but to "everyone in Israel."

Here, too, we are dealing with the revival of an ancient Jewish theme. Just as in antiquity the prophetic potential and priestly function of the individual were crucially important, so this basic principle of being a "nation of priests" had been preserved in the form that the father of the house consciously exercised priestly functions within the family on the Sabbath and feast days. The rebirth of this original priestliness takes place in the irreplaceability of the individual before God, in the latent tzaddikhood of each individual and in the central meaning gained by the individual as an individual for the entire lower and upper creation. However, it is worth pointing out once again that this revival, in its transvaluation, goes so far as to set aside the meaning of the exile by saying:

> Look, today, in the days of the galut, it is easier to reach the Holy Spirit than at the time of the Temple.[13]

Here re-emerges *Adam Kadmon*'s demand that every individual actualize his unrepeatable wholeness, with the result that tradition and the certainty of knowledge become relative. This relativizing of ethical values—pure and impure, good and evil, knowing and unknowing—is expressed in the principle of "good uncertainty."[14] And the tradition of "the merits of the fathers"[15] is also abolished, for what is needed is one's own light and the new revelation. At the same time, the principle of reward and punishment, which supports morality, is also abolished, because repentance, the transformation of human beings, which may and must occur at any time, creates an ever new relationship between humanity and God, consciousness and the unconscious. So, too, new and unforeseeable connections and possibilities are constantly discovered in the world.

The aspect of wholeness, which emerges in Judaism with the realization of *Adam Kadmon* as the Self, also leads, as we saw, to a reconstellation of the problem of masculine and feminine. The creation of wholeness presupposes a realization of the male and female aspect in every human being, which is also a central problem of the individuation process for modern people. And this creation of wholeness is possible only in a living relationship between consciousness and the unconscious, a relationship in which each of these authorities realizes both its male and its female aspects. Consciousness realizes this duality by actively relating to the unconscious and transforming it, while also reacting receptively to the contents of the unconscious, waiting, listening, letting in, accepting. At the same time, the unconscious constellates itself in its male–female aspect by responding in a feminine way to the "prior activity" of consciousness and proving to be fruitful, and also in a masculine way, by entering, transformingly, into this consciousness, now opened to it. This reciprocity of the changing relationships occurs under the sign of *Adam Kadmon*, of the balanced scales, the wholeness beyond opposition. Within and in the presence of this reciprocity, the opposites and the parts of the soul are unified.

Only now, in Hasidism, does a new connection take place between the principle of YHWH and that of the earth. Here, this pair of opposites does not lose its inner tension through reduction, nor does it break apart;[16] rather, it is overtaken by a new concept of wholeness.

In antiquity, this tension occurred at the collective level, in cosmic, collective symbolism, projected outwards as an opposition between JHWH and earth.

In the apocalypse, to be sure, the subjective component was strengthened, but the contrast between heaven and earth, above and below, was still projected into the psychic universe as heaven and hell. In Hasidism, this situation takes a new form.

We have already shown how the problem was taken inward, from the collective to the subjective and from outside to inside. It is very important that this problematic area was internalized for Judaism through the efforts of Hasidism.

The introversion of these problems leads to the extraordinary emphasis of Hasidism on the subject. The process once again takes place under the sign of *Adam Kadmon*, but this is no longer projected macrocosmically, as in the Kabbalah. Rather, what needs to be established now is the microcosmic meaning of *Adam Kadmon* as the Self, the inner human image.

With this internalizing, the character of collective projection comes to an end, and the symbolic and psychological meaning of the YHWH–earth polarity becomes real as a psychic constellation. The process of internalization is expressed in the whole worldview of Hasidism, with its emphasis on the inwardness of the world, its perception of the world as a symbol, and its relativizing of the relationship between inner and outer.

We have tried to show from various angles how the human relationship with God and the world depends on progressive processes of spiritual expansion and ascent. We have also explained that the world, in its relativity—even the real, outer world—becomes transparent to the human soul as its central authority, by which it is always being constituted in new and different ways. As a result of this inward shift in Judaism, precisely these aspects are enabled and realized.

This inward shift, in which the human being appears as the mid-point of the world, runs parallel to the process by which the divine migrates into humanity and appears there as the Self. It was only in this way that the relationship between God and humankind became psychologically tangible in its twin character, in its aspect as cause and as identity.

This shift from the collective to the single individual also changes the image of the messiah. The messianic era was made to depend directly on the individual's psychic development, on his ability "to bring about unifications and ascents." In Hasidism, this gave rise to what we have called "the actualizing of messianism."[17]

The principle of presentness removes the provisional nature of the Jewish-human existence that characterized existence in the galut. It shifts the emphasis that had hitherto been on the historical process, the subject of which was the collective, the people, to the course of life, the subject of which is the individual.

Until then, the history of salvation, the plan of salvation, had overshadowed all of life, because the contingency of the individual and of single generations was located somewhere in this superordinate but rationally unintelligible historical context; in this context, the ruler was YHWH, and paradoxical indeterminacy mocks all understanding.

Attempts to calculate the end-time, the messianic era, or to accelerate it, or, as happened in pseudo-messianic movements, to regard it as fulfilled, had proven to be incorrect and impossible. Only by internalizing even the messianic problem would the Jewish person be able to approach a new solution.

Jewish historiography understood world history up to then as a process that to some extent wrote itself and acted of itself. By moving outside of ordinary history,[18] Jewish history made itself into a mere object and a spectator. The Jewish person renounced the active role, because, although exile was regarded as a punishment, its end was seen as a gift of liberation, depending solely on the divine. To be sure, this end should be prepared for by the attitude of the Jews, but it could also happen, even without that, when the plan of salvation was fulfilled.

Here, too, an energetic counter-movement begins with the Kabbalah, because it saw as its highest goal to "push toward the end" through the individual's ascetic and mystical effort, that is, to exert an increasingly active influence on the meta-historical course.

In Hasidism, the collective aspect of messianism is not ended, but it is suspended, becoming dependent on the life of the individual and his capacity for fulfillment. The image of *Adam Kadmon* as the messiah and the symbolism of the messianic kingdom now emerge in the individual as the Self and its symbolism. At this level, psychologically formulated, the messiah and the messianic kingdom at the end of time prove to be a collective projection of the individuation process into the future.

Here, as everywhere, it becomes evident how important the historical factor is for Jewish people. Just as, in late Jewish antiquity, the process of human transformation and its images were projected onto the historical process,[19] now we see that individuation, the process of becoming human, and the creation of *Adam Kadmon*'s wholeness, was originally projected onto the process of the world's creation.

With the new central emphasis on the individual and on his introjection of collective psychic projections into his psychic space, the collective history of the world is replaced as the object of religious experience by the history of individual destiny. Depending on the comprehensiveness and depth of self-understanding, this individual history then becomes the object of religious experience.

This shift does not mean, as we have already suggested, that the destiny of the collective and of humanity loses this aspect—as little as the importance of the community disappears as a result of the central emphasis on the individual. But it turns out that from now on this more comprehensive aspect will become legitimate and available for experience only when the individual aspect is fully realized and fulfilled. Only a person whose individual life has become transparent, as destiny, can discern the destined meaning of the history of a people and of humanity. But, if an individual's destiny is meaningless, it cannot be compensated for by viewing the overarching, collective fate as directed by a plan of salvation, or as meaningful in some other way.

At the historical moment when this individual, in his irreplaceable religious importance and dignity, has become the unique place of divine revelation, there is no longer any collective aspect that can compensate for the fact of his refusal or his inadequate realization.

How this aspect of destiny appears in the psychology of the modern person, and what a decisive role it plays there, will occupy us elsewhere.[20] There, too, we shall see how a personal realization of collective destiny dissociates a person from the constraint of the outer collective, whereas it also leads to a rooted connection with the inner collective's creative forces.

The psychological process within Hasidism corresponds to something like a collective individuation event, in which many *tzaddikim* achieve this individuation process of realizing *Adam Kadmon*. They do this as individuals, while at the same time they prototypically appear to the people as mana-personalities. Beside which, however, Hasidism also represents (if such a thing exists) a collective individuation process for Judaism, for the previously dominant functions, thinking and intuition, were sacrificed, whereas the inferior function, with its close affiliation to the collective unconscious, was made conscious and realized through its connection with the feminine dimensions of feeling and earth.

This process failed collectively, as we shall explain. And it had to fail, for the same reasons that made it possible in the first place.

For a short time, the individuation process, which normally relates to the single subject, became woven into a collective phenomenon. This strange entanglement was possible only because the same kind of problem that one sees in the individuation process of single subjects, the dissociation of the individual from the collective, had become dominant within Jewish spiritual and psychic development. This problem also seized Judaism collectively, as a process in the history of ideas.

In this sense, the Hasidic period, by reinstalling the individual, anticipates the individualization of the Jewish person, dissociated from the primitive collective of the Jewish people. Thus, it marks the birth of the isolated modern Jew, needing the individuation process as the only escape from his crisis situation, which is the psychic situation of modern Jews. What makes Hasidism so significant for the modern Jew is precisely this, that it anticipates some essential questions of his problematic situation as an individual, while also answering them in a way that anchors the individuation event collectively, as it were. That is, by making it possible to reach the *inner* seedbed of Judaism through individuation, it prevents the individual from dissolving in the void of an individualistic atomization.

This inner rootedness does not mean recollectivization, in a regressive sense; it means only being grounded in a continuity of Jewish psychic space. For other peoples, this rootedness has been represented in real and concrete terms by land and culture, nation and community, such that every individuation is embedded in the self-evident existential space of life.

Hasidism's dynamic conception of the world and humankind seems to have broken the magical circle that the unconscious rule of the mother archetype and the dominance of rational consciousness had cast around the Jewish person. A religious life and a religious revelation became possible again in the sign of the bond between consciousness and the unconscious, that between YHWH as *Tiferet* and the *Shekhinah* as *Malkhut*, and the reconnection between YHWH and earth, spirit and life.

This development is dominated, in general and in particular, by the Self, the archetypal image of *Adam Kadmon*, which was once said to be identical with divinity; this is why the human being is said to have been created in the image of God, but about which it is also said:

> The true human being is the soul,[21]

and

> Within the human being lies the deep secret of the heavenly human being, *Adam Kadmon*.[22]

It is not our task to describe the decline of Hasidism, or to write a psychology of the nineteenth-century Jew. But here, let us briefly consider the development of the Jewish person in the period between Hasidism and modernity. For a series of related problems leads us to the psychology of the modern Jew, and various *leitmotifs*, which preoccupied us in our discussion of antiquity and Hasidism, can also be traced during this period.

The decline

The fact that Hasidism never seriously attempted to push the boundaries of legalistic Judaism, even externally, but always moved within its tight confines, hindered its influence on Judaism. Here, the tendency toward renewal, which was all too much directed toward inwardness, took its toll. Hasidism was also ruined because its self-awareness was not radical enough, and it knew too little about the real message that it brought.

The decline went in various directions. Early Hasidism rapidly deteriorated into tzaddikism. The way Hasidism declined recalls the way the prophetic potential of the individual was insufficiently realized in Jewish antiquity, and so the institution of prophetism compensated for the elevation of Moses to a mana-personality, on the one hand, and for the people's failure, on the other.[23]

The emphasis on the sacredness of the individual regressed now to the projection onto *tzaddikim*. Originally, there had been no substitution or replacement for the individual. Now, as mediators and representatives, the *tzaddikim* removed those traits from individuals, concentrating them on themselves instead. This eventually gave rise to a form of tzaddikism in which a mass of followers, stripped of selfhood, gathered around the mana-personality of a *tzaddik*, whose behavior ranged from primitive, magical, and mystical procedures to holding court in a worldly, dynastic, and grandly delusional manner.

Another historical trend in the decline took the form of regressing, going back to the rationalism of Kabbalistic rabbinism. For example, the Hasidic movement Chabad[24] went in this direction. It began by attempting to find a compromise with the Kabbalah and rabbinism, and in the end it was devoured by the same old dragon[25] of rational rabbinism, against which early Hasidism had aimed its original act of liberation and redemption.

Here, the "evil principle" was interpreted once again in the manner of medieval Christians and Jews, seeing, "body and blood"[26] as the source of evil, and body and world as hindrances to the soul. True, old orgiastic tendencies did break out once again in Hasidism, especially during its recollectivized period of decay, and the carnal enthusiasm of the Hasidim admittedly called forth justified objections, more or less reflecting early Hasidism. But this protest was also supported by the familiar arrogance of the Kabbalistic–aristocratic thinking type.[27]

Rabbi Nachman of Breslov, the descendant of the Baal Shem, attempted unsuccessfully to draw on early Hasidism, to create a renaissance of its primary tendencies. Not only did Nachman die too young,[28] but also his genius, which was powerful enough to gather a sect, no longer had the power to move a whole people. All the contents and currents of the Hasidic beginning were alive in him, and he shaped what are perhaps the most revolutionary formulations of the Hasidic movement. But he was already an individual, in the sense of deeper self-reverie and self-consciousness. Mystical and poetic elements were stronger in him, rather than the ones, present in the Baal Shem and the Great Maggid, that could embrace a world and form a people, seizing and transforming even outer reality.

At the far edge of Hasidism and its decline, we find figures of varying stature and depth. Descendants of the leaders and founders of Hasidism, they themselves were still *tzaddikim*, but they were seized by the historical period that operated underground, unshaped by the consciousness of Hasidic leaders, to drive the fate of Judaism away from Hasidism.

Mendel, the *tzaddik* of Kotzk, introduced a strangely un-Jewish, wild, and violent streak into Hasidism. His disciples were a brutal bodyguard, combining violence with rationalism. His dictatorial claim militantly radicalized the Leader principle, combining it with ancient Talmudism and an anarchic nihilism that finally enabled him to burst the boundaries. His unfolding of early Hasidism, in which he declared drives and desires to be parts of God,[29] led not only to the formal elimination of the separation between Sabbath and daily life, but also to atheism. He blew Judaism apart with Acher's saying: "There is no judge and no judgment." Thereafter, he retreated into thirteen years of solitude and isolation—or insanity. Around his barely recognizable figure flashes the same light that consumed Nietzsche.

Baer of Leowo of the Sadigura dynasty[30] is a weak final figure, but he, too, is a symbol of his time. A *tzaddik* who wanted to free himself from the deceptive tzaddikism of the declining period, he abandoned Law and religion and demonstratively escaped into superficial enlightenment. But instead of breaking free, he let himself be caught by it, just as he eventually let himself be recaptured by his tzaddikistic family. Treated as a standard bearer by the Enlightenment and also by Hasidism, celebrated as a spirit of progress and also as one who repented, he is actually insignificant as a person. If he is meaningful, nevertheless, it is because in him the development made strides, inexorably, and with inner justification, until it seized all of Judaism, that is, the development toward consciousness, the Enlightenment, Europe, and the western world.

2. The psychology of assimilation

As Hasidism declined, it relinquished to rabbinism the revolutionizing of Judaism that had been carried out within it. Thus, it actually helped to strengthen the medieval Jewish position. This brought it into the starkest contrast with the Enlightenment, which, in conformity with western European development, represented progress.

Through Hasidism's self-betrayal, the meaning of the individual and his relationship with the creative nothingness of the deity was lost, and the principle of inwardness and hiddenness degenerated into a deceptive lowering of mass intelligence. This gave the Enlightenment, even in its most superficial form, real legitimacy as the pioneer of Jewish intellectual development.

Secularization and atomization

It was a historical necessity that Judaism should leave medievalism behind, and also that the individual as an individual should loosen his primitive ties with the social, national, and religious collective. As a result, when the Hasidic revolution failed, there were no restraints on the secularizing and atomizing of the Jewish person.

Hasidism regressed to a stage that was morally below the level of rabbinism, because, along with its inner self-abandonment, it also abandoned the principle of consciousness. The danger facing any movement that represents a transmoral religious principle is that its decline will stir up primitive, pre-moral stages of culture. Hasidic superstition, amulets, exorcisms, magical cures—in short, all forms of power belonging to the mana-personalities—now begin to flourish, which makes the fanatical rejection of Hasidism by its opponents almost understandable.

From the legitimate principle of hiddenness, what followed was that any action of a *tzaddik*, no matter how unintelligible or immoral, could be interpreted as a higher mystery and revered. When this occurred, it showed the appalling danger in the saying:

> In every incomprehensible thing, there is a real part of God.[31]

This is a genuine principle of mysticism, which played an especially important role in Sabbatianism, for example. But here, in declining Hasidism, it became a veil that concealed deceiving and self-deceiving attitudes.

The focus of development now rightly shifted to the opponents of Hasidism. It must be added, of course, that, here as elsewhere, the anti-superstitious Enlightenment profoundly misunderstood the true meaning of religion and with it early Hasidism. Emancipation led to the extraversion of the Jewish person, who was bound to see in Europe, shaped by the French Revolution, the representatives of consciousness and human progress. With flying colors, Jews went over to this Europe, which represented liberty, equality, fraternity, the progress of consciousness, and individual freedom.

Nineteenth-century western humanity offered the Jewish person precisely those contents that he accepted as the supposedly governing values, values necessary and important for life, and for his development out of his own history. For this reason, a passionate assimilation now began, unprecedented in its energy, in which the Jewish person committed all his strength to assimilating the western world. Over the course of two to three generations, he achieved this, at least outwardly, to an extraordinary degree. As a result of this development, we see Judaism's conquest of western positions in all fields.

Memory loss and assimilation

This extraversion of Jewish energies, which was necessary to enable the assimilation of the western world in this short period of time, because it achieved a legitimate emancipation from the medieval Jewish collective, took place within the individual as an individual. Hand in hand with this development went a radical individualization and a phenomenon that might be called memory loss.

Every loosening of unconscious ties is followed by a stage in which consciousness isolates itself from the content that requires detachment. Affective suppression from consciousness usually characterizes the first stage of dissociation, in which consciousness wants nothing to do with its former ties, because detachment is difficult and not yet fully accomplished.

The Jew's loss of memory in the nineteenth century refers to his entire collective attachment to Judaism, both outer and inner. Forgetting and denying one's origin, and the violent tendency to exclude this collective layer, characterizes this era of Jewish attempts at assimilation. Only now does the second and real rootlessness of the Jewish person take place. As an atomized individual, he has also lost and abandoned the inner seedbed of his collective ties, which had until then, albeit with great difficulty, compensated for the loss of a real homeland and the foundation for a livelihood.

Many negative Jewish traits are determined by this historical situation of the Jewish person, who is on his own as never before, and as no member of any other people has been. Everywhere in the world, the community must provide the necessary corrective for the dubious quality of individual autonomy, so the absence of this corrective community poses a major threat. At this stage, because it suffers from memory loss, the Jewish community is powerless. To be sure, communities in which assimilation takes place do correct the Jewish person, but their corrections operate only through consciousness, the law, public opinion, etc. For every genuinely rooted person, there is an inner and unconscious communal correction, which comes partly in the form of instinct and custom, folk traditions and educational ideals, but partly also as a product of breeding, which is the basis of children's early learning. This inner communal correction is now always lacking for the Jewish person. It is lacking especially wherever Jewish assimilation faces strong resistance, whether this resistance comes from the host people or from the Jewish unconscious itself.

The Jew's staggering and honest attempt, collectively, to find his lost ground among other peoples and to take root there must be explained in terms of this context. We cannot go into detail here, but, as a general observation, his memory loss extends to the entire layer of the collective unconscious. And his lack of instinctive relationship with all collective contents, especially all *Jewish* collective contents, is symptomatic of this development.

Apart from the fact that it is a consequence of turning outward, this memory loss is a symptom of the Jewish person's unconscious self-rejection. We can understand the Jew's lack of self-knowledge, and his invariably astonishing refusal to gain this self-knowledge, only if we realize what it means for the individual to clash with the western world and its culture, while burdened with his inner Jewish structure, the historical and basic principles of some of which we have tried to elaborate. The average individual was in no position to carry out the fundamental struggle with the western European person that a self-aware Judaism would have had to battle its way through.

Memory loss for the sake of assimilation is the decisive direction of Jewish development in the nineteenth century, and we must understand its justification. The extraversion of assimilation means the de-ghettoizing of the medieval Jew and marks a partly successful attempt to incorporate the western world and its contents into one's own—unknown—structure.

The Jewish person's passionate and genuine love of the "world of others" arises from the semi-conscious awareness of his own structural deficiencies. After the ancient period,[32] Jewish development had led to outer rootlessness and the affirmation of this situation in principle. The earthly realm, both inner and outer, was largely lost, in terms of the affinity with nature and also of instinctive life. The psychic world, too, had become so repressed, so overgrown by the exaggerated emphasis on conscious intellection, that life became constricted in its scope—though not its intensity.

Life under the Law, with its conscious provisionality—awaiting the end, and paralyzing every present moment—was a matter of intellectual and dogmatic rigidity. This rigidity was radically systematized, so strongly that, apart from the various times of flourishing, when there was always an earthly contact with other cultures and it was possible to assimilate in their direction, the only counter-tendencies for which we have evidence were the powerful, messianic moods and collective movements. It was not until the seventeenth century that this artificial, rigid system began to be disrupted and dissolved from within, first by the Sabbatean–messianic movement, which seized large swaths of the people, and then by Hasidism.

The far-reaching exclusion of the intrapsychic region, which was rejected as the origin of inner revelation, had even managed to sterilize the Jewish person, to such an extent that he also became artistically unproductive. This, too, was in striking contrast to Jewish antiquity.

The assimilation and emancipation of Judaism occurred in two distinct directions. One of these was the *continuation* of Judaism's cultivated, rational attitude, with its emphasis on consciousness, which fitted the situation of the nineteenth-century western world. Wherever the development of reason and consciousness is valued, the Jewish person stands in the avant-garde, thanks to the cultivation[33] of his conscious structure. The development of the sciences, and all rational plans, penetrating judgments, and clarifications, are areas obviously well suited to the Jewish person. Here, he conformed with western development, especially during the nineteenth century, and adapted to it successfully. This was true of his achievements in science and technology and in the areas of sociology and law. It was also true of his political activities, aimed at new planning, and of the practical application of science and theory, both in his preferred liberal professions and in business.

The other direction to be noted was the Jewish people's remarkably strong dedication to art, stemming from their collectively unfulfilled psychic needs. In this regard, however, it is hardly accidental that they overemphasized the aspects of reproduction, empathy, and mediation, whereas the aspect of production was less developed.

The strong musical talent of Jewish people, which remained bound to religion until emancipation but found powerful, life-pervading expression in Hasidism, also expressed itself at first largely reproductively. An extraordinarily high proportion of Jews is active in the musical life of the world, especially as reproductive artists. They also play an important role in theater and artistic commentary. If the Jewish person is pulled toward western art, it is not on account of its existing collective presence; rather, it stems from his urge to compensate for what is missing and provide a field of action for his hitherto blocked energies. This need for compensation becomes particularly urgent for Jews who have lost even the remnants of the ground of inner, psychic rootedness. These were the remnants mediated to them by a national and religious collective existence—in customs and festivities, religious symbolism, and religiously permeated family life—up to the time of secularization and individualization.

Within Jewish development, Hasidism produced a groundbreaking reconnection with the previously excluded earthly aspect, the world's feminine side, which extends from earthly, bodily, and material reality to the creativity of feeling and the soul. This reconnection also helps to determine the development of the emancipated Jew, who, in his loss of memory, seems to have lost every collective tie.

The materialist leaning of Marx, like that of Freud, is characterized by this emphasis on the earth, which corresponds to a profound requirement of the Jewish person. But, once again, even this emphasis on the earth has a rational accent. This combination of rationalism and earth is typical of Jewish emancipation and is always accompanied by a strong idealistic ethos. Materialism belongs to the system that develops hitherto unrealized features, whereas the idealistic tendency of the Jewish person, which is equally strong and striking, belongs to the system that preserves existing dominants. Despite all of life's restrictions, even in the Middle Ages, morality and idealism have always characterized the Jewish conscious structure.

The memory loss associated with extraversion prevented access to the inner world and the creative layer of the unconscious. That is why, up to now, it has been impossible for so many Jews to gain the depth of their own resources. In this context, it is striking that even for Freud and Adler, the Jewish founders of depth psychology, the collective layer of the unconscious has remained largely undiscovered. This is not surprising in Adler's case, on account of his rationalism. But in the case of Freud, whose profound genius repeatedly touched on this layer from the outset, a special explanation is needed. This misconception was apparently based not only on the personal[34] but also on the collective Jewish problem, for Freud refused to acknowledge that the problem of the Jewish collective, which was then emerging, needed to be dealt with.[35]

We cannot begin to show here how attitudes typical of Jewish character derive from the collective situation. Some of these may result from Jewish memory loss. Others may be conditioned by the conflict, conscious and unconscious, between the tendency to assimilate and the unconsciously operating Jewish collective structure.

The great delusion

Only one point remains to be mentioned, because it has come to have far-reaching historical implications, especially for the psychology of the modern Jew.

This point concerns the great delusion in which the Jewish person has found himself in relation to the western world, and partly still finds himself. And this grand delusion is beginning to turn, dangerously, into a great disappointment.

The phenomenon of memory loss has made the Jew unhistorical. That is, it has not only alienated him from his own historical context but also blinded him to the fact that such a historical context exists. And the phenomenon of collective individualizing of the Jewish person has led him to turn toward "absolute" and "general" human values, to an extent that was bound to avenge itself most terribly.

Jewish emancipation took place during a historical era of the west in which the inherent movement of Jewish development coincided harmoniously with western development. This harmonious encounter significantly enhanced the illusion of possible assimilation, and indeed of its realization. It seemed as if the best strengths of the Jewish person had arrived at the perfect time to express themselves in the west, while excellently promoting its development, characterized by the advancement of consciousness and the values proclaimed in the French Revolution.

But western development is also based on the Christian and national pasts, which differ greatly among the various European peoples, in terms of both their cultural and civilizational stages and their psychological structure. Western development in the nineteenth century was characterized by the Enlightenment and, despite the process of nationalization, by the development of a common humanity. The direction of culture advances as far as the transpersonal concept of international connections. The concept of the European and western person emerges. And the initial signs of a common humanity begin to appear in all areas, even transcending the west.

Any such development could be affirmed and encouraged only by the Jewish person, according to his nature and situation.

Then, however, the historical development of the west begins to recede. As soon as this happens, indeed as soon as a dialectical counter-movement of nationalistically irrational, anti-conscious elements begins to determine development, nineteenth-century assimilation—to the extent it was naively taken for granted—must be exposed more and more starkly as a grand delusion.

But the grand delusion, which would lead Jews, especially in the twentieth century, to the brink of absolute despair, is also symptomatic of a loss of their own instinctive foundation. Only a Jewish consciousness restricted to rationalism, which failed to recognize the backgrounds and substrata of human nature, could, with touching unworldliness, have considered western ideals to be the only realities. This illusion was once again underpinned by the loss of memory, which made Jews forget their prior experiences with western people and led them to believe seriously in a superficial ideology of progress.

The atomization of the Jew caused the Jewish people, as a people, to ignore and discount both the intuitives, who saw the dangerous background and announced its impending approach, and the cultural pessimists, who drew attention to the negative structure of the human soul. As if blinded, this ancient people abandoned itself with the naive trust of a child to the enticing deception of the west, and no pogroms, no ritual murder trials, no anti-Semitic movements persuaded it otherwise.

One could frankly say that the wave of assimilation that seized the Jewish people was the wave of a new, hidden, pseudo-messianic movement, foreshadowing for them the long-awaited arrival of the messiah, albeit in enlightened, western garb. Only the passionate longing to have *finally* reached the shores of a peaceful and unbarbaric world explains the terrible blindness with which the Jews hurled themselves into the deadly light of deception by the west, a light that, in the annihilation of European Jewry, became a gruesome beacon for the victory of the primal fire, which nothing human has tamed.

If we hearken back to earlier historical eras in the western world, the Jews are necessarily excluded, for they did not share the experience of these western eras. The Jew is a historical novice in European existence, in almost everything that does not concern the development of western consciousness. Lacking a connection with the depth of one's own collective layer leads not only to a lack of creativity, but also to uncertainty about one's position in society, which leads to many misconceptions, both about the surrounding world and about oneself. The gradual neuroticizing of the Jewish person, however, and his efforts to compensate through counter-movements, no longer belong to nineteenth-century psychology; rather, they are aspects of the psychology of the modern Jew in general.

At this point, it is important only to recognize that Hasidism, the degeneration of which apparently rendered it historically powerless, and which plays absolutely no role in modern Jewish consciousness, nevertheless has a hidden, crucial meaning for the psychology of the modern Jew.

Here, we are not referring to subterranean influences or transmissions, but to the fact that, within every people, there is a continuity of psychic life. The set of inner problems that seized the Jewish people—still in its collective state—in Hasidism, and which expresses itself in the attitudes of Hasidism, is covered over for the modern Jew by other problems. But when one probes deep into the psyche of the individual modern Jew, detached from the collective and caught up in apparently highly individual crises, time and again one comes upon basic questions and answers about Jewish existence that were prefigured by Hasidism.

In our further attempt to say something about the modern Jewish situation, we must investigate to what extent Hasidism is relevant, not only to problems of the modern Jew, but also to those of modern people in general. If we find, however, that crucial distinctions lead the non-Jew and the Jew to solutions that are different in their emphasis, that discovery will teach us the whole significance of Hasidism for modern Jewish psychology.

Notes

1 *EN*: See Part One, pp.107f. [*Roots I*, pp. 79ff.: "The end of direct revelation."]
2 In translating, we treat "messiah" as a common noun, except when it is clearly meant as a title. (Cf. *Roots I*, p. 81, n. 28.)
3 *EN*: See Part One, pp. 168f. [*Roots I*, pp. 124f.: "The exclusion of inner experience."]
4 Hebrew: Ecclesiastes.
5 Cf. *Roots II*, pp. 111ff.: "Accepting the world."
6 Referring to his planned Part Three, Neumann adds: "This observation will occupy us in detail elsewhere."
7 *EN*: See Part One, p. 174. [*Roots I*, p. 129, under: "The loss of earth, inner and outer."]
8 Apparently alluding to Nietzsche's phrase: "*die Umwertung aller Werte*" ("the transvaluation of all values").
9 *EN*: See Part One, pp. 178ff. [*Roots I*, pp. 131ff.: "The secret victory of the mother archetype." Also, Neumann knew Jung's "Psychologische Aspekte des Mutterarchetyps" ("Psychological aspects of the mother archetype"), *EJ 1938*, portions of which are published in CW 9,i.4.]
10 Hebrew: "hair-splitting argumentation."
11 *EN*: Author, "Psychologie des Mythos" ("Psychology of myth"), op. cit. [Cf. *Roots II*, p. 127, n. 41. Perhaps referring to an early version of Part One of *Origins and History*. In that work, under "The Great Mother: The Ego under the Dominance of the Uroboros," a footnote reads: "Negative castration symbolism is typical of the hostility of the unconscious to the ego and consciousness, but is closely associated with the positive symbol of sacrifice, which stands for an active offering up of the ego to the unconscious" (*Origins and History*, pp. 53f., n. 16).]
12 Hebrew: "priests."
13 *EN*: *Great Maggid*, p. 160. [Cf. also *Roots II*, p. 104.]
14 Cf. *Roots II*, p. 90, under "Unknowing and belief."
15 Cf. *Roots II*, p. 103.
16 *EN*: See Part One, pp. 148ff. [*Roots I*, pp. 115ff.: "The dangerous ending of the YHWH–earth tension."]
17 *EN*: See Part Two, pp. 22ff. [*Roots II*, pp. 17ff.: "Contraction in time" and "The messiah soul und actualized messianism."]
18 *EN*: See Part One, pp. 150f. [*Roots I*, pp. 103f., "This historic upheaval in the history of humanity . . . . "]
19 *EN*: See Part One, pp. 138ff. [*Roots I*, pp. 96ff.: " Apocalypse and redemption in time."]

20 Apparently a reference to the author's planned Part Three.
21 *EN*: Zohar II 76a, Franck, 1844 (1913), p. 167. [Cf. *Roots II*, p. 155. Cf. also Appendix A, *Roots II*, p. 185.]
22 *EN*: Ibid. (paraphrased). [Franck's translation clarifies the verse by adding "*Adam*," which Neumann elaborates: "*Adam Kadmon*."]
23 *EN*: See Part One, p. 43. [*Roots I*, p. 27: "The elevation of Moses and the introduction of prophecy."]
24 From the Hebrew acronym, חבד, for wisdom, understanding, knowledge. The name of "a movement and tendency within Hasidism which places particular emphasis on the role of the intellect in the life of religion" (Louis Jacobs, *A Concise Companion to the Jewish Religion*, 1999, p. 77).
25 Neumann's first reference to being "unconsciously devoured by the dragon of the Torah" appears in *Roots I*, p. 132.
26 Neumann attributes to both Christians and Jews in the Middle Ages the idea that evil stems from "body and blood" ("*Leib und Blut*"), meaning that, in their orthodox teachings, medieval Christians and Jews shared a suspicion of physicality.
27 The excessive rationalism of rabbinical teaching is attributed, here and above, to a collective, dominant thinking function. Cf. *Roots II*, pp. 7f.)
28 Rabbi Nachman (1772–1810) lived and taught in Breslov, Ukraine.
29 *EN*: *Chassid Büch*, p. 403. [Buber describes Mendel of Kozk as "Rabbi Bunam's intellectually strong and wretched pupil," and quotes Mendel's radical statement: "Humanity is a part of God. Human beings have drives and desires. These, too, are a part of God."]
30 The lineage of the Sadigura dynasty may be traced back to the Baal Shem Tov in Ukraine. For a period, from 1850 to 1914, these *tzaddikim* were based in the city of Sadhora (Sadigura), Bukovina, then under Austrian rule. Dov Baer Friedman of Leovo (1822–1876) was a late, minor figure in this lineage.
31 *EN*: *Great Maggid*, p. 107.
32 Neumann sees the end of Jewish antiquity beginning with the destruction of the Solomonic Temple (cf. *Roots I*, p. 9, n. 24; p. 58, n. 156).
33 *Gezüchtetheit(?)*: handwritten correction, difficult to read. In typescript, the original word is *Űberlegenheit* (dominance, superiority).
34 *EN*: Michaëlis, op. cit. [This is Neumann's first reference to the 1925 book by Edgar Michaëlis, *Die Menschheitsproblematik der Freudschen Psychoanalyse: Urbild und Maske* (*The human problem of Freudian psychoanalysis: Primal image and mask*). No page cited.]
35 *EN*: Analyzing Freud's last book, *Moses and Monotheism*, in which, shortly before his death, he discussed the problem of the Jewish collective and accepted the collective unconscious as a fact, might make it clear to what extent his typical inner conflict also applied to the Jewish problem.

APPENDIX A

Passages from the Zohar in English translation

When Neumann quotes from the Zohar, his sources vary among three different German editions, all of them more paraphrases than translations. These three volumes, by Erich Bischoff (1913),[1] Adolphe Franck (1844/1913),[2] and Ernst Müller (1920),[3] were probably present in Neumann's own library, for he seems to have known them intimately. He skips freely among them, occasionally comparing different versions of a particular passage.

In preparing this volume, we felt it was vital to respect Neumann's creative process and train of thought, and so we could not substitute standard English translations for the paraphrased passages from the Zohar that he chose with such a free hand. His Zoharic passages have therefore been translated as they stand.

To assist the reader, this appendix provides alternate English translations of these Zoharic passages, mainly drawn from the masterful, newly available English translation of the Zohar, the twelve-volume Pritzker Edition:[4] *The Zohar* (ספר הזהר) (*Sefer ha-Zohar*) (2004/2016), translated from a critical Aramaic text by Daniel C. Matt.

It was not always possible to locate exact parallels in Matt's English translation, for two main reasons. First, the medieval Aramaic documents comprising the original text exist in many forms, with many variants, such that, even with years of critical reconstruction and reorganization, Daniel Matt cannot be said to have produced a "final" version. Also, his translation is deliberately imaginative and poetic. This is a major virtue, giving the Pritzker Edition much of its brilliance. But these features—the translator's reorganization and interpretation of texts—also mean that, when putting the Pritzker Edition side by side with other translations, one is sometimes hard pressed to establish close parallels.

Besides which, it appears that many of the passages Neumann cites are summaries, paraphrases, or variants of Zoharic texts. He normally names both his German source and the Zoharic passage that underlies it, but many of his footnotes are handwritten and difficult to read. For all these reasons, despite patient searching, a few alternate translations have proven impossible to locate.

To the extent possible, what follows are parallel passages from published English translations (primarily the Pritzker Edition), corresponding to the Zoharic texts quoted by Neumann. These passages are ordered by their location in the Zohar. They all come from the Pritzker Edition, except for one passage that was not found in Pritzker but in the older Soncino edition. Page numbers in square brackets indicate corresponding passages in *The Roots of Jewish Consciousness*.

Zohar I, 2a

Pritzker, v. 1, p. 8. [Cf. *Roots I,* p. 154, n. 76.]

> When Concealed of all Concealed verged on being revealed, it produced at first a single point, which ascended to become thought. Within, it drew [. . .] a deep structure emerging from thought, called מי (*Mi*), *Who*, origin of structure. Existent and non-existent, deep and hidden, called by no name but *Who*.
>
> Seeking to be revealed, to be named, it garbed itself in a splendid, radiant garment and created הלא (*elleh*), *these*. אלה (*Elleh*) attained the name: these letters joined with those, culminating in the name אלהים (*Elohim*). Until it created אלה (*elleh*), it did not attain the name אלהים (*Elohim*). Based on this mystery, those who sinned with the Golden Calf said 'אלה (*elleh*), *These, are your gods, O Israel!*' (Exodus 32:8). Just as מי (*mi*) is combined with אלה (*elleh),* so the name אלהים(*Elohim)* is constantly polysemous. Through this mystery, the universe exists.

Zohar I, 19a,b

Pritzker, v. 1, pp. 146f. [Cf. *Roots II,* p. 36.]

> The human being below has an image and figure, yet does not endure in the manner above. The figure and image above are drawn as they are, with no other garment to be drawn, so they endure constantly. The human figure below is drawn in a garment, in no other manner, so they endure for a set time. Every single night, the spirit strips itself of that garment and ascends, and the consuming fire consumes it. Later they are restored as before, figured in clothes. So they do not endure as those figures and images above, and of this is written: *New every morning* (Lamentations 3:23)—human beings who are *new* every single day. [19b] What is the reason? *Immense is Your faithfulness!*[5] (ibid.)—immense, not small. *Immense is Your faithfulness!—immense*, indeed! For it can grasp all creatures of the world, absorbing them in itself, higher and lower. A place immense and vast, absorbing all, filled no further. This is the mystery: *All the rivers flow into the sea, yet the sea is not full; to the place the rivers flow, they flow back again* (Ecclesiastes 1:7). They flow toward the sea, who grasps them, consumes them, and is filled no fuller. Then it pours them out as before, so they flow on.

Zohar I, 27b

Soncino,[6] v. 1, p. 105. [Cf. *Roots I,* p. 160, n. 117.]

> God commanded Israel: "thou shalt not uncover thy mother's nakedness" (Lev 18:7), and this captivity is the uncovering of the nakedness of the Shekinah, as it is written, "On account of your sins your mother has been

put away" (Is 50:1), i.e., for the sin of unchastity Israel has been sent into captivity, and the Shekinah also, and this is the uncovering of the Shekinah. This unchastity is Lilith, the mother of the "mixed multitude."

Zohar I, 51a

Pritzker, v. 1, pp. 282ff. [Cf. *Roots II,* pp. 77 and 84.][7]

Whoever desires to penetrate the wisdom of holy unification should contemplate the flame ascending from a glowing ember or a burning candle. For flame ascends only when grasped by coarse substance.

Come and see! In a flame ascending are two lights: one, a white light, radiant; the other, a light tinged with black or blue. The white light is above, ascending unswervingly, while beneath it is the blue or black light, a throne for the white, which rests upon it, each embracing the other, becoming one. This black light colored blue, below, is a throne of glory for the white—here lies the mystery of the thread of blue. This blue-black throne is grasped by another substance below, so it can flame, arousing it to embrace the white light. Sometimes this blue-black turns red, while the white light above never wavers, constantly white. This blue one, though, changes color: sometimes blue or black, sometimes red. This is grasped in two directions: above, by that while light; below, by what lies beneath, by which it is fueled, primed to glow. This constantly consumes and devours what is placed beneath it, for the blue light consumes anything cleaving below, anything it rests upon, since by nature it consumes and devours. On it depends destruction and death of all.

So it consumes anything cleaving below, while that white light hovering over it never devours or consumes, nor does its light waver. Therefore Moses said, '*For YHVH your God is a devouring fire*'—really *devouring*, devouring and consuming anything found below. That is why he said *your God*, not *our God*, for Moses inhabited that white light above, which does not consume or devour.

Zohar I, 51b

Pritzker, v. 1, p. 285. [Cf. *Roots II,* p. 84.]

Since this blue light by nature consumes and devours anything cleaving below, when favor prevails and the candle burns indivisibly, then this verse applies: *Fire descended from heaven and consumed the offering* . . . (1 Kings 18:38). Then it is known that the candle burns in a single union, a single bond: blue light cleaving to white light, and it is one. Below, it consumes fat and flesh of the offerings, though only when it ascends, joined to the white light. Then peace pervades all worlds, all linked inseparably.

Zohar I, 51b

Pritzker, v. 1, p. 286. [Cf. *Roots II,* p. 84.]

"In a dream all colors bode well, except blue," for it devours and consumes continuously. It is a tree of death spreading over the lower world, and since all abides beneath, it consumes and devours.

Now you might say, "It also prevails in heaven above, yet countless powers above endure." Come and see: All those above are encompassed by the blue light, but those below, not so, for they constitute coarse substance upon which it alights, so it devours and consumes them.

Zohar I, 55b

Pritzker, v. 1, p. 314. [Cf. *Roots II,* p. 82.]

Male and female He created them. From here we learn: Any image not embracing male and female is not fittingly supernal. So we have established in the mystery of our Mishnah.

Come and see: Anywhere male and female are not found as one, the blessed Holy One does not place His abode. Blessings are found solely where male and female are found, as is written: *He blessed them and named them Adam. . . .* It is not written: *He blessed him and named him Adam.* One is not even called אדם (*adam*), human, unless male and female are as one.

Zohar I, 191a

Pritzker, v. 3, p. 166. [Cf. *Roots II,* p. 155, n. 162 (approximately parallel).]

Rabbi El'azar said, "Even if a soul is not within him, the righteous never undergo a change from the original nature of their image."

Zohar II, 12a

Pritzker, v. 4, p. 57. [Cf. *Roots II,* p. 155.]

We have learned the mystery of the matter, for this implies that just as father and mother generate a body on earth, so all aspects—whether above or below—come into being from male and female. They have already established the secret that is written: *Let the earth bring forth a living soul* (Genesis 1:24). *The earth*—Assembly of Israel. *A living soul*—soul of supernal Adam, as has been said.

Zohar II, 20a

Pritzker, v. 10, p. 511. [Cf. *Roots II,* p. 69.]

He fashioned this world corresponding to the world above; all that is above has its counterpart below; and all that is below has its counterpart in the sea—all is one.

Zohar II, 70b

Pritzker, v. 4, p. 390. [Cf. *Roots II,* p. 155.]

For there are two *adams* recorded in this verse: one, mystery above; one, mystery below. [. . .] After the matter was revealed from the initial secrecy of the verse, He created *adam* below, as is written: *On the day of God's creating adam, a human, in the image of God He created him.*

Zohar II, 76a

Pritzker, v. 4, p. 409. [Cf. *Roots II,* pp. 155, 171.]

But surely, the human being is nothing but soul!

Zohar II, 76a

Pritzker, v. 4, pp. 409f. [Cf. *Roots II,* p. 171]

Bones and sinews are chariots and all those forces stationed within. All of them are garments for what is within: mystery of אדם (*adam*), human, who is innermost.

So too, mystery below. The human is the innermost within, his garments corresponding to what is above. Bones and sinews correspond, as we have said, to those chariots and camps. Flesh covers those camps and chariots, standing outside; this is the mystery conveyed to the Other Side. Skin, covering all, corresponds to those heavens covering all. All of them, garments clothing the innermost within, mystery of human. All a mystery, below corresponding above.

So, *Elohim created the human in His image; in the image of Elohim He created him* (Genesis 1:27)—twice here *Elohim,* one pertaining to male and one pertaining to female. Mystery of human below inheres entirely in mystery above.

Zohar II, 91b to Exodus 20:7

Pritzker, v. 4, pp. 525f. [Cf. *Roots I,* p. 143, n. 24.]

לא תשא (*Lo tissa*), *You shall not take* [*the name of YHVH your God in vain*] (Exodus 20:7). . . . For when the blessed Holy One planted the world, He sank into the depths a single stone, engraved with this Name, plunging it into the deep. When the waters desire to rise, they see the mystery of the Holy Name engraved on the stone, and they retreat and subside, turning back. This name endures to this day in the deep.

When human beings swear an oath truly, upholding the truth, that stone rises and receives that oath, then returns, established upon the deep. The world endures, maintained by that oath of truth.

When human beings swear a false oath, that stone rises to receive it—but it is false! Then the stone rising turns back; waters surge and the letters of that stone fly through the depths and scatter. The waters verge on rising and covering the world, returning it to its original state. But finally the blessed Holy One summons a prince, Ye'azriel [. . .]. He approaches that stone and engraves the letters upon it as before; then, the world endures, and the waters return to their place.

Zohar II, 113b to Exodus 32:19f

Pritzker, v. 5, pp. 133f. [Cf. *Roots I,* pp. 143f., n. 25.]

Come and see: In the moment of which is written *He smashed them at the bottom of the mountain* (Exodus 32:19), the Ocean overflowed, rising to flood. Moses saw the Ocean rising toward them, threatening to flood the world. Immediately, *He took the calf that they had made and burned it . . . and scattered it over the face of the water* (ibid., 20). Moses stood over the waters of the Ocean and said, "Waters, waters, what do you want?"

They replied, "Was not the world established solely by the Torah of the tablets? For the Torah betrayed by Israel—by making the Golden Calf—we intend to inundate the world."

Immediately, Moses said to them, "Look, all that they made is delivered to you! Those thousands of them who have fallen, is it not enough?" Immediately, *he scattered it over the face of the water*. Yet the waters did not subside until he took some and made them drink . . . .

Zohar II, 142a

Pritzker, v. 5, pp. 301f. [Cf. *Roots I,* pp. 40, 152; *Roots II,* pp. 74f.]

For all these form a single bond, corresponding to the pattern above in the mystery of *nefesh*, *ruaḥ*, and *neshamah*. All is one, one bond.

Nefesh has no light of her own at all. This is the one who shares in the mystery of a certain body, delighting and nourishing it with all that it needs, as is written: *She provides food for her house and a portion for her maidens* (Proverbs 31:15). *Her house* is that body, which She nourishes; *her maidens* are those limbs of the body, all of them.

Ruaḥ is the one who rides on this *nefesh*, controlling Her, illumining Her with all that She needs, and *nefesh* is a throne for this *ruaḥ*.

Neshamah is the one who generates this *ruaḥ*, controlling Him, illumining Him with the light of life, and that *ruaḥ* depends upon this *neshamah*.

Zohar II, 176b

Pritzker, v. 5, p. 535. [Cf. *Roots II,* p. 81.]

For until there was a balance, they did not gaze face-to-face, and the primordial kings died and their weapons vanished and the earth was nullified. Until the head of Desire of all Desires arranged and bestowed garments of glory.

This balance hangs in a place that is not; weighed upon it were those who did not exist. The balance stands on its own, ungrasped and unseen. Upon it rose and upon it rise those who were not, and who were, and who will be.

Zohar III, 10b

Pritzker, v. 7, p. 55. [Cf. *Roots II,* p. 80 (approximately parallel).]

. . . Daughter, *Matronita*, in whose hands all weapons are found. Hidden in all worlds—by Her they emerge and enter, by Her those below are nourished.

Zohar III, 48a

Pritzker, v. 7, pp. 301f. [Cf. *Roots II,* p. 155.]

Therefore, this image appeared only fittingly, as is written: *YHVH Elohim formed* האדם (*ha-adam*), *the human* [. . .] by a complete name, just as he is completion of all, consummation of all.

It has been taught: Adam was created on the sixth day, when the Throne was completed and called Throne, and it is written, *The Throne had six steps* (1 Kings 10:19)—*adam* appeared, who is worthy of sitting on the Throne. And it has been taught: Once Adam was created, all was perfected, all above and below, and all was included in Adam.

Zohar III, 65a

Pritzker, v. 7, p. 427. [Cf. *Roots II,* p. 79.]

Come and see: All those plants and all those burning lamps all shine and glow, are watered and blessed, from that flowing, gushing river, in which all is comprised, totality of all. This is called Mother of the Garden, above the garden, for Eden joins with Her, not parting from Her. Consequently, all springs issue, flow, and water in every direction, opening gateways in Her. So Compassion derives from Her, Compassion is opened in Her. Yet since we call Her Mother–Female–*Gevurah* and Judgment issue from Her. She is called Compassion in Her own right, yet from Her side judgments are aroused; so it is written as Compassion, yet vocalized as Judgment—letters in Compassion, yet Judgment drawn from Her side: יהוה. This is one rung.

Zohar III, 104a,b

Pritzker, v. 8, p. 170. [Cf. *Roots II,* p. 79.]

God created the human in His image. In the Book of King Solomon I found as follows: When coupling occurs below, the blessed Holy One sends a certain form—like a human visage, imprinted and engraved with an image, poised above that union. If the eye were empowered to see, one would glimpse above his head an image imprinted with a human visage. In that image the person is created; until that image, sent by his Lord, is poised above his head, hovering there, the person is not created—as is written: *God created the human in his image.*

That *image* remains present by him until he issues into the world. Once he does, in that *image* he grows, with that *image* he moves—as is written: *Only with an image does a human go about* (Psalms 39:7).

Zohar III, 144a

Pritzker, v. 8, p. 451. [Cf. *Roots II,* p. 72.]

In this array appears perfection, faith of all, poised upon the Throne, as is written: *an image like the appearance of a human being upon it above* (Ezekiel 1:26), and it is written: *Behold, with the clouds of heaven came one like a human being; he reached the Ancient of Days and was brought before Him* (Daniel 7:13).

Zohar III, 232a,b

Pritzker, v. 9, p. 569. [Cf. *Roots II,* p. 73 (approximately parallel).]

From within the liver and its lobe issues מרה (*marah*), bile, which is the sword of the Angel of Death, dripping those bitter drops to kill people, as is written:

In the end she is מרה *(marah), as bitter as wormwood, sharp [as a double-edged sword]* (Proverbs 5:4). [Bile] derives from the liver, and all fatal illnesses depend upon it.[8]

On that day, it roams the world, gathering all sins of the world. And all of Israel are in distress, and they take a shofar to arouse that *teru'ah*, alarm, and *teqi'ah*, blast—strict Judgment with Compassion and lenient Judgment with Compassion. Then they are aroused similarly above, and all are sweetened with one another. Whatever that liver obtains, it offers to the heart, who is king, to judge. But the heart is not drawn to, not does it desire, the foul deeds of its people. Rather, it obtains all that is pure and clear—all the merits and good deeds—whereas all that foulness and dirty filth it casts upon the other nations. Once the heart takes all those merits and good deeds—what is fittingly pure, choice, and clear—the liver takes all those sins and filthy dirty deeds, against its will, and casts them upon the other nations, as is written: *The goat shall bear upon it all their iniquities* (Leviticus 16:22). For so it is: once the heart takes all that is pure and clear, the liver takes all that is left—the filthy dirt and foulness—and casts it into all the other limbs, against its will.

Zohar III, 234a

Pritzker, v. 9, p. 580. [Cf. *Roots II,* p. 73 (approximately parallel).]

The spleen follows the nature of the liver; the latter was created on the second day, the former on the fourth in the act of Creation. Consequently, there is no good omen on the second or the fourth—death of adults, death of little ones.

Zohar III, 258b

Pritzker, v. 9, p. 646. [Cf. *Roots I,* p. 155, n. 94.]

This day is the day when the Bride enters the canopy, leaving all aspects of evil, having observed days of purification fittingly. This is the mystery of 'The King tastes the flavor of a virgin.' Therefore concerning [*Shavu'ot*] it is not written אשה (*isheh*), for another one did not approach the sanctuary, but rather was distanced from there. Thus there are no אישים (*ishim*) here, nor should there be, and Israel is distanced from the Evil Side, having counted days of purification—days and weeks—and having been absorbed into days of purification.

Zohar III, 296a

Pritzker, v. 9, p. 840. [Cf. *Roots II,* p. 82.]

In the hair of the Female, colors are mingled.

Zohar III, 296a

Pritzker, v. 9, pp. 842f. [Cf. *Roots II,* p. 82.]

The Male extends on the right and the left, through the inheritance that He receives. When colors combine, He is called *Tif'eret*, Beauty; and the entire body is arrayed as a great and mighty Tree, beautiful and fine. *Beneath it the beasts of the field find shade, and in its branches dwell the birds of heaven, and there is food for all in it* (Daniel 4:9).

His arms, right and left. In the right, life and *Hesed*; in the left, death and *Gevurah*.

Notes

1 Bischoff, Erich, *Elemente der Kabbalah, Teil I: Theoretische Kabbalah. Das Buch Jezira, Sohar-Auszüge, Spätere Kabbalah, Übersetzungen, Erläuterungen und Abhandlungen* (*Elements of Kabbalah, Part I: Theoretical Kabbalah, The Book of Creation, Zoharic excerpts, later Kabbalah, translations, commentaries, essays*), Berlin: Barsdorf, 1913.

2 Franck, Adolphe, *Die Kabbala, oder die Religions-Philosophie der Hebräer* (*The Kabbalah, or the Hebrew philosophy of religion*), *Aus dem Französischen übersetzt, verbessert und vermehrt von Adolf Gelinek* (translated from the French, revised and expanded by Adolf Jellinek), Leipzig: Hunger, 1844; 2nd edn, Berlin: Lamm, 1913. This work of French philosopher Adolphe Franck (1809–1893), *La Kabbale, ou philosophie religieuse des hébreux* (Paris 1843), was "the first attempt at a comprehensive scientific description of the beginnings and contents of the Kabbalah in popular form" (Skolnik, ed., *Encyclopaedia Judaica*, 2007, v. 7, p. 175).

3 Müller, Ernst, *Der Sohar: Das heilige Buch der Kabbala, nach dem Urtext herausgegeben* (*The Zohar: The sacred book of the Kabbalah*, edited from the original text), Wien: Glanz, 1932.

4 So named for its sponsor, Margot Pritzker, and the Pritzker Family Philanthropic Fund.

5 Daniel Matt notes: "*faithfulness* . . . One of the many names of *Shekhinah*. See Zohar 2:214a; 3:35b" (Pritzker, v. 1, p. 147n).

6 The Pritzker Edition has a gap between Zohar I, 22a and Zohar I, 29a.

7 In three places, Neumann quotes different versions of this passage.

8 Matt's footnote reads, in part: "Bile is secreted by the liver. In ancient and medieval physiology, it is one of the humors associated with anger and melancholy. Here it is identified with the sword of the Angel of Death. . . . The verse in Proverbs describes the seductive 'strange woman,' identified here with Lilith" (*Zohar, Pritzker Edition*, v. 9, 2016, p. 569, n. 207).

APPENDIX B

The importance of consciousness in the experience of depth psychology[1]

I. Symbols and stages of conscious development

To understand the psychological situation of the modern human being and, in particular, to clarify the specific nature of the relationship between his consciousness and the powers of the unconscious, one must give a general account of the development of human consciousness. The task that confronts the modern human being in the relationship between the ego and the unconscious,[2] as well as the nature of his rationalistic isolation from the instinctive world and the creative depth of the soul, can be grasped only in the context of the general development of consciousness within human history.

To the best of our present knowledge, the early state of humanity is strongly dominated by the unconscious, as we know about it from the animal world. But, in the end, this state is only ever available as a reconstruction, because it precedes the evidentiary record of human history. In this record, contained in inventories and traditions, customs and cults, we are dealing with an early state of consciousness, showing how both culture and the culture of consciousness began. But we also gain extensive insight into the beginnings of human existence by considering the developmental stages of primitive cultures, certain psychological conditions of contemporary persons, both healthy and sick, and the psychological world of the child.

The archetypal image that characterizes this state is the uroboros, the serpent forming the eternal circle and carrying its tail in its mouth. This ancient symbol, the origin of which can be traced to Egypt,[3] is the dark dragon of the primordial beginning, a basic symbol of Gnosticism and alchemy.[4] At the same time, however, it also represents the primeval parents, who appear in innumerable myths, who cohabit and form an undivided pre-worldly unity, in which heaven and earth, above and below, male and female, are inseparably connected.

This uroboros is the primordial union of opposites, the Taigetu of Chinese philosophy, the twilight of prehistoric times, which carries the opposites within itself. Here, there is no consciousness yet to constellate the opposites, no conscious sun to divide the world into day and night. Thus, yesterday and tomorrow, white and black, consciousness and the unconscious, good and evil are all undivided. Here, everything still lives in and with each other in generative chaotic abundance. It is Bachofen's swamp stage, in whose climate lives this primordial dragon, the self-entwined serpent, about which is said: *Draco interficit seipsum, maritat seipsum, impraegnat seipsum* (It slays itself, weds itself, and impregnates itself).[5]

I and Thou, humanity and the world, inside and outside, individual and group: here everything merges with everything else, participates with everything else, and is inseparable. Even today, this world lives in us as much as ever, as the world of the unconscious. A reflection of the primal human situation and the original confusion of existence still exists today in the intersections, confusions, and connections of the dream and its figures. It lives on in the almost inseparably linked images and symbols of the unconscious and their tropically proliferating abundance, the allusions, intimations, associations, and hints of which confront consciousness in an overwhelming flood.

As the experiences of primitive peoples teach us, the early state of humanity is characterized by the ego's lack of psychic detachment from the powers and contents of the unconscious and of the world, a state called *participation mystique*.[6] In this interwovenness, the ego, the individual, is not yet an independent entity, and the system of ego-consciousness has not yet differentiated itself from the outer world, the world of physical things, of other beings, plants, animals, and humans. There, for example, the group is the real "person," in which the individual, who is not yet an individual, possesses only a very partial reality, and the tribe or family is entitled to dispose of him as one of their parts. There, the ego does not yet have any freedom. Only the "great" individual, the mana-personality of the medicine man or chief, the priest or the king, represents, as a leader, the representative ego and consciousness of the group, which, as the psychology of the masses still demonstrates is an id, directed by unconscious forces. This group id integrates the individual entity, as far as one already exists. That is, it blots out what distinguishes individuals from each other, which is still relatively slight at this stage, and melts the group together into a unit. In matters of the outer world, this unit blindly surrenders to the representative leadership of the chief, and, in matters of the inner world, to that of the medicine man.

The rites, such as war dances, which produce this group unit through *participation mystique*, extinguish the individual as such. In our day, correspondingly, drills and trainings are used by the military and similar organizations to reduce the individual, reversing human development by making the individual once again into a blindly functioning part of the group, in whom personal consciousness is largely set aside. Today, we are still experiencing all the advantages and drawbacks of this psychic situation of participation, transforming the individual into part of a group soul, including reduced individual responsibility as well as the increased capacity for experience and intoxication. Today, and in all periods of civilization, the developed ego-consciousness must be re-collectivized, whereas, in early humanity, the group was primary and the individual person was still undeveloped. In early times, accordingly, orgiastic group experience led to a real increase in personality, as in the mysteries and the sacred festivals. But for civilized people, along with the sense of intensification, corresponding mass experiences always reduce ego-consciousness and lead to a loss of personality.

Just as, in early humanity, the individual was not yet completely separated from the group, so, even today, human beings are not completely differentiated from nature. We see frequent cases of identification with animals, plants, and things. The human relationship with ancestral animals, as we encounter it in totemism, is merely one example of this universal interwovenness of the primitive with surrounding nature. Early humans live in a world continuum, in which outer and inner, ego and non-ego are confused and interwoven. The world of the dead and the spirits interpenetrates the reality of life, which is directed and influenced by invisible magical powers. All bound together, here, are animated things, holy places, mystical identities with animal groups, and magical phenomena, by which the cosmos depends on human activity, and the sun cannot rise unless a human being performs the rite. The continuous fabric of the psychic space of the early human world is influenced in equal measure by objects, that is, parts of the outer world, and imagoes, that is, subjective reflections of this outer world. Parts of the outer world animated by projections, that is, contents of the world enlivened by the psyche, such as sacred animals, haunted places, etc., take up the same space in its existence as "complexes," unconscious part-souls, and things in the real outer world. Woven into the multitude of these participations, the ego's spark flares up only here and there.

As Ernst Cassirer[7] has shown, the discovery of this subjective reality, of the ego and the individual, is reflected in the various stages of unfolding mythical consciousness. The differentiation between inside and outside becomes possible only when human feelings of selfhood and self-awareness are distinguished from the primary feelings of unity and of life that connect him with the world. But it was only because of this distinction between human and world, between I and Thou, that ego-consciousness succeeded in separating from its original participation.

The fact that early humans were completely at the mercy of the dark superiority of the world and the unconscious inevitably created a sense of permanent danger. The primitive's psychic world is highly vague and uncertain, and the demonic dominance of what we call the outer world, rife with disease and death, hunger and flooding, droughts and earthquakes, is infinitely heightened by its confusion with what we call the inner world. The character of the world, with its irrational, arbitrary invasions, is gruesome enough in itself for the primitive, being unmodified by any knowledge of its regularity, and it is increased and made uncanny by the dead and ghosts, demons and gods, witches and wizards. Invisible effects emanate from all these beings, and the reality of this causation expresses itself in fears and emotions, orgiastic states of possession and psychological mass epidemics, irruptive spring urges, murderous impulses, visions, dreams, and hallucinations. If we are to understand, however rudimentarily, the primitive's fear of the world and feeling of existence, we must know how great is the westerner's primordial fear of the world even today, despite his relatively high level of consciousness.

The effects of the seasons and growth are no longer crucial questions for us, nor are we completely at the mercy of the weather, storms, lightning, hail, flooding, and droughts, as early humans were. Illness has also emerged from the irrational fate of magical, demonic arbitrariness and from the overwhelming power of the divine, to become something with which individual and collective consciousness struggles. It has already become more or less the object of knowledge and action, and not only something to be passively endured. Even today, destiny and "coincidence" are still the territory of superstition, the ghosts of which surround fortune and misfortune, success and failure in an ancient, primitive way, with divination and consultation. But these are merely wishful thinking for the modern person, and are dealt with incidentally, without the individual's total commitment, in the back yards of civilization. In contrast, the problem of destiny in early and primitive culture represented a fearful content, central to the sacral life of the community and the individual, whose invocation in worship and prophecy, spell and magic took forcible hold of the group.

Being "in the unconscious," this primal state of humanity, corresponds to the embryonic state of human consciousness, still dawning in the belly of the primordial male–female dragon, which possesses an encompassing, nourishing, and protective motherly character for that which it contains. And yet this feminine still has a masculine character, just as the paternal also shines through the maternal, because the opposites are still undifferentiated here. The embryo's individual germ experiences the influence—sometimes female, sometimes male, sometimes motherly, sometimes fatherly—of the surrounding world of the unconscious. The mother with male genitalia is a primordial image that belongs to this stage, and a host of psychic traits, which need to be interpreted as a tendency to return to the motherly uterus, point to this early, primordial state with its pre-differentiation. For just this reason, the archetype of the uroboros, and the return to its primeval belly, therefore often means renewal and rebirth rather than death and regressive downfall, because consciousness keeps experiencing itself as a child of this primordial dragon, from which it has been born time and again since time immemorial. Consciousness rightly knows itself as the child of the unconscious, for it is one of the late products of the unconscious, even apart from human history. The emergence of consciousness from the unconscious can be repeatedly observed, not only in every child's development, but also every night, when consciousness, dying with the sun, sinks back into the depths of the unconscious, in order to be reborn in the morning and begin its day with new strength. The unconscious is the creative mother of human existence. Every idea and every thought, every word and every image, the work of art and the technical invention, even the state institution and the religious movement, stem from its creative abundance. Not only drives, instincts and bodily events, but also psychic life and, as depth psychology has shown, spiritual life, have their foundation in the unconscious. Perfectly unconscious life, which distinguishes the world that we call nature, combines senseless murderous destruction with highly meaningful instinctive creativity. The meaningful unit of the organism is as much its product as the deadly cancer that consumes it. This is the unity of being in the uroboros, which, like the swamp, begets, kills, and gives birth in the endless ring of eternal self-enclosure. Experienced by the child's consciousness, this world is the world of Bachofen's matriarchy, the world of mothers and the spinning Norns of Fate. The devouring evil mother and the nurturing good mother are the two sides of the great Mother Goddess, who rules in this psychic situation. Here, we are not dealing so much with historical stages, although these can also be taken into account, but rather with the construction of the psychological structure, as experienced by a developing consciousness. The world and the unconscious, which, as we have seen, are experienced at first as unseparated, are comprehended by developing consciousness in terms of this symbol and these archetypal images. The archetypes are the self-representation of this experience in the psyche.

From this perspective, mythology is a self-representation of the human mind. If, as Freud has already recognized, myths are the dreams of the peoples, then—insofar as we acknowledge these dreams as representing the psyche—myths are the self-representation of the collective human unconscious. The deepest problem of the collective unconscious is the relationship between consciousness and the unconscious. For the primitive, in contrast, the world and the unconscious are fused together. In the interpretation of mythology, the extraverted aspect consequently emphasizes the importance of factors in the outer world. These range from astronomical–astrological theories through sociological ones to the milieu theory of Freud's family drama. An introverted aspect, on the other hand, which searches mythology for the workings of the psyche in the inner world, arrives at the archetypes of the collective unconscious. This search was attempted, without sufficient awareness, by a part of Freud's school; it was accomplished by Jung's psychology.

The overwhelming power of the unconscious, its devouring and destructive side, whatever its origin and manifestation, is depicted as an evil mother, be it as the bloody mistress of death or of the plague, hunger, or flooding, of violent impulses or the sweetness that lures humans to destruction. As a good mother, however, she is the fullness of the giving world, the beatifying giver of happiness, the nurturing soil of nature, and the cornucopia of the bearing womb. Experienced in their instinctive association, the depth and beauty of the world daily promise and fulfill the goodness and grace of the primal creative source, of redemption and resurrection, of revival and rebirth.

In relation to all this, the ego of the conscious individual remains small and powerless. He experiences himself as defenseless and minute, contained and hopelessly dependent, an island in the infinitely expanding primal ocean. At this stage, consciousness has not yet wrested solid ground to stand on from the flooding reality of the unconscious. For the primitive, everything still lies hidden in a bottomless pit, amid the vortices of which he is tossed back and forth, without orientation, without distance, almost without resistance to this primal whirlpool of eerie existence, arising simultaneously from his own depth and the depth of the world to overwhelm him.

The consciousness of a child, which continually renews its connection of dependence with its native ground, only gradually becomes a growing, independent system. So, bit by bit, consciousness attains self-consciousness, a reflective and self-aware ego emerges as the center of consciousness. Even before this centering of the ego, consciousness already exists, just as we see the child acting consciously, even before self-consciousness emerges. But until this ego experiences itself as different from the unconscious and separate from it, the childhood stage is not surmounted, and an autonomous system of consciousness cannot be formed. This early stage of consciousness in relation to the unconscious is reflected in the mythology of the Mother Goddess in relation to her son–lover. The figures of Attis, Adonis, Tamuz, and Osiris in the cycle of Near Eastern culture are not only borne by the mother (on the contrary, this aspect completely disappears), but are also her lovers, loved and killed by her, and buried, mourned, and reborn. This figure of the son–lover has left behind the embryonic stage and childhood. In his way of growing up and differentiating himself from the unconscious, in his masculine otherness, he becomes a partner to the maternal unconscious; he is a son, yet also a lover. But he is not yet equal to the motherly feminine. In dying, he succumbs to it; he returns to it, and is swallowed by it. Now, the mother and lover turns into the terrible goddess of death. She is still almost playing with him, with his life and death, and his rebirth is still overarched by her dominance. Wherever the dying and resurrecting god is symbolically connected with earth's fertility and vegetative existence, we see the dominance of the Earth Mother, while the autonomous existence of the god remains questionable. Here, the masculine is not yet procreative. It is not yet a balancing, fatherly tendency over against the motherly, the feminine. Rather, it remains youthful and spring-like, being only the beginning of a self-development that detaches itself from the place of origin and from the dependency of childish relatedness.

The struggle of consciousness with the unconscious becomes evident when the overwhelming threat of the unconscious confronts an ego core, which begins to resist this danger, sets itself apart as distinct and other, defines itself as an ego, and thus detaches itself from indiscriminate participation.

Before consciousness is systematized, all human acts, characteristics, and functions have no relationship with each other or with a center. Just as the psyche appears in the dream as an unfolding of seemingly uncentered and loosely juxtaposed figures, events, moods, and situations, this, too, is the unconscious situation of the early human being. Dissolved in states of participation, he consists of fragments, which function as if they were independent and self-reliant units. The best way to understand this state, which still exists in significant measure in modern people, will be to understand its opposite.

Gathering oneself from the state of distraction, considering, coming to oneself, and concentrating are aspects of a retracting tendency that forms and expands consciousness. With the early human being, we may speak of a general projection of psychic contents. To him, everything is "outside." He is scattered across the world. He is stuck partly in the ensoulments of physical reality, partly in the group's transpersonal collective powers, etc. To come to himself, find himself, and differentiate himself, he must first withdraw himself from wherever he was scattered. Only this process of retraction leads to consciousness with its centered ego. The introjection of projected contents as a path of conscious realization is only one typical application of this general development. The most extreme form of strengthening consciousness is Buddha's ascetic, meditative withdrawal from the world. Whereas the condition of being dissolved in the world and in the unconscious is also a condition of being at their mercy, centripetal retraction liberates one from entanglement in this trap.

Consciousness as redemption: this great slogan stands written above all human endeavors to liberate the individual from being entangled by the uroboros dragon. Regardless of whether this uroboros is lived and interpreted as the dragon of earthly, sinful existence, as matter, body, and the lower world, as the unconscious, as hell, as the dominance of nature, or in any other way, the uroboros always represents the threat and lawless supremacy of unknown powers. In contrast to this chaotic darkness, consciousness, even only its germ, represents the most valuable and sacred good and the light to be protected, upon whose strength and brightness the future of humanity depends.

Light and fire, the basic symbols of consciousness and illumination, are therefore the great object of the cosmogonic myth of all peoples. Thus, "in the creation legends of nearly all peoples and religions the process of creation merges with the dawning of the light."[8] And therefore, the sun, and after it the moon, are *the* object of myth. For space and *orientation*, that is, the experience of the world and the development of consciousness, depend on light, which makes differentiation, that is, knowledge, at all possible. Even today, this sun-relatedness, this orientation toward the contrast between light and darkness, is widely evident in language, especially in the affinity of consciousness with the eye, the act of seeing, and the lighted space.

We find light and fire symbolism throughout religious history as a center, a sacred mid-point, a holy fire or light, an image of the sun, or a sun-oriented cult. Equally, the hero and savior, the sacred redeemer figure of all times and peoples, is always the bringer of light. It is always the hero who defeats the dark dragon, the old, the past, and the unconscious (those whom no knowledge illumines), and who frees the treasure, the new thing. The hero is always the light bringer, who lifts the treasure out of darkness and brings it into the world. Whether the treasure is symbolized as a princess or as a prisoner that needs to liberated, as a doctrine of wisdom or as a ritual act, as a pearl or as the water of life, all these contents and symbols demonstrate that the hidden and liberated light is an essential element.

This struggle for the light of consciousness pervades not only myths and fairytales, but also the world of religion and science, from prehistoric times to the present. It may be the fire of Prometheus, the light in Iranian religion, the higher light of the mysteries and Gnosis, or the hidden spark of alchemy and Hasidism, the inner light of nature, or the flowing, divine light in mysticism, the illumination of religion, or the "bright" consciousness of modern knowledge. Light is always associated with consciousness, its opposite with the negative dimension, the anti-conscious aspect of the unconscious. This dark side is the unknown, evil, and unilluminated, which devours the light. It is night, death, chaos, the dragon and the serpent of the abyss, the monster of the primordial beginning, Satan, the lord of darkness and the underworld; it is the "ancient enemy" of the church hymn,[9] against whom every hero must fight his battle.

The many variations of the mythical fight against the dragon make consciousness diverge even more from the unconscious, to the point of conflict and struggle against the mother dragon's place of origin. Here, the unconscious has become entirely negative, because consciousness fiercely defends its independence against the dominance of the unconscious and its determination to overwhelm. The hero's deed is to overcome the mother dragon, which means regression and death, dissolution and the surrender of masculinity. The dragon represents the eternal danger of castration, which threatens from the unconscious side for masculinity and consciousness, emasculation being the mark of the Great Mother's priests. Only those who surrender completely to her and sacrifice their distinctive selfhood may serve as her priests. But the hero is the opposite. As the mythical son, he has torn apart the uroboros of the primal parents in their union. By committing this original sin against the primal parents, he has placed himself at the center of the resulting tension of opposites. The son's creative act, through which he, as sun and consciousness, has divided the twilight of the primeval dawn into the opposites of heaven and earth, father and mother, spirit and life, is the great offence through which he has gained autonomy and independence.[10] Two myths clearly illustrate the transition from the Great Mother's son and lover to the dragon-fighting hero. The first is the ambivalent story of Oedipus, and the second is the *Oresteia*.

At first glance, Oedipus's slaying of the dragon might seem unequivocally heroic. His victory over the sphinx undoubtedly adheres to this archetype. Seen progressively, patricide is the necessary elimination of fatherly authority by identifying with it, and marrying the mother corresponds to the definitive conquest of the stage of youth, during which the son is only a son–lover, never a valid husband. But beside this progressive interpretation, which represents the development of consciousness to the level of dragon slayer, another, regressive interpretation takes priority, based on other, equally important facts in the Oedipus myth. When Oedipus defeats, conquers, and rapes the sphinx of the mother dragon, thus demonstrating the superiority of the masculine principle of consciousness and spirit over the feminine unconscious, these are not only the acts of a hero. Having acted unconsciously, he is still only half a hero, and when he learns what has happened, he does not stand up for what he has done. The beloved, once she is recognized as his mother, regresses to the figure of the great mother–lover, and he regresses from being a man to being a youth and her son–lover. He blinds himself, thus performing the spiritual self-castration characteristic of the cult of the Great Mother. Oedipus sacrifices his spiritual and masculine principle of light, the eye, the power of vision, the symbol representing the spiritual and conscious side of the masculine, just as the phallus represents its instinctual and active side. Identification with the Great Mother leads to the self-castration of her priests and lovers, and to their destruction. Oedipus has indeed progressed to masculinity, becoming a hero and a dragon slayer; but after the deed he is gripped by the old shock and by fear of the mother, and he regresses to the Great Mother's son–lover, and to his downfall.

Both developments are still linked in Oedipus, although a tendency to overcome the Great Mother ultimately fails. In the *Oresteia*, however, we see a further step toward this detachment from the mother.[11] Here, the son sides with the paternal principle. Identification with it is positively accomplished and leads to matricide, the clearest separation of the son from the mother. Here, the maternal does not appear as a partial aspect of the dragon. Instead, because this maternal principle has committed a decisive sin against the paternal, spiritual principle; it is consciously slain, in full clarity, as the mother.

The victory of Athena's and Apollo's world of consciousness, which stands up for matricidal Orestes against the mother-world of the pursuing Eumenides, puts the seal on a development of consciousness, which has advanced from the unconscious, the mothers, to a consciousness that has now established its autonomy in relation to the unconscious. The mothers are always on the side of the collective, the bloody and earthy unconscious, that dull, instinctive being by which, in custom and practice, no rights whatever are conferred upon the individual, which is to say, the ego.

In its essence, the *participation mystique* of early human collective existence emphasizes the maternal, because it is dominated by the embryonic situation of the single human being, who is not an individual but part of a group entity.

We shall not pursue the problem of mothers any further here, but we must at least highlight a mythical feature that is immensely important for the development of male consciousness in particular and male psychology in general. In the male's struggle against the mother dragon, the hero is joined by a helpful new element—a feminine one, which makes it especially important—namely, the sister and the sisterly.[12]

Siblinghood is that part of the male–female relationship that emphasizes humanity and community, thus representing for the masculine an image of the feminine that is closer to the ego and more positively disposed toward consciousness. Here, we are considering typical relational forms, not actual relationships. In every male–female relationship, as discussed elsewhere, the natural elements are mother, sister, wife, and daughter. Not only are these relationships typologically different, but they also have their legitimate place in the individual's development or misdevelopment. In actual relationships, however, mixtures of these basic types may occur. For example, a maternal or spousal aspect may be mixed into the real relationship with a sister. That is not the issue here, however. In the present context, what matters is that the sister, as a female image of the soul, represents a spiritual being: Electra at the personal level, Athena at the transpersonal. In herself, as an individual with ego-consciousness, the sister's representation of the feminine contrasts with the collective feminine aspect of mothers.

This is why the sisterly helps the man to overcome his fear of the unconsciously female, the dragon aspect of the Erinyes. In relation to the daughter, what is emphasized is protective superiority; in relation to the wife, it is the tension between polar opposites. The sister, in contrast, is the image that counters the mother's dangerous dominance. Brotherhood and sisterhood, in the human and spiritual shape that these are given, for example, in Christianity, counterbalance and compensate for the threat of the mother dragon. The anima, and the male ego's positive relationship with her, creates the saving counterbalance against any flooding by the uroboros. Only when it is connected with the feminine, in the form of the anima, can male ego-consciousness pacify the Erinyes, the powers of the underworld.

Another form of confrontation with the dragon of the unconscious is the fight with the dragon, in which the mother represents only the regressive and negative sides of the unconscious. The positive side is represented as the anima figure, the princess to be liberated, the victor's prize. Here, the mother–lover of the earlier stage, with her fatal dominance, has separated into the mother, who is overcome as a negative dragon, and the lover, who is liberated and married by the masculine victor.

When Jung's typology distinguishes between rational and irrational functions of consciousness, these terms have a meaning specific to his psychology. It should be noted, however, that consciousness generally develops toward rationality in a different sense. Rationality here means a differentiating orientation, no matter which function of consciousness helps to achieve it. Jung's typology has shown that it is a mistake to equate consciousness with thinking, and that any of the functions of consciousness—thinking, feeling, intuition, or sensation—can serve as the guiding function of consciousness.

However, in the development of consciousness, emotional, feeling-toned, psychic states are characteristically suppressed in favor of rationality and the conscious capacity for discrimination, which contrasts with irrational existence in the unconscious. The irrationality of the unconscious consists in the fact that in the unconscious the ego, being disoriented and unable to differentiate, finds itself possessed and driven.

The early human being lives in an unconscious world distinguished chiefly by *participation mystique* and is undifferentiated from animals, things, and inner states, his life governed by affect and emotion. We should not forget that the complexes, the unconscious contents dominating early humanity and greatly influencing us, as well, have been characterized as "feeling-toned complexes."[13] As is generally known, the tendency of complexes to take charge of feeling—here in the sense of emotionality—is the basis of Jung's association experiments,[14] which led to the discovery of the complexes. Both disturbances in the rational structure of consciousness, which become apparent in the association and repetition experiment, and physical arousal, which forms the basis of the psycho-galvanic phenomenon, are based on the feeling-inducing, emotional part of the complexes. This is the part that led, in fact, to their discovery.

Human development proceeds from the primitive, emotional human being to the modern one, whose expanded consciousness is largely shielded from this primitive emotionality, or at least it strives in this direction.

To understand the development of consciousness, or to reach the unconscious through the conscious personality, one must differentiate, distinguishing carefully between two components of the unconscious. This involves separating a material component from a dynamic–emotional component of the collective unconscious. This separation will become even clearer in what follows. First, it implies that the archetype, as an image, represents a content to be grasped by consciousness. This content, however, is always found together with a dynamic component, which is emotional and takes charge of the personality.

As long as the early human being lived chiefly in *participation mystique* with the contents of the unconscious, and as long as his conscious system was unable to exist independent of the unconscious, material and dynamic components were so closely associated that one may speak of their identity and complete fusion. One may even say that the visual image and the instinctive reaction were one. The emerging image, the material component, and the instinctive reaction to this image, which seized the psychophysical organism as a whole, and the emotional–dynamic component, were coupled in the manner of a reflex.

Originally, the perceptual image thus led, either outwardly or inwardly, to an immediate instinctive reaction to that image. This means that the coupling of the image with the dynamic–emotional component led immediately to flight or attack, anger or paralysis, etc.

As consciousness gradually develops, this early human reaction, in which both components were connected, comes to an end. The instinctive reaction, which occurs like a reflex arc, is delayed with the increasing development of consciousness and the cerebrum, due to conscious interventions, such as deliberation and reflection, which conflict with instinctive reactions. The instinctive reaction is gradually suppressed in favor of consciousness.

Consciousness must necessarily confront the instinctive reactions occurring in the unconscious, because instinct is also an overwhelming dimension of the unconscious, from which developing ego-consciousness must differentiate itself. Although the instinctive reaction represents "purposeful behavior," conscious development conflicts with the development of the ego, on the one hand, and with the world of instincts, on the other. Consciousness always needs to replace instinctive reaction with its own distinct and differently oriented, intentional behavior, because collectively toned, instinctive reaction is by no means always aligned with the individual purposes of the ego and its preservation.

Instinct frequently adapts only inadequately to individual situations, serving merely as a primitive layer and a primitive ego, whereas it often remains highly unuseful for a developed one. A sudden affective reaction that leads to manslaughter, for example, can prove most useful among savages in the jungle; yet in the normal life of civilized people, who do not happen to be at war with each other, such instinctive reactions are not only inexpedient, but even life threatening. Mass psychology gives us more than enough evidence that instinctive actions not only frequently make no sense from the ego's perspective, but also, very often, bring the ego to ruin, even if the collective sometimes benefits.

For the primitive human being and in all primitive conditions, the conflict between individual ego-consciousness and the collective tendencies of the unconscious is always resolved in favor of the collective, at the individual's expense. The instinctive reactions of the unconscious are very often unrelated to the ego, but rather to the collective, the species, etc. Time and again, nature demonstrates its lack of interest in the individual. Or as Goethe wrote about nature: "She seems to have designed everything for individuality and makes nothing of individuals."[15]

In contrast, conscious development also serves the individual. In the ego's confrontation with the unconscious, ever-greater attempts are made to protect the personality, to strengthen the conscious system, and to stem the danger of flooding and irruption from the unconscious.

Thus, as the ego progressively develops, it must do all it can to prevent a situation in which an image from the unconscious, an archetype with its emotional and dynamic component, compels the ego to react instinctively, so that consciousness is flooded by unconscious content.

With the development of consciousness, there is a tendency to separate the reaction from the triggering perceptual image, thus breaking up the original reflexive unit. In the course of this development, the material and dynamic components of the collective unconscious move further apart. Thus, it is completely consistent with conscious development that an emerging archetype no longer elicits from the human being an immediate, reflexive, instinctive response.

Objective reality may be that of the outer world or that of the inner, psychic world, the collective unconscious. Discernment of either of these objective realities is disturbed, even prevented, by the activity of the emotional, dynamic component of the unconscious. But consciousness with all its four functions, in the extraverted as well as the introverted attitude, is a cognitive organ, and its differentiation and that of its functions are possible only if the emotional component of the unconscious is excluded. The accuracy of the differentiated function is always clouded by the interference of the emotional component.

For the ego to be in a state of rest, in which it can practice discernment, consciousness and the differentiated function must be as far removed as possible from the impact of the emotional component. This component is demonstrably disruptive to every differentiated function, but, of course, the disruption is most evident with thinking, which is naturally opposed to feeling, and even more to emotionality. More than any other function, differentiated thinking must be "cool headed" and "cold blooded."

In each of the possible types, the emotional and dynamic component therefore remains linked to the poorly differentiated, inferior function. It can be found in that function and wherever that function is tangibly at work. Part of the deflation of the unconscious, typical of human development, involves the inception of the conscious act that divides unconscious contents into their two components, by breaking apart the original connection between content and emotional impact. This process also successfully puts an end to the instinctive reaction, with its primitive state of affective possession. Basically, then, conscious development involves the more or less powerful suppression of the emotional and dynamic component.

Elsewhere, we attempt to show how this fact, which runs parallel to cultural development, is compensated for by the universal function of art. Especially in that domain, the emotional and dynamic component finds its specific field of expression and influence. Through these interconnections, one may come to understand more deeply the liberating and redeeming impact of art, its content, and the role of the creative person in the cultural environment.

Beyond the individual typology of attitude and function, however, the dynamic and emotional component, which is largely excluded from the conscious sphere, forms a specific characteristic of the unconscious. The atmosphere and . . .[16] *[remainder of paragraph is lost].*

If one considers what western people are like when they lose these conscious inhibitions and compensations, one understands the extreme anxiety among primitives to avoid such states. Their instinctuality is controlled and governed by elaborate sexual regulations, their anti-sociality by precise prescriptions of behavior within their group, and their inability or unwillingness to obey by exacting ceremonies toward those in authority. The law is always the instrument of consciousness against the "forbidden," which is forbidden precisely because it is an expression of the anti-conscious tendencies of the unconscious, and because what destroys consciousness must be prevented from breaking out.

It is a basic law of all psychic life that one can always infer, from the content and intensity of the prohibition, the unconscious reality that is supposed to be repressed, suppressed, and shut out. Having said this, however, we should not forget that not only is this diagnosis justified by what is forbidden, but also that the prohibition itself, which compensates for unconscious tendencies, is an expression of the psyche, especially of its compensating tendency toward wholeness. It would be utterly mistaken to infer nothing from a strong moral law but the strength of its opposing anti-moral forces. One would be entirely justified, however, in concluding here that the positions of unconsciousness and consciousness are always strongly in conflict.

It is important to realize that the unconscious is also the source of tendencies promoting consciousness and working toward the law, tendencies that are further represented in the development and strengthening of consciousness. The basic fact that the psyche is a self-regulating system is expressed, among other things, in the fact that, besides the instinctive powers, the forces forming and providing law, order, and meaning also spring from the unconscious, which contains the principle of opposites.[17]

What poses a threat in the early stage of humanity is not, as in modernity, the loss of instinct due to an overly powerful consciousness, but rather the reverse, that consciousness may be lost due to an all-too-powerful unconscious. That is why primitive life is so surprisingly restricted by all kinds of regulations, which are meant to guarantee protection for the light of consciousness, which must be carefully guarded.

The complete inconspicuousness of the personal and the private at this stage of humanity corresponds, as mentioned earlier, to the slight development of ego and consciousness. We need not present here how this life is lived in symbols, in collective ideas, under the control of the archetypes; it has been described in detail by the pertinent researchers.[18] To cite an important example, which we must also treat in another context, this basic fact of "living in the archetype" expresses itself, as may still be seen in infants today, in the way that parents are not experienced as individual personalities leading a unique and concrete existence, but as merged with collective ideas of what is "fatherly" and "motherly," that is, fused with the archetypal images of father and mother.

This transpersonal experience of parents is also strongly promoted, at this early stage of humanity, by the institutional role of the archetype. Thus, within the family, corresponding to collective demands, the primitive father is a patriarch. His individual traits, as far as they exist at all, disappear completely behind this role. This attitude is imposed on him by the collective, and he is forced by the institutions to identify with it. In fact, he becomes an archetypal being. He flourishes in his fatherhood. Everything else disappears behind his function as father figure, patriarch, and the family's father–king. He is the quasi-divine progenitor, master over life and death, representative of the ancestral line, legislator, and priest. In the primitive society, as we know, he often really performs all of these functions, and, for the child, his archetypal figure flows completely into his individuality, which in addition is scarcely developed.

Time and again, this manifestation of the fatherly is produced and revived in festival rites, in which heaven, spirit, ancestry, deity, tribal patriarch, king, and lawmaker become blurred, thus undoing any possible withdrawal of this factor into the background in private life. Not only does this same archetypal father image still appear in the psychology of the modern neurotic, but also the type is vividly present in every patriarchally inclined society and family. The degree to which this fact is crucial for the Jewish person, for example, must be explained elsewhere[19]—likewise, the general consequences and connections arising from this evolutionary situation.[20]

Only as human consciousness evolves does the individual stand out against the impersonal and the supra-individual. Here again, the transpersonal only gradually differentiates itself from the personal, as from the undefined interwovenness of inner and outer, I and Thou and It. Like all conscious progress and individualization, this development must struggle against the resistance of the old, the unconscious, the dominance of the collective, be it against the ideas of the inner collective, the archetypes, or those of the outer collective, the collective human norms. For within the individual himself, archetypal thinking instinctively resists the new, individual thinking of ego-consciousness, just as the collective thinking of surrounding society, in the guise of "opinion," defends itself against these new positions.

Conscious differentiation from the dominance of the unconscious occurs through a systematic expansion and stabilizing of the conscious system, which we can still trace in the individual's development from childhood to adulthood. In this process, consciousness deflates the unconscious in order to protect itself, collectively and individually, against overwhelming unconscious forces, the energetic charge of which, the power, is far superior to that of consciousness. This deflation involves a process of depletion, which deprives the unconscious of libido to the benefit of consciousness and its development. The development of consciousness deflates the unconscious, that is, it tends to progress, by differentiating, from the impersonal and the transpersonal to the limited determinacy and uniqueness of concepts, persons, things, and domains of the world. Conscious development, ego formation, and world orientation are therefore closely related.

Essential for conscious development, accompanying and at the same time facilitating it, is the process of personalization, which represents a basic law of what happens in the psyche. During early human existence, we are confronted everywhere with "powers," which are basically indeterminate in their nature and way of working. This indeterminacy, and the indefinable anonymity of these powers, actually characterizes the earliest psychic existence of humanity. Something pre-figured, still unfigured, and foreign to figuration here has the effect of mana[21] or *orenda*,[22] as power per se. The psychology of early humanity, in its blurry lack of definition, corresponds to a flowing together of world and human, person and condition.

The evolution of consciousness and the formation of the ego run parallel to the personalizing of the world.[23] From indeterminate powerfulness emerge powers, archetypes, gods, demons, spirits, magicians, holy places, and sacred objects, which become the focus of cult and ritual. They become easy to handle, and magic and incantation are human attempts to cope with the powers as something personal, as contents and substances. The indeterminate becomes the determinable, which can now be addressed, summoned, and formulated. Consciousness asserts power over it in the formula, in the spell, in the name, that is, in the formed structure. From the numinous come forth the numina, in the same measure as the structure of consciousness isolates itself from the unconscious.

For early humanity, the world is an intermingled, unformed, fluctuating, confused flowing together of those contents that we now call subjective and objective. Differentiation of this world occurs only very gradually, as a correlate of developing human consciousness.

As humanity develops, the outer world of objects—which western people tend to call the "world"—differentiates itself as an object of natural science. On the other hand, there emerges the inner world of objects, that is, the world of the collective unconscious, of ideas and archetypes, of the psychic images affecting humanity. Between these two parts of the world stands the individual, governed by ego-consciousness. This position of the human being as an individual, affected by the worlds of inner and outer objects and having to deal with both, forms the final stage in the development of human consciousness.

Conscious development is not limited to the period in which science or rational thought unfolds, but stretches back to much earlier times; and the sacral meaning of consciousness is often more obvious in the earlier than in the later phases.

But until this stage is reached, the germ of ego-consciousness must laboriously and tirelessly disentangle itself from the encompassing power of the unconscious world, in order to advance from embryonic containment to a position of autonomy. Religion, morality, philosophy, and psychology are only partial aspects of this ceaseless endeavor, which also expresses itself in myth and cult, rite and magic. The path to consciousness, and the development of consciousness, are *the* major theme in human history.

The fact that we experience psychic contents as units, figures, complexes, and personality fragments,[24] yet not as a diffuse continuum of flowing powers, or as indeterminate shapelessness, corresponds to the law of personalization. It is coordinated with the structure of our existence as an ego, which is personal and which, as the center of our consciousness, determines our experience. We experience in terms of figures, persons, things, beings, and ideas, because as an ego we are a form [*Gestalt*].

As consciousness develops, and as the unconscious becomes deflated, this process of primary personalization leads to secondary personalization, which represents a part of this devaluation of the unconscious. The transpersonal is now reduced to the personal, and the world is interpreted only by the ego, in terms of its most limited experience. The numinous, which had been experienced personally as powers, gods, and archetypal figures, is now entirely excluded. Typical in this respect are the attempts to derive gods from heroes, or to dismiss the powers as illusions.

The transformation of myth into fairytale, for which Egyptian culture provides a beautiful example, is a similar process. Here, we can follow in detail the transformation of the myth of Osiris and Set, the hostile divine twins, into the tale of Bata and his brother, a family romance now played out purely by personal, individually characterized figures.[25]

In early humanity, when myth is produced, it is experienced as an impersonal and transpersonal event. In mythologizing humanity, the productions of the collective unconscious, through the medium of the formulating groups, are relatively unimpeded. The lower the level of consciousness, the lower its share of the product, which then passes through the producer as it were. We are still aware of such processes today, as when, for instance, images emerge from the deep unconscious and pass through the person to whom they occur, without his or her consciousness being able to access those images at first, and without their being reduced to or derived from any contents of the personal unconscious. We find the same processes throughout early humanity, in myths and in some customs, rituals, etc. They are direct projections of the unconscious, for instance, into the heavens. Whatever knowledge we have about what we call the collective unconscious comes to us only through these projections.

As consciousness grows, and the ego develops progressively into the center of consciousness, what we call secondary personalization occurs. We can observe this process in general as well as in individual development. Now that the ego has begun to expand its scope, events that had been relatively neutral and indifferently transpersonal are "personalized" by the ego's growing participation. They are experienced and represented in their relationship to the ego. The gods change shape and descend, as divine events first become quasi-human and eventually human ones. The myth of the hostile twin brothers turns into the family drama,[26] the features of which now depend on the personal structure of the one who produces it.

Secondary personalization, which occurs under the dominance of ego-consciousness, now also changes the original transpersonal conflict of opposites by introducing "themes." The original mythological opposition between brothers is simply "there," standing "at the beginning of the world," as it were. The question of themes, being a question of consciousness and causality, only arises at the stage of secondary personalization. Here, themes begin to enrich the conflict between the brothers; depending on personal structure, these may be themes of sexuality or power, or other themes, including the problems of the first-born child and the sister. Once more, it is characteristic how the previously indefinable object of contention now becomes tangible and able to be personally grasped.

Earlier, the object of the struggle was entirely unmentioned, or it was indefinably pregnant with symbolism. The treasure to be attained still scintillated in the midst of infinite variety, being simultaneously soul, woman, mother, beloved, power, treasure, gold, sun, philosopher's stone, water of life, and water of death, liberation from life, death, birth and rebirth, all at once, nothing and everything.

The transformation of the object at the heart of the struggle, from symbol into content, from the indeterminate into something tangible, is typical of secondary personalization and the direction of ego development.

Rationalization and secondary personalization are parts of the deflationary tendency, with which consciousness asserts itself against the unconscious. The tendency "away from the unconscious," and towards the "principle of reality," is an essential building block of the wall that is erected, with the help of suppression and displacement, between the conscious and unconscious systems. This wall is necessary to safeguard consciousness against the negative forces of the unconscious. It is an integral part of what we call culture.

The development of western culture, however, has turned consciousness so radically outward that a catastrophic reinforcement of this dividing wall has occurred, and thus also a dangerous isolation of the ego and consciousness. Western consciousness is so self-absorbed that the ego knows only itself and its conscious world. In this state, the knowledge has almost been lost that consciousness and its territory are only a part of psychic existence as a whole. The immense world of the psychic background, the world of the mothers and powers, the gods and archetypes, has now become the "unconscious," about which the ego knows nothing.

Even in this state of self-absorption, the individual and humanity can still live healthily, as long as the compensatory balance provided by the unconscious, although unconscious, is still effective. The blindness and one-sidedness of consciousness, for which the world has become merely the world of consciousness, are counterbalanced by the unconscious, instinctive side, which represents the unconscious, the immense unconscious power of which is revealed by modern depth psychology. Illness occurs only when the permeable membrane between consciousness and the unconscious has become an impenetrable wall, and the unconscious compensation degenerates into a split between consciousness and the unconscious. When the side of the mothers is not merely fought against, but also disavowed, we truly have a crisis.

Just as the Eumenides, the dark mothers, were pacified in the *Oresteia* only when a shrine had been erected for their veneration, so the conscious world, if it wishes to remain healthy, must preserve the shrine of motherhood, venerating the power of the primordial dragon and offering it sacrifices. But when this shrine is destroyed and no longer venerated in the everyday world of consciousness, the old mothers once again become the Erinyes. They break into the human world, snake girdled, as a devastating flood from the unconscious, bringing sickness and death into the world of humankind that has forgotten them.

Erich Neumann
1943

Notes

1 This four-lecture series, previously unpublished, was written in 1942–43. The first three lectures date from 1943. The fourth, dated 1942, is Neumann's revised and expanded version of a lecture of April 1940 (cf. editorial comment, Appendix B.IV, *Roots II*, p. 256).
2 *EN*: *Beziehungen*. [Cf. CW 7,2.]
3 *EN*: Günther Goldschmidt, "Alchemie der Aegypter" ("Alchemy of the Egyptians"), *Der Ursprung der Alchemie* (*The origins of alchemy*). *Ciba-Zeitschrift*, Basel und Leipzig, 1938, No. 57.
4 *EN*: Herbert Silberer, *Probleme der Mystik und ihrer Symbolik* (*Problems of mysticism and its symbolism*), 1914 (hereafter: *Probleme der Mystik*). [Silberer discusses the dragon as an alchemical symbol, pp. 76, 83f., 128f., 175f.]
5 *EN*: Jung, "Einige Bemerkungen zu den Visionen des Zosimos" ("Some comments on the visions of Zosimos"), *EJ 1937*, p. 37; and *Integration*. [Cf. CW 13,2, "The Visions of Zosimos," ¶105. The reference to Jung's *Integration* is undefined.]
6 *EN:* Lévy-Bruhl, *Das Denken der Naturvölker* (*How Natives Think*), Chapter 2. [In *How Natives Think* (trans. by Lilian Ada Clare), Chapter 2 is titled "The Law of Participation." Robert Segal advises that the term "mystic relationship" is given on p. 61, and "mystic participation" on p. 82. Jung and Neumann take the original phrase from Lévy-Bruhl's *Les fonctions mentales dans les sociétés inférieures* (1910). (Cf. also *Roots I*, p. 25, n. 38.)]
7 *EN*: Ernst Cassirer, *Philosophie der symbolischen Formen* (*Philosophy of symbolic forms*), v. 2. [Title of v. 2: *Das mythische Denken* (*Mythical thinking*). A relevant passage occurs in Chapter 2, third section. (In the English edition: "The Concept of the Personality and the Personal Gods: The Phases of the Mythical Concept of the I," pp. 199ff.)]
8 *EN*: Cassirer, op. cit. p. 123. [Cited as p. 3. In the 1997 German edition, cf. p. 119. In the English edition, cf. p. 96.]
9 Probably referring to Martin Luther's famous hymn, "Ein' feste Burg" ("A mighty fortress"), which refers to Satan: "Der alt' böse Feind, mit Ernst er's jetzt meint." ("For still our ancient foe doth seek to work us woe.")

10 *EN*: See "Die Schöpfungssage der Maori" ("The creation saga of the Maori"), in Eckart von Sydow, *Kunst und Religion der Naturvölker* (*Art and religion of native peoples*).

11 *EN*: Lucy Heyer, "Erinyen und Eumeniden: Der Kampf zwischen Geist und Erde in der antiken Tragödie" ("Erinyes and Eumenides: The struggle between spirit and earth in ancient tragedy"), in Heyer and Seifert [1937], *Reich der Seele* (*The psychic realm*), v. 1, pp. 39–51. [A crucial passage in this paper concerns the trial of Orestes, over which Athena presides. Orestes' ultimate pardon gives priority to patriarchal rights over matriarchal; yet Athena is still able to make peace with the Erinyes (the Furies), the darkly feminine earth-powers, by giving them a shrine in Athens, where they will be worshiped, placatingly, as the Eumenides (the Kindly Ones) (ibid., p. 49).]

12 *EN*: Author: "Erscheinungsformen mann-weiblichen Bezogenseins" ("Forms of relationship between masculine and feminine"). [An unpublished writing by Neumann, not found to date.]

13 *EN*: Cf. Jung: *Diagnostische Assoziationsstudien: Beiträge zur experimentellen Psychopathologie* (*Diagnostic association studies: Contributions to experimental psychopathology*) (1909). [Cf. CW 2,9, "Disturbances of Reproduction in the Association Experiment," ¶918–38.]

14 *EN*: Ibid.

15 *EN*: Cf. Goethe, "Die Natur," *Aphoristisches* ("Nature", *Aphorisms*), 1780. [Although commonly attributed to Goethe, the source of this passage appears to be a fragment by Georg Christoph Tobler, "Die Natur" (1780). The false attribution seems to stem partly from the fact that the piece contains handwritten corrections by Goethe, who later claimed authorship.]

16 In the raw typescript of this lecture, p. 12b is a cut half-page, the final sentence of which is incomplete, as shown. A new paragraph begins on p. 13.

17 *EN*: Jung, *Energetik*, pp. 87ff. [Cf. CW 8,1, "On Psychic Energy," ¶104ff. In this passage Jung argues: "The spiritual appears in the psyche also as an instinct, indeed as a real passion .... It is not derived from any other instinct, ... but is a principle *sui generis*, a specific and necessary form of instinctual power" (¶108).]

18 *EN*: Lévy-Bruhl, Cassirer, et al.

19 *EN*: Author: "Die Bedeutung des Weiblichen für die Zukunft des Judentums" ("The importance of the feminine for the future of Judaism"). [An unpublished writing by Neumann, not found to date.]

20 *EN*: Author: "The Development of Consciousness and Stages of Life." [Cf. Appendix B.II, *Roots II*, p. 209.]

21 Polynesian: supernatural force. (Cf. Jung's "The Mana Personality," CW 7,2, ¶374–406, cited above by Neumann, pp. IA-104 and IIC-54 in working translation.

22 Latin: "objects of prayer."

23 Cassirer, op. cit., p. 123. [Cited as p. 3. In the 1997 German edition, cf. p. 119. In the English edition, p. 96.]

24 Jung: "Allgemeines zur Komplextheorie" ("A review of the complex theory"), 1934. [Cf. CW 8,3, ¶202.]

25 *EN*: Adolf Ermann, *Die Literatur der Aegypter: Gedichte, Erzählungen und Lehrbücher aus dem 3. und 2. Jahrtausend v. Chr.* (*Egyptian literature: Poems, stories and schoolbooks from the 3rd and 2nd centuries* BC).

26 Neumann here echoes his earlier essay, the then-unpublished *Jacob & Esau,* where the concept of secondary personalization had been introduced and defined: "In this process, an originally suprapersonal or impersonal content, namely, the opposition between Horus and Seth, the hostile twin deities, is transformed into a personal story, a family story involving individual characters" (*Jacob & Esau,* p. 84.) In his introduction to that work, Erel Shalit discusses how emerging ego-consciousness moves the story of Jacob and Esau, another pair of hostile twins, from its original meaning at the mythical and archetypal level to one that can be experienced subjectively and personally (ibid., p. lv). Neumann's concept of secondary personalization is further developed in *Origins and History*.

II. The development of consciousness and the stages of life

The cultural situation of modern humanity is determined largely by a development in which consciousness stakes a one-sided, unambiguous claim to power, as the unconscious and its contents are predominantly "unconscious," that is, kept out of conscious view. This primacy of consciousness has led western humanity, collectively and individually, into a crisis, as yet unresolved, the effects of which also threaten the lives of ordinary people. Only when we understand the development of the individual, in relation to consciousness and differentiation, can we clearly grasp the threat and simultaneously the opportunity that is presented by this situation of western consciousness.

For every human being, the first half of life stands under the sign of the collective. Education and increasing life experience work toward an adaptation to reality, which is largely identical with adaptation to the collective. However varied the collective orientation might be at different times, the individual is compelled to develop a one-sidedness that is acceptable to the collective in question.

This necessary adaptation involves the cooperation of various factors, the common trait of which is to strengthen consciousness and its ability to act, along with a parallel tendency to exclude the forces of the unconscious as disturbances.

One of these factors is typological differentiation, that is, the fact that each individual adopts a certain attitude toward the world, which is related either extravertedly to physical reality or introvertedly to psychic reality. Beside this habitual attitude, one function of consciousness tends to be preferred and differentiated. In one individual, it may be thinking, in another feeling, etc.[1]

This differentiation of one's type, whether it is determined by constitution or in some other way, affords the individual the greatest chance of adaptation, because the function that is most capable and best suited is generally developed as the individual's primary function.

The development of persona,[2] the part of the personality consciously and unconsciously tailored to the collective, corresponds to a second necessary adaptation process, which suppresses and disguises individually significant traits and gifts in favor of factors that are collectively more effective and desired.

The development of the will, the training of purposeful and disciplined action at the expense of instinctive, unconscious reaction, is another necessary adaptation to reality to be achieved by the growing human being.

Although, by natural disposition, every individual is physically and psychologically bisexual, development eventually forces the individual to push the contrasexual part into the unconscious. Just as typological differentiation and the formation of the persona cause essential individual components to be suppressed into the domain of the shadow and the inferior function,[3] so the one-sided emphasis on one's own gender ends by constellating the contrasexual part in the unconscious, as the anima in a man, and the animus in a woman.[4]

In their systematizing, all of these factors demand the development of ego, consciousness, and will. Their relative blockage of the instinctual side of the unconscious heightens intrapersonal tension. The splitting of consciousness from the unconscious creates a tension between these systems, but, by identifying with only one side of the opposition, the ego also loses contact, consciously or unconsciously, with psychic wholeness. Consciousness now claims to represent unity, even though it is confined to a partial region of the psyche. In reality, this unity is merely the relative unity of consciousness; it is not yet a unity of personality. Psychic wholeness is lost and replaced by the dualistic principle of opposition, which dominates the systems of consciousness and the unconscious.

These developments do not, however, form the basis on which a neurotically ill personality develops. On the contrary, they are normative, and, should they be absent or undeveloped, their incompleteness leads to illness. This one-sided developmental direction, which privileges consciousness, seems, at least to some degree, to constitute the specific western structure, which thus includes sacrifice and conflict from the outset.

As we shall see, however, this psychic structure also contains a corresponding ability to make sacrifice meaningful and conflict fruitful. A holistic tendency is normally at work within it, such that, over one's lifespan, the early sacrifice and one-sidedness are balanced out by a compensatory development in the second half of life. The conflict between consciousness and the unconscious, which arises as consciousness becomes differentiated, leads gradually, if the natural compensatory tendencies of the unconscious are respected, to a lasting growth of personality. As the relationship between consciousness and the unconscious intensifies, it is accompanied by an ever more encompassing synthesis, replacing the original conflict.

The basic fact that the development of individual consciousness passes through the same stages as the evolution of consciousness in humanity, and moves in the same direction, is still evident today in the development of the western child. Essentially, western humanity is oriented toward the outer world. To this day, even childhood education is conducted largely under the motto "develop the reality principle," in the one-sided meaning of adaptation to the outer world.

Western consciousness reaches a turning point only in modern depth psychology; only here does consciousness begin to reflect on itself. The inner dimension of the world now emerges as an objective world, an objective psyche, which can be engaged in a conscious working through. Until this point, however, which is a decisive moment in the psychological history of humanity, designated by the term "individuation process,"[5] the outward orientation of consciousness was characterized, even in individual development, by the developmental stages and processes through which collective consciousness had passed.

In particular, these stages are the original uroboric situation, the deflation of the unconscious, and secondary personalization. The original situation is the embryonic containment of consciousness in the parental uroboros. As the personal psychology of the child teaches us,[6] the parents' unconscious is crucial in this respect. The infant's *participation mystique* with its parents goes on for a long time. That is, for a long time the child does not have its own psychology, meaning the psychological experience of an ego. Instead, just as the child was previously a part of the mother's body, after birth it is a part of the parents' psychic space, from which it detaches and frees itself only gradually.

A purely personalistic psychology is therefore incapable of adequately grasping the child's psychological state. Only gradually does the child awaken to consciousness, later to external consciousness, and only in puberty does it make its own ego-consciousness system, relatively independent of parental influences.

To begin with, the all-powerful uroboros is dominant, in the indefinite and shapeless world of the intertwined primal parents. From this confusion, with increasing ego development, when the great figures of the primal parents, the father and the mother, emerge, they emerge not as individuals but as archetypes.

The first stage of the parental relationship is impersonal and unconscious, dominated by *participation mystique* with the parental archetypes. That is, the field of the child's experience is governed as described above, for example, by the image of the Father archetype.[7] Here, the form of an archetypally determined life corresponds to an ego-consciousness that is still undeveloped. Only in the second stage of the parent–child relationship, with the process of secondary personalization, do we move out of the unconscious connection with parental archetypes, into the personal story of the family romance and the so-called Oedipus complex.[8]

The final outcome of this process is personalization, in which the real, personal parents come to the fore, and their archetypal component recedes, that is, the transpersonal aspect of their behavior, which is powerful and real for the child, independent of the parents' private, personal existence.

The parental archetypes, primal images that tower into the transpersonal, affect the small child, whose consciousness is still minimal, lacking any real or personal experience. Working partly through the real parents, whom the child does not experience personally, they imprint themselves on the child, who is wide open to unconscious forces and images, having as yet no consciousness that can differentiate the mother, for instance, as a part of the outer world. Rather, at this point, the mother still contains, protects, and nurtures everything; she is the world, and at the same time she is the inner dimension, and these aspects flow together in the infinite background.

Life that is not centered by ego-consciousness is life in the world of the collective unconscious, in the mythological world of primal time. The child's ego lives among these primal images just as the adult's conscious ego lives among people.

The sphere of personalization is reached only at a late stage. A long development is needed for a world to emerge, consisting of father, mother, brother, and sister as individual, unique, and concrete living beings, as objects; it presupposes experience of the world and awareness of reality. This adaptation to the world is achieved with great difficulty. For in personalization, ego-consciousness is already demanded and promoted, and a piece of the objective world is formulated, as personal figures are detached from the overlapping form of the primal images.

This early phase of infantile containment in the collective unconscious is difficult to define, precisely because of the phenomenon of secondary personalization, which also causes adult consciousness to see its early childhood experiences transposed into the merely personal context of the family romance. Behind the ciphers of the family romance, consistent with the general tendency of the unconscious to become deflated, the great figures of the primal images can no longer be recognized or experienced.

Whereas the archetypal forms of the unconscious are projected onto the parents in the first stage, that is, are experienced through them, the child's growing ego-consciousness gradually perceives the real figures of the parents. Insofar as the parents are personalized, part of the child's participation with them, which dominates his life to such an extent,[9] also comes to an end.

This second stage normally extends to puberty, in which a conscious relationship between the ego and the real parents is permanently established. In the transition from the first stage to the second, the child begins to differentiate himself[10] from the powers of the unconscious, and the real, outer world begins to appear. The projection of the archetypes onto the real parents, and the child's unconscious dependency on and identity with them, makes way for a process of differentiation, in which the child experiences himself as an intentional ego, separate from his parents, whose reality character grows to the degree that the child recognizes their non-identity with the archetypes.

The child's psychic space divides into the outer world of the real parents and the experiencing ego, on the one hand, and the archetypes, on the other. Then the archetypes either (for instance, in religion) continue to play a major role in the life of consciousness, or—and this is not without danger—they are ousted from consciousness by the deflationary tendency. Either way, ego-consciousness draws part of its energy from the ending of participation with the parents. But, and this is the essence of secondary personalization, because the real parents now emerge as differentiated from the ego and as part of the outer world, the family romance becomes the first chapter in the child's adaptation to reality. The secondary personalization of the parental archetypes deprives the unconscious of libido, which is used to expand ego-consciousness and to conquer the outer world, the prototype of which is here the family.

Consistent with Freud's purely personalistic concept of the psyche, his treatment of the child's oedipal situation remains limited to investigating the infant's relationship with the real parents. Moreover, he makes later psychic development depend largely on the solutions found by the child's ego in this situation. Freud fails to recognize the archetypal character of the situation, because he has overlooked both the phenomenon of secondary personalization and its effects and implications. That is, he fails to recognize that, when the problem is transferred to the real, personal parents, this simply represents a late stage in the ego's relationship with the primal parents.

As the child's consciousness develops further, the ego begins to differentiate itself from consciousness. The original uroboros situation, the stage when the child is contained within the primal parents, is now replaced by the son–lover phase, in which the ego experiences itself as both the son and the lover of the motherly unconscious. This process of differentiation is always accompanied by experiences of projections onto the personal mother or corresponding figures.

This stage also belongs to the Oedipus complex, if one understands this complex in its entirety. Normally, this stage begins to shift into a new phase at approximately the time of entering school. With the tendency to separate from the motherly unconscious, connected with the child's entrance into the masculine and fatherly cultural sphere of school, a psychological state is reached in the development of consciousness that we characterize as the battle with the dragon. This struggle against the overwhelming power of the unconscious, in favor of the fatherly spirit, ends with the separation of the night-time world of the maternal unconscious from the daytime world. In western culture, this day-world of consciousness is dominated by the paternal spirit, which excludes and devalues the mother's night-time world as far as possible.

A developmental direction from the mother's world to the father's normally corresponds to the general development of human consciousness, and—if we overlook the morbid degenerations of our own time, where the two sides are completely split off from each other—this direction does not necessarily lead to disaster. Only if the unconscious is too radically, rationally, and one-sidedly cut off, with a resulting lack of psychological nourishment, are the consequences individually and collectively destructive.

The direction of childhood development is normally from the pleasure principle to the reality principle, from playing to learning, from the mother's child to the school child. But, with this development, one of the typical symptoms of impoverishment, not determined by any historical period, is the waning of the imagination and of the powers of artistic creation that children naturally possess in great measure. Emotional vitality and original reactions are gradually lost, in favor of learning what counts for the collective as "appropriate" and "good" behavior. The development of competency in life (for collective utility), at the expense of life's full range, are typical milestones in this necessary process of impoverishment, through which the child must go until he reaches adulthood.

Growing ego-consciousness leads to an increasing transference of libido onto the world, to occupying the world of objects in ever greater dimensions, while the unconscious is simultaneously deflated.

The deflation of the unconscious is clearly seen in normal child development. Here, the child's primal world of the unconscious, which is characteristically found in fairy tales and children's drawings and games, retreats more and more in the face of the real, outer world. This development, which school, of course, strongly and consciously supports, leads to a permanent growth of the ego and consciousness. The libido, having been withdrawn from the lively unconscious, is put to work building up and expanding the conscious system. This process, practiced piecemeal at first, characterizes the transition from playing to learning, and the school is the collectively assigned architect, whose task is to erect the wall between the deflated unconscious and the reality adaptation of consciousness.

During puberty, this process is normally completed, to the point where attachment to the parental imagos is also dissolved or ready to be dissolved. Activation of the unconscious, which always occurs at this time, now takes place in the unconscious, behind the wall that separates the ego and the unconscious; thus, only the emanations of this activation reach and stimulate consciousness. This causes the unconscious contents to be projected, to emerge outside, in the world of objects. These projected contents draw the libido even further outward, promoting the outward tendency of development.

Thus, for instance, from the initially hermaphroditic nature of the child, whose psyche need not yet contain an unequivocal, one-sided sexual emphasis, a fixation on one sex usually forms, as consciousness expands, with the progressive suppression of the opposite side into the unconscious. This means that the boy, nurtured by the collective and its corresponding demand, develops his masculinity by suppressing his feminine aspect into the unconscious, whereas the reverse happens in the girl. This differentiation, which is often accompanied by the typical forms of rejecting the opposite sex, culminates during puberty.

(To a large extent, however, this development seems to be culturally and historically contingent, at least in its radical one-sidedness. Cultural education in cultures and periods that more strongly emphasize the feminine principle, and thus do not over-emphasize masculine dominance so much, will promote other outcomes and individual developments.)

Running parallel to this psycho-physical transformation, there is an activation of the unconscious, which is shown by a strengthening in the collective unconscious, the archetypes. This strengthening far exceeds the activation of the sexual sphere. It expresses itself not only in the heightened risk of psychotic break, evident in the frequency of psychosis during this period of life, but especially in the newly emerging and vivid interest in everything that is transpersonal, universal, and ideational, which many people experience only during this time of greater unconscious power. Normally, this period is also characterized by a changed attitude toward life and the world, resembling the attitude of early humanity, with its affinity for the world, much more than that of modern adults. The lyrical ensoulment of the world, and the relatively frequent appearance of mythological themes in dreams and poems of this age, are typical expressions of this activation of the collective unconscious layer.

As a rule, however, only strongly introverted or creative natures directly perceive this movement in the unconscious, because consciousness also increases its compensatory working through during puberty. In general, as mentioned above, this leads to the emanation of the unconscious into interest and feeling. But this activation of the unconscious manifests itself essentially in fascinating projections, which initiate and guarantee further normal development.

One projection characteristic of this period is that of the anima or the animus, that is, the imago of the opposite sex, slumbering in the unconscious, which is now activated. Its image, crowned by the splendor of the unconscious, is projected into the world, where it must be searched for. And thus, the partner problem is constellated, which is a major theme of the first half of life.

As a rule, detachment from the parental imagos, the real parents, must be achieved in puberty. But, as primitive puberty rites show, this detachment in no way contradicts the fact that the archetypes of the primal, transpersonal parents are especially energized at this time. This energy is utilized institutionally, however, by and for the collective, which supports and demands the projection of parental archetypes onto transpersonal, or rather *as* transpersonal contents. Now, the relationship with the figure of the teacher, the master and leader, the mana-personality,[11] as a projection of the father-archetype, becomes as important as the projection of the mother-archetype onto homeland, community, church, or movement. From now on, the life of the one—the adult—who has stepped out of the family circle and entered the collective will be claimed and consumed largely by these contents.

The criterion of adulthood is just this rebirth, which leads out of the family circle and initiates the individual into the larger world, the great parents of life.

As primitive puberty rites and their remnants in our time suggest, the time of puberty corresponds to a period of rebirth and to a symbolism representing the hero's self-generation in his fight with the dragon. The purpose of all these rites, from communion to *bar mitzvah*, is a renewal of personality through a night sea voyage, in which the mother dragon is defeated by the principle of spirit and consciousness, and the attachment to mother and childhood is broken. The one who is reborn is reborn mainly by the representative fatherly principle, with which he identifies in the initiation. He now becomes the son of the father, without the mother; and so, being identical with the father, he becomes his own father.[12]

This self-generation of the masculine is the victory. The victor, like the dragon-fighter, is rewarded with the princess. Now that he is an adult, and admitted into sexuality, the mother's place must be taken by the wife, for whom in principle the victorious young man represents the masculine and the spiritual side. Today, just as in the primitive collective, the adult male must now play his masculine role. Thus, we also come here to the problem of persona, which is characteristic of adult psychology.

The first half of life is devoted largely to adapting to these forces of the outer world and their transpersonal claim. The only thing that initially enables consciousness to develop toward the outer world is the outward projection of these archetypes, the primal parents and the anima. Fascination by these archetypal images, which are alive behind the outer reality that must be conquered, is what gives the psyche the outward inclination that is characteristic of any normal development in the first half of life.

In this period of life, consciousness continuously unfolds, and the reality relationship to the outer world expands. The deflation of the unconscious, for which secondary personalization is the first stage, progresses to a relative alienation from the unconscious. Parallel with this, there is a stabilizing of ego-consciousness, volition, and the adaptation to reality. This developmental tendency is natural. It corresponds to the instincts and psychic mechanisms of the human species, which foster the development and stabilization of consciousness. Corresponding to this inherent developmental tendency is the fact that, through natural processes of working through and projection, even the pronounced activation of the unconscious that we see in puberty ultimately leads toward further outward development. Analysis of developmental disturbances and adult neurotic disorders also proves that this development is given by nature.

After puberty, as adults we should normally have a stable, yet elastic ego-consciousness, with a large amount of free libido. Our ego-consciousness should be strongly sealed off against the influence of the unconscious, yet without being encapsulated, and, depending on the scope of consciousness and the amount of libido, it should be directed toward a relatively large share of the world of objects. Progressive conquest of and adaptation to this world of objects forms consciousness and personality in both extraverts and introverts.[13] The only exceptions are creative people, on the one hand, those with an overload of unconscious activity, yet whose capacity for consciousness is able to cope with this overload, and neurotics, on the other, those in whom—for whatever reasons—the development of consciousness is disturbed.

The development of consciousness leads from the early human's prelogical[14] state of unconscious connection with the world to the autonomous consciousness of modern humanity, where the ego confronts the world as an object and makes it the object of knowledge. The original, unfree connection of the unbounded ego to a world in which it lived unconsciously, in one-sided states of identification, turns into the free act of ego-consciousness, which turns voluntarily toward objects.

All the activities and abilities freely available to the modern human as functions of his consciousness, subject to the ego and its will, were once harnessed to this consciousness only in laborious "yoga." What now appears as a self-evident capacity of consciousness was originally deprived of free choice and conscious volition, as much as the weather or the ripening of seeds.

This primordial state expresses itself in the fact that, in their early stages, not only did religions associate a god with every outer event, lightning or rain, the stars, or the seasons, but also every human act stood under divine auspices. "One god helps with the ploughing, another with the sowing, a third with the seed's sprouting, with the growing, ripening, harvesting, threshing, grinding, and baking the flour."[15]

Here, not only the humanly undetermined events of nature are subject to a god, but so are human activities like harvesting, threshing, and baking. Pious modern parlance, which imploringly includes the phrase "with God's help," is the last, fading remnant of this original situation, when every action rested in the hands of a god, because, for early human beings, conscious intention and will were still extremely uncertain and unreliable.

Jung has often referred to this basic disposition of human nature, its laziness,[16] which manifests itself, for example, in the fact that early humans make a conscious, intentional effort and engage in volitional acts only with difficulty and reluctantly. Special preparations and cultic actions are required *rites d'entrées,*[17] relating specifically to the powers of the inner world, which invoke and address the responsible god and thus enable the unconscious libido to be directed toward action, toward the object, toward the outer world.[18] Slowly, over the course of development, these unique and conspicuous acts turn into functions of consciousness. Only gradually does it become unnecessary in every case to lure the energy for action out of the unconscious; rather, the energy of the will becomes available to the ego and freely disposable.

But when challenges surpass the normal scope, the modern person, like the primitive, needs ceremony, the mass gathering, the summoning of divinity, the display of holy symbols, and the invocation of the great magic words, in order to release the amount of libido required for the activity.[19]

Basically, consciousness increasingly tends to assimilate autonomous outer and inner contents, that is, contents that function independently of it, and to unite them under its rule. In some sense, however, this wrests these contents from the hand of God and his inscrutability. In this way, ever-larger strips of conscious knowledge are won from the infinite territory of the unknown, the land of God, or no man's land.

This tendency of consciousness is quite legitimate. To raise doubts about it would undermine the existence of western humanity. That would mean, for example, abandoning all conscious interference with the power of illness, which is "heaven sent." In both contexts, consciousness assumes the right to expand its domain. (The multitude of special gods and function-related gods is confronted by an uncentered human being, who is a receptacle of behaviors and instincts dependent on random happenings. In the history of religion, the special gods have combined into god-figures, each of which unites many special gods. This process corresponds to the centering of ego-consciousness and the coordination with it, as abilities of consciousness, of hitherto autonomous, unconscious functions, which had been assigned to the function-related gods. It would be most revealing, even if impossible at this point, to investigate the association between the dimension of conscious development and that of changing god images, to see if there are correspondences with the growth of consciousness, not only in a growing worldview but also in a growing god image.)

The ego is helped to install itself as the center of consciousness by its developing powers of differentiation and abstraction, which cut up the continuum of the inner and outer worlds. Apart from the increases in libido that are gained, as we have seen, from the deflation of the unconscious, consciousness expands through the withdrawal of projections cathected in the outer world. On the one hand, this makes the objects of outer reality visible; on the other, the projected contents are taken inward, as abilities and contents, and personal space, especially the conscious system, expands.

The development of consciousness, as we shall show, has led to a strong emphasis on the differentiating function of thinking. In this sense, the "rationality" of consciousness, as against the "irrationality" of the unconscious, is a truism.. And yet, Jung's typology specifically demonstrates that it is wrong to equate consciousness with thinking. Each of the different functions, thinking and feeling, sensation and intuition, can represent the guiding function of consciousness.

Nevertheless, a process is evident in the deflation of the unconscious, that is, in the retreat of the unconscious, and above all, of the archetypes, which makes this customary equation of rationality with consciousness, and of irrationality with the unconscious, more understandable. This process is particularly important for the path of individuation and for bringing the unconscious into awareness. But it also characterizes a significant part of the development of human consciousness, from prehistory to modernity.

To understand the development of consciousness, and to bring the unconscious into awareness through the conscious personality, requires an act of differentiation, making a fundamental distinction between two components of the unconscious. This involves separating two aspects of the collective unconscious: the material and the dynamic–emotional component. This separation will become even clearer in what follows. What this means, first, is that the archetype, as an image, represents a content to be grasped by consciousness, but also that it is always originally accompanied by a dynamic, emotionally powerful component that seizes the personality.

As long as early humanity lived largely in *participation mystique* with the contents of the unconscious, and as long as the conscious system of humanity was unable to exist independent isolation from the unconscious, the material and dynamic components were so closely interlinked that one could speak of an identity. Visible image and instinctive reaction were one and the same. The emergence of the image was coupled with the reaction to it, which seized the entire psychophysical organism like a kind of reflex.

Jung states[20] that the primordial image, the archetype, is the counterpart of instinct. Purposive action, represented by instinct, captures the momentary situation with the help of the image that exists *a priori*, the archetype, "which not only gives expression to the energic process but facilitates its operation."[21] This reflexive reaction of the early human being, in which material and dynamic components are tightly connected as instinctive reactions and begin moving, *uno actu*,[22] with the image, ceases with the increasing development of consciousness. As the cerebrum and consciousness develop, and according to the type of reflex arc, the instinctive reaction becomes delayed by the activation of conscious intervention. Reflection, premeditation, stands in opposition to instinctive reaction and finally, at least to some extent, detaches from it.

Consciousness also opposes the instinctive reactions occurring in the unconscious, because instinct itself is an ego-overwhelming dimension of the unconscious, against which the developing system of ego-consciousness must set a boundary. It is consistent with this development of consciousness to separate the reaction from the triggering perceptual image, thus breaking up the original reflex unit. In the context of this development, the material and dynamic components of the collective unconscious came apart. In other words, the fact that the human being did not respond immediately, reflexively and instinctively, to the appearance of an archetype was perfectly consistent with his developing consciousness.

Early human participation, indeed all *participation mystique*, is distinguished by the special feeling character of its emotionality and affectivity. For this reason, the development of consciousness stands and has always stood under the primacy of reason and thinking. We should not forget that the "complexes" of the unconscious are characterized primarily as "feeling-toned complexes," that is, as contents that, by their nature, seize hold of feeling. This may occur in disturbances of the rational conscious structure or in the generation of emotions, which then lead to the discovery of these complexes, for instance, in the association experiment.[23]

Just as in childhood the irrational functions—sensation and intuition—develop before the rational ones—thinking and feeling—so rationality also seems to be a late product of human development. Perception of the outer world of objects, as achieved by sensation, and that of the inner world of objects, as achieved by intuition, are in no fundamental conflict with emotionality. Both functions can work in a differentiated way, undisturbed by the interference of emotional and dynamic components.

As a differentiated rational function, however, thinking depends to a great extent for its accuracy on the absence of interference by dynamic and emotional components. (To simplify matters here, we are representing rationality as limited to thinking, and are not elaborating on the corresponding conclusions about feeling.[24]) As the rational functions are more active, more ego related, than the irrational ones, for which consciousness is more receptive, their functioning requires them to maintain an essential distance from the dynamic–emotional components, and thus to preserve the tranquility of the ego. Differentiated thinking requires a "cool" head and "cold" blood.

The activation of thinking over the primary, affective state of possession is thus a symptom of conscious development, tendeing toward the deflation of the unconscious, as typified by its way of splitting up the original unity of perception and affect into a material component, on the one hand, and a dynamic component, on the other. From the ego's viewpoint, as we learn often enough from mass psychology and would do well to remember, instincts do not always have meaningful results.

Originally, an outer perception or an inner intuition, aided by the dynamic components of the collective unconscious, led reflexively to an instinctive reaction to the perceptual image, for example, to fight or flight, an outburst of anger or of helplessness. With the development of rational consciousness, however, came a more or less strong suppression of the dynamic–emotional component. These dynamic and emotional components constitute a specific characteristic of the unconscious, apart from the individual's attitude and functional type. Independent of momentary content, that is, independent of material components, the dynamic and emotional components of the unconscious are expressed through its atmosphere and color, its emanating fascination, its indefinable attraction and repulsion, and also its creeping insistence, by which every ego is determined and imprinted.

But consciousness, ego, and will, the shock troops of human development—in the west, at least—are crucially intent, first, on loosening the connection between the material and the dynamic components of the unconscious. And then, having suppressed the dynamic components, the instinctive reactions and actions, they can take charge of the material components, the contents of the unconscious, and work them through. This suppression of the dynamic and emotional parts of the collective unconscious is inevitable, because the development of thinking and consciousness first requires that the ego become detached and liberated from the clutches of emotion and instinct.

The human being's attempt to free himself from the power of the unconscious by developing consciousness, in the development from prelogical[25] to logical thinking, leads to replacing the archetype with the idea for which it is the precursor. In this process, the idea is the result of an abstraction. It expresses "the meaning of a primordial image, a meaning that has been abstracted from the concretism of the image" and is "a product of thought."[26]

Development proceeds from the primitive human state of total possession through the image, to a final state in which unconscious deflation has progressed so far that the idea is considered a content of consciousness. Being seized by the archetype has become "having an idea," or, at best, "following it." This late stage of development poses a danger, even aside from the fact that it often involves self-deception by consciousness, which is unaware of the enduring power of the archetypes.

Although the split into these two components is consistent with the development of consciousness, it is also one of the critical points of an overdeveloped consciousness, one that is split off from the unconscious. It implies a conscious reluctance to react to perceptual images, a factor particularly noticeable in modern people. This also means that moderns are defended against the appearance of an unconscious image or situation. In contrast to the immediate reflexive reactions of primitive people, the interval between reaction and situation is now significantly extended, if not altogether suspended.

This delayed or absent reaction is highly characteristic of the modern person's behavior when faced with manifestations of the unconscious. It corresponds to the deflating tendency of consciousness, its apotropaic, defensive magic, its tendency to weaken and devalue the unconscious. This is particularly the reaction of the thinking type; but it is not limited to him. Rather, it follows from the essential differentiation of consciousness into a primary and an auxiliary function, at the expense of the other functions and at the cost of wholeness.[27]

The modern person's pigeon-hole psychology expresses itself in the fact that he reacts and functions only partially. In doing so, he is even conscious of ensuring that these partial reactions remain independent of each other. For example, he is different as a political person than as a religious person; he has different morals in his profession than in war or in the family; he thinks differently as a scientist than as an educator. This sort of pigeon-hole psychology makes sense, in that it protects the individual from being overwhelmed by contents that could make absolute claims on him, and thus it safeguards the small, partial sovereignty of ego-consciousness.

The holistic reaction of the primitive human being is dominated by the unconscious. He is completely contained in every situation and reaction, but he is also totally unconscious, possessed in his wholeness. He cannot distinguish what possesses him and where it takes him, because consciousness and the ego have been almost completely obliterated. Standing in contrast to this primitive blindness and helplessness, however, the modern person's freedom and independence are purchased at the price of surrendering his wholeness. His ego and consciousness depend on constricting the unconscious as far as possible, dividing life into fragments. As these fragmentary domains are so small and isolated, they protect from the state of total possession, which is dangerous because it renders unconscious. Thus, the ego, within its system, can decide arbitrarily and deliberately.

This situation of being less than whole remains unnoticed and undisturbing, as long as the individual is preoccupied with and fully engrossed by the claims of the world. Thus, as long as the demands of the collective, in the form of community and civilization, are unsatisfied, the individual must more or less forsake his own individuality, in order to achieve his adaptation to life. This is the task of the first half of life: on the one hand, to resolve the partner problem and start a family and, on the other, to achieve professionally and integrate into the community. These are the two sides of the collective's demand to be a "normal" person.

This adaptation to life takes place, as we have seen, with the help of conscious differentiation, by developing the differentiated function and suppressing the inferior one. From another perspective, this corresponds to the formation of the persona and the unconscious formation of the shadow. Finally, this process is characterized by intrapsychically polarizing the original male–female disposition.

Here, consciousness acknowledges and emphasizes only the character that corresponds to the outer sexual characteristic, whereas its opposite remains unconscious, as the system of anima or animus, and governs the relationship between the unconscious and consciousness. As Jung has shown,[28] a reversal of this situation is one of the natural problems of the second half of life and most frequently stands behind its crisis.

The absence of puberty rites, to facilitate the young person's transition into the world, is the most common cause of adolescent neuroses, insofar as their common difficulty is finding this transition into the world, in adapting to the collective and to the partner. Similarly, the absence of rites associated with the climacteric,[29] rituals of aging, is expressed in the climacteric neuroses of the second half of life. The common difficulty at this stage is to disentangle oneself from the world, which is necessary for maturation and achievement in old age.

The important problem of the second half of life and the cultural significance of the individuation process, for the individual but also for the collective, cannot be dealt with here. Jung has devoted a substantial part of his work to this problem. Here, as we are concerned with the development of consciousness as a special problem, we need address only the processes characterizing development in the first half of life. This reversal, the contents of which we have considered elsewhere,[30] can also be dealt with here in regard of a particular aspect.

To characterize the different developmental directions of old age, we must highlight the major pairs of opposites that belong to this development. In the first half of life, the deflation of the unconscious leads, as we have seen, to the constriction of the unconscious and the emergence of the necessary inclination toward the collective and the world. Conversely, the development of old age requires a deflation of the world, a detachment from the collective and its values, and the reappearance of the unconscious in a new and heightened form. The pre-personal aspect of the child's unconscious existence was replaced by the personal, ego-centered existence of the adult, who proves his worth in and for the collective, putting the domain of his ego at the center, making it visible in one worldly domain or another, whether as power or achievement, relationship or work.

If development is natural, however, this purely egoistic existence is followed in turn by existence of a post-personal kind, in which the ego's domain is replaced by the transpersonal. Here the decisive role is played by archetypal powers, the unconscious, the world's "background," or ideas and one's engagement with them. The elderly, the grey-haired, are the bearers of culture and custodians of transpersonal existence. Their maturity lies in the fact that they have the necessary distance from the world, the empirical collective, and the domain of ego. They receive their light from the other side, and convey transpersonal and impersonal aspects of the background of existence to the community.

But with this cultural achievement, their own individuality also unfolds. In confronting old age and death, the other side of individual existence now develops, just as the personal aspect of the ego developed at the beginning, in the confrontation with adulthood and life.

Jung has often shown how the individuation process is based on sacrificing the differentiated function and developing the inferior function, that is, on the reversal of the youthful process that had led to the differentiation of the functions. Similarly, the individuation process includes the acceptance of the unconscious contrasexual side. The assimilation of anima or animus relativizes one's single-sex identity and develops the opposite position.

The fact that a feminine soul is unconsciously at work in the masculine, and a masculine spirit in the feminine, now comes to consciousness. As the personality moves toward wholeness, its embrace of the contrasexual side enriches the onesidedness of a life that up to now has stood under the primacy of a single-sex identity. It completes itself psychologically, by realizing the original, natural tendency toward bipolarity.

Finally, too, in the process of individuation, we regularly find that secondary personalization is reversed. That is, every deep analysis arrives at the Oedipus complex, which, however, as development deepens, reveals its symbolic and impersonal character.[31] This means that, behind the personal figures of the parents and their imagos, the parental archetypes emerge as the basic powers with which the child's ego-consciousness, and that of the adult, too, has had to struggle. But now, their confusion with the personal parental imagos comes progressively to an end.

Behind all these manifestations of the world's deflation, the sacrifice of the differentiated and development of the inferior function, in the acceptance of the contrasexual side of the psyche and the shadow, a tendency toward wholeness is at work in normal psychological events, which is of utmost importance. In the reversal of secondary personalization, however, this same tendency causes a struggle to emerge between the world of consciousness and the transpersonal world of the unconscious.

As typology has shown, consciousness and the act of thinking cannot be equated, even if the development of consciousness and the splitting off of the material from the dynamic components of the unconscious are largely governed, as we can see, by the primacy of thinking. The basic fact that consciousness and thinking are not identical is one of the main problems, however, on the path into the depths, for it has been shown that it is entirely insufficient to work through the unconscious with thinking alone. The essence of the individuation process is to bring the whole personality to reality, that is, to work not only with the attitude opposing the conscious attitude, but also with the inferior, undifferentiated functions, in order to liberate them from the unconscious. The problem of "realization" is thus very different from using just *one* function to bring things to consciousness. The contents of the unconscious should not become "familiar"; they should not be "felt," or "seen," etc. Rather, they must be experienced by the whole personality. The high points of this experience are different for each individual and each type. But when such experiences occur, their shared character is that they are not confined to partial areas or partial functions; instead, they progressively seize and transform the whole person.

It is necessary to compare the materials that emerge from the unconscious with the psychic heritage of humanity in general. This is the only way we can, for example, interpret many dreams and other contents, in order to promote a broad expansion of consciousness. But this method reaches only the contents and material components of the collective unconscious, i.e., only one aspect of its archetypal and symbolic elements.

Besides these material components, which can be perceived, evaluated, and understood, and the possibilities of which can and must be investigated, there are also the dynamic–emotional components, in the unconscious, which represent instinctive behavioral patterns and impulses for action. When the unconscious is no longer deflated by the ego, its contents are activated; then its part personalities, its material components, can emerge. And, beyond this, the dynamic and emotional components of the collective unconscious are also enlivened. That is, the instincts reappear, the typical forms of reaction, which up to then had been alien to the ego and outside its responsive range.

"Civilization and its discontents"[32] lead the human being into crisis and, through it, via the path of the depths, back to the unconscious, where he now re-experiences all these stages of conscious development in the opposite direction, under the constant control and participation of the ego. As mentioned, not only does this reactivate the complex nature of the unconscious, making its dynamic–emotional components reappear, but it also reunites them with the material components of the collective unconscious.

The path through the deep layers of the unconscious not only expands consciousness but also leads to an expansion and transformation of the whole personality, described by Jung as integration and individuation.[33] Becoming whole is achieved not least by reactivating the dynamic components, as expressed in the capacity to be possessed and set in motion by this state of possession.

What analytical psychology calls the "realization of the unconscious" refers to this state of affairs. A typical example is the introverted intuitive, that is, a person to whom the images of the unconscious, the archetypes, become visible as images. For example, in an intuition he sees an image of the "terrible mother," the mother's devouring aspect. Not only can he perceive this image, he can also shape it. without being touched by it. He beholds it, amazed, as something foreign, with no reference to himself or his situation, because he stops with the perception. He reacts to the suggestion that this being, this image, lives in the depth of his psyche with surprise and interest, but without being able to put it to any use. He functions entirely as a differentiated part personality, as an intuitive, to the exclusion of the other functions, and completely lacks any instinctive reaction to the image.

(The case with dreaming, for example, is different. There, too, on account of lowered consciousness, the dynamic–emotional component is less well suppressed, so the whole personality can be taken over by the dream. This can happen even to highly differentiated egos. Although the deflation of the unconscious promotes forgetting and disregarding one's dream life, such persons sometimes experience a therapeutic and cathartic effect from a dream that has a powerful impact, even without interpretation.)

As long as the intuitive remains in this situation, he has perceived only the material and content component of the archetype, not its other, energetic side, which is dynamic and emotional. But, if the intuitive now proceeds, by thinking his way through the archetypal image, that is, if he adds the corresponding mythological, religious–historical, philosophical contents, etc., he can understand the scope and meaning of the image of the "terrible mother" with their help. Then his consciousness expands, and the hitherto unconscious content gains access to his life and his conscious world. This process may not only benefit but also save him, by preventing the archetype from exploding or flooding consciousness. But even this working through does not amount to a full realization. The situation changes fundamentally only when the less-differentiated functions are included in the reaction. (In our example, these would be the judging function of feeling and the reality-perceiving function of sensation.)

Regardless of typology,[34] the situation changes in exactly the same way, because the inferior function is always connected with the emotional and dynamic components of the unconscious. In other words, whenever the inferior function is involved—and a large part of depth analysis is devoted to its involvement and development—the dynamic component is reactivated, and there is a holistic reaction to real experience.

This activation of the inferior function and its associated dynamic and emotional components (feeling, as noted, forms the exception) always leads ultimately to a connection between the material and the dynamic components, and thus to a resurgence of the deeper instinctive reactions. This reconnection with deep instinctuality contributes decisively to the personality in its recovery of wholeness. It is a therapy for modern people, whose consciousness is split off in its isolation, estranged from both instinct and nature.

Now comes a direct experience of the unconscious. To stay with our example, this means that the ego regresses to the level of early humanity. There it is overcome, with the overwhelming power that we know from dreams and nightmares, by the image of the terrible mother, and the ego reacts to the image with emotion. Thus, its intuition becomes reality.

Activation of the unconscious, however, means undergoing a primal experience and being transformed by it. This is why the development of the inferior function, the unconscious side of the personality, is the core element of any journey into the depths, for only this development allows the personality to become transformed and whole. In the inferior function, every human being is a primitive, because this side, which is turned away from ego-consciousness, is the shadow region of the personality and connected with the unconscious in *participation mystique*. Therefore, the realization of this side means that, through the mediation of the "dark brother," consciousness experiences the prehistory and early history of humanity. By including this primitive part and its emotional–dynamic components, and by moving through the earlier stages of humanity that preceded conscious development, the ego itself is transformed.

The original unity is restored between the emerging unconscious content and emotionality. At the same time, however, the splitting of the modern human being into parts—partial functions, partial attitudes, and partial reactions—is also reversed. For this reason, the process of achieving wholeness and integration is so often associated with alchemical symbolism,[35] because the basic problem of alchemy is represented in just this way, in the remelting and reuniting of fragments. The symbolism of fire, which is crucial in this process, corresponds to the emergence of the dynamic and emotional components of the unconscious in depth-psychological development. The cathartic phenomenon, so important in modern psychotherapy, where it is known as either a goal or a symptom, occurs explosively. On the path of analytical psychology into the depths, on the other hand, this phenomenon basically accompanies the whole process. Thus, it no longer has to do with a therapeutic shock or the abreaction of blocked affects; rather, it is about the fundamental reconnection of life and consciousness with the contents and emotionality of the unconscious.

Reconnection with the instincts, as the dynamic components of the unconscious, takes place within the individuation process in such a way that the ego, aided by its primitive aspect and partially identical with it, repeats the primal experience of the early human being. Ego-consciousness, however, is not recollectivized; it is not dragged back, reflexively and explosively, into the instinctive, holistic reaction of the unconscious. This new form of reconnection with the instincts involves the active participation of the system of consciousness. Thus, it establishes a conscious connection between consciousness and the unconscious.

This process means that consciousness experiences the unconscious as if in slow motion. It is a gradual process of synthesis, and therefore it is always accompanied by the symbolism of vegetative growth. The reconnection between material and dynamic components enables the personality to react as a whole, including ego-consciousness. It is no longer an explosive, holistic reaction of the reflex, excluding the ego and consciousness.

In this experiential process, the instincts are reflected to some extent. The dynamic, strongly emotional components seize consciousness, but they do not flood it. They transform, and yet do not dissolve, ego-consciousness. Nevertheless, the unconscious can be realized only insofar as the ego lets itself be affected by the depth of the unconscious, and only insofar as consciousness is willing, in this process of realization, to revise its worldview, and submits to being decisively reshaped by the experience of the depths.

The natural authority that enables this transformation and the realization of the unconscious is the symbol. The emergence of the symbolism of the unconscious makes it possible for consciousness to approach the side of the psyche that is alien to consciousness. For the symbol, by its very nature, mediates between consciousness and the unconscious.

In the primitive human being, as Jung has shown,[36] the symbol mediates the transition of psychic energy from the unconscious to a conscious application and activity. Jung understands the symbol as "the psychological mechanism that transforms energy."[37] With its help, instinctual energy is diverted "from its natural river-bed of everyday habit into some unaccustomed activity."[38]

The everyday habit here is the unconscious existence of the primitive human, whose libido habitually adheres to the world in the *participation mystique* within which his natural life takes place. The symbols release the energy from this adherence and conduct it toward conscious activity and the achievement of work. Only the symbol, as a transformer of energy, enables the transformation of libido, which makes achievement possible for early humans in the first place. This explains why a multitude of cultic and symbolic measures precede and accompany every early human activity, be it agriculture, hunting, fishing, or any other "unaccustomed," non-everyday activity. Only with help from the libido-capturing, fascinating, and ego-engrossing capacity of the symbol is it possible to tackle an unaccustomed activity.

The same conditions are still partially at work in modern people, except that we are not aware of them. Even today, the way to persuade people to change from their everyday habit to a necessary but unaccustomed activity is to "hallow" the unaccustomed activity. For example, the transformation of a small office clerk into the responsible commander of a death-sowing fighter squadron is probably one of the most radical psychic transformations demanded of the modern human being. This transformation of the normal, peaceful person into a warrior is possible, even today, only with the help of symbols. Invoking the symbols—God, king, fatherland, freedom, the "holiest goods of the nation"—in heavily symbolic, communal acts of dedication, aided by all the themes of religion and art that have power for the individual: this remains the primary enabling path for this transformation of personality. Only this makes it psychologically possible to divert psychic energy from the "natural river-bed" of peaceful, private life into the "unaccustomed activity" of killing.

Claiming that these symbols have a more rational character than the symbols of the primitives fails to recognize that the power of each symbol, in particular its power to influence the modern human being, is based on its irrational side. Like the individual symbol, the social symbol, that is, one that applies to the group, "never [has] an exclusively conscious or an exclusively unconscious source, but arise[s] from the equal collaboration of both."[39] This means it has a rational side, "that accords with reason, but it has another side that does not; for it is composed not only of rational but also of irrational data supplied by pure inner and outer perception."[40]

In other words, the sensuous, pictorial component of the symbol, generated by the irrational functions of sensation and intuition, cannot be grasped by reason. Although this is immediately apparent in the case of concrete symbols, such as the flag, the cross, etc., it is equally true of more abstract ideas, insofar as they involve symbolic realities. The idea of "fatherland," for example, undoubtedly has a rational aspect, but its importance as a symbol far exceeds anything about it that reason can grasp. An unconscious, emotional factor, which is also called into action when the symbol is invoked, is actually its source of power and shows the symbol to be a transformer of energy, using fascination to release the libido from its old ways.

In general, the symbol works in opposite directions for early and for modern humanity. In evolutionary terms, in early humanity the symbol led to conscious development, adaptation to reality, and the discovery of the outer world of objects. For example, as we know today, the sacred animal comes into evidence earlier than the domestication of cattle, and the sacral meaning of values and things is older than their profane meanings. Time and again, an object's meaning in reality emerges only long after its symbolic meaning.

During the early era of humanity, the part of the symbol that can be rationalized is of crucial importance. Here, the image of the world develops from the symbolic to the rational, and the progress from prelogical to logical thought is facilitated by the symbol. Similarly, it can be shown that the gradual differentiation of philosophical and scientific thought has been made possible only by symbolic thinking, with ongoing emancipation from the emotional and dynamic components of the unconscious.

For the modern human being, the symbols appearing on his inward journey have a completely different meaning and function. The mediating position of the symbol, based on its combination of unconscious and conscious elements, is proven here. For just as consciousness developed out of the unconscious for early human beings, now, going in the other direction, the reconnection of consciousness with the unconscious is once again accomplished through symbols.

With the help of the symbol, the modern person's psychic energy is also diverted "from its natural river-bed of everyday habit into some unaccustomed activity." Conversely, however, it is now diverted and directed inward by the consciously controlled field of outer accomplishment and adaptation to reality.

Whereas the symbol was instrumental for early humanity in the extraversion of libido, for the modern person it accomplishes an introversion. For early humans, the world was animated by the outward projection of symbols. Now, going in the opposite direction, an "internalization"[41] is achieved; the unconscious is activated through the symbol's introjection. On both the outbound path of the primitive human being and the return path of the modern person, the symbol gives evidence of its lively power as a mediator between the sphere of ego-consciousness and the deep layer of the unconscious, which, as the name implies,[42] "fall together" in it, sharing equally in its structure.

The meaning of the symbol lies in the fact that it represents a unity and a wholeness in which rational and irrational elements are synthetically combined. The essence of the symbol is synthesis. The instinctual aspect of the unconscious and its spiritual aspect, which corresponds to reason, are both effective side by side, yet here they are merged into an operative unit. This synthetic nature appeals to the human tendency toward wholeness and synthesis, which is aroused by the appearance of the "living symbol."[43] The potential wholeness of a personality, in which the conscious and unconscious systems still function separately, is set in motion by the natural synthesis of conscious and unconscious components in the living symbol. In the symbol's wholeness and completeness, the demand for wholeness and completeness confronts the individual as something like a task.

Not only does the symbol preoccupy, it also fascinates. It does not let go, it asserts its claim, and it forces the human being to keep returning to it. In depth analysis, it is not unusual to work on a symbolic drawing or series of images for years. The individual may return to it time and again and, by devoting himself to it, may experience and understand the new meaning of this symbolism through a new approach to its content.

In this way, the constantly changing contents of the unconscious, which have formulated themselves symbolically, are conveyed to consciousness, which expands itself through them. At the same time, the individual is increasingly exposed to the power of the unconscious. Its contents are progressively brought into reality, as the material dimension of the symbols—their knowable content—is joined with their emotional and dynamic dimension, by which the individual is seized.

This realization is a greater form of becoming whole; it is the synthesis of the individuation journey, on which the opposites are united and the morbid dissociation of consciousness from the unconscious is healed and overcome. The healing and hallowing power of the symbol is taught to us by humanity's history of religions. This history could almost be described as a salvation history of the symbol, because all religious existence depends on the whole-making, healing effect of the living symbol.

The disquiet, appeal, and activation emanating from the symbol are due to its effect on any parts of the personality that may be undifferentiated and unconscious. For every symbol "formulates an essential unconscious factor."[44]

When Jung says, "The symbol is always a product of data from every psychic function,"[45] this means that, for every individual, every living symbol contains components that are alien to consciousness. Thus, the symbol not only addresses the differentiated part of the personality, its consciousness and developed functions, but also activates the other side of the personality.

Thus, for every individual, the living symbol contains some of the vitality of the inferior function, and its excitement arises from its powerful impact on whatever side of the personality is undeveloped. Regardless of its content, its material component, the symbol activates the emotionality and dynamism that are always closely linked to the inferior function.

One illustration of this factual situation is that, especially in primitive human beings, dominated by irrationality and the unconscious, the symbol leads to the development of reason and consciousness. In modern people, on the other hand, in whom rational consciousness dominates, the symbol is what brings about the development of the irrational and the unconscious.

The compensatory function of the symbol, which guides the individual toward wholeness, far exceeds any experience of being addressed at the personal level. For beyond the personal aspect, the symbol always also expresses the spiritual aspect, the principle of the unconscious that gives form, for "the spiritual appears in the psyche also as an instinct," as a "principle *sui generis*."[46] Together with the experience of instinctuality of the unconscious, and just as important, is that of its spirituality. These two basic tendencies of the human psyche are synthesized in the symbol, with its combination of the rational and the irrational. Sometimes one component and sometimes the other is more important for the consciousness of the individual to work through.

The power of the living symbol to constellate wholeness is most obvious in the phenomenon described by Jung as the unifying symbol and the "transcendent function."[47] Unlike a natural symbol, which is mainly the product of the unconscious, the unifying symbol is the product of a special situation, in which ego-stability, the attitude of consciousness toward the unconscious, is a decisive factor. As a product of the transcendent function, the unifying symbol overcomes the energetic and material tension that exists between conscious ego-stability, on the one hand, and the unconscious, opposing it, on the other, the tendency of which is to overwhelm consciousness.

The unifying symbol is a manifestation of the wholeness of the individual, which combines and thus overcomes—"transcends"—the conscious and unconscious positions, by productively, that is, creatively, incorporating new and hitherto unused elements. This makes the unifying symbol the highest form of the synthesis that we have already encountered in the natural symbol. It is the most perfect product of the holistic and self-healing tendency of the psyche, which not only uses a creative process to heal every conflict, provided it is seriously borne, but also makes it the starting point for an expansion of the whole personality.

With the unifying symbol, the conscious situation is not only compensated and completed, as with the natural symbol, but is also taken into specific account. Whereas the natural symbol is produced by the creative nature of the unconscious, which compensates for consciousness, the unifying symbol is produced by the creative nature of the whole psyche, including both consciousness and the unconscious. It is the product of a structure that includes consciousness—here, in the form of the ego-stability that rejects the unconscious.

Jung surmises "that the stability and determinacy of individuality and the superior power of unconscious expression are nothing but indications of one and the same factual situation"[48]—the stability and determinacy of individuality: this means strength and integrity, as well as the moral integrity of consciousness, which does not allow itself to be overturned by the demands of the unconscious. But the superior power of unconscious expression is the transcendent function. It corresponds to the creative component of the psyche, which overcomes a conflict that consciousness cannot solve, by creating a new path, value, or image. Taken together, both express an attained and effective wholeness of personality, in which the creative side of the psyche and the determinacy of individuality, of consciousness, no longer function as two opposing systems, split off from each other, but have achieved a synthesis.

This synthesis of the psyche, achieved in the individuation process, represents a connection of two opposing systems: consciousness and the unconscious. This synthesis therefore often appears among symbols representing a newly unified principle of opposites, such as the hermaphrodite, the union of male and female. The hermaphroditic nature of the uroboros appears here on a new level.

Just as the alchemical process of transformation elevates the original hermaphroditic situation of primordial matter, the *prima materia*, to the final hermaphroditic situation of the philosopher's stone, the *rebis*,[49] so individuation, the path of human transformation, leads to a higher synthesis of ego, consciousness, and the unconscious. Whereas, in the beginning, the embryonic ego lay trapped in the enveloping hermaphroditic uroboros, in the end the Self is the golden mean of the elevated uroboros, the union of male and female, conscious and unconscious elements, in which the ego does not perish, but experiences itself as the unifying symbol, the Self.

The Self and its symbolism represent the central aspect of wholeness, the midpoint and creative source of the psyche.[50] But this Self is not an archetypal content of the unconscious. Rather, as the center of the individuation process, it is the unique, individual synthesis that has arisen from the transpersonal structure of the unconscious and the personal structure of consciousness. For this reason, the ego has this special and unique relationship to the Self, to something that is more comprehensive than the ego, yet which the ego nevertheless experiences as "I myself," my very essence.

On the one hand, this Self is the symbol of the transformed personality, formulated symbolically as the new ego, reborn, sublimated, and extracted from the alchemical process. Yet, on the other hand, it is also the treasure acquired by the personality in the confrontation of life, in the struggle with the world and its own unconscious.

The self-generating act, in which ego-consciousness frees itself from the entangling power of the dragon of the unconscious at the beginning of life, corresponds in the second half of life to the self-generating rebirth of the ego as the Self, in which it frees itself from the entangling power of the dragon of the world. The dragon fight in the first half of life begins with the path through the world of the unconscious and ends with the heroic birth of the ego. The night sea journey of the second half of life begins with the path through the world and ends with the heroic birth of the Self.

Puberty rites conclude the process in which the ego and the conscious world emerge from the unconscious. Correspondingly, the rites of aging in the second half of life are those in which the ego detaches itself from the world, is initiated into the transpersonal world, and assumes a new form through rebirth as the Self. The initiation mysteries of the ancient world, like those of the Middle Ages, the initiation into the Kabbalah, and the secret teachings of India, are intended for adults. That is, they are only for those who have already, in their profession or their family, performed their service to the collective.

Whereas the ascending arc of conscious development in the first half of life occurs under the principle of differentiation and the primacy of the ego, the descending arc of development in the second half of life occurs under the primacy of the Self and is governed by the principle of integration. Only together do they form the structure of wholeness, which tends toward fulfilment in every psyche.

This emerging wholeness, as a result of the individuation process, is an intensified structuring, a forming of the personality, which contrasts with the process of differentiation at the beginning of life. Development during the first half of life tends toward differentiation and increasing tension, at the expense of wholeness, but the integration process moves toward increased stability and diminishing tension. This developmental trait accords with the natural aging process of every living structure. It has its biological and physiological equivalents. This formation, consolidation, structuring, and stabilization are therefore also connected with a symbolism that includes the perfect form, balance, harmony, and stability. The mandala, as circle and sphere, as pearl and perfect blossom, unites all these elements, whereas symbols of the Self, like the diamond, stone, or rock, represent the indestructibility and stability that can no longer be dissolved by the opposites.

It is important to emphasize that this stability of the psyche—as long as the emphasis is not placed on indestructibility, eternity, and immortality—always emerges as a living, renewing structure that grows and evolves. When the tension between opposites is reduced, it means, in this case, a binding and shaping of these powerful forces, that is, their qualitative transformation, not just their quantitative weakening. Here, as elsewere, maturation seems to correspond to the transformation of quantitatively strong potential tensions into qualitatively higher and more stable structures.

The holistic structure at the center of which stands the Self as the mid-point of the psyche, as the unity of consciousness and the unconscious, often symbolizes itself as a mandala, a centered circle, or the uroboros of hermaphroditic existence. Now, however, this circle is centered on the luminous core of the Self. In the beginning, the uroboros exists on its animal level, and the ego, as the center contained in it, is almost concealed. But in the unfolding of the mandala blossom, this animal tension of the opposites is overcome, transcended by a Self that extends out into the opposites. At the beginning of development, consciousness is almost obliterated by the superiority of the unconscious, but at the end it is expanded and empowered by its connection with the Self. Because the Self cooperates with the stability of the ego, the contents of the world and of the unconscious, of what is outside and what is inside, are tamed and controlled.

Corresponding to the unified structure of the psyche, which differentiates itself in the first stage, the world has differentiated itself under the principle of opposites, into inside and outside, consciousness and the unconscious, spirit and life, male and female, individual and collective. But, to the maturing psyche, which, overcoming the principle of opposites, integrates itself under the sign of the hermaphrodite, the world also proves to be a hermaphroditic circle of existence, in which a human center is realized, as the individual who realizes himself between the inner and the outer worlds, or as humanity itself. For humanity as a whole has the same task as the individual, namely, to realize itself as a unity. Both the individual and humanity are thrust into a reality, one half of which confronts them as nature and the outside world, the other half as the psyche and the unconscious, as spirit and powers. And both of them must experience themselves as the center of this reality.

In the beginning, the ego lay hidden, as an embryo in the belly of the dragon, the primal parents, the uroboros, with its confusion of inner and outer, the world and the unconscious. In the end, as in alchemical images, the hermaphrodite stands on this dragon, having overcome the primal situation by existing as a synthesis, while above it floats the crown of the Self, and the diamond shines in its heart. But only when the consciousness of humanity as a whole, not just of some individuals, has developed to this stage of synthesis, is the supra-individual uroboric situation overcome, and with it the collective threat of the dragon.

Human consciousness must experience the collective unconscious, the unconsciousness shared by all humankind, and bring it to awareness as the common primal ground. Only when the differentiation of humankind into races, nations, tribes, and groups is once again resynthesized, by a process of integration, will the threat of the primeval dragon, the flooding unconscious, be conquered for humanity. A future humanity will then know in reality the same center, the core of humanity, that the individual ego experiences today as its center: the superordinate Self, at whose appearing the primal threat of the uroboros dragon is overcome.

Erich Neumann
1943

Notes

1 *EN*: *Typen*. [Cf. CW 6.]
2 *EN*: *Beziehungen*. [Cf. CW 7,2.]
3 *EN*: *Typen*.
4 *EN*: *Beziehungen*.
5 *EN*: Ibid.
6 *EN*: Wickes [1931], *The Inner World of Childhood*, op. cit.

7 *EN*: Author: "Symbols and Stages of Conscious Development," p. 3. [Cf. above, Appendix B.I, *Roots II*, p. 211.]
8 *EN*: Author: "Die symbolische Bedeutung des Oedipuskomplexes" ("The symbolic meaning of the Oedipus complex"). [Another of Neumann's writings, not found to date.]
9 *EN*: Wickes, op. cit.
10 *EN*: We limit ourselves here to the male child. The developmental situation and problem of the female child will need to be addressed separately.
11 *EN*: *Beziehungen*.
12 *EN*: Transposition of these puberty rites into early childhood is a typical feature of cultures that emphasize the male and the spirit. In circumcision and baptism, the mother is already replaced by the father at the beginning of life, by which the mother's domain is deliberately and decisively reduced, as the author has explained elsewhere. [Cf. *Roots I*, pp. 155ff.]
13 *EN*: *Typen*.
14 Neumann annotates the word "prelogical" in a later paragraph. Cf. Appendix B.II, *Roots II*, p. 220, n. 25.
15 *EN*: P.D. Chantepie de la Saussaye [et al., 1925], *Lehrbuch der Religionsgeschichte* (*Primer on the history of religions*), v. 1.
16 Jung describes the libido's typical "inertia, which will relinquish no object of the past" (CW 5, ¶253 (p. 174).
17 French: "rites of passage."
18 *EN*: *Wandlungen*. [Discussions of libido are numerous in this work, which Neumann knew in the 1912 or the 1925 edition. Later, much revised and expanded, it was published as CW 5, *Symbols of Transformation*. A relevant passage may be found in "The Battle for Deliverance from the Mother," CW 5, ¶450.]
19 *EN*: *Energetik*, p. 74. [Neumann's note, at the bottom of a long typewritten page, is difficult to connect with the text on that page. The closest match between his text and p. 74 in Jung's *Energetik* is a passage that reads, in Hull's translation: "All major undertakings and efforts, such as tilling the soil, hunting, war, etc., are entered upon with ceremonies of magical analogy or with preparatory incantations which quite obviously have the psychological aim of canalizing libido into the necessary activity" (CW 8,1, ¶86). Andreas Jung kindly allowed me to study p. 74 in Jung's edition of *Energetik*.]
20 *EN*: *Typen*, p. 603. [Cf. CW 6, ¶754.]
21 *EN*: Ibid.
22 Latin: in one action.
23 *EN*: Jung [1909], *Diagnostische Assoziationstudien* (*Diagnostic association studies*). [Cf. CW 2,9.]
24 This statement assumes readers know that Jung defines both thinking and feeling as rational functions (cf. e.g., CW 6, ¶518).
25 *EN*: Cassirer, 1925[/1997], *Philosophie der symbolischen Formen* (*Philosophy of symbolic forms*), v. 2, *Das mythische Denken* (*Mythical thinking*); and Lévy-Bruhl [1926], *Das Denken der Naturvölker* (*How Natives Think*). [Nico Fehlbaum advises that Cassirer does not use the word *prälogisch* (prelogical), which Neumann annotates here, except when discussing the writings of Lévy-Bruhl. In *How Natives Think* (*Das Denken der Naturvölker*), Lévy-Bruhl titles Chapter 1 "The Functioning of Prelogical Mentality." He defines "prelogical" in Chapter 2, "The Law of Participation" (cf. p. 63). Robert Segal advises that in this context the term refers to a mixture of identity and separateness and is used synonymously with "mystic."]
26 *EN*: *Typen*, p. 630. [Cf. CW 6, ¶732.]
27 *EN*: Ibid.
28 *EN*: *Seelenprobleme*. [Probably referring to "Die Lebenswende" ("The Stages of Life"), as cited above, *Roots II*, p. 124, n. 26. (Cf. also CW 8,16.)]
29 *EN*: Jung speaks of the first and second half of life and sets the midlife crisis point at the age of 35 to 40. Apart from this classification, however, the subdivision into quarters is of

great practical importance, since the time of puberty falls at the approximate middle of the first half of life, and the climacteric at the approximate middle of the second half.

30 *EN*: Author: "Stages of religious experience on the path of depth psychology." [Neumann's 1942 lecture is published here under its original title, "The religious meaning of the path of depth psychology," Appendix B.IV, *Roots II*, pp. 256ff.]

31 *EN*: Author: "Symbolische Bedeutung des Oedipuskomplexes." [Cf. note 8, above.]

32 "*Unbehagen in der Kultur*" (*Civilization and its Discontents*): Allusion to Sigmund Freud's book, originally published 1930. A groundbreaking essay on cultural theory, Freud's work explores the inevitable conflict between the demands of culture and those of human instinctuality.

33 *EN*: *Beziehungen*, and *Integration of the Personality* (hereafter: *Integration*). [*Integration* is a collection of Jung's papers, published in English in 1939, trans. by Stanley Dell. Various chapters are now found in CW 9,i, CW 12, and CW 17.]

34 *EN*: The feeling type is an exception. Here, the process is reversed. A feeling type starts from the dynamic–emotional component and discovers in the unconscious the material component, thus arriving at their reconnection from the other side.

35 *EN*: Jung, *Integration* and *Psych & Rel*; Silberer [1914], *Probleme der Mystik*.

36 *EN*: *Wandlungen*. [Cf. CW 5, e.g., ¶338–44.]

37 *EN*: *Energetik*, p. 76. [Cf. CW 8, ¶88.]

38 Cf. CW 8, ¶87. Here, Jung refers to the power of ceremonies and rituals.

39 *EN*: *Typen*, p. 679. [Cf. CW 6, ¶821.]

40 *EN*: Ibid. [Cf. CW 6, ¶823.]

41 *EN*: Silberer, *Probleme der Mystik*, pp. 154ff. [On p. 154 Silberer mentions *Verinnerlichung* (internalization). On the following pages, in a discussion of Jung's writings, he links this concept to introversion.]

42 The etymology of "symbol" in Greek: *syn-*, "with," and *ballein*, "to throw."

43 *EN*: *Typen*, p. 679 [Cf. CW 6, ¶819f.]

44 *EN*: Ibid. [Cf. CW 6, ¶820.]

45 *EN*: Ibid, p. 681. [Cf. CW 6, ¶823, paraphrased. In Hull's translation, Jung's full statement reads: "The symbol is always a product of an extremely complex nature, since data from every psychic function go into its making."]

46 *EN*: *Energetik*, p. 98. [Cf. CW 8, ¶108.]

47 *EN*: *Typen*, p. 683. [Cf. CW 6, ¶825-28.]

48 Although Neumann encloses these words in quotation marks, a citation is lacking. He may be paraphrasing a passage in CW 6, which reads in Hull's translation: "Sometimes it seems as though the stability of the inborn *individuality* (q.v.) were the decisive factor, sometimes as though the mediatory product possessed a superior power that determines the ego's absolute stability. In reality it may be that the stability of the one and the superior power of the other are two sides of the same coin" (CW 6, ¶826).

49 *EN*: Jung, ______; Silberer, *Probleme der Mystik*. [Neumann's note omits the title of Jung's work. From context, he may have intended to refer to a passage in *Integration*, Chapter 4, "Dream Symbols of the Process of Individuation," describing the *rebis* as "compounded of two parts and therefore frequently hermaphroditic as an amalgam of Sol and Luna" (cf. CW 12, ¶305).]

50 This paragraph and the next correspond to Neumann's discussions of the ego–Self relationship in this volume, *Hasidism*. Cf. *Roots II*, pp. 81ff., pp. 106f., pp. 136ff., and 152f.

III. The path of depth psychology and consciousness

The threat to the individual is one of the critical dangers of our time. The collectivization of modern human beings, in whatever guise, threatens to extinguish the individual as a bearer of responsibility and ultimately to destroy his importance as an ego, conscious of representing the collective, the nation, and humankind.

The atomizing and collectivizing of western humanity is seen in the increasing tendency of the individual to put himself at the mercy of powerful events, without trying to influence or even understand them. In their dependence on the collective, individuals today feel *outwardly* helpless, to the same extent that primitive human beings felt *inwardly* helpless in relation to the powers of the unconscious. The myriad monstrous machines of death that crawl and fly over the world's horizon fill modern human beings with the same horror that filled medieval people, in the face of a myriad of demons, witches, and devils creeping forth from the maw of hell. But that fear is mild in comparison with the emptiness that is beginning to hollow out human beings today. Medieval people had the security of religion and salvation, which promised to rescue them from the evil enemy. But modern people have nothing that they can effectively set against the conspicuous power of evil. None of the political and sociological efforts to interpret and explain can reach deep enough to banish the deep, primal fear that now surges around modern humanity.

The danger of being swallowed up by the collective powers is extraordinarily great. It threatens to consume the future of humanity in the west, unless the overwhelming perspective of collective domination is compensated by an equally momentous conception of the importance of consciousness and the individual. Capitulation to the opaque power of the transpersonal reduces the ego and consciousness to an experience of helplessness, which is felt all the more sharply because, up to now, western people were fully persuaded of the strength and mastery of these authorities.

The extraordinary increase in the human species in recent centuries has led to an amassing of densely populated cities and industrial regions. It is also seen in the consolidation of small, insular states, which had existed as such for two hundred years, into national, continental, and intercontinental entities. The process culminates psychologically in two phenomena that contradict each other, although the relationship is evident.

On the one hand, parallel with this amassing of the species, the development of natural science and technology leads to an amazing rise in western ego-consciousness, which identifies itself with the consciousness of humanity and finds itself to be the final, highest point of a long developmental sequence. On the other hand, it leads in the contrary direction, to a growing depotentiation of the individual as a personality. Individuals now discover that they are atoms in the enormous world of collective humanity. Their self-consciousness is overpowered by the weight of a historical and physical image of the world, demoting contemporary humanity to a tiny grain of dust in the infinity of time and space.

Until now, there has been too little recognition of how profoundly human self-estimation has been shaken by modern science, especially by the history of evolution in its popular, Darwinian form. Human beings are now assigned to the animal world, with mammalian and primate ancestry. Discoveries about genetic randomness, by which human dispositions are thrown together like dice, raise profound questions for western people, who no longer have the sacred certainty of being made in God's image and occupying a central place in the world. These questions also threaten a loss of intrinsic value, through the transformation of the physical image of the world, which has banished both the earth and humanity from the center of the world to a random, lost, and meaningless point in infinity. The earlier orientation within a cosmos has become impossible. The process of disintegration, which no longer knows above or below, and for which heaven no longer arches over the earth or concentrically encloses it, is also made absolute by the fact that, beside the macro-world with its billions of light years, the micro-world of matter now confronts us with exactly the same universal dimensions. In ghostly fashion, research into atomic structure dissolves what is nearest and most concrete into infinity, just as, on a large scale, the formed image of a geocentric and anthropocentric cosmos has dissolved into infinity.

When we consider the contrast between this modern concept of the world and that of the medieval person, who felt like the responsible center of a religiously ordered cosmos, we shall recognize the full extent to which the western person is existentially shaken and devalued.

In this total dissolution of everything solid in the physical world of things, the human being is forcibly thrown back upon himself. He is overwhelmed by a new infinity, that of collective humanity, and thus shattered in his very existence as an individual. In an empty universe, as a tiny fragment of the species "human animal," the individual finds himself in a historical situation that teaches him that mass movements, earthly and subterranean migrations, determine his destiny. The basic layers of the ground in which he is rooted have begun to shift. These layers in which he is enmeshed, layers of race, nation, and human group, surround him and determine his existence, apparently without the possibility of escape.

The compensation for no longer being at the center of a world concentrically ordered around humanity, came with the modern discovery that the human being is the crowning end-point of a developmental sequence of unknown duration, and that this ending culminated, not unjustly, in the proud possession of human consciousness. The positive line of this development in the western sense of self stretches from the Renaissance to the Enlightenment, and manifests itself in the progressive widening of the world's horizon and the emergence of the historical unity of the western world. Self-emancipating ego-consciousness released itself from the strictures of religion and crowned itself in the French Revolution as the goddess Reason. In the nineteenth century, this development reached its negative phase, in which the flood of new contents and the simultaneous destruction of old orientations could no longer be compensated by modern western ego-emphasis.

The expanded horizon now led to a growing feeling of inferiority on the part of the individual, who renounced fulfilling the universal human image and was consciously subjected to the narrow existence of a specialist. This renunciation, as well as the loss of guiding values that enable personality formation, led to a self-established independence of partial contents, less and less subordinated to a higher principle. This created the "compartmental psychology" of modern people, which no longer reacts as a whole, but divides life into separate spheres—profession, private life, politics, religion, hobby—and has a different psychology, a different form of behavior, for each of them, under the motto that the right hand does not need to know what the left hand is doing.

Since the Renaissance, the extraverted orientation to life, directed toward the world of outer reality, has become so completely dominant in the west that the inner world has begun to retreat from consciousness. This is especially true because the emphasis in cultural education has also gradually shifted to the study and conquest of the outer world. The original continuum in which early humanity lived was an equal mixture of inner-world and outer-world factors. That is, objects and their influence are no longer involved in its composition as inner-world factors—part-souls, images, ideas, symbolic and religious givens, etc. Beside objects and their influence stands the inner world, the subject, the human structure; and its influence is in no way less than that of the outer world. For human experience depends as much on the subject as on the experienced object. The development of the west, which turned its attention mainly to the world of outer objects, has been one-sided and incomplete, to be sure, but it was still far from being diseased or damaging. Indeed, one might even say that the radicality and one-sidedness were necessary, in order to enable both the turning of libido toward the outer world and the exploration of its objects. It must be emphasized that, with the emergence of natural science and the discovery of the earth, of social and biological research, etc., it became necessary to detach oneself from the medieval values of the inner world by turning outward. This extraversion of libido among western people unfolded entirely according to the heroic epic, which always portrays the development of consciousness.

The struggle against the Church, by Galileo, Giordano Bruno, Kepler, etc., absolutely expresses the mythical struggle of the bringers of light against the dragon. We must not forget this fact, even if our world's present situation compels us to place the accent elsewhere. Today, for the development of consciousness, the character of progress lies in a turn toward the inner dimension, just as earlier it lay in a turn toward the outer dimension of the world. Turning toward the inner aspect today allows, in fact demands, that we derive much important material and content from the medieval spirit. This fact must not mislead us, however, into believing that medievalism is reactionary against the modern development of consciousness or, vice versa, that the turn toward inwardness must occur with the expanded consciousness acquired in the post-medieval and anti-medieval period.

The development of modern consciousness, with the withdrawal of psychological projections from the outer world, leads to the objective, physical world of natural science, a world emptied of soul.[1] Simultaneously, however, it also leads to a strong (even if at first unconscious) enlivening of the psyche, which is visible as the "reality of the soul," that is, as the native soil of all projections. All that was once projected outside, enlivening and investing the world with soul,[2] is now taken back again. Whatever soulfulness was lost in today's world has been won, unconsciously but powerfully, in the soulfulness of the human being.

This process was without danger until the dissolving of projections led to a complete loss of orientation for modern people and a revolution in their entire system of values and views. The transition from medieval to modern humanity progressed without any visible catastrophe, as long as the highest religious values, and moral and social values, remained untouched. So, even as the individual's attention shifted to the outer world, these values still guaranteed an orientation for the collective. As long as the great powers of the inner world were experienced through projection, and people were duly in touch with them through religion, manners, and custom, the radical extraversion of westerners was balanced by an unconscious counterweight.

The development of consciousness, however, which led to the natural sciences and the modern idea of the world, made it more and more impossible to experience the great contents of the unconscious as outer projections. With this critical destruction of projections, what necessarily followed for the western person was a serious loss of balance, for the repressed inner aspect now also forfeited its compensatory effectiveness in the existing religious systems.

Only now did a split emerge between the unconscious inner world and the extraverted direction of life and consciousness. The contents of the inner world could now no longer be experienced in projection, because consciousness had seen through these projections as having no reality in the outer world.

The dominants of the collective unconscious, the archetypes, the projection of which is the essential concern of religion, are distinguished precisely, however, by their possession of an energetic charge, which far exceeds that of consciousness. For this reason, it was and is impossible, in principle, to assimilate these contents into consciousness. Rather, when the projections of religious systems were destroyed, they fell back into the human psychic space from which they had been projected, and stimulated it.

The stimulation of the western person's inner world is the hallmark of our epoch. Its collective epidemics, its twilights of gods and values, are the symptom of a fundamentally changed constellation in this inner world. The stimulation of the collective psychic layers of the unconscious in the west has been growing ever clearer in the past 150 years. It expresses itself first in a change of worldview, which must include more and more of the dark side of life and of humankind. In every area one may discern this irruption, which has profoundly transformed the structure of western people and laid ruin to their whole system of values and orientation.

Running parallel to this emergence of the dark side, however, is an extraordinary widening of the human horizon, which embraces the whole of humankind, all of humanity, in relation to geography, history, the history of evolution, and politics.

Thus, with the invading force of the collective unconscious came a simultaneous expansion of human consciousness, even if not to the same extent. This compensatory process has placed humanity in a better position to assimilate the emerging unconscious powers.

Not by coincidence, depth psychology came into existence at this time, as the necessary and ever more intensive attempt of humankind, with the help of consciousness the sacral instrument of the western person, to understand and take control of the activated and violently invading inner world. In depth psychology, this activated inner space presented itself, confronting human consciousness as the objective psyche, and became an object of consciousness and scientific knowledge.

In this new struggle that confronts it, the ego, which sees itself facing the powers and worlds of the collective unconscious, has no intention of abandoning its dignity or allowing itself to be regressively undone. We see here a decisive characteristic of modern human development, in that consciousness, which has not capitulated to the superior power of the outer world, is equally unwilling to capitulate to that of the inner.

Holding fast to the principle of consciousness, while simultaneously turning inward to experience the objective psyche, results in what is called the individuation process.[3] This process is distinguished from the religious experience of earlier times exactly by emphasizing and retaining the dignity of this principle of consciousness, which knows itself to be the highest good of humankind. From the connection between the contents of the collective unconscious and the maintained consciousness comes the individuation process, which leads to a transformation of the entire personality. The path inward runs in a direction that is the reverse of the development of human consciousness. It is a path backward, which temporarily, step by step, reverses all the positions that consciousness has constructed. First, it progressively undoes the devaluation of the inner world, which was connected to the development of western consciousness, and pulls down the wall, piece by piece, which the emerging ego-consciousness had erected between itself and the world of the unconscious.[4]

The wall,[5] which is meant to protect emerging consciousness from the superior force of the unconscious powers, is also the protection that the individual erects against the danger of being swallowed up by the mass psyche in *participation mystique*. Consciousness, ego, and individuality are products of the process of detachment from the unconscious, and at the same time they are the instruments of its realization. Only their development makes the human person an individual who differentiates himself, and only insofar as he differentiates himself is he separate and an individual. As we have shown elsewhere,[6] the process of "secondary personalization" plays an important role in the development of consciousness, as an operation in which the archetypal images, for example, the Great Parents, are gradually replaced by the images of the real, personal parents. Here, the child's original form of experience, which resembles that of early humanity, is gradually replaced by the experience of the adult and the cultured person in our civilization, who no longer deals with archetypes, images, symbols, and collective ideas, but with objects, persons, and things.

On the return path leading inward, this secondary personalization is also undone again, and, beyond the personal, the world of the great powers grows ever more strongly visible as a background reality, determining the life of the collective and the individual. Anamnesis, the remembering of childhood and the search for the childish and infantile sides of the personality, always necessarily leads back to the sources of vitality, in which the world of the transpersonal feeds the childhood world, and in which this transpersonal world has touched the growing individual in decisive ways, preforming future developments.

The return path is not only a regression, in which old stages of development are revived. Rather, it is always also (this especially distinguishes the individuation process) a unique individual form, in which the collective contents are experienced in new ways. Comparative methods help to reveal these contents as contents of the collective unconscious, that is, as the common psychological property of humanity. But for every individual they appear in an individual variation, a different guise, with different accentuation. The range of modifications in which the primal symbols can appear to each individual is legion. Not only the sequence and canon of appearing symbols, the group of symbols, can vary, but also, the meaning of a particular symbol varies for the individual, because it is compensatory only to the conscious constellation of the one for whom it arises.

In collective initiation rites, as we see, for instance, in ancient mystery religions, the same content (for example, rebirth from the earth) applies for those to be initiated, whereas, for modern people, the path of the depths is characterized by the variability of content for each individual. The individual structure, for instance the typological structure of each person, the differentiated function of each one's consciousness, and thus also the specificity of the inferior function, has crucial significance for content and function.[7]

The way the ego and its specific form of consciousness fit together also puts its stamp on the experiential process of consciousness. Only insofar as the uniqueness of the individual, reflected in his typological structure, is kept intact is there valid, individual experience. Individuality and consciousness belong together, as do the collective and the unconscious. Only in the individuation process is a synthesis created in which both the productivity of the collective unconscious and the individuality of consciousness are preserved. Whereas one aspect usually asserts itself at the expense of the other, both these aspects achieve a creative progression in the unifying symbol,[8] thus permitting the expansion of consciousness as well as the self-realization of the unconscious.

Individuality is ultimately realized only in the individuation process. Although the return path preserves individuality, on this path the old, limited form of the ego, which had been closed off from the unconscious, is destroyed once and for all. The ego's delusional grandiosity, its belief in its sole dominance, had already begun to falter due to the crisis or illness that led it into the depths. And now, to the degree that the barriers fall, which had segregated the narrow world of the merely personal from the totality of psychic space and the inner cosmic background, this former grandiosity of the ego is pushed to the limits of absurdity.

This is not the place to present the ways in which self-esteem is necessarily transformed on this path into the depths.[9] As the process moves inward, the wall between ego-consciousness and the unconscious is gradually dismantled, the deflation of the inner world is reversed, and the fullness of psychic reality becomes visible again and available to direct experience. This activation of the unconscious expresses itself at first in the form of psychic dissociation, as the emergence of a multiplicity of complexes, often frightening to the ego,[10] and of part-personalities, images, and instincts. The deflation of the inner world, which was so important to the development and self-confidence of the ego, is now suspended, and, as a result, ego-consciousness can easily become deflated instead. A considerable share of neurotic symptoms, all depressions, anxieties, compulsions, and complex reactions, down to simple behavioral slips, are symptoms of ego-weakness and uncertainty in the system of consciousness, thus observably demonstrating the superior power of the inner world. Now, contrary to the hubristic belief in the ego's sole sovereignty, there emerges a belief in the ego's impotence, which is just as one-sided and false as its opposite. One may describe and show evidence for a whole series of stages, in which the relationship of the ego to the unconscious shifts toward ever greater unconscious influence and, parallel with this, the ego's increasing weakness and dissolution.

We find these phases, for example, in the various forms of mental illness. In simple cases, the ego loses only specific areas and functions, which are subject to the influence of the unconscious; but more severe illnesses involve an extensive subjugation of ego-consciousness to the unconscious, as, for example, in mania and depression. In the most serious case—cases of schizophrenia among others—we see a complete depotentiation of ego-consciousness, in which all that remains to be seen of this sphere is a relatively powerless complex. Here, ego and consciousness can no longer function as the basis of a total personality and are no longer capable of assimilating contents into consciousness, but are only a powerless, isolated complex among the multitude of psychic parts.

We find the same phenomena, however, independent of any pathological event, in the exceptional psychic conditions that accompany any state of possession. Mystical ecstasy, with its dissolution of ego and consciousness, is only the extreme case, in which the psychic background, in the form of a deity, appearing as nothingness, or as an overpowering vision of light, dissolves the differentiating capacity of the separate ego. With the onset of a mass condition or *participation mystique*, every orgy, every kind of mass intoxication, whether this be religious, political, or otherwise engineered, leads to an *abaissement du niveau mental.* That is, it produces a weakening of ego and consciousness, symptomatized by, among other things, the lowered moral and intellectual level of the mass of people. And it culminates in a take-over by unconscious powers, which then determine the emotionally toned behavior of this mass.

But even if we speak of being obsessed with an idea, a task, or a creative act, the same phenomenon is in effect. The creative principle, the idea, and the work often assert themselves as autonomous contents of the unconscious, against the individuality and the ego of the "possessed" person. This can be seen in the numerous self-depictions of these people, in which the autonomy of the controlling process is described time and again, even confronting the conscious intention of the so-called creator. It is positively characteristic of the creative process that the ego recognizes itself as being "seized" by something other, something of superior rank and power, and feels itself to be an instrument in the hand of this creative "It," which is described as god, genius, muse, daimon, etc. However this in-breathing spirit of inspiration is named, it demonstrates its ego-alienness and otherness not least by compelling the possessed ego, often with cruel ruthlessness, to materialize the content, the idea, or the task, without regard for the individuality of the possessed, their life situation, their well-being, their health, or their degree of strength. The biographies of almost all creative people illustrate this mania—divine though it may be—and its often disastrous consequences for the individual.

We assign positive value to the relative disempowerment of the domain of ego-consciousness in the case of creative people, because what makes them productive is that, in their state of possession, they make the contents of the unconscious accessible to the collective. But this does not change the association of these creative processes with the phenomena in question. The religious awe of the primitive toward one who is mad, who is seized by the deity and communicates the divine will to the collective, is a variant of this function of creativity for the collective. Only the higher and very highest forms of creativity are characterized by greater participation on the part of the receptive and formative core of ego and personality. As a general matter, this participation is fairly strong in art and philosophy. Among the creative doers, those personalities who move history and found religions, for example, it is by no means always so great.

Whether the ego is swallowed and dissolved by the powers of the unconscious depends, on the one hand, on how the deep layer of the unconscious makes an appearance; on the other hand, it depends on the breadth and solidity of ego-consciousness. The disintegrative power of the unconscious contents is greater, in other words, the closer they are to the collective unconscious and to the archetypes. For normal ego-consciousness, the contents of the personal unconscious generally only come up as fairly minor disturbances. Archetypes, however, always cause strong, decisive disruptions and transformations in consciousness. A developed and ego-stable consciousness will assimilate minor unconscious disturbances without difficulty, especially those involving personal contents. It is even able, under favorable circumstances, not only to ward off the ego-dissolving tendency of the deep layers but also to reshape it productively and thereby to regenerate the whole personality.

During the history of development, consciousness and rationality stood against the unconscious, trying to become as independent of it as possible. They became neurotic only at that point in time when differentiation and the turn to the outside were pushed so far that, with the deflation of the inner world, not only the drives and instinctive constellations of the unconscious but also its creative and spiritual side were lost. As these constellations are actually the locus of power, however, they have broken out violently, reducing the life of the western individual and that of the western collective to ruins, over which the negative Wotan-spirit of the irrational[11] triumphs. We find that, for either the individual or the collective, if neurotic consciousness closes itself against all attempts at compensation on the part of the unconscious, the compensatory relationship of the unconscious to consciousness then turns negative, leading to a powerful, destructive irruption into consciousness.

Ego-stability here turns into an ego-spasm and constellates the unconscious in such a way that it degenerates from compensation into spasmodic destruction.

Those for whom these collective problems have become a personal problem, and a problem of consciousness, are the vanguard of the collective, no matter whether the overwhelming situation seized them as a result of crisis or of illness. They make the journey into the unconscious in the same way that, centuries ago, seafarers journeyed over the earth's oceans to discover new continents. What is learned on these individual journeys, which must be undertaken due to affliction,[12] and for the sake of individual health, is of crucial importance also for the future of the collective, for this affliction and illness are deeply connected with the affliction and illness of the collective. In later times, the life of the community will appropriate as much from the experiences of these individuals as was appropriated by the community from the conquests of the explorers, who, on their own authority, as a vanguard, conquered new territory in every region of the outer world, in science and in politics, on ships and sleds, with telescopes and microscopes, and added it to the consciousness of humanity.

The path of introversion leads in the opposite direction, through all the stages and deep layers that had to be traversed by ego-consciousness in its development out of the unconscious. Hand in hand with the weakening tendency of consciousness to deflate the unconscious, layers of the unconscious now become animated. This leads to the emergence of contents, figures and forms of relationship, analogous to those we know from the phenomenology of religions and corresponding in detail to the various stages of humanity's religious and psychic development.

All these stages in which humankind realized itself, and which then determined the world at each level of humanity, all systems of life, whether their emphasis was pre-animistic, animistic, demonological, magical, or ritual, all these stages are present in the unconscious as systems of psychic preparedness and functionality. They are enlivened by every development in the depths, and they determine the ego's experience of the unconscious, for better or worse. This fact is also of great importance for its practical application, in that the collective contents that come up today, in the dreams, images, and fantasies of modern people, can be interpreted only through reference to the corresponding materials of religious history, folklore, and mythology.

What is decisively new about this psychic return path is not that consciousness is disintegrated and dissolved, as happens with other extraordinary psychic phenomena, but rather that ego-consciousness is protected here at every stage from being dimmed and extinguished, thanks to the cooperating consciousness of the analyst who accompanies the process. This "roping together"[13] is indispensable, especially for the parts of depth analysis in which the ego is confronted by the collective unconscious, because otherwise the ego is almost certain to be overwhelmed by the archetypes. The fact that every initiation, in all tribes and at all times, is directed by an initiate, one who has already had the corresponding experience of the depths through initiation and who stands beside the novice to explain, is most deeply based on this necessary support of consciousness.

An essential characteristic, however, which distinguishes the modern person's path into the depths from all initiation rites of earlier times, is that this path is not collectively prescribed but is individual and unrepeatable. That means that—unlike the ancient mysteries, Gnosticism, Indian and Chinese yoga, or the fixed canon of images laid out by Loyola—contents and experiences are not transmitted consciously by initiates. On the contrary, here the two who are bound together on the depth-psychological journey, analysand and analyst, attempt to travel an unforeseeable path. During this process, the analyst cannot guarantee protection for the consciousness of the analysand with help from a fixed system of consciousness, for example, from a scholastic dogma. He must be able continually to ensure the living self-renewal of personality through the assimilation of unconscious contents, by which consciousness is fundamentally challenged, time and again, and must newly reconstitute itself, over and over, in response to the demands of the unconscious.

This is not the place to present what such a process looks like, or the position of the ego in such a process, or the manner in which it is transformed.[14]

The reconnection of consciousness with the unconscious in the individuation process is essentially dependent on a hierarchy of experiences, which the ego has to undergo with the archetypal figures of the unconscious. The ego's return path through the earlier stages of consciousness,[15] its encounters with the figures of the unconscious, the collective powers, and its experiences with them, do not unfold systematically, although one can speak of a hierarchy of experiences. In the reality of this path, the stages blend into each other, and the path often zigzags between the various figures and deep layers. But when one reviews the path in its wholeness, despite the endless multiplicity of individual variations, it is still possible, time and again, to determine this hierarchy of experiential levels.

As Jung has explained more than once,[16] the sequence of these figures, which must be experienced, leads from the shadow to the anima or animus, and finally to the mana-personality of the unconscious. But before we characterize what is general and universal about these experiences, we must emphasize again that these experiences look different for every individual. To be sure, the experience of the shadow always comes first, but how this shadow looks, what characterizes it and makes it so uncanny or "negative," where its center of gravity lies, for what reason it is so unacceptable to the ego, all of this is different for every individual. In the analysis of the shadow personality, the reduction to the general structure of drives, for example, to sexuality and the power drive (Freud and Adler), no doubt plays a major part. But the typological structure of the individual and of groups is so diversified that new and different accents always become visible here. Osiris and Seth, Abel and Cain, Jacob and Esau, Jesus and Judas, Prometheus and Epimetheus, Baldur and Loki, Siegfried and Hagen, Faust and Mephisto, the shadow problem of the hostile brothers has been represented by the collective in the most varied forms, according to the mythology of the group that is being expounded.

The individualizing of modern people, which expresses itself in the individuation process, has led, however, to a differentiation that far surpasses this diversity. This differentiation and specialization of the ego and the individual are also expressed in modernity, of course, in the shadow's corresponding individualization, which must be made conscious. Beyond making the personal shadow conscious, the shadow world then leads in all of us to the problem of the collective human being. This collective human being confronts the ego as a representative of the universally human shadow structure, which the individual, as an ego, fears.[17]

The lowest, more or less primitive level of religious experience encounters the ego or the dream-ego—the dream-ego, with its lowered consciousness is of course always primitive—whenever it fears being overpowered by the invisible. Everyone knows those dreams of emptiness and silence, with a background of anxiety, where the creaking stair or the rustling paper is uncanny, and the ego is irradiated by the invisible. Taking on solid form, this anxiety condenses into animals and figures, beggars and Arabs, robbers and burglars, strangers and murderers. But it can also be something disguised and strange, a weird shape of the unconscious, which seizes the ego with fear in a dream, a fantasy, or the light-and-dark shimmering landscape of a vision.

Aside from the moral problem, the world of the shadow always comes back within us as the world of primitive humanity. This primitive human being raises his head at night. Our brother and neighbor, he lives inside us on the other side of the wall of our consciousness, hardly affected by the development of human consciousness over the past few centuries. He wakens when we sleep, just as he sleeps when we are waking. His terror of demons, of night and darkness, lives in us, as do his superstition and compulsive cruelty, but also his closeness to nature and his longing for the morning. This is known to anyone who awakes at night from a heavy dream and feels afraid, or who has lain, sick, at night, wakeful and waiting: when will it be light, when will the sun come up? From the beginning of time, the connection between the shadow and the dark of night has been as close as that for consciousness, the ego, and the sun. At night, we sink back into the *participation mystique* of the primal world, which surrounds us in dreams. There we are a shape among shapes, sucked into the collective world of psychic space, which overgrows and receives us, takes us back, renews and transforms us.

The experience of early human beings, their idea of the world, becomes our own whenever we enter the fear-arousing spell of the unconscious. The shadow realm and its ever-present collective component is especially able to transmit to us the religious experience of primitives as if it were our own. Everyone knows oppressive dreams of the primeval forest, swamps and snakes, where the solitary dream-ego feels the desolation of the abandoned animal-creature amid the cosmic chaos. But also, there is the exciting noise of drums in the night, which call together the tribe, the group, the sacredness of fire in the dark, the help and counsel of the Old One, the magician, and the murmuring voices of initiation. All of this arises in the dream and touches us. It is under our skin, as close as the fiery core under the earth's crust.

Within us live the many kinds of religious experience known to primal and early humanity, and they create, even today, the foundation of all numinous experience. Magic and charm, anathema and consecration, conjuring and ceremony, all of these are still as powerful within us today as ever. The basic experience of an encounter with the unconscious is that "it happens to you." The ego divests itself of its executive activity. It provides only the initial tension; then, the creative unconscious asserts itself of its own accord, forming, constructing, speaking. Every depth analysis is founded on this process of the ego's self-preparation and the manifestation of creative spontaneity. Whether we have an inner conversation, in the free upwelling of images in meditation, whether we model with clay, or paint, or write, in every case, the ego must relinquish its masculine activity and allow things to happen. There is room for revelation. The *na'aseh v'nishma,*[18] "we do, we hear," applies in the small as in the large. First, the process itself happens through us; then, as an after-effect, understanding follows.[19]

What is true for the world of the shadow is also true for that of the anima.[20] The anima, a man's "soul," his feminine side, which is open to the unconscious and which encounters him in the form of a woman, leads the ego into a new world and specifically to a changed basic attitude, which corresponds to the re-emergence of a primal instinct. The ego changes its modern, western form of reaction, which is marked by a masculine, outward-directed activity of the will. Another, more original attitude of the ego institutes itself, one of hearing and receiving, of opening and preparation. Something unfamiliar is meant to be experienced; a revelation is to be received. This inward listening, which is the precondition of every creative process, this permission for the psychic feminine to be actualized, is identical with the realization of the anima. The ego experiences this figure in her positive character as a priestess and prophetess, who, coming from the depths, where she is known and the secret of which she knows, brings the ego tidings and a revelation.

Thus, when the anima is made conscious, the process is always accompanied by a psychic loosening, a release of the blocked, masculine structure of consciousness, with its exclusively outward-focused activity. And it always expresses itself—disregarding the fact that it is often, but by no means always, artistically meaningless in an objective sense—in a production that brings to the ego a wealth of life-giving revelations, new contents, changed aspects, and new psychic qualities. Whether this "new thing" manifests itself in fantasies, visions and images, drawings or plastic modelings, in words, dance, or music, the ego immediately experiences the soul, the anima, as the great inspiring female, mistress, or herald. She reveals herself in a saying that the ego perceives, in an image that the ego sees, in a figure that the hand forms, and in the stories and occurrences that the ego writes without recognizing their content, a content that is new, strange and incomprehensible, and which only later becomes accessible to the ego, slowly and with difficulty.

This state of being deeply moved is the reality of the new experience that the ego, now conscious, encounters when the world of the anima emerges. This state is the newly realized, feminine side of the personality. Always, when this capacity is demonstrated, it is the anima at work. Like all unconscious contents, as long as the anima system is unconscious, it operates as an autonomous complex, in which case it has to be projected outward by the masculine ego, as a part personality, onto a woman, or else it is perceived within as a psychic image. The ego is engaged by this figure, which has its place deep inside the personality. And the instinctive reaction of this ego, being directed by the anima system, expresses itself in shifting, affective–emotional moods, in outbursts and waves of feeling, that incapacitate the conscious masculine attitude. Only when the anima is made conscious does the ego reach a new attitude, compensating for the old masculine activity with a feminine receptivity. Only then does the anima change from being the autonomous content of the unconscious to a function of consciousness, which the ego can now apply, by using the feminine side of the personality, like an organ of perception or a seismograph, to experience both the outer world and the inner.

Each of the great figures that one meets on the path into the depths rules over its own territory, and anyone who takes this path must pass through and assimilate a hierarchy of psychic realms and their associated experiences. It is strange, and yet revealing, that this path is a path of ascending experience.

If these things were the products of speculation, and not a summary of daily experience, then one would necessarily have to encounter more and more primitive stages of religious experience the deeper one went on the path. This holds true, however, only to a certain extent, because the path into the depths is not, and cannot be, a laboratory experiment in which the unconscious is laid bare layer by layer.

The ascension mysteries of antiquity, whether these concern the Gnostic–Iranian transcending of the seven heavens, or the chambers of the kingdom of death, or the ascending mysticism of early Kabbalah,[21] always have the magically accented character of transformation. Consciousness, which enables one to pass through the new level, and by which alone one may overcome the threat of the guardians at the gates, or the negative aspect of the deity, is always mediated by an initiating person. Whether this knowledge consists of a magic spell, a key that opens the gate, or a secret name that must be used to address deities, angels, archons, or daimons, whether it is concealed in a sacral action or woven into a garment that contains a name of God[22] which the ascending one must put on or take off, it is always the summoning power of conscious knowledge that makes the path possible in the first place. But, in any case, this knowledge is fixed, and may largely be handed down.

With the modern path into the depths, in contrast, there is no content to be handed down and no helpful magical knowledge. The person to be initiated, if we may use this term, cannot be transformed by watching a mystery play or, as in the Isis mysteries, by walking a symbolic path on which he identifies himself with the rebirth of the sun. Rather, he himself is stage, actor, and audience in the mystery play of his own transformation. He is in the paradoxical situation of simultaneously having to suffer the experience of the archetypes of the unconscious, while not being allowed ever to give up his conscious ego-stability. That is, the ego may not entrust itself to the unconscious blindly, without consciousness, for, if it does, it will be flooded, recollectivized, and dissolved by the powers of the unconscious. Equally, however, it may not surrender itself to consciousness, for, then, it will be isolated, infertile, and constricted. The generative function of the unconscious, which becomes visible in the unifying symbol as the "transcendent function,"[23] is only the product of a preserved consciousness, which defends its own position with a stable ego and does not sacrifice it to the momentary demands of the unconscious, and yet at the same time holds itself open to the counter-position of the unconscious, that is, it does not repress this counter-position, but accepts it as a conflict.[24]

As the ego travels into the depths, with a system of consciousness that is maintained and yet constantly transformed by this depth experience, it constellates ever deeper and broader layers of consciousness. At the same time, the path of the ego, passing through this broadening of personality, not only circles into the depths but also rises from a primitive religious experience to one that is higher. When Silberer says, "True mysticism is characterized by an expansion, false mysticism by a constriction of personality,"[25] he is referring to this state of affairs on the path to the depths. But he confuses matters with the term "mysticism," which is far too narrow in this context, for mysticism represents only a particular variety of this basic experience. The whole realm of this experience, which we designated for just that reason as "religious experience," is embraced by the Jungian formulation of *religio*, as:

> . . . a careful consideration and observation of certain dynamic factors, understood to be "powers," spirits, demons, gods, laws, ideas, ideals or whatever name man has given to such factors as he has found in his world powerful, dangerous or helpful enough to be taken into careful consideration, or grand, beautiful and meaningful enough to be devoutly adored and loved.[26]

The world of the shadow, with its demons and terrors, is the mirror image of an ego entangled in the world, bereft of insight, and confused; this is a genuine but primitive religious experience. The world of the anima, mirror image of an ego that has become self-transforming, listening, more open and solitary, contains a higher, divinatory experience, which is no longer primitive. The difference between these worlds is the difference between the savage, hunted by terrors and invoking cruel demons, and the Greek, who consults the Pythia of Delphic Apollo. The worlds of the unconscious and its associated forms of inner experience, with their hierarchical order, are the levels of personality transformation. But, at the same time, they are circles of an expanding consciousness that affiliates itself to new inner and outer realms of the world. How ego-consciousness arrives in this way at its own symbols and rites, its own cultic forms, belongs to the particularities of the individuation process.

In general, one may say that, when working psychologically in the individual realm, with all the alertness that is necessary on this path, there emerges a wealth of analogies to actions and contents that are familiar from the history of religion. Today, it seems as if the growing decay of religious institutions in the collective, outer world, must correspond inwardly, in compensation, to the religious attitude of the individual. Meditation and contemplation, for example, are basic practices on the path of psychological development, the effectiveness of which does not depend, for understandable reasons, on the collective, religious character of these behaviors. Inner dialogue takes the place of prayer, which is no different in essence. As Jung and his disciples have shown, with the multitude of examples they have collected,[27] the individuation process involves experiences analogous to conjuring spirits and the experience of mysteries through the cultic image. But central religious experiences, too, such as vocation and consecration, the making of laws, prophecy and theophany, correspond to the psychological events of modern individuals. To work out the analogies and differences in these phenomena would be the task of a separate work, which cannot be undertaken here. What is crucial is that the psychic background, which encounters the ego on its path into the depths, can, and remarkably often does, take on a fundamentally revelatory character.[28]

The wealth and depth of these revelatory background forms, ranging from the obscurity and confusion of hybrid and distorted beings to the cosmic vision and the bursting clarity and directness of the *neum Adonai*,[29] are infinite. All these experiences of the ego, however, and all the revelations that approach it have those features that Rudolf Otto has already demonstrated as being characteristic of the numinous or the divine, and as giving it its particularity.[30]

Otto designated the holy, which is the center of every religious experience, as the *numinosum*. This anonymous neutrality is characteristic. It belongs to the core of this experience and not only refers to the *numen*, the deity, but also undertakes to make itself formlessly present, as something even more essential, in the *numinosum*.

The *mysterium tremendum*, the "terrifying mystery," forms one side of the experiential core of the holy. It stretches from shuddering before the ghastly and terrible all the way to the ego's feeling of annihilation, from shivering with horror at the overpowering gruesomeness of the divine all the way to a state of paralysis before the strangeness of the uncanny *numen*. The idols and masked figures of primitives belong here, this ghostly jumble of beings piled upon each other, whose uncanny inner tension freezes our blood even today. But so do the millions of slaughtered people, who have bled to death on all the altars, before the images of all the gods in the world, from the gods of the Incas to the bloody cult of the Khalidhurga in India, and from the funeral piles of the Inquisition to the Moloch sacrifices of Carthage. The scale of this experience is very large. It includes the kindling and devouring fire of YHWH's wrath and vengeance, the paradox of his callings, his compulsion of the prophets, the fear of YHWH, the terror of Isaac, but also divinity in animal form, the non-human wherever it occurs, that which seizes in the storm, which strikes in the lightning, and the mysterious hovering of the divine spirit, brooding over the waters of creation.

But the numinous is also the totally other, the incommensurable. Ungraspable and beyond experience, it is emptiness and nothingness, anti-reason, the super- and unnatural, that which confounds and astounds, which paralyzes like the Gorgon. It is the paradoxical, which is suddenly, astonishingly, speechlessly perceived in the half-dark. It rises up as majesty, devaluing the ego, annihilating, shattering with its superior power. As the grandiose and gigantically overwhelming, it burns up the ego, makes it tiny and humble, unreal and disoriented. But just as this holy *numinosum* shines in the emptiness of cathedrals, so it burns with the glow of passion, seizes the human being as the irresistible will of the divine, drives him away from father and mother, away from the plow and out of his homeland, compels him into pilgrimage and into the wilderness. It burns within him; it is desert wind and waterfall, earthquake and cloudy darkness. "The lion roars, who should not be afraid. YHWH speaks, who should not prophesy."[31] Thus divinity is compulsion and power, horror that robs consciousness, and greatness that causes trembling.

But it is also the *fascinans* of captivation, the endless sweetness of ecstasy, the sense-beguiling flame, in which the mysticism of all times enchants, befuddles, blesses, and dissolves in grace. It is the boundless fullness, the unspeakable blessedness around which all religions circle. It is the grace that confuses, pulls away from the world, and gives meaning; it is the spring of miracle and rebirth, of transfiguration and establishment. And it is the *sanctum*, which gives reconciliation and imposes obligation, which blesses and assigns value, which leaves the profane outside and keeps it away from holiness.

All of this taken together is the numinous. It is the counterpart of human religious emotion, toward which human creatureliness feels itself to be servant and friend, child and sacrifice. It is the concept-shattering ungraspability, which pulverizes all human certainty, which forbids murder and commands it, and which, as the ruling power of the numinous, amounts to the central point of religion.

In the experience of the unconscious, all these aspects become not only activated, not only perceptible, but, rather, it seems as if the world of the unconscious were nothing else than the extension of this *numinosum*, as if the ungraspable diversity of these aspects of the numinous had put itself on display in the figures of the collective unconscious, simultaneously and sequentially, in order that it may be experienced at all by the ego. Or conversely, this *numinosum* is the quintessence, the unity, the form, and the summary of that which the ego and the person experience about and in the unconscious. At the same time, it also reflects the inadequacy of this experience, the incommensurability of ego and consciousness, which stands trembling before this insurmountable fullness and authority, while on all sides and everywhere it sees its limits overleaped, overgrown, and overwhelmed. Now, in the ego's recognition of its own failure, this encounter is constellated as the totally other, the foreign, which can only be verbalized in paradox, as containing the opposites. And, because consciousness can only approach it by speaking of nothingness and emptiness, while also stammering of fullness and the all, and can only pronounce the creative word while taking it back, it is silence.

The experiences of the ego on its return path are so overwhelming, because this path returns to the primeval; it goes back to the origin, to the mother. Human consciousness is a son of the deep unconscious, and its path outward, to the world, is hard and exhausting. The path that the westerner travels is violent; it is the path of voluntarily renouncing the mother. The cruel, sharp, driven face of the western person is marked by the torment of this path into distance and foreignness. For that very reason, it is so seductive, when fear is overcome, to turn back toward inwardness. For that reason, everywhere today, one sees how the westerner, suffering from his tragic inner split, seizes the possibility of regression and lets go of his ego-consciousness, lets go of his western conscious development, and allows himself to be sucked back into the womb of the great mother, the unconscious, there to find peace.

Blood and soil, people and community, collective, totality, these are the *fascinans* of the collective unconscious, the great, holy mother-dragon, which tempts and seduces in the form of church and nation. The temptation here is the deluding possibility that makes every intoxication intoxicating, the surrender of the ego, of individuality and responsibility. This is the great ambiguity of the unconscious, the Janus-head of each of its elements: that what was once root, renewal, and rebirth suddenly turns, for an ego that has lost its footing, into the consuming power of the devouring mother. In place of the ego of consciousness, in its necessary solitude and uniqueness, the figure of the mediator now emerges, the salvific mana-personality. This figure relieves the individual of the cross of individuality, but, thereby, it also removes the meaning and dignity of his existence and degrades the redeemed person to a mass particle.

The individuation process, however, signifies the Other. It is the opposite of this tendency toward regression. It continues western conscious development, and it is also the path inward. The religious aspect does not make its appearance here as the analogy to an already traversed level of human development or a previously achieved religious experience. It is something entirely new, an unrepeatable and unique thing that occurs from time to time in individual depth experience. The reactivated stages of earlier human levels are all melted together into the alchemical process of self-transformation, in which a new center, the human image, becomes visible within the Self as a divinity.

The consciousness of the modern person is no longer prepared to project the divine outward into the cosmos, as something independent of humanity. But, equally, precisely because of the discoveries of depth psychology, it is incapable of denying the phenomenon of the divine. For this phenomenon crops up everywhere, for everyone, as soon as a person approaches the deep layers of the psyche. For this reason, we must maintain an attitude consistent with the state of our knowledge, and recognize that this phenomenon emerges within the realm of what can be experienced. That is, we must research this phenomenon as belonging to human beings, and draw the consequences of its presence and its power for them. To study this phenomenon outside of its human connection has to be left to a metaphysics brave enough to regard such an approach as meaningful.

When it occurs in the presence of a fully maintained consciousness, that is, not in a mystical state or any other state of possession that dissolves the ego or impairs its competence, the emergence and power of the numinous are the decisive characteristic of the individuation process.

The individuation process leads to a transformation of personality, in which the original situation of a split, between an ego that functions as the center of consciousness and an unconscious that operates in the dark, is basically laid to rest. The mutual interpenetration of conscious and unconscious ends with an integration of the personality, whose center is no longer the ego, but that which analytical psychology calls the Self. This center exists in living connection with the ego and consciousness, but it has the quality of a superior factor. It is superior not only in the sense of being the dominant power, in that the ego repeatedly encounters this *numinosum* and the Self as its own center of life and destiny, and as victoriously making its way against the limitations of conscious intention. Rather, it is also superior because the Self is always "right," that is, it always represents higher consciousness, the "greater reason," contrasting with the "lesser reason" of ego-consciousness.

When the center shifts in the individuation process, from ego to Self, this does not dethrone the ego, that is, the sacral meaning of consciousness is in no way cancelled. Nor does it install a foreign authority or destroy the autonomy of the personality. The phenomenon of the transcendent function, the prerequisite for individual revelation in the unifying symbol, is based precisely on the autonomy of ego-consciousness and its associated ego-stability. It is based on the fact that the individual stands by his limited, unique, incomplete situation, and that he defends his daytime world and its limited abilities against the claims of the unconscious—be they the demands of the idea or the fascination of images—which pay no heed to the individual. This situation of consciousness may relativize itself, insofar as it is convinced of its own relativity, that is, the ego may know that in another half year it will perhaps take another position. But it must protect the present time and its own finitude against the overwhelming demand of the unconscious, which knows only the infinite. Only when this dialectic between the ego and the unconscious is accepted does the Self constellate itself as a center in which transpersonal and personal, individual elements paradoxically coincide. In this constellation, the sacral meaning of consciousness is not only preserved; rather now, for the first time, it becomes recognizable in its central importance. Consciousness alone is the partner of the Self, which is to say, the phenomenon of the Self—not to be identified with a collectively projected divine theophany—is based on ego-consciousness, standing up for itself.

What is decisive is that the Self, with all its otherness, all its existence as non-ego, is nevertheless experienced as the center and wholeness of the personality, as a "myself" that encloses the ego, as something that one feels is more truly oneself than the ego. The personality experiences itself as stretched between ego and Self, and this paradoxical, uncategorizable state corresponds exactly to the deepest experience of the individuation process, which is to discover oneself as a whole, personal and transpersonal at once, in which the ego sphere of the personal is no longer split off from the non-ego sphere of the transpersonal.

Someone undergoing transformation in the individuation process has not only become aware, with astonishment, of the paradox of divinity but also exists personally in the paradox. Such a person experiences himself gaining experience as an ego-consciousness, but, at the same time, he experiences himself as the Self. With amazement, he becomes aware of himself as the wholly other. He does not give up his ego identity, however, for if he relinquished this ego, he would also lose himself, and with that also the Self, which did not act in vain when it brought forth the ego from itself, in order to unfold dialogically. When a person learns from his own life the connection between being and destiny, and recognizes the encroaching power of his own existence in relation to the world, from which this very existence constellates its own destiny, then he understands, terrified by the numinous, that he too is numinous, and he recognizes his own reflection in the depth of the creative source. When, in the dialogue between day and night, in the continuity of the dream sequence with life, he experiences the Self as the redactor of dreams, he does not identify with the Self. How could he, when he keeps having trouble understanding what this redactor means? And yet this Self remains in a relationship with the ego, about which Judaism declares: "God and the human being are twins."[32]

The dialogue with this Self gradually becomes an experience of leading. But leader and led are not only in covenant with each other; their secret intimacy is greater than in the word of Jesus of Nazareth: "I and the Father are one."[33] Yet even now, the phenomenon of God-forsakenness can occur. But then the ego knows better, because it stands in a connection with this Self, and with itself, which theology designates as faith, although it is actually something quite different, namely, a knowledge born of experience. The Baal Shem tells a story about Noah: "When the Father became distant from him, Noah knew: 'This is so that I may learn to walk.'" Here the accent is placed directly on this knowledge, which is more than the faith of theology, for it is the personal experience of the Self, which absolutely cannot be lost.

If we endeavor to say something about consciousness, individuation, and the religious aspect, that is an endless field. It will be impossible to come to an end or achieve any sort of conclusion. It is a strange moment in human history, when people face the task of taking into themselves everything that once filled heavens and hells, a moment when divinity reveals itself in human beings and, more than that, in every person. We realize, of course, that the divine lives neither in heaven nor under the earth. But what results for humanity from experiencing the divine as something within the human being, indeed as his living center, of this we have no knowledge at all.

Western people speak and think in a way that a Jew once formulated to me as follows: "I heard from Nietzsche that God is dead, and I was satisfied with that." But it appears as though something in the people of today is not at all satisfied with that, and their dissatisfaction is reaching the point of catastrophic expression.

To follow the expressions of this dissatisfaction and to recognize the ways in which it might be eased—or, better, to recognize how this very dissatisfaction within people is seeking and finding new ways to achieve a higher satisfaction—this is one of the tasks assigned to us.

Erich Neumann
1943

Notes

1 *zu einer entseelten Welt*: alternatively, "to a world emptied of psyche."
2 *die Welt beseelend*: Alternatively, "investing the world with psyche."
3 *EN*: *Beziehungen*. [Perhaps referring to Jung's first discussion of the objective psyche in relation to the process of individuation. Cf. CW 7, ¶184–6.]
4 *EN*: Author: "The Development of Consciousness and Stages of Life." [Cf. Appendix B.II, *Roots II*, pp. 209ff.]
5 Cf. *Roots II*, p. 137; p. 151.
6 Cf. above, Appendices B.I and B.II, *Roots II*, pp. 190ff.; pp. 209ff.
7 *EN*: *Types*. [Apparently referring to Jung's book as a whole.]
8 *EN*: Ibid., 1.3. ["The Significance of the Uniting Symbol," CW 6, ¶318–74.]
9 *EN*: Author: "Stages of religious experience on the path of depth psychology." [Cf. Appendix B.IV, *Roots II*, pp. 256ff. Beneath handwritten corrections, the original title can be read: "Zur religiösen Bedeutung des tiefenpsychologischen Weges" ("The religious meaning of the path of depth psychology"). This title, echoing the title of the April 1940 lecture from which it comes, is the one used in the present edition.]
10 *EN*: Jung: "Allgemeines zur Komplextheorie" ("A Review of Complex Theory"). [Cf. CW 8, ¶211f.]
11 *EN*: H. G. Baynes [1941]: *Germany Possessed*. [Perhaps referring to Chapter 2, "Wotan, God and Daemon," pp. 62–98, with its discussion of Jung's "Wotan" (*Neue Schweizer Rundschau*, 1936). Baynes writes: "For [Jung] Wotan is the hypothesis which expresses the most significant dynamic of present-day Germany. He is the god who is the 'possessor' of the German people, a fundamental and irrational quality of the German soul which remains latent in the unconscious until the time arrives when it emerges like a cyclone, dispersing all culture and reason and rousing the nation to a state of fury" (*Germany Possessed*, p. 78).
12 *aus Not*: or, "out of necessity." In this sentence, pointing out that individual affliction (necessity) is tied up with that of the collective, Neumann repeats *Not* three times.
13 "*Anseilung*": the term is borrowed from mountaineering.
14 *EN*: Cf. especially Jung, *Integration*. [Perhaps referring to Chapter 2, "A Study in the Process of Individuation," which included two black-and-white prints of paintings by a patient. The later, revised version (CW 9,i, ¶525–626) includes a longer series of paintings, reproduced in color.]
15 *EN*: Author: "Stages of religious experience on the path of depth psychology." [Appendix B.IV, *Roots II*, pp. 256ff. The original title is hand-corrected. Cf. note 9, above.]
16 *EN*: Jung, *Beziehungen* and "Archetypen des kollektiven Unbewussten" ("Archetypes of the Collective Unconscious"). [Cf. CW 7, II and CW 9.i, I. "Űber die Archetypen des kollektiven Unbewussten" was Jung's 1934 Eranos lecture, later published in *Integration*, trans. by Stanley Dell.]
17 *EN*: Author: *Tiefenpsychologische Beiträge zu einer neuen Ethik* (*Depth psychological contributions to a new ethic*), I. [Neumann's monograph was published in 1949, under the title, *Tiefenpsychologie und neue Ethik* (*Depth Psychology and a New Ethic*). Most of the work was finished in 1943, including its first chapter, "Die alte Ethik" ("The old ethics").]

18 Hebrew: "we do and we hear" (Ex 24:7).
19 *EN*: *Beziehungen*. [Cf. CW 7, ¶292.]
20 *EN*: To avoid over-complication, the corresponding world of the animus, in women, is omitted from discussion here.
21 *EN*: Gershom Scholem, *Major Trends*, Chapter 3. [Scholem's discussion of "Merkabah (chariot) mysticism," is actually found in Chapter 2, pp. 40–79. His discussion of the "mystical ascent" appears on pp. 49ff.]
22 *EN*: Ibid., p. 77. [Cited as p. 76.]
23 *EN*: *Typen*. [Cf. CW 6, ¶828.]
24 *EN*: Ibid., part II. [The second chapter of Jung's *Types*, "Schiller's Ideas on the Type Problem," contains a pertinent passage. Cf. CW 6, ¶112–15.]
25 *EN*: Silberer, *Probleme der Mystik*, p. 182.
26 *EN*: *Psych & Rel*, p. 14. [Cf. CW 11.1, ¶8.]
27 *EN*: Wilhelm/Jung, *Geheimnis*; Jung, *Integration*; Heyer [1932], *Organismus der Seele* (*The psychic organism*); Frances Wickes [1938], *The Inner World of Man*.
28 *EN*: Author: "Religiöse Stadien" ("Religious stages"). [Cf. Appendix B.IV, *Roots II*, pp. 256ff. Neumann also explores these themes in "The depth of the revelatory layer and the conscious attitude," *Roots I*, pp. 47ff.]
29 Hebrew: "speech of the Lord."
30 *EN*: Rudolf Otto, *Das Heilige* (*The Idea of the Holy*).
31 Amos 3:8, slightly paraphrased. Cf. also Neumann's references to Häussermann, *Roots I*, p. 38, n. 84; p. 47, n. 125; p. 139, n. 5.
32 Cf. *Roots II*, p. 155, n. 164. Paraphrased from Rashi's comment, *Bab Tlm*: *Sanhedrin* 46b.
33 John 10:30.

IV. The religious meaning of the path of depth psychology

Neumann wrote this lecture in 1942. It is a revision, expanded and renamed, of his earlier lecture, "Religious Experience in Depth Psychology," dated April 1940. Later, Neumann appears to have changed the title to "Stages of religious experience on the path of depth psychology," but the original title, more closely echoing that of the 1940 lecture, is published here. Although the main content of the earlier version is folded into this one, the interpretive framework and writing style show that Neumann's thinking had matured. When he sent the April 1940 version to Jung, he commented, "The talk belongs to a certain extent in the third section of my book: On the Depth Psychology of the Modern Jew*" (11 May 1940,* J-N Corresp*, p. 156). In 1943 he decided to treat the expanded version as the final lecture in a four-lecture series, and then wrote the three lectures that introduce it. These four lectures give a glimpse of what his Part Three might have contained.*

Total loss of orientation is the decisive characteristic of our time. The ancient tablets are broken, and the values that oriented humanity for centuries, indeed millennia, have collapsed. But the downfall of the gods is always at the same time the downfall of a world and endangers those who were living in it.

The psychic health of humanity depends on the people's spiritual energies being held and shaped by ideas and values, symbols and religions. When these energies are freed through the shattering of the ancient tablets, the breaking of the vessels, it leads to a flood of energy, which determines the life of our time in the form of deluge, chaos, and the end of the world. The abundance of repeated dreams about flooding and the end of the world illustrates our catastrophic situation, into which illnesses, crises, and the collapse of individuals are merely embedded. Whether it is the collapse of moral values on a larger scale, which determined the coexistence of the peoples, or on smaller scale the decline of the sacrament of marriage, which determined the coexistence of individuals—after the twilight of values the human being is flooded by powers that now, having lost their direction, make nations and individuals their playthings. The consequences of this decline are mass epidemics and world wars, mental illnesses and suicides.

The decline of values, and the ever more obvious flooding of humanity by insurmountable, chaotic energies, is a process that has been clearly traceable for about 150 years, since the French Revolution. It is, however, accompanied by an event, the significance of which has not yet been sufficiently recognized, namely, the irruption of the psychological into western consciousness.

An unceasing current, at first underground but increasingly visible, brought ever new contents from the prehistoric and primordial world of humanity into the western world. The discovery of mythology, which began with Herder and Romanticism and extends to C. G. Jung's discovery of the collective unconscious, is only one of the many lines of development, the richness of which enables this new continent, the psyche, to emerge.

Psychological and biological research, ethnological studies, research in the history of religions, and sociological research, with their many diverse approaches, are all involved in the discovery of this great, unknown being, into which the human being has suddenly turned. The discovery of the world of primitives and of mass psychology, mythology, and depth psychology, are all only parts of this image of the human being that has recently emerged into human self-awareness.

The horizon of the western world has widened tremendously in these 150 years, to encompass the whole breadth of the earth. Alongside the western Christian world, for which paganism and Judaism were merely the prelude, appear the major cultures of Asia, America, Africa, and the primeval world of early humanity. At the same time, however, historical and prehistorical research connects the image of the human being with early history and prehistory, and beyond that, through the world of primitive humanity, links it to the animal world. Thus, to the broadening of the horizon is added the dimension of depth.

The new image of humanity and the human being, still fragmented and buried in research's many small boxes, nevertheless moves humanity as something psychologically alive and makes itself felt in the destruction of the old values and orders. The psychological is no longer seen merely as a theoretical content, or as a psychic background or underground that is of interest only for the study of individual pathologies. Instead, it is experienced more and more as a force that shapes humanity. Human beings are increasingly conscious of the significance of the psyche as an active factor, perhaps even as the decisive historical factor, whether as the power of the unconscious that determines the life of the individual or, in collective psychological epidemics, the historical behavior of nations.

The collapse of the old world, which is taking place collectively in the revolutions and world wars of our time, expresses itself individually in the modern person's confusion, which is apparent not only in the exceptionally high and growing number of mentally ill people, but even more in the progressive neuroticization of the individual.

The destruction of authorities who once provided orientation leads almost everywhere to the futility and lack of direction in today's existence, at the mercy of which the individual feels blind and powerless, no matter whether he experiences them as an isolated individual or as an atom immersed in a collective movement. The present attempt to escape the catastrophic situation through collectivization, to divest oneself of responsibility as a part of the masses, is futile, because, as historical and current events teach us, the masses are the preferred sphere of action of those same chaotic powers from which the individual has fled. This endangered situation of the modern human being led to the birth of depth psychology as an attempt to help the human being find a way out of himself.

The still very short history of depth psychology is a path from outer to inner. The psyche was discovered only on the way, so to speak, and the limits and objectives of research shifted inward over several decades. The development of depth psychology as a science corresponds exactly, as we shall see, to the path that the individual has to follow. Unconscious psychological reality was seen at first only as disturbing, negative and primitive, something to watch out for, that ultimately stands in irreconcilable contradiction to the outer world, which, as "reality," represents the highest principle of being. Only gradually did it become clear that turning inward, that is, introversion, is not merely a step backward, a regression, but also the path to another world, the reality of which is as valid and powerful as that of the outer world, and that the health of human beings and humanity can be guaranteed only by an adaptation to reality that includes both worlds, outer and inner, as equal factors.

Our present attempt is somewhat abstract, for it omits the abundance of material and the diversity of individual contents, as it seeks to depict the stages of this inner path, travelled together by analysand and analyst in the work of depth psychology. It is not without danger to renounce the information of first-hand experience, such as one gains through intimate insight into the vivid self-unfolding of psychological development. The suspicion that this generalizing account amounts to an applied philosophy, an ideology, or a "conception" can be countered only by referring to the materials from which these stages are abstracted and to the personal experience of people of all times, especially our own, who have travelled this path. The fact that these materials are still unknown, and that these experiences are not common knowledge, is the fate of every new scientific discovery. Its impact is always delayed at first by the custodians of the old, who, following the principle of psychological inertia, fight the new as "heretical," as it was called in the Middle Ages, or as "unscientific," as it is called in modern times.

Obviously, not everyone who undergoes depth-psychological treatment will travel the spiritual path outlined here. Many experience only partial domains, whether because they are permitted to travel only part of the path, or because their life situation, a specific constellation of forces, or a weak consciousness prevents them from travelling the path in its entirety. But anyone who walks the entire path, whatever his age, gender, or typological disposition, will be transformed by his experiences and by the contents that confront him on it.

When we draw contrasts between certain stages of this inward path, we are essentially trying to characterize a transformation that occurs in this process regarding the feeling of ego and Self. These stages encompass the multiplicity of individual situations. That is, no matter the fateful constellations in which this process takes place, the process itself remains unaffected. Whatever stands at the beginning of the path, whether a parental conflict or a crisis in world-view, an apparently unfounded breakdown or a marital tragedy, and whatever sequential or simultaneous contents determine the course of the psychological work, the ego always passes through these transformative stages in its relationship to itself and to the psychic background.

Laws of deep psychological development are beginning to become apparent to human consciousness. The experiences of religions, the mysteries of antiquity, the psychology of Indian and Chinese yoga or of Hellenistic and medieval alchemy, and the personal experiences of modern humanity prove merely to be different forms of a universal structure of the human psyche. The psychic processes represented by such an inner path are neither arbitrarily without direction nor fundamentally different for every individual. The structure of the human soul, which is essentially the same, despite all apparent differences, requires that, as the experience of depth psychology teaches, a certain regularity determine this path, the unequivocal and universal nature of which is only gradually entering consciousness.

Our account must seem strange to the contemporary westerner, insofar as he is still captive to the rationalistic–materialistic prejudices that he considers particularly modern, because they originated only in the second half of the last (the nineteenth) century. For the normal person of our time, dreams and other manifestations of the unconscious are only disturbing foreign bodies, which occasionally intrude into the closed world of his daytime existence. It is only natural that he has a completely different idea of the psyche to someone for whom the inner human dimension is the daily content of his work and whose image of the psyche is formed in part by his occupation with thousands of dreams.

It is only when we recognize our time as the background to depth psychology that we understand that a considerable number of those people who show up for psychological work are not sick or disturbed in the usual sense. Not only the sick seek recovery on this path. Those who are disoriented, and for whom institutional support has become insufficient, in the form of religious or political dogmas, also follow this path as a way to themselves, and to a deeper and more creative state of perfection and health.

What most frequently drives people into the work of depth psychology is an illness or crisis, and the contents of these crises are as manifold as life itself. They range from acute disturbances caused by a concrete situation to despair at the futility of human existence. But there are fluid transitions from an actual illness, behind which lies an unresolved psychic problem, to a conscious crisis in worldview, behind which looms a mental illness.

In almost all cases, the first stage of analysis is filled with personal and private material. The personal sphere has priority; its relationship to the environment has to be examined and clarified. Profession and marriage, friends and relatives, these are the first circle and environment to be considered. Here, we traverse the greater or smaller expanse of consciousness, for only a precise knowledge of the ego-world enables us to understand the Other, which we call the unconscious.

Even in this domain, which exists under the dominant of the ego, other factors gradually emerge. An important part of analysis is devoted to anamnesis, recollection, taking stock of one's own life. This return path always involves encountering oneself in a very peculiar way. Even if at this stage we relied solely (which of course we do not) on the work of consciousness, on the memories that surface and the clarification of connections with earlier encounters and experiences, time and again, an experience occurs here that could be called "the hiddenness of determination." Endeavoring to understand oneself, to understand one's own reactions and misreactions, gaining insight into typically recurring situations, the appearance of previously unnoticed turning points, of decisions with concealed importance, all this leads to the experience of a hidden lack of freedom, a contingency and dependency of the ego, which shakes and often even endangers the security of consciousness.

The fact of post-hypnotic suggestion is prototypical for people at this stage. For us, the most important aspect of this phenomenon is that, after waking up from hypnosis, in which a suggestion, an order, was given to him, a human being carries out this command, but believes that his actions, which were compelled by hypnotic suggestion, stem from his own free will. At this stage of experience, which we have called *hidden determination*, if a person is inclined to self-reflection, he might feel, depressingly, as if he were merely a puppet on the stage, his strings being pulled and his existence directed by unknown forces. This idea will suggest itself to anyone who engages with the phenomenon of the unconscious. For the ego and consciousness are actually far less masters in their own house than the average European assumes. In this context, we must mention the countless dreams in which one locks the front door but cannot lock the back door, dreams about the neighbor knocking on one's door, or the foreign tenant.

This stage is usually associated with a causalistic and fatalistic conception of psychic life, which regards the complexes of the unconscious as fateful determiners before which the ego and consciousness are helpless. It is only a variant of this view if these complexes are projected into parts of the outer world, so that parents, educators, the milieu, or childhood experiences are now regarded as the factors ultimately determining the ego. The arrogance of the ego before analysis, which saw only itself and its world of choices and values, is now replaced by an equally erroneous devaluation, which sees the world of the ego and consciousness as a mere epiphenomenon of a superior constellation of unconscious forces. Nevertheless, this stage of devaluation marks an important transition, because this is where the deep layer opens up, at least in the sense that consciousness is detached from its self-encapsulation and begins to realize its fateful connection with the psychic background.

Ego-consciousness, accustomed to viewing the outer world of the everyday, begins to understand that this is only one side of the world. At first, unaccustomed to the new experience and resisting it, the ego tends to acknowledge this other side only as a disturbance of ego-continuity, as a darkness breaking into the world of daylight, and as an invasion of primitive and infantile layers into the cultural brightness of consciousness. What comes up inwardly has for the most part a truly negative character. It consists of the contents, memories, qualities, and aspects of life that make self-preoccupation frowned upon and despised in our day. It is the aversion to the shadow, the slimy and the jellylike, the nauseating and the wicked, the "ugliest person," on account of which we equate "rummaging around in oneself" with self-reflection. We are repeatedly assured that no one can really be expected to grapple with themselves unless absolutely necessary. The self-evident way in which one's own psyche is considered a garbage dump is a striking characteristic of our time. The negative one-sidedness of psychoanalysis is only a symptom, but not a cause of this trait, which compensates remarkably for the degree to which the modern person is unburdened by sin. The psychology of the negative, of the shadow, is one of the great barriers that prevent consciousness from turning inward. The reductive part of the psychological work, with its elaboration of the instinctual psychic underground, is part of this first phase, which is experienced repeatedly as the dethroning and devaluation of the ego and its world.

The negative aspect of the inner dimension begins to disappear and become unimportant to the extent that the ego realizes that all these contents, the contents of the personal unconscious, are important and fruitful components of the personality. The negative shock subsides, and a completely different phenomenon attracts the interest of consciousness.

At the same time, along with a more encompassing self-understanding and self-encounter, which widens the boundary of the personality, the ego also begins to experience itself as part of an unknown inner world, a psychic space that encompasses and affects it, just as the outer world encompasses and influences the ego of humanity. The experience of *the ego as a dream-ego* strikes me as prototypical of this stage. In the dream, the ego enters the psychic space as a dream-ego, where it moves like an ego in the outer world. As a dream-ego, the ego lives in a world that forms its existential landscape, whether this world is strange or natural, remote from reality or a cosmic exaltation of it. But the entire landscape and form of the dream are the content of psychic space. Gods and demons, witches and goblins, animals and humans, colors and events that the dream-ego experiences and endures as destiny occur exclusively in the inner space.

But this world, like the everyday world, has a continuity of its own. On awakening, we once again find ourselves, with conscious matter of factness, in the world that we left when we fell asleep hours before and pick up where we left off. So likewise, in dreaming, we immerse ourselves as a dream-consciousness into the psychic space. It is where we left it hours ago, and we pick up where we left off dreaming.

Although the ego, in dealing with the unconscious, at first puts up with the analyst's interpretation of a dream as with the odd procedures performed by a medicine man, half astonished and half curious, it gradually realizes the new situation. It begins to experience the continuity of the psyche.

Often, what initiates this adjustment is the simple, everyday fact of a dream *series* and the return of particular dream figures. Generally speaking, the dream series implies that a dream cannot be interpreted in isolation, but that the problem of the unconscious asserts itself and becomes apparent only in the continuity of dream texts. This experience, that tonight's dream continues what last night's dream began, makes it clear to the ego for the first time that grappling with the unconscious is a dialogue. Although the next dream is also the continuation of the previous one, it is at the same time the reaction, the answer, to a conscious working through. Thus, the dream sequence is not only a great story in installments. Rather, statements and replies move back and forth between the conscious ego that interprets and understands and the unconscious that produces texts. The wholeness of a lifetime comes about only when the life lived by day is combined with the one lived by night. The ego now no longer feels lost and unfree, at the mercy of an overwhelming foreign psychic world. It no longer experiences itself as standing opposed to a negative, hostile inner world, but as part of a continuity, in which it is embedded and interwoven like a solo voice into the orchestra's many voices.

Nevertheless, what has priority in the beginning is the association of this psychic world with the personal and private sphere. Here, to be sure, we have mostly overcome the originally prevailing view, that the day's residue, the connection with outer events, determines the dream. The often-overwhelming genius of the dream, orchestrating its intentions by linking them to the day's residue, has already been experienced, but the domain of the personal unconscious has not yet been surpassed. The imagos, images of friends and relatives that emerge in the psychic space, surely belong to this sphere. But also constituting this personal sphere are the imagos of strangers and unfamiliar persons, which may prove to be personified parts of one's own personality, split-off and repressed parts, former egos and attitudes, undeveloped dispositions and the still-infantile germs of future developments.

Now, however, something different and new begins, the *encounter with the transpersonal*, the world of the "great figures,"[1] the collective unconscious. These great figures, the archetypes, are the dominants of the unconscious. They are the active powers, which humankind has always feared and worshipped, as gods, demons, and spirits, by carefully cultivating its contact with them in cult, ritual, and custom, as with overwhelming constellations of forces. The attempt to protect consciousness, with the help of religions, from the influence of these highly charged contents of collective psyche, takes up an enormous amount of space in human history. All races and peoples have always and everywhere taken great pains to behave in such a way that the gods, demons, and spirits, the invisible powers, protected and promoted human life. Even this universal human endeavor, the fact that cultural and intellectual history is essentially full of gradual variations on these efforts, should teach us that the forces involved here are "real," even if by necessity they no longer appear to western consciousness in the same way as they did to primitive, early, or medieval humanity.

To early humanity, these contents of the unconscious appeared outside, projected, as theophanies, because the outer and inner worlds were not as strongly separated as with a more developed consciousness. But the fact that these forces no longer appear outside implies nothing about their lack of power. On the contrary, the same primordial powers direct modern humanity as they did earlier humanity, but we are exposed to these influences blindly, as individuals as well as in the collective, and suffer them uncomprehendingly and unconsciously. The old, institutional, and cultic approach to these forces as "external circumstances," in heavens and hells, has become impossible, but a new approach, treating these forces as individual psychic constellations, is only just emerging. Insight, that is, looking inward, leads us to encounter the causative powers, which then become visible as figures—as they have always done, according to the nature of the psyche—and their hidden effectiveness can be grasped.

The appearance of these figures is not limited to early and pre-history. They not only appear in mythology, religion, and fairytales; rather, they still determine the lives of children, who, with their low level of consciousness, still live mainly in the unconscious early world.[2] This also characterizes the psychology of the mentally ill, whose consciousness is destroyed by the process of illness, and it is alive in the creative power of art.

Until recently, the power of this collective psychic background still lay outside the average experience of the individual. But today, for example, the magical and mystical importance of the medicine man, and his inspiration as an active collective factor that fascinates mass psychology, has leapt visibly into the midst of European historical existence. The medicine man, the mana-personality, is also one of the figures of the collective unconscious,[3] who has stepped from psychic space into the historical "outer" world. Its roots lie in the source layer of this unknown psychic dimension, which remains dangerous as long as western consciousness fails to adequately address it, and for that very reason can be seized by it "from behind."

The emergence of this world of transpersonal powers into visibility is one of the most decisive experiences for those who encounter it. The consciousness of the modern person is always adapted more or less strongly to the western, outward orientation. Often, in particular when consciousness is strongly developed, lengthy work must be undertaken before the turn toward the psychic background is accomplished, and the descent is dared. Long stretches of the initial process often go on under a drought. The ego, inhibited by fear and repugnance, barely escapes the vicious circle of nihilism, and consciousness is, at first, more than willing to "let something happen" to it. Only illness, pathlessness, and despair bring it to the point, finally, of surrendering to its own depths.

It is always an overwhelming experience when, after the initial stages have been passed through, the deep probing reaches the source layer of the soul, and the polymorphous fullness of a previously hidden world emerges. When the symbol of the source of life appears, the fountain of the depths or the water of life, then the experience of the soul's creative primal ground constellates itself, in many individual variations.

For consciousness, what matters most basically about its experience of this world, with its manifold powers and forms, symbols and images, are not the details of the emerging content, nor the meaning of one symbol or another—as much as this may determine development—but the fact of the psyche's spontaneity.

The ego now experiences the unconscious as the "wholly other," as the non-ego, as a swirling world of shapes and forces, the living fullness of which, as an infinite ocean forever generating new form, is the mother of all that lives. The creative power of this realm of the mothers, which exists independent of the world of consciousness, forms the bubbling underground from which consciousness is always being born anew, and to which its roots always keep it tied. Consciousness experiences itself as the son of the great mother, which is the unconscious, from which it originates, in which it immerses itself night after night, and into which it enters once again in death. The ego sees itself in a world that is constantly nurtured by this source of nature, which pulsates and moves through the life of the ego in dark, urging instincts and drives, as sudden impulse and inspiration, as mood and irrupting vision. Inherent in this psychic vitality is the creative diversity of forces and gods. The light of nature, which shines equally over all that lives, the just and the unjust, man and beast, near and far, in the alternation of light and darkness, day and night, good and evil, weaves the sacred garment of the mother goddess, which no mortal is able to lift. A wealth of cosmic images seizes the ego and overwhelms it with the depth and breadth of emerging horizons. Here belong the many dreams with mythological themes, proving that human history, religious symbols, primitive customs, and the cosmic anxiety of all living creatures are both possible and powerful for every human soul. Here, the individual ego knows itself to be part of nature and the human species, a small link in an endless chain of development, which, starting from primeval times, leads to the isolation of the modern person. The stages of this development are not only evident in the complexity of every human psyche, but remain alive and powerful in it today.

But irrespective of the aspects that it turns toward those who enter it, from this domain of the depths radiates the numinous, the god-like. To this depth belong all the attributes and forms of power that have been described as "the holy."[4] Contact with this world, or with parts of it, is a destiny, for every consciousness is either transformed or destroyed by the overwhelming power of this layer, the energetic charge of which far exceeds that of consciousness. For even psychosis, the destruction of consciousness, occurs through contact with this layer and its contents. But contact with this deep layer of the psyche also means life, because it has the aspects of healing and regeneration, of rebirth and the future.

For the modern human being, who is always "doing" and feels obliged to "make" the world, it is highly important to experience the psyche's implicit activity. It is always a healing and holy experience to learn that the human being grows and develops, independent of the responsibility and willfulness of ego-consciousness, that a creative force is living in the deep layer of the psyche, generating, balancing, regenerating, and building up, of its own accord, beyond any intervention of consciousness, beyond any intervention of the ego, and that it is possible to let go, to entrust oneself to the flow of life and let oneself be carried by it.

After the negative side of the unconscious has been experienced in all its weight, and all the dangerous consequences of the dominant unconscious forces have been recognized, then the psyche's natural tendency toward wholeness and healing is even more significant.

But the cosmically anonymous form of the wholly other, when it encounters the ego on this level as the infinite realm of the psyche, constitutes only one stage in the experience of the depths.

The ego's participation and importance turn out to be extraordinary. Despite the need to learn to let things happen, the ego has to constantly intervene and control, contradict and yield. The ego, which feels almost lost in the infinity of the soul, takes note of the fact that dreams and all other manifestations of the unconscious have a relationship with the ego. If it is true, as the Talmud says, that "an uninterpreted dream is an unread letter," this ego has both a responsibility and a task. At some point on its path into the depths, the ego has the important experience of being "meant." It is the recognition that no outward or inward event is about the blind turning of the world; rather, the ego must grasp and realize everything that happens in a specific and individual way. The characteristic of significance that emerges here is only a preliminary stage of the fullness of meaning. But the ego, which earlier realized its dependence and smallness, now sees itself as the object of a relationality that is somehow directed toward it, and suddenly it experiences its irreplaceable and unique value.

To begin with, the experience of being "meant" has the effect that the ego takes itself seriously in a new and profound way. Compared with the nihilizing tendency of our time, which atomizes the individual and thus deprives him of the inner basis of existence by degrading him to the senseless and meaningless particle of an unseen mass event, taking oneself seriously has great constructive importance. This new seriousness alone legitimizes all these efforts to penetrate one's own life, as well as the egoistic and seemingly unimportant occupation with oneself and with the circumstances of one's small, private existence. The profound feeling of powerlessness, which today threatens every individual who experiences the collective upheavals of our present time with its mass murders, seduces the individual over and over again, with the result that he does not take himself seriously, thus sacrificing the basis of any responsibility. This tendency finds its clearest expression in the *Führer*-cult of our time, in which the individual gives up being responsible and installs the leader as a superman, "the individual as such," who alone is to be taken seriously and alone bears all responsibility.

The inner experience of being "meant" means more than taking oneself seriously, however; it is the recognition that one is being taken seriously. The ego experiences the world in terms of relationship, the psychotic form of which is paranoid delusion. The accidental nature of biographical data, both inner and outer, fades away as one gains insight into the connection between inner constellation and outer givenness, that is, as it becomes clearer that, for each person, the outer world is not something alien and accidental, but rather, something belonging to the ego. The deeper the path leads into the psychic background, and the more strongly the personality transforms itself through and on this path, the more coherent and less accidental each life proves to be. The ego then experiences the givens of the inner and outer world as parts of a whole. A wealth of seemingly random data becomes meaningful. What was previously meaningless proves to be meaningful, the incomprehensible falls into perspective, and, just as illnesses and crises, for instance, prove intelligible and meaningful for a person's life, so what has been experienced only negatively now becomes transparent as the occurrence of justice. Justice and grace do not remain abstract metaphysical concepts, the contents of remote philosophical studies, but prove rather to be forces that determine life from within.

When it learns to recognize the hidden efficacy of the soul, the ego experiences an inexorable law of justice. Deeper research into every psychic disease reveals the overwhelming power with which the deep layers repeatedly assert themselves and mercilessly conduct the "trial" against the resistance of consciousness. But, just as Franz Kafka's work is misinterpreted, overlooking the mysterious justice at work in the plot,[5] so the ego only gradually learns to recognize, behind blatant meaninglessness, the subtle way meaning does its work. Rabbi Nachman's sentence stands not only behind every neurosis, but also behind every life that understands itself correctly: "If a person does not judge himself, all things judge him, and all things become the messengers of God."

The very driving quality of the forces, the directionality of the things that the suffering ego experiences as justice, proves to be a "messenger" or, in other words, a mission that, if understood, shows the ego a new direction and a new path. Thus the ego also sees the occurrence of justice as embedded in grace. True to its nature, the human soul reveals itself to be created in such a way that, in the interdependence of consciousness and the unconscious, it tends to let the human being travel a guided path, as if it were directed by a wholeness superior to the ego.

As a wheel that rolls of itself, nature is experienced in the juxtaposition of black and white, day and night, good and evil, as the world of the great mother, knowing neither justice nor mercy as the law of the world. Its hallmark is precisely the balanced coexistence of construction and destruction, life and death. It is indifferent, unrelated to the ego and the human being. This defines its greatness, but also its inhumanity. The ego, with its experience of being "meant" and taken seriously, overcomes this stage of anonymous life and attains new self-esteem, which finds new expression in knowing that the world is structured in terms of grace and justice.

Jung described the path into the depths as a centering process for the personality, as a path of individuation.[6] Essentially, this process means that the merely superficial unity of consciousness, based on a dissociated multitude of autonomous psychic parts, is replaced by a real integration of the personality. From this process of integration, the interpenetration of consciousness and the unconscious, arises a wholeness, the center of which, the "Self," appears as the mid-point of the psyche's totality.[7]

> Sensing the self as something irrational, as an indefinable existent, to which the ego is neither opposed nor subjected, but merely attached, and about which it revolves very much as the earth revolves round the sun—thus we come to the goal of individuation.[8]

The relationship between ego and Self[9] underlies everything that encounters the ego, either as justice or as grace, on its path through the depths. The following assertion about the Self captures the unique situation of the modern human being: "The individuated ego senses itself as the object of an unknown and supraordinate subject."[10] This state of affairs appears in the theology of every era, as an essential expression of the God–human relationship. On the other hand, however, the Self is experienced precisely in terms of the specific uniqueness of its individual correspondence to the ego. That is, the Self is experienced as an ego-Self, dominating the ego, which emerges individually and exercises a unique impact within a person's psychic structure. The Self is not a metaphysical construct, but a psychological boundary concept, the very nature of which means that it cannot be fully grasped by consciousness, because, as a dimension including the unconscious, it must remain largely un-conscious.

With the appearance of the Self, the anonymous aspect of nature, which dominates the image of the great mother goddess, for example, is overcome, and a more comprehensive aspect of meaning opens up, resting on the ego's experience of relationship and encompassing the world's structure of justice and grace.

The dialogue between ego-consciousness and dreams—for dreams are the preferred, though by no means exclusive, form of unconscious expression with which we are dealing—is experienced more and more as a dialogue with an unknown Thou. On account of the fact that dreams come in series, the ego begins to recognize that it is having a lively dialogue with something we might call the dream "redactor."[11]

One can gauge the meaning of this experience only if one has some rough idea of the inspirations, messages, and texts that may come to an individual through dreams. The redactor has absolute command, always assembling his text from the infinite material of individual and collective life, so that, when correctly understood, his intentions are compellingly clear. Time and again, coming face to face with this superior wisdom inside oneself, one can only marvel. The universality of dream orchestration reaches from the punch line and joke to the humorous aside, from historical illustration to cosmic vision, from a personal address to an impersonal vision that allows the individual to be only an eye.

Rarely, and only in fateful moments, does this redactor override the defective attitude of consciousness and breach the ego's defensive barricade. Then, suddenly, a big dream breaks into the life of someone who "never dreamed," and who now listens, horrified, to the message that is addressed to him. Most of the time, however, the redactor adapts himself; he corresponds to the ego and answers when a real question occupies a person's consciousness. Otherwise, however, when consciousness is decentered and fragmented by everyday vagueness, he, too, answers merely with fragments and blurred texts. But even then, if consciousness attempts—and this is the purpose of dream interpretation—to trace the actual intention of the dream, the dream text becomes clearer and less ambiguous.

The experience of dialogue gradually becomes something more. The ego now has the central experience of guidance. But this does not mean that the ego and consciousness must sacrifice the right of self-determination and simply surrender to the intention of the unconscious or the redactor. On the contrary, it is only when the ego exercises its proper right of self-determination that the unconscious constellates itself to bring about the religious phenomenon of guidance. In contrast to earlier times, the responsible light of consciousness is the *conditio sine qua non*[12] of this experience. Letting oneself be guided, here, does not mean being overcome by just any part of the unconscious and following it submissively. Not just any unconscious divine image, or idea, or primal image, has to assume the guiding role. Were this to happen, we would once again be dealing with obsession, an unconscious state exhibiting all the symptoms of a dogmatic and fanatical restriction of consciousness. But the constantly repeating experience teaches us that listening to the voice, and *engaging* with it, causes an orientation to dawn, which is able to point the way through the depth of the unconscious and the darkness of life.

The key aspect of religious experience, as it emerges in this form on the path through the depths, is that it leaves the integrity of consciousness unaffected. The modern human being is not allowed to sacrifice consciousness, or he will be hopelessly exposed to the chaotic forces of the unconscious. For the unconscious centers itself only according to the centeredness of the personality. When we survey the succession of different stages that the ego passes through on its path through the depths, we recognize how the gradual ordering and centering of the personality correspond to a gradual ordering and centering of the unconscious world.

The constellation of the Self, as a subject supraordinate to the ego,[13] brings forth a new stage of realization and a wider form of knowledge. This experience of meaning emerging in the depths, the power of unfigured shapelessness beyond figures, which leads to them, through them, and against them, is a living, direct revelation and at the same time a meaningful transformation of the personality.

The paradox of the inner situation consists of this: on the one hand, the path into the depths activates unconscious forces and exposes the ego to their dangerous supremacy, because it is only through this experience of the depths, in the encounter with numinous powers, that the process of direct revelation can occur. On the other hand, however, consciousness must prove steadfast in the face of this danger. Ego-stability, which may change but must not be eliminated, is precisely the condition for this process of melting and recasting, which leads to a revolution in the personality, renewal of consciousness, and emerging wholeness for the human being.

Some people who must travel this path move very close to the edge of the abyss. Falling into the hands of the living God is as terrible today as it has ever been. Of the four men who entered the Garden of the Secret Teaching, the *pardes*,[14] the garden of the collective unconscious, it is said: "Four [men] entered the garden; one looked and died, one looked and became mad, one looked and hacked at the plants,[15] and only one entered in peace and left in peace."[16] It is the old dangers, then and now, that threaten the one who enters the *pardes*, because health and psychosis, life and death, becoming whole and being split, all of these possibilities often lie very close together when experiences play out in this deep layer.

Presenting the final stages of this development goes beyond the scope of this essay, which should be treated as a brief report of an expedition into an area, the exploration of which has only recently begun. Knowledge of the deeper structure of the psyche is still quite limited. For this reason, in writing this report, I expect that many people continue to doubt the very existence of this territory, the layers and boundaries of which I am seeking to establish.

I am concluding with a number of dreams that illustrate part of what I have tried to explain. In them, we come across the particular Jewish religious problem, which forms part of the general problem of modern humanity and especially of the modern Jew. To show the relationship between the psychological situation of the modern Jew and his inner history, on the one hand, and the general problem of history, on the other, while also clarifying these connections, is one of the most important and relevant tasks of analytical psychology. It proves especially suited to this task, because its conceptual framework is able to explain how and why the personal situation of the individual turns out to depend on the constellation of the collective unconscious, both in the individual and in the group.

It is, of course, impossible to treat these questions as some sort of an appendix, but at least let me exemplify a small part of the problem with a dream series. This is not the place for me to demonstrate that the living revelation looks, and must look, different to the modern Jew than to the ancient Jew, or to tell you all that can be said about it today. I must, however, make at least one point in this context. Whereas in ancient and apocalyptic literature, the place of revelation was mostly "above," in heaven and coming from heaven, this orientation has changed in the inner history of Judaism. The modern person must dare to descend into the unconscious; the heavenly place of revelation lies "deep down." Just as the *olei ha-Merkavah*,[17] those who mystically ascended to God's chariot, have become the *yordei ha-Merkavah*, those who descend to it,[18] so it is today. Undoubtedly, Mephisto's words partly apply here:

> Then, descend! I might as easily say rise!
> It's all the same. Escape from what exists,
> into the boundless realm where all Form lies![19]

The direction is not quite the same, however, for given with it at the same time is a hierarchy of experiences, which the ego must go through in order to attain revelation.

But whether this place can be found in the depths of the unconscious, in the fount of the instincts, or in the heavenly places of the mind and ideas makes a crucial difference. This difference is given by the various levels of consciousness on which revelation should occur. A basic law of the living revelation is its relative coordination with the conscious system. But as the Jewish system of consciousness 4,000 years ago was different from the one of today, the kind, place, and content of revelation have necessarily changed as well.

It is not possible here to present the context of these dreams, as part of an individual development, nor can I lay out the whole breadth of their fundamental meaning. The first dream, which precedes the group of three other dreams, is reported here only because of its general aspect, its direction, which seems to apply to all events on the path into the depths.

> A divine judgment was laid upon me—if I manage, using a burning candle, to carry the light of the upper world into the eternal darkness of the shadow kingdom and there to light the extinguished lamp of God, I shall be acquitted of my guilt. I walk down a terrible path—indescribable dangers and ghostly apparitions waylay me from all sides—and I heed nothing but the tiny, flickering light, which I protect with my hands from the storm and wet. . . . I am not really afraid, or horror has frozen me so much that I lack all sensitivity. I know that if I didn't have the light as a task, I would have long since collapsed—but I have it, and so a gentle current of love and hope keeps flowing from it into me.

The problem of guilt, which underlies the dream as a basic situation, need not be interpreted here. What matters in our context is that the light of the upper world, of consciousness, is carried down into the depths, and then there is the meaning of this light, which is both a task, needing protection, and also a magical source of power. With the task, to use this light to light "the once extinguished lamp of God," we are in the middle of the religious problem of our age. For deep in the psyche of our age, the light of God has been extinguished. This dream, however, should be seen only as introducing the series of three other dreams. In them, the problem of prophetic vocation, already broached in this dream, becomes absolutely clear.

As the modern human being is inclined from the outset to reduce such contents to an illegitimate claim to power, to megalomania or else to a wish, I should emphasize from the outset that, in these dreams, as in human development in general, we see the individual's attempt—rightly and for the best of reasons—to resist this task of delivering the prophetic message of the psychic background to the world. This task threatens to destroy the person's natural, collectively embedded life, and, like the ancient prophets from Moses to Jonah, the human being is still trying to defend himself and flee from this thing that assaults him.

The events of the dream series, dreams occurring on three consecutive nights, are so transparent that just a few elucidating remarks will suffice for understanding. The archetypal symbolism of the dreams can only be mentioned here, for demonstrating parallel passages and discussing the groups of symbols belonging to these archetypes would fill a work of its own.

> I'm standing in a deep, narrow ditch. High above and far away, some event is taking place, and its outcome is fast approaching.
>
> Immediately before me a voice rings out, so powerful and urgent that it is hard to imagine it is the voice of a human being. "The people who walk in darkness see a great light; those who live in the shadow of death, upon them light is shining" (Isaiah 9).[20] I retain this sentence, simply, because I already know it. The speech as a whole tells us that a person should be prepared to become the bearer of the light and of its proclamation among the peoples, so that they do not lose themselves in despair.
>
> I know that the voice is here addressing me and only me—but I don't answer. Ahead of me a light shines in the trench wall and keeps drawing closer. I recognize that it is a gemstone, which captures even the slightest ray of light and transforms it into a dazzling glow. The very small stone draws closer and closer to me, and, when it is within grasp, I close my eyes—its brightness has painfully bored into them. Then, a hand moves across my forehead, I feel a brief, burning pain and reach up protectively. The stone is sitting in the middle of my forehead as if ingrown.
>
> I scream, full of despair—now I will never again be able return to the company of other people, because if people don't want to see the light, they won't spare its bearer. God can withdraw from people if they do not receive him; but I am fair game for God and human beings.

Light, the gemstone, and the middle of the forehead are all associated with each other here. Light, as the symbol of insight, of knowledge, of "enlightenment," is as archetypal as the gemstone or pearl that bears it. The stone in the middle of the forehead is known in India as the third eye, for instance, that of Shiva or Buddha. It is often represented as a gemstone, symbolizing the higher wisdom, the highest knowledge that distinguishes the enlightened. It is the unity of life and consciousness that occurs in Chinese culture under the symbol of the Tao. Associated with it is the "central white light," described by Jung in his "Commentary on 'The Secret of the Golden Flower,'" as follows: "This light dwells in the 'square inch' or in the 'face,' that is, between the eyes. It is a visualization of the 'creative point,' of that which has intensity without extension, in conjunction with the 'field of the square inch,' the symbol for that which has extension."[21]

Characteristically, this point not only is seen in India as a very high spiritual and emotional center,[22] but also is the place for the symbol of affiliation with YHWH. It is the same point between the eyes that bears the sign of the prophets,[23] which is affixed as a sign of protection upon those faithful to YHWH,[24] and which, finally, as a sign of Cain in the negative sense—the prohibition to kill Cain—guarantees affiliation with YHWH and his protection. It is just this combination of the two meanings of *kadosh*,[25] being chosen and enlightened, on the one hand, and the meaning of Cain, on the other, that constitutes the content of the dream event, as it crystallizes around the sign on the forehead.

The ego struggles in vain against being chosen as the bearer of light, who is compelled to take on the assignment of the "voice" to the collective. The problem of chosenness was always alive as a fateful reality in times when people were familiar with the soul and aware of the danger of the religious task. The dream that follows on the next night shows that this chosenness still has the same dangerous power today, albeit in altered guise. It highlights the catastrophic situation into which the personal and private life of a human being was thrown, when forcibly taken possession of by the transpersonal, and that the ego resisted this claim of the "voice" with it all its might.

> I am lying in the hospital, seriously ill with meningitis. Nobody knows the real cause of my illness. Dr. N. must also rely on conjecture. After I have lain unconscious for a long time, Dr. N. decides to try something and asks X. to come to me. As he bends over me, I recognize him. It looks to me as if his face were repeatedly destroying a circle that I am struggling to complete, because I know that then I will have peace. I want to strike at him, but I have no strength for that either. Helpless, I let myself sink back into unconsciousness.

Meningitis, as a life-threatening disease, is the organism's reaction to the foreign body, the gemstone, embedded in the forehead. Nevertheless, this dream must be seen as a "corrective dream," one that corrects the work of analysis. The unconscious, compensating for the situation of consciousness, expresses the wisdom of the totality of personality and thus corrects the analyst's attitude. To balance out the danger constellated by the intrusive collective unconscious, in the form of the voice, the gemstone, and the mission, the analyst had tried to create a counterweight by strengthening the dreamer's personal contact with life. (This is what is meant, in the dream, by the bedside visit at the analyst's request.) This attempt is rejected by the unconscious of the sick person who is fighting for his life.

Recovery depends solely on the gemstone's incorporation, that is, on the assimilation of the foreign body of transpersonal experience, which thereby loses its foreignness. Emphasizing the personal and endeavoring more or less to neutralize the impersonal and transpersonal disrupts the "formation of a circle," which alone can bring peace. This formation of a circle again represents an archetypal symbol, the mandala,[26] which guarantees psychic wholeness. The circle, the mandala, known as the sphere of magic and spell, the perfect circle, and that which is tightly closed around a center, is the symbol of the psychic wholeness that must be created.[27] In the situation of the individual, the content symbolized by the gemstone can no longer be eliminated. Rather, it must be assimilated; the personality must accept and absorb this content. Only in this way can the circle, the protective wholeness, be formed. Rejecting the gemstone and its contents and attempting to split it off are what cause the life-threatening disease. Beyond the obvious explanation, the foreign body in the forehead, we need not be concerned here with the reasons why this disease is precisely meningitis, with its loss of consciousness and mortal danger.

> I am lying completely exhausted on a bed and sense some kind of movement around me. But I lack the strength to lift my head to get my bearings. I sink back into a state of weakness; when I regain consciousness, I can barely open my eyes, as so much light is flooding me. I am lying as if in a world of light, for not only does infinite light rain in from above, but it is also reflected on all sides.
>
> I think I'm exposed to the midday sun in a winter landscape, so my bed must have been brought up here from the depths.
>
> Suddenly, I remember that terrible things have happened to me. I reach for my forehead—there's a hard lump, but I don't know if it's the stone or a scar. However, I have no strength to struggle with this fact again. I think that I must somehow find the strength to endure my life—and I give myself over again to sleep.

This dream on the third night brings recovery, the incorporation of the stone, the trusting to destiny, and acceptance. It is still a first convalescence, a beginning; consciousness is still very weak, exhaustion still great. The process of illness overwhelmed ego-consciousness and pulled it down into the depths of the unconscious, for in this illness the resisting ego was attacked "from behind" by the transpersonal, which pushed it to the loss and nearly the destruction of consciousness.

Now, however, events take place on a different level: "My bed must have been brought up here from the depths." Together with rebirth and recovery, there has also been a transformation of the world. In the first dream, the fullness of light, reflected from all sides, was associated with the gemstone, "which captures even the slightest ray of light and transforms it into a dazzling glow." On the new level, it encounters the ego, into which the stone has become incorporated, as something "outside," for the world has become transformed into a world of light.[28]

These three dreams illustrate what I have described above as a dream series, the fundamental importance of which I have tried to characterize. But they also reveal what I have called the special situation of the modern human being.

The fact that consciousness, the burning candle, the light of the upper world, must be preserved, necessarily leads to a resistance against the overwhelming demand of the transpersonal. This resistance . . .

[three final pages are missing]

Erich Neumann
1942

Notes

1 *EN*: *Beziehungen*; *Integration*; *Psych & Rel.*
2 *EN*: Frances Wickes [1931], *Analyse der Kindesseele* (*Analysis of the child's psyche*).
3 *EN*: *Beziehungen*, p. 184.
4 *EN*: R. Otto [1917]: *Das Heilige* (*The Idea of the Holy*).
5 *EN*: This world of the law and its power in Kafka's work is shown in a commentary by the author. [Neumann's youthful, still-unpublished essays use Kabbalistic categories to interpret Kafka's themes, especially that of judgment. (Cf. above, *Roots II*, **p. IIBb-60**, note **109**.)]
6 *EN*: *Beziehungen*.
7 *EN*: Ibid.
8 *EN*: Ibid. [Cf. CW 7, ¶405f.]
9 Concerning the ego–Self relationship, cf. also *Roots II*, pp. 81ff.; pp. 106f.; pp. 136ff.; and pp. 152f.
10 Cf. CW 7, ¶405f.
11 *EN*: This redactor contrasts sharply with Freud's questionable figure of the censor who, close to consciousness, allegedly falsifies the texts of the unconscious.
12 Latin: "essential condition."
13 As cited above, the phrase echoes CW 7, ¶405f.
14 Hebrew: "orchard"; figuratively, paradise. Referring to the classic work by Moshe Cordovero, *Pardes Rimmonim* (*Orchard of Pomegranates*) (1548). Cf. *Roots I*, p. 20, n. 19.
15 *EN*: This means that he became a Gnostic and denied the unity of God. [Legend referring to the first- and second-century Rabbi Elisha ben Abuyah, called *ha-Acher* (the Other One).]
16 *EN*: *Jer Tlm*: *Hagigah* 2a.
17 Hebrew: "those who ascend to the chariot" (cf. Ezek 1:15ff). Gershom Scholem writes frequently about "*Merkabah* mysticism." One source that Neumann would have known at the time of writing was Scholem's doctoral dissertation, *Das Buch Bahir* (1923), a critical edition of an early Zoharic work, which Scholem elsewhere describes as "the highly obscure and awkward book *Bahir*, . . . edited in Provence during the twelfth century" (*Major Trends*, p. 74).

18 *EN*: Scholem: *Major Trends*, pp. 45f. [Hebrew: "those who descend to the chariot" (cf. Ezek 1:15ff). In his chapter on "*Merkabah* Mysticism and Jewish Gnosticism," Scholem writes that "the mystical school of the *Yorde Merkabah* . . . may have been in existence in Palestine during the fourth century" (ibid., p. 61).]
19 Spoken by Mephistopheles to Faust in "The Mothers' Scene," in Goethe's *Faust*: Part Two, Act One, Scene 5 (trans. by Philip Wayne. London: Penguin Books, 1959, p. 78). (Cf. *Roots I*, p. 95, n. 98.)
20 Isaiah 9:2. Following the Hebrew, Neumann sets this verse in the present tense.
21 *EN*: Wilhelm/Jung, *Geheimnis*, p. 35, and the whole context of this passage. [Cf. Jung's "Commentary on *The Secret of the Golden Flower*," CW 13, ¶37.]
22 *EN*: Evidence for the sacred meaning of these points can be found almost everywhere in humanity.
23 *EN*: Kings 20:38ff.
24 *EN*: Ezekiel 9:4ff.
25 Hebrew: "holy."
26 *EN*: *Integration*; *Psych & Rel* (as cited above, note 1).
27 *EN*: Heinrich Zimmer: *Kunstform und Yoga* (*Artistic Form and Yoga*).
28 *EN*: In the present context, we cannot go into the significance of this phenomenon or its association with a specific stage of inner development, found among all peoples and at all times.

EDITORIAL NOTE

Working with the materials for this book, I observed something about Neumann's writing method. His handwriting was nearly illegible. Perhaps for that reason, he typed up his own manuscripts, using sheets of carbon paper to produce a master copy with three carbon copies. The existence of four identical typescripts allowed him to revise his work by hand. When he finished revising one of the lower carbon copies, he transferred his changes to a better one, revising again in the process. Last of all, he entered final revisions, either neatly printed or else typed on slips of paper and pasted into the master copy. This "fair copy" was presumably meant for the publisher.

So, Neumann created multiple, nearly identical copies of his manuscript, all of which he kept. Thanks to his painstaking method, his thrift in keeping duplicate copies, and his family's careful oversight, today we have the benefit of being able to compare different versions of his work. More than once, when transcribing this book, I could only decipher Neumann's nearly illegible handwritten revisions by studying an alternate copy.

The most dramatic instance arose with "Life in this world," the missing 36-page section in Part Two, printed here as Chapter Three of *Hasidism*. That chapter exists today because I was able to reconstruct it from Neumann's poorest carbon copy, amended by comparison with his earlier version of Part Two.

In recent years, the existence of multiple, nearly identical copies produced an anomaly, one that may be typical of the vicissitudes that beset old and valuable manuscripts. Documents for Parts One and Two, essentially identical to those on which this work is based, are now privately owned by a company in California, which bought them at auction in 2006. The auction catalogue described them:

> Two volumes . . . some typed and manuscript corrections on strips of paper affixed to the typescript, cloth-backed card wrappers, repairs to a few pages with translucent adhesive tape, some small tears, browning, creasing to second title, small tears to wrappers.
>
> *(Sotheby's, London, 2006)*

Although the unnamed buyers have declined to respond to repeated inquiries, no harm resulted for the present work, because the complete, original materials were still accessible. As explained, multiple copies of Neumann's typescripts, held by the Erich Neumann Estate, were available for editing. I might have liked to compare passages in these typescripts with the same passages in the auctioned copies, but as it turned out, such comparisons were not essential.

I could not have prepared this book for publication without help from several learned consultants. Erel Shalit had intended to be my primary consultant, in addition to overseeing the whole endeavor, but he fell ill, tragically, a few months after our work began. Through illness and treatments, he used his strength strategically, establishing the work's editorial direction in essential ways. For example, he pondered and then accepted the title I proposed for the work, and later the volume subtitles. He reviewed English-language options for transliteration from Hebrew, and we worked together to set transliteration conventions for the work. At a crucial point, Erel made it clear that the translation must be flexible, because Neumann's youthful style required vigorous editing. He invited Professor Moshe Idel to write the Foreword for Volume Two. As his last editorial contribution, in January 2018, Erel sent out a set of electronic images, Neumann's "Torah" watercolors. From these paintings, after his death, Nancy Furlotti and I selected the two cover images.

The Roots of Jewish Consciousness is heavily annotated, for good reasons. The challenge of bringing a work from the early twentieth-century German–Jewish thought-world into the English-language world of today required extensive annotation. To mention only one example, in the early 1930s, when the Hitler era began, the German language went through a transition. For instance, at Neumann's time of writing, the word *völkisch* still had its old meaning, "national" ("pertaining to a people"), as well as its newer one, "nationalist" (or, in Nazi jargon, "racially German"). In his "Introduction to the work," Neumann uses the term twice in one sentence, giving it both meanings (*Roots I*, p. 2, n. 4).

While working as translator, Mark Kyburz contributed to annotations and helped the editorial process in other ways, with a fine copy-editor's eye. And, as noted in the Acknowledgments section, several other scholars have responded to my queries during the past three years, generously lending time and attention to this project.

A special challenge arose early in the editorial process, because Neumann's personal library is lost. His books were given away years ago, and their whereabouts are no longer known. To track down his many citations to German-language works that are, in some cases, rarely read today, I turned at various times to the resources of the Dorot Reading Room at the New York Public Library, the libraries of the Jewish Theological Seminary and the Leo Baeck Institute, and—frequently, in the last eighteen months—the vast Judaica collection at the library of Brandeis University, where I found invaluable help in the office of head librarian and Hebraist, Jim Rosenbloom.

In the annotations to this work, Neumann's original notes are introduced with his initials: *EN*. Editorial additions to his notes are enclosed in square brackets.

Unsigned notes are by the editor, with occasional contributions from Mark Kyburz. Unless otherwise marked, all German-to-English translations are the collaborative work of Mark Kyburz and Ann Conrad Lammers. Mark, who translated Neumann's *Jacob and Esau*, began the translation process for the present work by systematically comparing key terms in *The Roots of Jewish Consciousness* with the translations of those terms in Neumann's previously published works. Over time, he prepared initial drafts of almost every document of *Roots*. He then graciously allowed me to revise his English texts, to bring them to a stylistic standard that I strongly felt, with support from Nancy Furlotti and Erel Shalit, was appropriate for this publication. As a consequence, Mark and I have collaborated intensively on every part of *Roots*, balancing our shared concern for accuracy and faithfulness to the original with the need for accessible, idiomatic, and readable English.

When it came to Neumann's quotations from published sources in German, we found three situations requiring special attention. First, when quoting the Bible, he favored the translations of Buber and Rosenzweig, then newly published, which have a distinctive character. Second, when quoting from the *Zohar*, Neumann draws from three German translations, which vary in their interpretations of the medieval Aramaic texts. Third, he quotes copiously from Buber's *Die chassidischen Bücher* (*Hasidic tales*). Mark and I had to decide how best to honor the author's choices, as we brought these and other quoted materials into English.

Dr. Everett Fox's biblical translations, *The Five Books of Moses* (1983, 1997) and *The Early Prophets* (2014), represent the best equivalent we could find of the translations undertaken in the 1920s by Martin Buber and Franz Rosenzweig. Dr. Fox's English version follows approximately the same principles as those of Buber and Rosenzweig, because it is meant to be read aloud and conveys—as far as possible—the aural and poetic qualities of the original Hebrew texts. As the B&R translations differ from other German Bibles, the voice in Fox's translations is different from that of other English-language translations.

Daniel Matt's English translations of the *Zohar*, in the Pritzker Edition, are now widely accepted as standard. In contrast, Neumann alternates among three German editions of the *Zohar*, all of them freely paraphrased and based on now-dated research. The advice of Tamar Kron and Erel Shalit was to substitute Matt's translations for our renderings of these passages. By following this suggestion, however, we would have introduced another problem. Neumann was deliberate in his use of sources, sometimes comparing one version with another. If his choices had been hidden behind a "standard" version, his nuances and associations would have been lost. Our compromise, therefore, was to be faithful in translating the passages Neumann quoted, while also—to the extent possible—printing Daniel Matt's versions of corresponding passages at the end of *Roots II* (Appendix A).

Neumann quotes heavily from Buber's collected stories of great Hasidic teachers, *Die chassidischen Bücher*, published in 1927/1928. For English versions of these passages, we were fortunate to have the two-volume translation by Olga Marx, *Tales of the Hasidim: The Early Masters* (1947) and *The Later Masters* (1948). Marx reorganizes Buber's text, however. Her edition includes passages from his other books, while omitting passages from *Die chassidischen Bücher*. Passages not found in *Tales of the Hasidim* are translated by Kyburz and Lammers. Neumann's citations to Buber's book are maintained as he gave them. *Tales I* and *II* are also cited when appropriate.

While we worked on the English edition, Neumann's book was being translated into Hebrew by Tamar Kron and David Wieler, whose judicious suggestions and corrections have often made our English translations more accurate. Dr. Kron is a Jungian analyst and a leading professor of Jewish mysticism. With her guidance, I located several elusive passages in the Talmud and Mishnah. It was she who first referred me to the Pritzker *Zohar*, and who helped me direct an artist's recreations of Neumann's drawings of the Sefirotic Tree.

BIBLIOGRAPHY

I. Primary sources

This section shows works cited by Erich Neumann in the text and notes of Volumes One and Two of *The Roots of Jewish Consciousness*. Translations and related editions, including abbreviated references to Jung's Collected Works (CW), appear immediately after the editions to which they correspond, enclosed in square brackets.

A few sources that Neumann regularly consulted and quoted are missing from this list, including his German edition of the Talmud. In the absence of his personal library, it is hard to say which of the then-available editions should be listed here. Editions of the Talmud consulted by the editor are listed under **Secondary sources**, together with sources cited by contributors to *Roots I* and *II*.

Apuleius, Lucius, *Der Goldene Esel: Metamorphosen*, translated by August Rode, Berlin: Propyläen, 1920. [Originally published 170 CE.]

[— *The Golden Ass, or Metamorphoses*, translated and introduced by E. J. Kenney, London and New York: Penguin Classics, 1999.]

Auerbach, Elias, *Wüste und Gelobtes Land*, v. 1: *Geschichte Israels von den Anfängen bis zum Tode Salomos*, v. 2: *Geschichte Israels vom Tode Salomos bis Ezra und Nehemia*, Berlin: Schocken, 1938.

Azulai, Avraham b. Mordecai, *Chesed l'Avraham*, Amsterdam: Emanuel Athias, 1785.

Baader, Franz, *Franz von Baaders Vorlesungen und Erläuterungen zu Jacob Böhmes Lehre*, edited by Julius Hamberger, Leipzig: Bethmann, 1855.

Baer, Yizchak, *Galuth*, Berlin: Schocken, 1936.

[— *Galut*, translated by Robert Warshaw, Lanham, MD: University Press of America, 1988.]

Baldensperger, Wilhelm, *Die messianischen-apokalyptischen Hoffnungen des Judentums*, 3rd edn, Strassburg: Heitz & Mündel, 1903.

Baudissin, Wolf Wilhelm Graf von, *Kyrios als Gottesname im Judentum und seine Stelle in der Religionsgeschichte*, v. 3, 4, Giessen: Eißfeldt, 1929.

Baumann, Hans, "Tier und Pflanze als Symbole," *Zentralblatt für Psychotherapie und ihre Grenzgebiete*, v. 10(3), Leipzig: Hirzel, 1938, pp. 149–65.

Baynes, H. G., *Germany Possessed*, introduction by Hermann Rauschning, London: Jonathan Cape, 1941.

Bergel, Joseph, *Mythologie der alten Hebräer*, v. 1, Leipzig: Friedrich, 1882.

Bin Gorion, Micha Josef, *Die Sagen der Juden: Von der Urzeit*, v. 1; *Sefer Hamaassioth CLVII*, v. 5; *Sefer Jezira*, v. 1, Frankfurt am Main: Rütten und Loenig, 1913.

— *Sinai und Garizim: Über den Ursprung der israelitischen Religion, Forschung zum Hexateuch auf Grund rabbinischer Quellen*, Berlin: Morgenland, 1926.

Birnbaum, Salomo, *Leben und Worte des Balschemm nach chassidischen Schriften, Auswahl und Übertragung von Salomo Birnbaum*, Berlin: Welt, 1920.

Bischoff, Erich, *Elemente der Kabbalah*, Teil I: *Theoretische Kabbalah. Das Buch Jezira, Sohar-Auszüge, Spätere Kabbalah. Übersetzungen, Erläuterungen und Abhandlungen*, Berlin: Barsdorf, 1913.

Blau, Ludwig, *Das altjüdische Zauberwesen*, Budapest: Jahresbericht der Landes-Rabbinerschule in Budapest, 1898. (2nd edn, Berlin: Lamm, 1914.)

Bloch, Chajim, *Priester der Liebe: Die Welt der Chassidim*, Zürich: Amalthea, 1930.

[— *Aus Mirjams Brunnen*, introduction by Salcia Landmann, Darmstadt: Melzer, 1966.]

Brecher, Gideon, *Das Transzendentale, Magie und magische Heilarten im Talmud*, Wien: Klopf & Eurich, 1850.

Buber, Martin, *Des Baal-Schem-Tow Unterweisung im Umgang mit Gott*, Hellerau: Hegner, 1927.

— *Die chassidischen Bücher*, Berlin: Schocken, 1928.

[— *Tales of the Hasidim*, Volume One: *The Early Masters*, translated by Olga Marx, New York: Schocken, 1947.]

[— *Tales of the Hasidim*, Volume Two: *The Later Masters*, translated by Olga Marx, New York: Schocken, 1948.]

[— *Tales of the Hasidim*. I. *The Early Masters*; II. *The Later Masters*, translated by Olga Marx, Foreword by Chaim Potok, New York: Schocken, 1991.]

— *Ich und D*, Leipzig: Insel, 1923.

[— *I and Thou,* translated by Walter Kaufmann, New York: Scribner, 1970.]

— *Königtum Gottes*, v. 1: *Das Kommende*, Berlin: Schocken, 1932/1936.

[— *Kingship of God*, 3rd edn, translated by Richard Scheimann, New York: Harper & Row, 1967.]

— *Moses*, *משה*, Jerusalem: Schocken, 1945.

[— *Moses: The Revelation and the Covenant*, New York: Harper & Brothers, 1958.]

— *Reden über das Judentum: Gesamtausgabe*, Berlin: Schocken, 1932.

— *Der Weg des Menschen: nach der chassidischen Lehre*, Heidelberg: Lambert Schneider, 1948, 1960.

[— *The Way of Man According to the Teaching of Hasidism*, translator unidentified, Secaucus, NJ: Citadel, 1966.]

Buber, Martin und Rosenzweig, Franz, *Die Schrift*, v. 1: *Die Fünf Bücher der Weisung* (Im Anfang, Namen, Er rief, In der Wüste, Reden); v. 2: *Künder: Bücher der Geschichte* (Jehoschua, Richter, Schmuel, Könige); v. 3: *Künder: Bücher der Kündung* (Jeschajahu, Jirmejahu, Jecheskel, Die Zwölf), Berlin: Schocken, 1934.

— *Die Schrift und ihre Verdeutschung*, Berlin: Schocken, 1936.

[— *Scripture and Translation*, translated by Lawrence Rosenwald, with Everett Fox, Bloomington and Indianapolis, IN: Indiana University Press, 1994.]

Cassirer, Ernst, *Philosophie der symbolischen Formen*, v. 2, *Das mythische Denken*, Berlin: Bruno Cassirer, 1925. [Facsimile edition, Darmstadt: Primus, 1997.]

[— *The Philosophy of Symbolic Forms*, vol. 2, *Mythical Thought*, translated by Ralph Manheim, preface and introduction by Charles W. Hendel, New Haven, CT: Yale University Press, 1955.]

Chantepie de la Saussaye, P.D., Bertholet, A., Lehmann, E., et al. *Lehrbuch der Religionsgeschichte*, v. 1. Tübingen: Mohr, 1925.

Cordovero, Moshe, *Pardes Rimmonim*, Safed, Israel: [n.p.], 1548.

Diels, Herman, trans., *Herakleitos von Ephesos*, Berlin: Weidmann, 1909.

Eisler, Robert, "Das Rätsel des Johannes-Evangeliums," *Eranos-Jahrbuch 1935*, Zürich: Rhein, 1936, pp. 323–512.

Ermann, Adolf, *Die Literatur der Ägypter: Gedichte, Erzählungen und Lehrbücher aus dem 3. und 2. Jahrtausend v. Chr.*, Leipzig: Historische Buchhandlung, 1923.

Evans-Wentz, W. Y., ed., *Das Tibetanische Totenbuch*, mit Einleitung von C. G. Jung, Zürich: Rascher, 1935.

[— ed., *The Tibetan Book of the Dead*, with Psychological Commentary by C. G. Jung, London, Oxford, New York: Oxford University Press, 1960.]

— ed., *Yoga und Geheimlehren Tibets*, v. 3, München: Barth, 1937.

Fankhauser, Alfred, *Das wahre Gesicht der Astrologie*, Zürich und Leipzig: Orell Füssli, 1932.

Franck, Adolphe, *Die Kabbala, oder die Religions-Philosophie der Hebräer*, aus dem Französischen übersetzt, verbessert und vermehrt von Adolf Gelinek, Leipzig: Hunger, 1844. [2nd edn, Berlin: Lamm, 1913.]

Freud, Sigmund, *Der Mann Moses und die monotheistische Religion*, Amsterdam: Allert de Lange, 1939.

Geitel, Charlotte, "Das introvertierte Kind." *Reich der Seele: Arbeiten aus dem Münchener psychologischen Arbeitskreis*, v. 2, edited by G. R. Heyer, München: Lehmanns, 1937.

Gesenius, Heinrich Friedrich Wilhelm, "Mischkaf," *Neues Hebräisch-deutsches Handwörterbuch*, Leipzig: [n.p.], 1815/1823/1828.

Glatzer, Nahum Norbert, *Untersuchung zur Geschichtslehre der Tannaiten*, Berlin: Schocken, 1933.

Glatzer, Nahum Norbert and Strauss, Ludwig, *Ein jüdisches Lesebuch. Sendung und Schicksal. Aus dem Schrifttum des nachbiblischen Judentums*, Berlin: Schocken, 1931.

[— *Time and Eternity: A Jewish Reader*, translated by Olga Marx, New York: Schocken, 1946.]

Goethe, Johann Wolfgang, *Faust*: Zweiter Teil, Aarau: Sauerländer, 1832/1960.

[— *Faust*: Part Two, translated by Philip Wayne, London: Penguin, 1959.]

Goldberg, Oskar, *Die Wirklichkeit der Hebräer: Einleitung in das System des Pentateuch*, Berlin: David, 1925.

Goldschmidt, G., "Alchemie der Ägypter," *Ciba-Zeitschrift*, no. 57: *Der Ursprung der Alchemie*, Basel und Leipzig: Gesellschaft für Chemische Industrie in Basel, 1938.

Grunwald, Max, ed., *Mitteilungen zur jüdischen Volkskunde*, v. 9, Berlin: Calvary, 1909.

Gunkel, Hermann, trans., "Das vierte Buch Esra," *Apokryphen und Pseudepigraphen des Alten Testaments*, v. 2: *Die Pseudepigraphen des Alten Testaments*, edited by E. F. Kautzsch, Tübingen: Mohr, 1900, pp. 331–401.

Häussermann, Friedrich, *Wortempfang und Symbol in der alttestamentlichen Prophetie: Eine Untersuchung zur Psychologie des prophetischen Erlebnisses*, Giessen: Töpelmann, 1932.

Heiler, Friedrich, *Das Gebet: Eine religionsgeschichtliche und religionspsychologische Untersuchung*, 2nd edn, München: Reinhardt, 1920.

Hennecke, Edgar, ed., *Neutestamentliche Apokryphen, in Verbindung mit Fachgelehrten in deutscher Uebersetzung und mit Einleitungen*, 2nd edn, Tübingen: Mohr, 1924.

Heyer, Gustav Richard, *Organismus der Seele*, München: Lehmanns, 1932.

Heyer, Gustav Richard and Seifert, Friedrich, eds, *Reich der Seele: Arbeiten aus dem Münchener psychologischen Arbeitskreis*, v. 1, 2, München: Lehmanns, 1937.

Heyer, Lucy, "Erinyen und Eumeniden: Der Kampf zwischen Geist und Erde in der antiken Tragödie," *Reich der Seele: Arbeiten aus dem Münchener psychologischen Arbeitskreis*, v. 1, edited by Heyer & Seifert, München: Lehmanns, 1937, pp. 39–51.

Holzinger, Heinrich, "Einleitung, Numeri 18," *Die Heilige Schrift des Alten Testaments*, v. 1, translated by Emil Kautzsch, 4th edn, edited by Bertholet, Tübingen: Mohr, 1922, p. 228.

Hornstein, Maria,"Der Mensch und sein Tier," *Reich der Seele: Arbeiten aus dem Münchener psychologischen Arbeitskreis,* v. 2, edited by Heyer & Seifert, München: Lehmanns, 1937, pp. 119–58.

Horodezky, Samuel A., "Baal-Schem-Tob (בעש"ט), Israel ben Elieser," *Encyclopaedia Judaica: Das Judentum in Geschichte und Gegenwart*, v. 3, edited by Jakob Klatzkin, Berlin: Eschkol, 1929, cols 835–42.

— "Lilith," *Encyclopaedia Judaica: Das Judentum in Geschichte und Gegenwart,* v. 10, edited by Jakob Klatzkin et al., Berlin: Eschkol, 1934, cols 972–4.

— *Mystisch-religiöse Strömungen unter den Juden in Polen im 16.-18. Jhdt*, Leipzig: Engel, 1914.

— *Torat ha-magid mi-Mezerits ve-sihotav*. תורת ה "מגיד" ממזריטש ושיחיתיו. (*The teaching of the Maggid of Meseritz and his conversations*), Berlin: Ajanoth, 1923.

— *Torat Rabi Nahman mi-Bratslav ve-sihotav*. תירת רבי נחמן מברצלב ושיחיתיו. (*The teaching of R. Nachman of Bretzlav and his conversations*), Berlin: Ajanoth, 1923.

Jeremias, Alfred, *Das alte Testament im Lichte des alten Orients: Handbuch zur biblisch-orientalischen Altertumskunde*, Leipzig: Hinrich, 1906.

Jonas, Hans, *Gnosis und spätantiker Geist*, v. 1: *Die mythologische Gnosis,* with foreword by Rudolf Bultmann, Göttingen: Vandenhoeck & Ruprecht, 1934.

Jung, C. G., *Analytische Psychologie und Erziehung: Drei Vorlesungen gehalten in London im Mai 1924*, Heidelberg: Kampmann, 1926. [Reprint, 1936.] [CW 17,3]

— *Die Beziehungen zwischen dem Ich und dem Unbewussten*, Darmstadt: Reichl, 1928. [CW 7,2]

— "Bruder Klaus," *Neue Schweizer Rundschau*, August 1933, pp. 223–9. [CW 11,6]

— *Diagnostische Assoziationsstudien*, v. 2: *Beiträge zur experimentellen Psychopathologie*, Leipzig: Barth, 1909. [CW 2,9]

— "Einführung," *Das Geheimnis der Goldenen Blüte: Ein chinesisches Lebensbuch*, Übersetzt und erläutert von Richard Wilhelm mit einem europäischen Kommentar von C. G. Jung, München: Dorn, 1929, pp. 7–88. [2nd edn, Berlin: Dorn, 1936.]

— "Einführung," *Das Tibetanische Totenbuch*, edited by W. Y. Evans-Wentz, Zürich: Rascher, 1935, pp. 15–35. [CW 11,11]

— "Einige Bemerkungen zu den Visionen des Zosimos," *Eranos-Jahrbuch 1937*, Zürich: Rhein, 1938, pp. 15–54. [CW 13,2]

— "Zur Empirie des Individuationsprozesses," *Eranos-Jahrbuch 1933*, Zürich: Rhein, 1934, pp. 201–14. [CW 9.i,11]

— "Die Erlösungsvorstellungen in der Alchemie," *Eranos-Jahrbuch 1936*, Zürich: Rhein, 1937, pp. 13–112. [CW 12,3,III]

— "Zum Gedächtnis Richard Wilhelms," *Das Geheimnis der goldenen Blüte: Ein chinesisches Lebensbuch*, 2nd edn, edited by R. Wilhelm and C. G. Jung, translated by R. Wilhelm, Berlin: Dorn, 1936, pp. ix–xviii. [CW 15,5]

— *The Integration of the Personality*, translated by Stanley M. Dell, New York: Farrar and Reinhart, 1939. [CW 9,i, CW 12, CW 17.]

— "Die Lebenswende," *Seelenprobleme der Gegenwart*, Zürich: Rascher, 1931, pp. 248–74. [CW 8,16]

— "Psychological Analysis of Nietzsche's Zarathustra: Notes on the Seminar." Unpublished, typed transcriptions of English-language seminars, edited by Mary Foote, 1934–1939.

— "Psychologische Grundlagen des Geisterglaubens," *Über die Energetik der Seele*, Zürich: Rascher, 1928. pp. 200–24. [CW 8.11]

— *Psychologische Typen*, Zürich: Rascher, 1921. [2nd edn, 1930.] [CW 6]

— "Die Psychologischen Aspekte des Mutterarchetypus," *Eranos-Jahrbuch 1938*, Zürich: Rhein, 1939, pp. 403–44. [CW 9.i,4]

— *Psychology and Religion: The Terry Lectures*, New Haven, CT and Oxford: Yale University Press, 1938. [CW 11,1]

[— *Psychologie und Religion: Die Terry Lectures, gehalten an der Yale University*, translated by F. Froboese and T. Wolff, Zürich: Rascher, 1940.]

— *Seelenprobleme der Gegenwart*, Zürich: Rascher, 1931. [CW 4, CW 6, CW 8, CW 10, CW 15, CW 16, CW 17.]

— "Die Struktur der Seele," *Seelenprobleme der Gegenwart*, Zürich: Rascher, 1931, pp. 114–75. [CW 8,7]

— "Traumsymbole des Individuationsprozesses," *Eranos-Jahrbuch 1935*, Zürich: Rhein, 1936, pp. 13–134. [CW 12,3,II]

— "Über die Archetypen des kollektiven Unbewussten," *Eranos-Jahrbuch 1934*, Zürich: Rhein, 1935, pp. 179–230. [CW 9.i,1]

— *Über die Energetik der Seele*, Zürich: Rascher, 1928. [CW 8,1; 8,6; 8,9; 8,11]

— "Die verschiedenen Aspekte der Wiedergeburt," *Eranos-Jahrbuch 1939*, Zürich: Rhein, 1940, pp. 399–447. [CW 9.i,5]

— *Wandlungen und Symbole der Libido: Beiträge zur Entwicklungsgeschichte des Denkens*, Leipzig, Vienna: Franz Deuticke, 1912/1925. [CW 5]

— *Wirklichkeit der Seele: Anwendungen und Fortschritte der neueren Psychologie*, with contributions by H. Rosenthal, E. Jung, and W. M. Kranefeldt, Zürich: Rascher, 1934. [CW 8, CW 10, CW 15, CW 16, CW 17, CW 18.]

— "Wotan," *Neue Schweizer Rundschau*, March 1936, pp. 657–69. [CW 10,10]

Kautzsch, Emil F., *Apokryphen und Pseudepigraphen des Alten Testaments*, v. 2: *Die Pseudepigraphen des Alten Testaments*, Tübingen: Mohr, 1900.

— *Biblische Theologie des Alten Testaments*, 4th edn, Tübingen: Mohr, 1922.

Klatzkin, Jakob, eds, *Encyclopaedia Judaica: Das Judentum in Geschichte und Gegenwart*, v. 1–10 (A–Lyra), Berlin: Eschkol, 1928–34.

Lévy-Bruhl, Lucien, *Das Denken der Naturvölker*, Wien, Leipzig: Braunmüller, 1926. [*Les fonctions mentales dans les sociétés inférieures*, 1910.]

[— *How Natives Think*, translated by Lilian Ada Clare, New York: Washington Square Press, 1966.]

— *Die geistige Welt der Primitiven*, München: Bruckmann, 1927. [Originally published, *La mentalité primitive*, 1922.]

— *Die Seele der Primitiven*, Wien und Leipzig: Braunmüller, 1930. [Originally published, *L'âme primitive*, 1927.]

Lidzbarski, Mark, *Das Johannesbuch der Mandäer*, v. 2, Giessen: Töpelmann, 1905.

Michaëlis, Edgar, *Die Menschheitsproblematik der Freudschen Psychoanalyse: Urbild und Maske*, Leipzig: Barth, 1925.

Molitor, Franz Joseph, *Philosophie der Geschichte oder über die Tradition in dem alten Bunde und ihre Beziehung zur Kirche des neuen Bundes. Mit vorzüglicher Rücksicht auf die Kabbalah*, v. 3, Münster: Theissing, 1839.

Müller, Ernst, *Der Sohar: Das heilige Buch der Kabbala, nach dem Urtext herausgegeben*, Wien: Glanz, 1932.

— *Der Sohar und seine Lehre: Einleitung in die Gedankenwelt der Kabbalah*, Wien, Berlin: Löwit, 1920.

Neumann, Erich, "Beiträge zur Symbolik des Jakob-Esau-Gegensatzes," typescript, 1934, pp. 1–99.

[— *Jacob and Esau: On the Collective Symbolism of the Brother Motif*, edited and introduced by Erel Shalit, translated by Mark Kyburz, Asheville, NC: Chiron, 2015.]

— "Das Bewusstsein und der religiöse Aspekt: Als Einleitung in einen Kurs über 'Das Unbewusste und der religiöse Aspekt'," unpublished typescript of lecture, November 1940, pp. 1–27 (now missing pp. 5–11).

— "Bewusstseins-Entwicklung und Psychologie der Lebensalter," typescript, 1943, pp. 1–27.

[— "The Development of Consciousness and Stages of Life," second lecture in four-lecture series, "The Importance of Consciousness in the Experience of Depth Psychology," *Roots II, Hasidism*, Appendix B.II, pp. 209–34.]

— "David und Saul," unpublished typescript of short story, n.d., pp. 1–15.

— "Eros und Psyche: Ein Beitrag zur seelischen Entwicklung des Weiblichen," in Apuleius, *Amor und Psyche*, Zürich: Rascher, 1952, pp. 75–217.

[— *Amor and Psyche: The Psychic Development of the Feminine. A Commentary on the Tale by Apuleius*, translated by Ralph Manheim, Princeton, NJ: Princeton University Press, 1956.]

— "Die religiöse Erfahrung in der Psychoanalyse," unpublished typescript of lecture, April 1940, pp. 1–20.

— "Zur religiösen Bedeutung des tiefenpsychologischen Weges," typescript, 1942, pp. 1–26 (missing pp. 27–29).

[— "The Religious Meaning of the Path of Depth Psychology," fourth lecture in four-lecture series, "The Importance of Consciousness in the Experience of Depth Psychology," *Roots II, Hasidism*, Appendix B.IV, pp. 256–74.]

— "Symbole und Stadien der Bewusstseins-Entwicklung," typescript, 1943, pp. 1–20.

[— "Symbols and Stages of Conscious Development," first lecture in four-lecture series, "The Importance of Consciousness in the Experience of Depth Psychology," *Roots II, Hasidism*, Appendix B.I, pp. 190–208.]

— *Tiefenpsychologie und neue Ethik*, Zürich: Rascher, 1949.

[— *Depth Psychology and a New Ethic*, with forewords by C. G. Jung, Gerhard Adler, and James Yandell, translated by Eugene Rolfe, Boston & London: Shambhala, 1969/1990.]

— "Der tiefenpsychologische Weg und das Bewusstsein," typescript, 1943, pp. 1–20.

[— "The Path of Depth Psychology and Consciousness," third lecture in four-lecture series, "The Importance of Consciousness in the Experience of Depth Psychology," *Roots II, Hasidism*, Appendix B.III, pp. 235–55.]

— *Ursprungsgeschichte des Bewusstseins*, mit einem Vorwort von C. G. Jung, Zürich: Rascher, 1949.

[— *The Origins and History of Consciousness*, with a foreword by C. G. Jung. translated by R. F. C. Hull, Princeton, NJ: Princeton University Press, 1954.]

Ninck, Martin, *Götter- und Jenseitsglauben der Germanen*, Jena: Diederichs, 1937.

— *Wodan und germanischer Schicksalsglaube*, Jena: Diederichs, 1935.

Otto, Rudolf, *Das Heilige: Über das Irrationale in der Idee des Göttlichen und sein Verhältnis zum Rationalen*, München: Beck, 1917.

[— *The Idea of the Holy: An Inquiry into the Non-Rational Factor in the Idea of the Divine and its Relation to the Rational*, translated by J. W. Harvey, London: Oxford University Press, 1923.]

— *Sünde und Urschuld und andere Aufsätze zur Theologie*, München: Beck, 1932.

Przyluski, Jan, "Ursprünge und Entwicklung des Kults der Muttergöttin," *Eranos-Jahrbuch 1938*, Zürich: Rhein, 1939, pp. 93–136.

Puech, Henri-Charles, "Der Begriff der Erlösung im Manichäismus," *Eranos-Jahrbuch 1936*, Zürich: Rhein, 1937, pp. 183–286.

Ramakrishna, Sri, *The Teachings of Sri Ramakrishna*, edited by Swami Budhananda, Calcutta: Advaita Ashrama, 1971. (Combines two volumes.)

Scheftelowitz, Isidor Isaac, *Altpalästinischer Bauernglaube in religionsvergleichender Beleuchtung*, Hannover: [n.p.], 1924.

— *Altpersische Religion und Judentum: Unterschiede, Übereinstimmungen und gegenseitige Beeinflüssungen*, Giessen: Töpelmann, 1920.

Scholem, Gershom Gerhard, *Bibliographia Kabbalistica: Die jüdische Mystik (Gnosis, Kabbala, Sabbatianismus, Frankismus, Chassidismus) behandelnde Bücher und Aufsätze von Reuchlin bis zur Gegenwart*, Leipzig: Drugulin, 1927. [Rev. edn, Berlin: Schocken, 1933.]

— *Das Buch Bahir: Ein Schriftdenkmal aus der Frühzeit der Kabbala auf Grund der kritischen Neuausgabe von Dr. Gerhard Scholem*, Leipzig: Drugulin, 1923.

— *Die Geheimnisse der Schöpfung: Ein Kapitel aus dem Sohar*, Berlin: Schocken, 1935.

— "Kabbala," *Encyclopaedia Judaica: Das Judentum in Geschichte und Gegenwart*, v. 9, edited by Jakob Klatzkin et al., Berlin: Eschkol, 1932, cols 630–732.

— *Major Trends in Jewish Mysticism*, Jerusalem and New York: Schocken, 1941.

— "Zum Verständnis des Sabbatianismus: Zugleich ein Beitrag zur Geschichte der Aufklärung," *Almanach des Schocken Verlags 5697*, Berlin: Schocken, 1936/37, pp. 30–42.

Silberer, H., *Probleme der Mystik und ihrer Symbolik*, Wien: Leipzig & Heller, 1914.

Soldan, W. G. and Heppe, Heinrich, eds, *Soldan's Geschichte der Hexenprozesse, neubearbeitet von Dr. Heinrich Heppe*, v. 1, Stuttgart: Cotta, 1880.

Steinmann, E. רבי נחמן מברסלב ("Rabbi Nachman of Brezlav"), *Davar*, 11 October 1940, Tel Aviv, p. 3.

Trumbull, H. C., *The Blood Covenant: A Primitive Rite and its Bearings on Scripture*, Philadelphia, PA: Wattles, 1898.

Virolleaud, Charles, *L'Astrologie Chaldéenne: le livre intitulé "Enuma (Anu) ilu.Bel"* (transliteration and translation of an ancient Mesopotamian text), Paris: Paul Geuthner, 1908.

— "Die grosse Göttin in Babylonien, Ägypten und Phönizien," *Eranos-Jahrbuch 1938*, Zürich: Rhein, 1939, pp. 121–60.

Volz, Paul, *Das Dämonische in Jahwe*, Tübingen: Mohr, 1924.

— *Die Eschatologie der jüdischen Gemeinde im neutestamentlichen Zeitalter nach den Quellen der rabbinischen, apokalyptischen und apokryphen Literatur*, Tübingen: Mohr, 1934.

— *Der Geist Gottes und die verwandten Erscheinungen im Alten Testament und im anschliessenden Judentum*, Tübingen: Mohr, 1910.

— *Mose und sein Werk*, Tübingen: Mohr, 1907/1932.

von Sydow, Eckart, *Kunst und Religion der Naturvölker*, Oldenburg: Gerhard Stalling/ Sacramentum Artis, 1926.

Weber, Max, *Gesammelte Aufsätze zur Religionssoziologie*, v. 3: *Das antike Judentum*, Tübingen: Mohr, 1923.

[— *Ancient Judaism*, translated and edited by Hans H. Gerth and Don Martindale, New York: Free Press; London: Collier-Macmillan, 1952.]

— *Wirtschaft und Gesellschaft: Grundriss der verstehenden Soziologie*, Abteilung III: *Grundriss der Sozialökonomik*, Tübingen: Mohr, 1922.

Wellhausen, Julius, *Abriss der Geschichte Israels und Juda's*, Berlin: Reimer, 1884.

— *Israelitische und Jüdische Geschichte*, Berlin: Reimer, 1894. [8th edn, Berlin & Leipzig: DeGruyter, 1921.]

— *Prolegomena zur Geschichte Israels*, 2nd edn, Berlin: Reimer, 1883.

Wickes, Frances, *Analyse der Kindesseele: Untersuchung und Behandlung nach den Grundlagen der Jung'schen Theorie*, Einleitung von C. G Jung, Stuttgart: Hoffmann, 1931.

— *The Inner World of Childhood: A Study in Analytical Psychology*, with introduction by C. G. Jung, New York: Appleton, 1927.

— *The Inner World of Man, With Psychological Drawings and Paintings*, New York: Farrar & Rinehart, 1938.

Wilhelm, Richard & Jung, C. G., eds, *Das Geheimnis der Goldenen Blüte: Ein chinesisches Lebensbuch*, translated by Richard Wilhelm, with a European commentary by C. G. Jung, München: Dorn, 1929. [2nd edn, including Jung's memorial to Richard Wilhelm, Berlin: Dorn, 1936.]

[— *The Secret of the Golden Flower: A Chinese Book of Life*, with European commentary by C. G. Jung, translated by Cary F. Baynes, London: Kegan Paul, 1935.]

Wolff, Toni, "Betrachtung und Besprechung von 'Reich der Seele'," *Zentralblatt für Psychotherapie und ihre Grenzgebiete*, v. 10,4/5, Leipzig: Hirzel, 1938, pp. 239–78.

Wünsche, August, trans., "Von der Bildung des Kindes," *Aus Israels Lehrhallen: kleine Midraschim zur späteren legendärischen Literatur des Alten Testaments übersetzt von Aug. Wünsche, nach der Buberschen Textausgabe*, Leipzig: Pfeiffer, 1907.

Zimmer, Heinrich, *Kunstform und Yoga im indischen Kultbild*, Berlin: Frankfurter, 1926.

[— *Artistic Form and Yoga in the Sacred Images of India*, translated and edited by Gerald Chapple, Princeton, NJ: Princeton University Press, 1984.]

II. Secondary sources

Sources used in the scholarly apparatus of *The Roots of Jewish Consciousness*.

Abelson, J., ed., *The Zohar, Soncino Edition*, v. 1–5, translated by H. Sperling and M. Simon, London and New York: Soncino Press, 1933.

The Aramaic Bible, Targum, Pseudo-Jonathan, v. 2: *Exodus*; v. 5b: *Deuteronomy*; v. 15: *Job*, translated by M. Maher, Collegeville, MN: Liturgical Press, 1987–1991.

Der Babylonische Talmud, mit Einschluss der vollständigen Mišnah, v. 7, translated by L. Goldschmidt, Haag: Nijoff, 1933.

Berman, Samuel A., *Midrash Tanhuma Yelammedenu: An English Translation of Genesis and Exodus from the Printed Version of Tanhuma Yelammedenu with an Introduction, Notes and Indexes*, Hoboken, NJ: KTAV, 1996.

Bialik, H. N. and Ravnitzky, Y. H, eds, *The Book of Legends: Sefer ha-Haggadah. Legends from the Talmud and Midrash*, translated by William G. Braude, introduction by David Stern, New York: Schocken, 1992.

Buber, Martin, *For the Sake of Heaven*, translated by Ludwig Lewisohn, Philadelphia, PA: Jewish Publication Society of America, 1945.

Catane, Moshe, ed., *Bibliography of the Works of Gershom G. Scholem*, Jerusalem: Magnes Press, The Hebrew University, 1977.

Charlesworth, James H., ed., *The Old Testament Pseudepigrapha*, v. 1: *Apocalyptic Literature and Testaments*, v. 2: *Expansions of the "Old Testament" and Legends, Wisdom and Philosophical Literature, Prayers, Psalms, and Odes, Fragments of Lost Judeo-Hellenistic Works*, Peabody, MA: Hendrickson, 1983.

Corrigan, K., "Soul and the Sensible World." *Reading Plotinus: A Practical Introduction to Neoplatonism*, West Lafayette, IN: Purdue University Press, 2005, pp. 38–41.

Corney, Richard W., private email correspondence and telephone consultation, 2015–18.

Dennis, Geoffrey W., *The Encyclopedia of Jewish myth, magic and mysticism*, Woodbury, MN: Llewellyn, 2007.

Dreifuss, Gustav, "Erich Neumanns jüdisches Bewusstsein," *Kreativität des Unbewussten: Zum 75. Geburtstag von Erich Neumann (1905–1960). Analytische Psychologie*, v. 11, 3–4, edited by H. Dieckmann and C. A. Meier, Basel, München, Paris, London, New York, Sydney: Karger, 1980, pp. 239–47.

Drob, Sanford, *Kabbalistic Visions: C. G. Jung and Jewish Mysticism*, New Orleans, LA: Spring Journal Books, 2010.

Ephrayyim, Moshe Hayyim, *Degel Mahaneh 'Efrayyim*, Jerusalem: Mir, 1994.

Epstein, I., ed., *The Hebrew–English Edition of the Babylonian Talmud: Shabbath, Pesahim, Yoma, Sukkah, Ta'anith, Hagigah, Sotah, Baba Bathra, Baba Mezia, Sanhedrin, Abodah Zara, Abboth, Niddah*, translated by H. Freedman, L. Jung, J. Rabinowitz, et al., London: Soncino, 1967–1989.

Fehlbaum, Nico, private email correspondence, 2018.

Fishbane, Michael, *The Garments of Torah: Essays in biblical hermeneutics*, Bloomington and Indianapolis, IN: Indiana University Press, 1989.

Fox, Everett, "The Book in its Contexts," introduction to Martin Buber and Franz Rosenzweig, *Scripture and Translation*, translated by Lawrence Rosenwald with Everett Fox, Bloomington & Indianapolis, IN: Indiana University Press, 1994, pp. xiii–xxvii.

— trans., *The Schocken Bible*, Volume I: *The Five Books of Moses* (Genesis, Exodus, Leviticus, Numbers, Deuteronomy): *A New Translation with Introductions, Commentary and Notes by Everett Fox*, New York: Schocken, 1983/1986/1990/1995.

— trans., *The Schocken Bible*, Volume II: *The Early Prophets* (Joshua, Judges, Samuel, and Kings): *A New Translation with Introductions, Commentary and Notes by Everett Fox*, New York: Schocken, 2014.

— private email correspondence and telephone consultation, 2015–16.

Friedmann, Dov Baer Mimezeritch, *Magid devarav le-Yaakov*, edited by Rivka Schatz-Uffenheimer, Yerushalayim: Hotsa'at sefarim 'a. sh, Y.L. Magnes, ha-Universitah ha-Ivrit, 1976. [Originally published, 1780.]

— *'Or ha-'Emmet*, Bnei Braq: Yahadut, 1967.

Furlotti, Nancy Swift, "Preface," *The Roots of Jewish Consciousness, Volume One: Revelation and Apocalypse*, edited by Ann Conrad Lammers, translated by Mark Kyburz and Ann Conrad Lammers, London and New York: Routledge, 2019, pp. xi–xv.

— private email correspondence, 2015–18.

Garb, Jonathan, *Yearnings of the Soul: Psychological Thought in Modern Kabbalah*, Chicago, IL and London: University of Chicago Press, 2015.

Gellman, Jerome, "Buber's Blunder: Buber's Replies to Scholem and Schatz-Uffenheimer," *Modern Judaism*, v. 20, 1, 2000, pp. 20–40.

Greenstein, Edward. L., *Essays on Biblical Method and Translation*, Atlanta, GA: Scholars Press, 1989.

Gunkel, H. & Zimmern, H., *Schöpfung und Chaos in Urzeit und Endzeit: Eine religionsgeschichtliche Untersuchung über Gen 1 und Ap Joh 12*, Göttingen: Vandenhoeck & Ruprecht, 1895.

Heschel, Abraham Yehoshu'a, *'Ohev Israel*, Zhitomir: Hanina Lipa and Joshua Heschel Shapira Printers, 1863.

Holtz, B. W., ed., *Back to the Sources: Reading the Classic Jewish Texts*, New York: Summit Books, 1984.

Hurwitz, Siegmund, "Psychological Aspects in Early Hasidic Literature," *Timeless Documents of the Soul*, edited by H. Jakobsohn, translated by H. Nagel, Evanston, IL: Northwestern University Press.

Idel, Moshe, "Foreword: On Erich Neumann and Hasidism," *The Roots of Jewish Consciousness*, v. 2: *Hasidism*, edited by Ann Conrad Lammers, translated by Mark Kyburz and Ann Conrad Lammers, London and New York: Routledge, 2019, pp. xiii–xviii.

— *Hasidism: Between Ecstasy and Magic*, Albany, NY: State University of New York Press, 1995.

— *Kabbalah: New Perspectives*, New Haven, CT and London: Yale University Press, 1988.

— "Martin Buber and Gershom Scholem on Hasidism: A Critical Appraisal," *Hasidism Reappraised*, edited by Ada Rapoport-Albert, London and Portland, OR: The Littman Library of Jewish Civilization, 1997, pp. 389–403.

Jacobs, Louis. *A Concise Companion to the Jewish Religion*, Oxford: Oxford University Press, 1999.

Jaffé, Aniela, *From the Life and Work of C. G. Jung*, expanded edition, translated by R. F. C. Hull and Murray Stein, Einsiedeln: Daimon, 1989.

Joseph, Steven, private email correspondence, 2016, 2018.

Jung, C. G., *Answer to Job*, translated by R. F. C. Hull, London: Routledge & Kegan Paul, 1954. [CW 11,9]

— *Dream Analysis: Notes of the seminar given in 1928–1930*, edited by William McGuire, London: Routledge and Kegan Paul, 1984.

— "An Eightieth Birthday Interview," *C. G. Jung Speaking: Interviews and Encounters*, edited by William McGuire and R. F. C. Hull, Princeton, NJ: Princeton University Press, 1977, pp. 268–72.

Jung, C. G. and Kirsch, James, *The Jung–Kirsch Letters: The Correspondence of C. G. Jung and James Kirsch*, edited by Ann Conrad Lammers, translated by Ursula Egli and Ann Conrad Lammers, London: Routledge, 2011. [Rev. edn, London: Routledge, 2016.]

Jung, C. G. and Neumann, Erich, *Analytical Psychology in Exile: The Correspondence of C. G. Jung and Erich Neumann*, edited and introduced by Martin Liebscher, translated by Heather McCartney, Princeton, NJ: Princeton University Press, 2015.

Jung, C. G. and White, Victor, *The Jung–White Letters*, edited by Ann Conrad Lammers and Adrian Cunningham, London and New York: Routledge, 2007.

Kafka, Franz, *Der Prozess*, Frankfurt am Main and Hamburg: Fischer, 1960. [Originally published 1925.]

Kravitz, Leonard and Olitzky, Kerry M., trans. and eds., *Pirke Avot: A Modern Commentary on Jewish Ethics*, with foreword by W. Gunther Plaut, New York: UAHC Press, 1993.

Lammers, Ann Conrad, "James Kirsch's Religious Debt to C. G. Jung," *Jung Journal: Culture and Psyche*, Vol. 6, No. 1, Winter 2012, pp. 21–34.

Lancaster, Brian, *The Essence of Kabbbalah*, London: Eagle Editions, 2005.

Leshem, Zvi, private email correspondence, 2018.

Lévy-Bruhl, Lucien, *How Natives Think*, translated by Lilian Ada Clare, New York: Washington Square Press, 1966.

Löwe, Angelica, *"Auf Seiten der inneren Stimme . . . " Erich Neumann—Leben und Werk*, Freiburg und München: Alber, 2014.

Malamud, René, "Gedanken zu Exodus 4:24," *Drei Aufsätze*, edited by Monica Malamud-Matter, Zürich: Daimon, 2017.

Matt, Daniel C., ed. and trans., *The Zohar* (ספר הזהר), *Pritzker Edition,* v. 1–12; v. 1–9 translated by Daniel Matt; v. 10–11 by Nathan Wolski, Palo Alto, CA: Stanford University Press, 2004–17.

Naor, Bezalel, *Lights of Prophecy*, New York: Union of Orthodox Jewish Congregations of America, 1990.

Neumann, Erich, "Die Angst vor dem Weiblichen," *Die Angst*, Studien aus dem C. G. Jung-Institut, v. 10, Zürich: Rascher, 1959, pp. 67–112.

[— "The Fear of the Feminine," *Fear of the Feminine and other essays on feminine psychology*, edited by William McGuire, translated by Boris Matthews, Princeton, NJ: Princeton University Press, 1994, pp. 227–82.]

— *Das Kind: Struktur und Dynamik der werdenden Persönlichkeit*, Zürich: Rhein, 1963.
[— *The Child: Structure and Dynamics of the Nascent Personality*, translated by Ralph Manheim, New York: Putnam, for C. G. Jung Foundation for Analytical Psychology, 1973.
— *Die große Mutter: Der Archetyp des großen Weiblichen*, Zürich: Rhein, 1956.
[— *The Great Mother: An Analysis of the Archetype*, translated by Ralph Manheim, Princeton, NJ: Princeton University Press, 1955. (2nd edn, 1963.)]
— "Der mystische Mensch," *Eranos-Jahrbuch 1948*, Zürich: Rhein, 1949, pp. 317–74.
[— "Mystical Man," *The Mystic Vision: Papers from the Eranos Yearbooks*, v. 6, edited by Joseph Campbell, translated by Ralph Manheim, Princeton, NJ: Princeton University Press, 1968, pp. 375–415.]
— "Die Psyche und die Wandlung der Wirklichkeitsebenen: Ein metapsychologischer Versuch," *Eranos-Jahrbuch 1952*, Zürich: Rhein, 1953, pp. 169–216.
[— "The Psyche and the Transformation of the Reality Planes: A Metapsychological Essay," *The Place of Creation*, edited by William McGuire, translated by H. Nagel, E. Rolfe, J. van Heurck, and K. Winston, Princeton, NJ: Princeton University Press, 1989, pp. 3–62.]
— *Tiefenpsychologie und Neue Ethik*, Zürich: Rascher, 1949.
[— *Depth Psychology and a New Ethic*, with forewords by C. G. Jung, Gerhard Adler, and James Yandell, translated by Eugene Rolfe, Boston and London: Shambhala, 1990.] [First published, with forewords by C. G. Jung and Gerhard Adler, London: Hodder & Stoughton, 1969.]
— *Ursprungsgeschichte des Bewusstseins*, mit einem Vorwort von C. G. Jung, Zürich: Rascher, 1949.
[— *The Origins and History of Consciousness*, with foreword by C. G. Jung, translated by R. F. C. Hull, Princeton, NJ: Princeton University Press, 1954.]
Neumann, Erich, and Jung, C. G., *Analytical Psychology in Exile: The Correspondence of C. G. Jung and Erich Neumann*, edited and introduced by Martin Liebscher, translated by Heather McCartney, Princeton, NJ: Princeton University Press, 2015.
Neumann-Loewenthal, Rali, interview, Jerusalem, 29 April 2015; telephone consultations, June 2018.
Neusner, Jacob, ed. and trans., *The Talmud of the Land of Israel: A Preliminary Translation and Explanation: Yoma, Ta'anith, Megillah, Sotah*, Chicago, IL: University of Chicago Press, 1984–1990.
Omer-Man, Jonathan, private email correspondence and telephone consultation, March 2018.
Rapoport-Albert, Ada, ed., *Hasidism Reappraised*, London; Portland, OR: The Littman Library of Jewish Civilization, 1997.
Rosenzweig, Franz, "The Unity of the Bible," *Scripture and Translation*, translated by Lawrence Rosenwald, with Everett Fox, Bloomington and Indianapolis, IN: Indiana University Press, 1994, pp. 22–6.
Schiffman, Lawrence. H., *From Text to Tradition: A History of Second Temple & Rabbinic Judaism*, Hoboken, NJ: KTAV, 1991.
Scholem, Gershom Gerhard, *Bibliographia Kabbalistica: Verzeichnis der gedruckten die jüdische Mystik—Gnosis, Kabbala, Sabbatianismus, Frankismus, Chassidismus—behandelnden Bücher und Aufsätze, von Reuchlin bis zur Gegenwart*, Leipzig: Drugulin, 1927.
— *Sabbatai Sevi: The Mystical Messiah*, translated by Zwi Werblowsky, Princeton, NJ: Princeton University Press, 1973.
— "The Unconscious and the Concept *Qadmut ha-Sekhel* in Hasidic Literature," *The Latest Phase: Essays on Hasidism*, edited by D. Assaf and E. Liebes, Jerusalem: Am Oved-Magnes, 2008 (Hebrew).
Segal, Robert, private email correspondence, 2015, 2018.

Shalit, Erel, "Introduction," *Jacob and Esau: On the Collective Symbolism of the Brother Motif*, edited and introduced by Erel Shalit, translated by Mark Kyburz, Asheville, NC: Chiron, 2016, pp. xix–lvii.

— private email correspondence, 2015–18.

Shalit, Erel and Stein, Murray, eds, *Turbulent Times, Creative Minds: Erich Neumann and C. G. Jung in Relationship (1933–1960)*, Asheville, NC: Chiron, 2016.

Skolnik, Fred, eds, *Encyclopaedia Judaica*, 2nd edn, v. 1–22, New York: Macmillan Reference; Jerusalem: Keter, 2007.

Wigoder, Geoffrey, eds, *Encyclopedic Dictionary of Judaica*, New York and Paris: Leon Amiel; Jerusalem: Keter, 1974.

Worch, J. Hershy, trans., *Sefer Yetzira: Chronicles of Desire. A New Hebrew/English Translation & Commentary*, Lanham, MD: University Press of America, 2010.

Zemmelman, Steve, "C. G. Jung and Erich Neumann: Conflict, Philia, and Finding the Other in Oneself," *Jung Journal: Culture and Psyche*, Summer 2016, v. 10(3), pp. 77–83.

The Zohar, Pritzker Edition, v. 1–12, translated and edited by Daniel C. Matt (v. 1–9); translated by Nathan Wolski (v. 10–11), Palo Alto, CA: Stanford University Press, 2004–17.

The Zohar, Soncino Edition, v. 1–5, edited by J. Abelson, translated by H. Sperling and M. Simon, London and New York: Soncino Press, 1933.

INDEX

Volumes One and Two

Note: This index covers both Volumes One and Two. Volume One page numbers are introduced with a superscript 1; Volume Two page numbers are introduced with a superscript 2. Page entries followed by & *n* indicate that the note relating to that text is also relevant. Page entries followed by *n* and a number, such as 169*n*102, indicate a specific endnote of relevance.

SCRIPTURAL INDEX

Note: This index covers both Volumes One and Two. Volume One page numbers are introduced with a superscript 1; Volume Two page numbers are introduced with a superscript 2.

Bible

Apocrypha and Pseudepigrapha

Babylonian Talmud

Jerusalem Talmud

Zohar

For Product Safety Concerns and Information,
please contact our EU representative GPSR@taylorandfrancis.com
Taylor & Francis Verlag GmbH, Kaufingerstraße 24,
80331 München, Germany

Printed by Integrated Books International,
United States of America